The Works
of the
Gawain-Poet

CHARLES MOORMAN

UNIVERSITY PRESS OF MISSISSIPPI
JACKSON

THIS VOLUME IS AUTHORIZED
AND SPONSORED BY THE
UNIVERSITY OF SOUTHERN MISSISSIPPI
HATTIESBURG, MISSISSIPPI

Library of Congress Cataloging in Publication Data

Main entry under title:

The Works of the Gawain-Poet.

    Bibliography: p.
    CONTENTS: Introduction.—Patience.—Purity.—Pearl.
[etc.]
    1. English poetry—Middle English, 1100–1500.
I. Moorman, Charles.
PR1203.W67   821'.1   76–40190
ISBN 0–87805–028–0

THE WORKS OF THE *GAWAIN*-POET

For Ruth

· Contents ·

Acknowledgments   ix

Table of Abbreviations   xi

Introduction   3

Bibliography   52

Frequently Cited Sources   63

Patience   67

Purity   101

Pearl   197

Sir Gawain and the Green Knight   281

Glossary   445

· Plates ·

Jonah cast into the sea   66

Jonah preaching to the Ninevites   91

Noah and his family   122

Daniel expounding the wall writing   191

The dreamer asleep   196

The dreamer standing by the stream   210

The dreamer and the child   253

The dreamer and the New Jerusalem   270

The headless Green Knight   314

Gawain and the lady   363

Gawain at the Green Chapel   428

Gawain and Arthur's Court   441

· Acknowledgments ·

In reviewing a project ranging somewhat unsteadily over ten years it is difficult to thank properly all those who have contributed meaningfully to its progress. If I should thus fail to mention some particular helper, it is not from willful negligence but from simple forgetfulness (which is probably worse!) that I do so.

First, I should like to thank the American Council of Learned Societies, which has probably long ago abandoned hope of seeing its faith in the project justified. Without its sponsorship I could never have begun the work. Second, I should like to thank the University of Southern Mississippi, and particularly its former president and dean, W. D. McCain and John H. Allen, as well as its present head, Aubrey K. Lucas, for its active support over a great many years.

Among those colleagues who have read and commented on the manuscript, Professors Morton Bloomfield and Thomas Ross have helped the most, though they should not be held accountable for the errors which eagle-eyed young scholars will doubtless discover.

The list of amanuenses is long, but three deserve the title of editoral assistant—Mrs. Catherine Rhodes Adams, Mrs. Perry Lou Milner Barrio-Garay, and Mrs. Patricia Trimble Gregory.

Finally I should like to thank J. Barney McKee, Director of the University Press of Mississippi, who personally edited a manuscript which, first typed twelve years ago, had never been retyped, only corrected and emended.

The dedication page acknowledges a debt that I can never repay and on which the interest accumulates daily.

· Table of Abbreviations ·

Academy
American Benedictine Review
AngB   Anglia Beiblatt
Angl   Anglia
Ant   Antiquity
CE   College English
ChaucR   The Chaucer Review
Criticism
EC   Etudes Celtiques
EETS   Early English Text Society
ELH   Journal of English Literary History
ELN   English Literary Notes
EM   English Miscellany
ES   English Studies
E Stn   Englische Studien
FMLA   Forum for Modern Language Studies
JEGP   Journal of English and Germanic Philology
LanM   Les Langues Modernes
The Library
The Lock Haven Review
MÆ   Medium Ævum
Manuscripta
Mass. Studies in English
      Massachusetts Studies in English
MLN   Modern Language Notes
MLR   Modern Language Review
MLQ   Modern Language Quarterly

· TABLE OF ABBREVIATIONS ·

MP	Modern Philology
MS	Mediaeval Studies
MSpr	Moderna Sprok
N&Q	Notes and Queries
Neophil	Neophilologus
NEQ	New England Quarterly
NM	Neuphilologische Mitteilungen
Orbis Litterarum	
PQ	Philological Quarterly
PLL	Papers on Language and Literature
PMLA	Publications of the Modern Language Association
RES	Review of English Studies
RPh	Romance Philology
RR	Romantic Review
SLI	Studi Linguistici Italiani
SN	Studia Neophilologica
SoQ	Southern Quarterly
SP	Studies in Philology
Spec	Speculum
Trad	Traditio
Tulane Studies in English	
UTQ	University of Toronto Quarterly

THE WORKS OF THE *GAWAIN*-POET

· Introduction ·

As far as the editor can determine, this is the first "collected edition" of Cotton Nero A.x. since the MS itself. It is hoped that this work will contribute to the study of the *Gawain*-poet in that it will facilitate studies of the whole poet, in addition to those of his individual works, will provide a basis for comparative study, and will aid in an evaluation of the poet's development. The book should prove useful both as a reading and a reference edition and as a graduate text.

The paleographer and textual critic should approach his task with two caveats ringing in his ears, the first by a Latinist:

> There are many useful jobs which can be done by men who do not like to think. They can dig ditches, clean automobiles, and compile concordances. They cannot, however, become good textual critics. (Willis, 1972:3)

The second by a Latinist-cum-poet:

> A textual critic engaged upon his business is not at all like Newton investigating the motions of the planets; he is much more like a dog hunting for fleas. If a dog hunted for fleas on mathematical principles, basing his researches on statistics of area and density of population, he would never catch a flea, except by accident. They require to be treated as individuals; and every problem which presents itself to the textual critic must be regarded as possibly unique. (Housman, 1961:132–3)

Having had fair warning, the editor may then proceed to plunge—not immediately into the intricacies of the text before him, but into the morass of conflicting philosophies of textual criticism which he finds reflected in the work and comments of his predecessors and from which he must somehow pluck a working method of his own. There are, broadly speaking, two basically opposed approaches to the preparation of critical editions of English literary MSS, between which there exist an infinite number of shadings. One approach aims at restoring the text to the state in which it was first delivered to the scribe, who is *ipso facto* an unreliable copyist. The other refuses to allow personal judgments to override the editor's respect for the authority of the manuscript and of a scribe who, whatever his deficiencies, was closer to the event than even the most erudite modern scholar and who may have had before him an actual autograph.

Both approaches have their advocates and their critics. The first can lead to excesses of subjective emendation, the second to the zenith, or depth, of editorial objectivity. James Willis presents the distinction sharply, along with its attendant dilemma:

> The ultimate goal of conjectural criticism is to present what the author wrote, no matter how much the credit of the scribes may suffer; conservative criticism, in its extremest form, aims at proving that the manuscripts were always right. The successful defence of a manuscript reading pleases the conservative critic as a matter of principle; he must therefore, if he is to be consistent, welcome the successful defence of every suspected reading in a text. But if this goal is attained, and the attested readings are one and all accepted, what has the conservative critic in fact achieved? He has shown that the manuscript (either real or reconstructed) which conveyed the text of the work concerned contained no single error of any kind. Now it is almost certain that no such manuscript has ever existed . . . . What then of conjectural criticism? Has it not been guilty of crimes against grammar, metre, sense, and style as heinous as any that can be laid at the door of conservatism? It can be indeed. (Willis, 1972:11)

Both basic viewpoints have been held by the editors of the poems of Cotton Nero A.x. Sir Israel Gollancz, who edited all four poems, was of the first school, and his editions are the most provocative, and infuriating, of all modern versions. Robert Menner's edition of *Purity*, on the other hand, is very cautious in changing the text, though, strangely enough, most free in altering its orthography. The other editors range the hills and valleys between, now conservative and cautious, now conjectural and almost revolutionary.

The writer's own feeling, reflected I hope in the following text, is that the editor should wherever possible accept the MS reading and attempt to justify it. The problem of editing the unique MS (such as Cotton Nero A.x.) is at once simpler and more complex than that of editing a work for which a number of MSS exist. On the one hand, the editor is spared the harrowing task of MSS classification by any one of several usually unsatisfactory methods; on the other, he has no choice of readings or standards of comparison. One again needs to recall Housman:

> Authors surviving in a solitary MS are by far the easiest to edit, because their editor is relieved from one of the most exacting offices of criticism, from the balancing of evidence and the choice of variants. They are the easiest, and for a fool they are the safest. One field at least for the display of folly is denied him: others are open, and in defending, correcting, and explaining the written text he may yet aspire to make a scarecrow of the author and a byword of himself. (Housman, 1961:35)

I have thus made no changes for purely metrical reasons or in order to correct the alliterative pattern or to fill out a short line which otherwise makes good sense. Neither have I suggested a great many new readings, though I have, I think, corrected some old ones. In considering the changes proposed by other students of the poems, I have tried to choose that reading which seemed most in harmony both with the immediate textual environment and with the meaning and intention of the poem.

I have made, however, one rather great change; I have followed what would seem to be the chronological order of the poems— *Patience, Purity, Pearl, Sir Gawain and the Green Knight*—both in the text and in the various discussions in the Introduction. The reasons for this arrangement are that the best means of presenting the poems for reading and study is chronological and that, conversely, no good purpose would seem to be served by following the apparently arbitrary order of the MS.

Following the practice of the two Early English Text Society editions of *Sir Gawain and the Green Knight*, here and in the other three poems I have reproduced the traditional divisions of earlier editions, but I have indicated by 24-point capitals the MS divisions in *Sir Gawain* at 619, 763, 1421, 1893, and 2259 as well as the usual divisions at 491, 1126, and 1998. In spite of Laurita A. Hill's arguments that these capitals represent the true structure of the poem, the traditional arrangement seems to me to follow best the manuscript division (the capitals of 491, 1126, and 1998 being larger and more ornate than the other five) and the natural divisions of the argument. It will be apparent also that I have followed in *Patience* and *Purity* the quatrain arrangement advocated by Gollancz (See notes to *Patience*, 1, and *Purity*, 1).

I have attempted everywhere, moreover—in text, notes, and glossary—to provide an edition which will be of use to the general student of literature as well as to the specialist. Thus I have tried to make the text as readable, the notes as succinct and informative, and the glossary as usable as possible.

As to the mechanics of editing, therefore:

(1) I have re-edited the text of the four poems from the Gollancz facsimile, from photographs and microfilms of the MS, and at all cruces from the MS itself.

(2) I have not italicized my expansions of the scribe's abbreviations. The Gollancz editions of the poem do this accurately, and needless italics mar the appearance of the printed text. Certainly uniformity of type is less distracting. The poet's abbreviations for *and, with, þou, þat,* and other common words are quite ordinary. Scribal *qt* has been rendered as *quoþ* and *õ(r)* as *our*.

(3) The apparatus includes MS readings not adopted in the text and what I consider to be significant variants adopted by previous editors (though I have not collated Morris's *Early English Alliterative Poems*). It does not include those changes made by either one of the two scribes. The term "illegible" in the apparatus does not necessarily mean that an entire line is illegible, but that a portion of the

line has been reconstructed by offsets (mirror-image blots on oppos-
ing pages) or, more often, from context. The abbreviations used in
the apparatus are as follows:

Patience	:	A = Anderson
		B = Bateson (2nd edition)
		Go = Gollancz (2nd edition)
Purity	:	Go = Gollancz
		M = Menner
Pearl	:	O = Osgood
		Gn = Gordon
		H = Hillmann
		Go = Gollancz
Sir Gawain and the Green Knight	:	D = Tolkien and Gordon (2nd edition, rev. Davis)
		Go = Gollancz
		W = Waldron
		TG = Tolkien and Gordon (1st edition)

(4) I have refrained from punctuating the text since the manu-
script punctuation is minimal and since *any* punctuation, scribal
or modern, occasionally dictates interpretation.

(5) I have printed as single words those words divided in the text
which are now regarded as single words (*e.g., vp on=vpon*) and
vice versa (*e.g., nwȝeres=Nw ȝeres*). I have also followed modern
practices of capitalization (proper names, the deity, holidays, etc.),
though I have not capitalized pronouns and synonyms referring to
the Trinity.

(6) I have followed the MS's use of *u* and *v* and short and long *i*
(where distinguishable) except for the pronoun *I* and words such as
iwysse and *ichose*.

The notes make use of all the important scholarship on the poems.
But since I am not attempting a variorum edition and thus cannot

record every comment ever made, the choice of what is included is my responsibility. Neither do I make any attempt to reproduce details of commentary and argument included in the notes of previous editions; the major comments of other editors are summarized, and the reader is simply referred to these editions as to any other book or article.

There already exist detailed etymological glossaries for each of the four poems listing each meaning, if not each instance, of every word used, and a concordance which is thorough, even if occasionally confusing—in short, ample aid for the philologist-specialist engaged in a study of the *Gawain*-poet. It seemed gratuitous, therefore, to repeat the labors of my predecessors, who are more learned and talented in language than am I and whose efforts are available. I have therefore glossed the "hard" words, the unfamiliar ones, to the side of the text the first few times they appear in each poem, and I have provided in the back of the book a basic vocabulary, based on the Kottler and Markman frequency count, as supplement. A given word may appear in both places. I would hope that every word not immediately clear to the reader is somewhat glossed, though I shall doubtless be proved mistaken. My model is that of Robert Pratt's *The Tales of Canterbury*. I would hope that this method of glossing, though it unfortunately tends to solidify a single reading by neglecting ambiguities, will prove as successful here as it does in Pratt's text in increasing both the speed and comprehension of the reader. At any rate, the students who read the text in typescript seemed to agree that it did.

Some explanation of the form taken by the Introduction may be also necessary. A cursory glance at the 500 or so items devoted to the poet should convince even the most demanding critic that anything resembling an adequate exposition in narrative form of the particular forms, sources, themes, etc. of each of the four poems would be impossible in less than several hundred pages, a luxury which not even one's "own" university press can afford. My answer to the problem has been to furnish the reader with a brief and wholly introductory, though carefully organized, statement to each of the major topics traditionally dealt with in an edition of this kind, and then to present him with a decently comprehensive, though still selective, bibliography of the major contributions on the subject. The reader should then be able to formulate his own expository account of the current state of criticism on any given topic. The bibliographies are necessarily limited to general and interpretive studies, and no attempt is made to cross-refer items dealing with more than one topic. For more detailed bibliographies the reader is directed to the bibliographies of the various editions and translations, to the new *Cambridge Bibliography of English Literature*, to the bibliographies in John Edwin Wells' *Manual*, to the continuing bibliographies in *PMLA* and *Speculum* (until October, 1972), to the Modern Humanities Research Association *Bibliography*, and to *The Year's Work in English Studies*.

Such an introduction is the antithesis of R. A. Waldron's lengthy introduction to the York Medieval Texts edition of *Sir Gawain and the Green Knight* or of John Gardner's introduction to his translation. For whatever the validity of Waldron's and Gardner's commentaries, they are in essence discussions more appropriate to journal essays than to editions. The editor of this volume feels that an introduction to what he hopes will be a widely accepted and used edition will serve merely to define areas of discussion and to indicate problems. It thus nowhere consciously takes advantage of its position to favor prejudices or introduce novelties, not, at least, in its general introduction.

The list of frequently cited sources which precedes each set of notes should prove a convenience to the reader in that it vastly simplifies the Notes section. Its drawbacks are that the reader must consult the list for any complete reference to these items (though it is doubtful that he will do so very often) and that precise page references are not given in the notes. On the other hand, the only books and articles included in this list are editions and great compilations of short notes, and the endless repetition of bibliographical data on such items would be tedious and unrewarding. Where authors or

titles only are given in the Introduction and Notes, the full bib-
liographical reference is included in the introductory bibliographies,
though even here the simplest possible bibliographical forms (basi-
cally those of the American Anthropological Association) are used.

THE MANUSCRIPT

The four poems contained in this volume are to be found on folios
43–130 (formerly 37–126)[1] of a unique vellum MS contained in the
British Museum where it bears the designation Cotton Nero A.x.,
Art. 3. The MS is bound in a small quarto volume 118mm in width
and between 163 and 172 mm in height; prior to 1964, it was bound
together with two unrelated texts. The gatherings in the new binding
are so stitched that the collation can be traced: the MS begins with
a bifolium containing four illustrations to *Pearl*, there follow seven
gatherings of twelve leaves each, and the MS concludes with a gather-
ing of four leaves. Folios 39–55 contain *Pearl*, 56 two illustrations to
Purity, 57–82a *Purity*, 82a a half-page illustration to *Patience*, 82b an
illustration to *Patience*, 83–90a *Patience*, 90b an illustration to *Sir
Gawain and the Green Knight*, 91–124 *GGK*, 125–126a three illus-
trations to *GGK*. Each of the twelve-leaf gatherings concludes with a
catchword.

The illustrations are strongly colored and are almost certainly
contemporaneous with the MS. The poems are not entitled in the
MS; *Pearl, Purity* (or *Cleanness*), *Patience*, and *Sir Gawain and the
Green Knight* are the designations of early modern editors. The be-
ginnings of the poems are marked by illuminated initials in red and
blue; smaller initials in the same colors are occasionally used within
the poems.

The writing is a late fourteenth-century Gothic minuscule, quite
small, somewhat uneven, and generally angular. There are 36 lines
of writing to the page. The chief difficulties in reading the MS

---

1. This edition retains the older numbering in order to facilitate collation with
previous editions.

are due to the faded state of the ink and to its having occasionally blotted on opposing pages, though these passages can often be deciphered with a mirror. The scribe himself frequently seems hurried and careless, as seen in his too rapid turning of still wet pages, and at the best of times his short and long *i*'s, *u*'s, and *v*'s, *bo*'s and *lo*'s, and *ha*'s and *la*'s are virtually indistinguishable. There is evidence also of the hand of a corrector, who for the most part simply retraces the original scribe's letters, but occasionally corrects his predecessor.

The history of the MS is largely undetermined. It was acquired by the British Museum in 1753, having escaped the Ashburnham House fire of 1731, with the MS collection of the seventeenth-century bibliophile Sir Robert Cotton, who arranged his volumes in cases under the busts of Roman emperors and so catalogued them. Cotton presumably acquired his Nero A.x. from Henry Savile (1568–1617), a great Yorkshire collector whose catalogue describes the work as "an owld booke in English verse beginning Perle pleasants to princes pay in 4° limned."

There is no evidence of another copy of the poem ever having existed, though Gollancz states "it may be safely inferred that, after allowing for scribal errors, our MS is not an exact transcript of the originals" (1923:8). J. J. Anderson notes that "there is minor palaeographical and linguistic variation from poem to poem, suggesting that at some time the poems existed in separate manuscripts" (1969:2). J. P. Oakden even suggested that the four poems had undergone copying by no less than seven scribes, an argument rebutted by W. W. Greg and reaffirmed by Oakden. Certainly, however, the evidence of the unique manuscript does not permit a reconstruction of its sources.

THE ALLITERATIVE REVIVAL

The four poems of Cotton Nero A.x. are a part of the so-called Alliterative Revival of the late fourteenth century, a literary movement centering in the west and north of England. This revival was marked by its use of an alliterative accentual meter, by a predilection on the whole for natural subjects, by a rich Anglo-Saxon vocabulary, by a distinctively moral and heroic point of view, and, at times, by a heightened social consciousness. In all these features, the poetry of the Alliterative School, though certainly written for an aristocratic audience, contrasts with the more artificial poetry of Chaucer's London and its fragile continental mannerisms.

At least two critics have seen in the poetry of the Alliterative Revival a political and moral as well as an artistic reaction, sponsored by the great conservative country barons, against the irresponsibility and extravagance of the Ricardian court. This literary movement may thus be a part of the long-standing baronial opposition to the crown which had existed from the times of Magna Carta. Indeed, these poems with their insistence upon pre-invasion metrical forms and values may well be symptomatic of the growing breach between the increasingly nationalistic country barons and the culturally francophile London court in the period 1350–1400.

Whatever the reason for their sudden appearance in the mid-fourteenth century, these poems owe their metrical forms and their themes not to a sudden rediscovery of the past, but to a poetic tradition which had come down, probably by means of an unbroken oral tradition, with very few changes from Anglo-Saxon times. There can be little doubt that the chief features of Alliterative Revival poetry—the alliterative accentual verse, the formulaic diction, the stern moral outlook, the essentially pagan and pessimistic view of nature beneath the faint Christian coloration—reflect their common origins in pre-invasion verse.

It is in this tradition that the works of the *Gawain*-poet—like the chronicle poems of Alexander and Troy, the romances of William of Palerne and Arthur, and the social protests of *Wynnere and Wastoure* and *Piers Plowman*—viewed in historical perspective belong and within which they are best judged. Though it does not, like *Piers Plowman*, sound the clarion of social justice, the poetry of Cotton Nero A.x. does indeed share with the other alliterative poems of the movement, though in infinitely varied and faceted forms, their common music and themes.

The evidence for common authorship of the poems of Cotton Nero A.x. is very strong. The poems are written in precisely the same Northwest Midland dialect, and they share a number of colloquial and peculiar forms and words which are not a part of the formulaic tradition. The poems are stylistically similar in their use of framing devices, in their avoidance of stereotyped formulaic half-lines, in their grouping of similes, in their rather unusual paraphrasing of "God" and "Lord" by means of relative clauses, in their repeated mention of the beatific vision, and in their vivid landscape drawing.

Most striking, however, is the concern throughout the four poems with chastity and with its relation to patience, humility, and obedience. All four poems, in fact, have at their centers failures in purity and/or obedience, and all display man's incapability of achieving salvation by obeying the commandments of God. Thus in all four poems one is conscious, even amidst the laughter of Bercilak's court, of the same deeply moral poet whose chief concern is not with the superficialities of story-telling, but with the suffering of man and with what Graham Greene in *Brighton Rock* calls the "appalling strangeness of the mercy of God." While the comparison to a disillusioned, twentieth-century post-Romantic may seem inappropriate, yet in raising questions which apparently never even occurred to Walter Hilton or to Richard Rolle or even to Geoffrey Chaucer, the *Gawain*-poet steps out of his age into ours.

One wishes that the evidence identifying the author were equally convincing. From the poems themselves something of his background and interests may be inferred—that he was well trained, probably professionally, in theology and rhetoric, that he was widely read in works ranging from the *Roman de la Rose* to the church fathers, that he was intimately acquainted with life at court, with law and medicine, with hunting and heraldry, and with music. And something of his personality may be seen, provided such evidence is ever valid, in his work. He seems more than usually conscious of man's frailties and his inability to measure up to the standards imposed on him by God, and, as a natural corollary, more than uncommonly sympathetic towards the sufferings of men who must endure in a fallen world grief and humiliation and failure.

He was, to judge again from his poems, a man singularly conscious of the changing face of physical nature and particularly of its destructive menace, of storms at sea and boiling inland waters and frozen forest wastes, although he can equally well describe the burial mound of a child where paradoxically grow "gilofre, gyngure, & gromylyoun / & pyonys powdered ay bytwene."

A number of early commentators, however, went well beyond these general characteristics in order to see in the poems a tragic biography. Having lost, they said, a two-year-old daughter (*Pearl*), the poet abandoned the gay courtly life of his youth (celebrated in *Sir Gawain and the Green Knight*) in order to find solace and consolation in religion, particularly in obedience to and harmony with God (*Purity* and *Patience*). No recent critic, however, has chosen to defend this position, mainly because it assumes an order of composition which places the most accomplished of the four poems first and the least accomplished last.

Efforts, largely unsuccessful, have been made to identify positively the *Gawain*-poet. Assuming, on what one might assert to be rather firm evidence, that he was a university-trained clerk, he has been assigned to the households of John of Gaunt, of Enguerrand de Coucy, one of the Earls of Bedford, and of John Hastings, Earl of Pembroke, whose daughter, conveniently to the theory named Margaret, died at age two, thus doubly qualifying her as the *Pearl* maiden. On the basis of his library he has been identified as one John of Erghome. His works have also, on slim evidence indeed, been attributed to two vague literary figures of the period—the "philosophical Strode" of

Troilus and Criseyde and to that "universal genius," Huchown of the Awle Ryale.

The dating of the four poems has met with little better success. The arrangement of the poems in the manuscript—*Pearl, Purity, Patience, Sir Gawain and the Green Knight*—almost certainly does not represent the order of composition; one hesitates to place the elegantly structured *Pearl* before the comparatively amateurish *Patience*. Since the relative chronology of the poems is thus uncertain, the dating of the individual poems becomes even more difficult. By metrical, stylistic, and thematic standards, certainly the best arrangement is *Patience, Purity, Pearl,* and *Sir Gawain and the Green Knight*, but this order, based wholly upon internal evidence, offers no help in dating the individual poems. *Pearl* almost certainly was composed after 1360, the date of Boccaccio's *Olympia*, its principal source. *Sir Gawain and the Green Knight* can be dated only after 1345, the probable date of the founding of the Order of the Garter, and *Purity* only after 1356, the probable date of the French version of Mandeville's *Travels*, which the poem may reflect. On the other hand, *Patience* seemingly must be placed before 1377, the date of the B-text of *Piers Plowman*, which echoes it. It should be apparent that these few scattered dates, most of which are themselves conjectural, are of no help in establishing either the relative or positive chronology of the Cotton Nero poems. Thus, the best one can say is that the poems were probably written during the period 1360–90. Such a lengthy period leads naturally to the supposition that the poet wrote other poems, but aside from *St. Erkenwald*, the evidence for the authorship of which is inconclusive, no poems resembling those of the *Gawain*-poet in theme and manner have appeared.

Concerning the place of their composition, something more positive may be said, though again the problems outnumber the solutions. The common dialect of the poems is that of the Northwest Midlands, probably of Lancashire or Cheshire. Internal evidence also demonstrates that the poet was familiar with the geography and countryside of northern Wales and with the Wirral, a forest in northwestern Cheshire, then a haunt of outlaws.

It is thus impossible to identify positively the poet or to ascertain with any certainty the date and place of the composition of his poems, nor would it seem that a further sifting of the available evidence will reveal further information.

SOURCES AND ANALOGUES

Before attempting any generalizations regarding the poet's handling of his sources, it might be well to review briefly the sources of the individual poems.

A. *Patience*

The principal source of the homiletic *Patience* is the Vulgate Old Testament Book of Jonah. The poet also uses scriptural passages— the beatitudes (Matt. 5:3–12), verses 8 and 9 of Psalm 93—to express the stupidity of Jonah's flight from God, and perhaps verses 2–5 of Psalm 6 for Jonah's penitential prayer inside the whale.

There is evidence also that the poet made use of three Latin poems —*De Jona et Nineve*, sometimes attributed to Tertullian, Bishop Marbod's *Naufragium Jonae Prophetae* (both of which deal with the Jonah story), and Prudentius' "Hymnus Ieiunantium," the seventh hymn of the *Liber Cathemerinon*. From the first of these, the poet draws heavily for descriptive detail in expanding the Vulgate account of the storm at sea and the whale. The other two poems are used to a far lesser extent to supply small details of character and incident. A single parallel links the poem to *Alexander C*, but only the fact that a few parallels to the same poem exist in *Purity* gives credence to this claim. Finally, the poet would seem to make some small use of St. Jerome's commentary on the Book of Jonah in developing the anguish and sorrow of Jonah and of Tertullian's *Liber de Patientia* in analyzing the virtue of patience.

B. *Purity*

The chief sources of *Purity* are the Vulgate and popular religious tradition. Whereas in *Patience*, the poet draws only upon one biblical tale (that of Jonah) in order to illustrate his theme of obedience, he here draws upon the stories of Lucifer, Adam, Noah, Abraham and Sarah, Sodom and Gomorrah, Zedekiah, Nebuchadnezzar, and Belshazzar's feast, and he makes use as well of the beatitudes, the parable of the wedding feast, and a number of scriptural images, particularly that of the purity of Christ and Mary. In all, he makes use of a dozen of the books of the Bible.

Aside from a highly doubtful use of a Latin poem *De Sodoma*, sometimes ascribed to Tertullian, the poet calls upon two secular sources, the French version of Mandeville's *Travels* and the Jean de Meun section of the *Roman de la Rose*. From the first of these he takes his vivid description of the Dead Sea and from the second he adapts to the Christian situation a line advising the lover to conform to his lady's tastes. It has been argued also that the poem was influenced by *Le Livre du Chevalier de la Tour Landry* and by the *Cursor Mundi*, but the evidence is of too general a nature to indicate precise indebtedness.

C. *Pearl*

The major source for the narrative framework of *Pearl* is probably Boccaccio's "Fourteenth Eclogue," the *Olympia*, written in 1361 to commemorate the death of the poet's five-year-old daughter, Violante, though there is no direct connection between the two poems. In the tradition of the pastoral elegy, Boccaccio's central figure, the grieving shepherd Silvius, wakes to a vision of his radiant daughter, here called Olympia, who comforts him and reconciles him to God's will. The *Olympia*, however, even if a source, supplies the poet only with a particular narrative situation, one which, according to the proponents of the elegiac school, paralleled very closely his own experience. The overall structure of the poem, the dream-vision, is far older than Boccaccio's work and so widely diffused that the poet was probably familiar with a number of its appearances, including that in the *Roman de la Rose*, and so saw in it an ideal framework for the sort of fantasy he wished to present. There are also present in the structure of the poem elements of the debate, of the heavenly vision as seen in the saints' lives, of the dialogues and spiritual journey of the *Divine Comedy*, and of Boethius's *Consolatio*.

The substance of the poem, like its structure, reflects a variety of sources. The Vulgate is the source of about one-third of the poem, especially in the theological debate between narrator and child and this debate reflect the writings of the church fathers, especially St. in the vision of the New Jerusalem. It is clear that the arguments of Augustine. There is at least one clear reference to the *Roman de la Rose,* and the poem is studded with reminiscences of the liturgy and with symbolic references (the pearl, the other jewels, the garden, the spices, etc.), all of them commonplaces from medieval herbals, treatises on gems, and the like.

D. *Sir Gawain and the Green Knight*

While the immediate source or sources of *Sir Gawain and the Green Knight* are unknown, it is clear, as G. L. Kittredge established, that the poem is a fusion of two ancient and oft-repeated motifs of Celtic literature usually referred to as the Beheading Game, or Challenge, and the Temptation.

Although the earliest forms of both stories are forever lost, a few early versions of each have come down. The first of these stories, the Beheading Game, has the clearest history of transmission. Its first appearance in written form is in an eighth- or ninth-century Irish epic of Cuchulainn (who may well be the same person as the Welsh Gawain) called *Fled Bricend* or *Bricriu's Feast,* though its oral form must be at least a century older. In a segment of this epic usually called "The Champion's Bargain," a magician, Uath Mac Imomain, proposes a beheading game to Cuchulainn and two companions, the three of whom are vying for the "champion's portion." Cuchulainn accepts the challenge and successfully cuts off the magician's head. Twenty-four hours later, according to the agreement, Cuchulainn appears before the magician, who declares the contest finished after striking three light blows and praises Cuchulainn's great valor. In another episode of the epic, a savage churl appears at court and proposes another beheading game. One hero, Munremur, accepts the challenge, beheads the *bachlach*, and then fails to keep the agreement. Two other heroes also fail to keep the pledge; but on the fourth night Cuchulainn appears, accepts the challenge, and returns on schedule to face the churl. The churl then strikes Cuchulainn once with the blunt edge of his ax, declares Cuchulainn to be the best warrior of the court, and vanishes. The bard reveals the churl's true identity—Curoi mac Dairi, the judge of the "champion's bargain."

At some time between the ninth and the late twelfth centuries, the Beheading Game motif passed from Irish folklore into the French romance tradition, though no one has been able to trace exactly the stages of this early transmission. It appears, however, in several French romances of the twelfth and thirteenth centuries—*Livre de Caradoc, La Mule sanz Frain* ("The Mule without a Bridle"), *Perlesvaus,* and *Gawain et Humbaut*—works in which the Beheading Game motif was in all probability derived not directly from Celtic sources, but from a group of earlier French romances now lost.

The story pattern, however, and its relation to *Sir Gawain and the Green Knight* are perfectly clear. In the *Livre de Caradoc,* Arthur is portrayed at his Whitsuntide assembly awaiting, according to his custom, some adventure. Soon a knight comes into the hall and initiates the beheading game. Caradoc responds and is told to be ready in a year to receive a blow in return. The knight returns at the appointed time, and, when he finds Caradoc waiting, strikes him with the hilt of his sword and praises his courage.

The other romances in the tradition tell approximately the same story but with minor variations. In *Perlesvaus,* for example, Lancelot is the hero, and the detail of the hero's flinching at the first blow is included. Gawain is the hero of both *La Mule sanz Frain* and *Gawain et Humbaut.*

These brief summaries demonstrate the closeness with which the *Gawain*-poet follows the thirteenth-century romance form of the legend. The relationship of *Sir Gawain and the Green Knight* and the *Livre de Caradoc* is so close, in fact, that one scholar has claimed *Caradoc* to be the immediate source of the English poem.

The Temptation story, like the Beheading Game, almost certainly goes back to Celtic oral tradition, but we have no ninth-century epic to provide an archetypal form of the tale. The earliest example of the Temptation motif is perhaps that detected by R. S. Loomis in the "mabinogi" or bardic tale of *Pwyll*, an early twelfth-century Welsh work; but it is unlikely that it is one of the progenitors of the English poem. The version of the tale closest to *Sir Gawain and the Green Knight* is found in *The Carl of Carlisle*, an English romance written sometime after *Sir Gawain and the Green Knight*, but derived presumably from a lost French original older than *Sir Gawain and the Green Knight*. In *The Carl of Carlisle*, Gawain, as part of a test of his obedience, successfully resists the overtures of his host's wife, who has deliberately been sent to tempt him by his host. In *Le Chevalier a L'Epée* Gawain resists the overtures of his host's daughter, and in *Yder* the advances of his host's wife, though this time he must resort to kicking her in the stomach to protect himself. The presence of the Temptation motif in *Lanzelet*, a twelfth-century German romance, also demonstrates its popularity.

The greatest single problem concerning the sources of *Sir Gawain and the Green Knight* is the manner in which the two source motifs were combined. Kittredge believed that the Beheading Game and the Temptation were first joined in a single poem by an unknown French romancer in a now-lost romance. Kittredge's principal evidence lies in the fact that a later English version of the combined stories, *The Turk and Gawain*, seemed to him to have been derived not from *Sir Gawain and the Green Knight* but from a similarly combined version, probably in French and certainly not extant, which he reasoned to have been also the source of *Sir Gawain and the Green Knight.*

J. R. Hulbert, whose work on the poem appeared at almost the same time as that of Kittredge, believed that the Temptation and the Beheading Game were originally part of the same oral Celtic fairy legend. This legend recounted how Gawain was enticed by a fairy to her Other-World domain, but was entertained by an emissary before his arrival (the Temptation) and was faced with the Beheading Game as a condition of entrance to the Other World. However, since Hulbert's theory is almost entirely hypothetical and can be supported by no written version of the story, it has gained few supporters.

The most severe modification of Kittredge's theory of transmission has been suggested by Else von Schaubert, whose attractive theory is that the two motifs were first joined by the *Gawain*-poet himself. Hence, according to Schaubert, there is no need to hypothesize a missing French source, for the existence of which there is so little evidence in the text. Schaubert's principal argument for the originality of the *Gawain*-poet's work is that the method of enlarging an existing romance by the addition of a second plot strain is wholly English in practice and is to be found in none of the French courtly romances.

Yet other circumstances under which the Beheading Game and the Temptation might have been joined have been suggested. Alice Buchanan argues that there are strong suggestions of the Beheading Game mixed in with the Temptation theme in *The Carl of Carlisle* and in two other Arthurian episodes, and that the *Gawain*-poet thus needed no combined French source. Laura Hibbard Loomis, on the other hand, finds the two motifs combined in the twelfth-century German *Lanzelet*, though she sees no possibility that the German poet ever influenced the *Gawain*-poet.

It is clear, moreover, that many elements of the poem other than the two main plot lines go back to Celtic and other ancient sources. Almost certainly the Green Knight's name, Bercilak de Hautdesert, is a corruption of the Irish *bachlach* (churl), a three-syllable name repeatedly applied to the challenger of Cuchulainn in *Bricriu's Feast*. And, as would be expected, the origins of the Green Chapel, the Green Girdle, the pentangle, and particularly the figure of Morgan le Fay have all been found in Celtic folklore. The greenness of the Green Knight has been explained in terms both of its possible connections with early vegetation myth and with its Celtic origins.

Nor does the mythic ancestry of the poem end with its Celtic origins. The great Indian scholar Ananda Coomaraswamy found that the Beheading Game had many parallels in Indian myth and ritual. Heinrich Zimmer, in the midst of a psychoanalytical investigation of the poem, managed to discover in the details of *Sir Gawain and the Green Knight* analogues to the folklore of East and West alike. The Green Knight has also been identified with the Lord of Hades, about whom vestiges of the public executioner still hover, and with a "fende" from hell sent to test a Christian knight. There have also been efforts, as might be expected, to identify the Green Knight of the poem with an historical figure. Thus scholars have seen in the poem possible allusions to one Ralph Holmes, a captain of the White Companies in Spain in 1369, and to one Simon Newton, often referred to as the "Green Squire." These attempts at identification, however (somewhat like the attempts to link the last line of the poem—*Hony Soyt Qui Mal Pence*—with the founding of the Order of the Garter), are in the end only hypotheses and have no bearing upon the literary effects and merits of the poem.

E. *General*

If the poems are placed in their probable order of composition, a progression from simplicity to complexity can be noted in the poet's combination of sources. *Patience* draws on one Bible story, *Purity* on a number of scriptural tales. *Pearl* pulls together material as needed from sources as apparently unrelated as St. Augustine and the *Roman de la Rose*, and *Sir Gawain and the Green Knight* weaves together two folk motifs in such a complex fashion that the outcome of the Beheading Game depends upon Sir Gawain's reaction to the Temptation.

From the beginning, however, one notes that the poet is no mere redactor. In addition to using his sources in all sorts of unexpected combinations, he both contracts and expands his inherited materials in order to suit them to his theme or to his desired dramatic effect or, usually, to both. *Patience* provides an illuminating example. Having announced in a sixty-line preamble that his chief theme is to illustrate through the tale of Jonah the virtues of patience and poverty, and having defined these terms through reference to the Beatitudes, the poet reinforces at every opportunity throughout the narrative the point of the prologue by the elaboration of scenes not in the Vulgate.

Thus, the preacher's main point—Jonah's lack of humility—is enforced immediately by Jonah's response to God's first command, to rise and go to Nineveh. "Whenas that sound was still, that marvel brought,/ Wrathful he waxed, and angry" (73–74). Jonah is both full of "wrath" at God's presumption in ordering him about and fearful for his life at the hands of the Ninevites; and his monologue, beginning with line 75, shows all too clearly his lack of humility, of "poverty in spirit." Jonah's most considered evaluation of the situation is full of pride and self-aggrandizement: God has singled him out for punishment and will ignore him when he is persecuted by the Ninevites. He is determined, however, to outwit God by hiding in Tarshish since "when he is lost [God] will let [him] alone" (88). Jonah thus goes to Joppa, "swearing for naught he'd suffer much pain" (90), the very picture of the complaining fool defined in the prologue.

The function of such expansions and digressions as these is obvious. The poet's commentary upon Jonah's imprisonment in the whale's belly, his elaboration of the Vulgate's meager descriptions of the storm and of the whale's belly, his contrasting of the immediate conversion of the King of Nineveh with the continuing wrath and pride of Jonah, his great elaboration of the conclusion of the worm and gourd story as typical of the mercy and loving–kindness of God—all these are means of emphasizing throughout the tale the point of the prologue: the uselessness of complaining against the apparent injustice of life, and the need for patience and poverty of spirit as antidotes to the kind of false pride which leads to "grouching" which in turn engenders more cause for suffering.

The same point, that of the dramatic and thematic use of sources, can be made of *Purity*. There can be no doubt that the poet was well grounded in the Vulgate text. So thoroughly familiar was he with the Scriptures that in many places he interjects into a biblical paraphrase words and phrases from another part of the Bible, presumably from memory. Moreover, his general use of the Bible is highly creative. While he never changes the basic sense of the narrative line of a scriptural passage, he is always willing to embellish biblical passages in order to emphasize whatever thematic aspect of the source he wishes to bring out.

In *Purity* the poet's most extensive additions are to the accounts of the punishment meted out to impure men. Such passages of course invite graphic elaboration, but they also carry the major theme of the poem: God's wrathful treatment of the impure.

Mandeville's *Travels*, the most popular though also the most wholly fictional of the medieval travel books, provides the poet with his account of the Dead Sea (1022 ff.) and with the marvelous ornamentation of the description of the sacred temple vessels (1439 ff.). In both cases the *Gawain*-poet borrows graphic detail which lifts his work far above the humdrum biblical paraphrase common in his time. The Dead Sea is seen as a pit filled with pitch, "broad and bottomless and bitter as gall" (1022), where nothing may live, a place where lead floats and feathers sink, where trees bear fruits of wondrous color, "red and ripe and richly hued" (1045), with cores of ashes. The temple vessels are marvelously ornate—cups in the forms of turreted castles and candlesticks with pillars of brass and branches decorated with figures of birds.

From popular religious tradition the poet borrows the detailed account of the fall of Lucifer with its localization of his throne in the northern part of heaven (211), the failure of the raven to return to the ark because of its discovery of dead flesh (459), the disobedience of Lot's wife in putting salt into the food of the angelic visitors (819 ff.), and Christ's breaking of the bread as evenly as a knife could cut it (1103 ff.). Besides adding vividness and interest to the paraphrase, three of these details supply thematic significance as well. The perfidy of the raven and of Lot's wife are reminiscences of the theme of unfaithfulness in the midst of tales dealing with impurity, and the legend of Christ's breaking the bread is used to enforce the picture of the cleanness of Christ's every action.

When the *Gawain*-poet alludes to Jean de Meun's portion of *Roman de la Rose*, the allusion is made remarkable in that the poet identifies it by author within the poem (1056 ff.). The passage from the *Roman* paraphrased in *Purity* contains a piece of advice given by the Lover's Friend to the Lover, its rather cynically taken point being that the Lover should observe closely the personality of his beloved and then suit his actions accordingly. The *Gawain*-poet, however, allows none of this worldly wisdom to creep into his paraphrase, but recommends the Friend's advice to the Lover to the soul seeking God: "Conform to Christ," he says, "and make yourself clean." The allusion to this highly secular passage of the *Roman de la Rose* in the midst of an intensely emotional section of *Purity* helps the poet to reveal, by means of a startling juxtaposition of religious and secular images, the relation of sinful man to perfect God.

Although *Pearl* makes some slight use of literary sources—the parable of the vineyard, Boccaccio's *Olympia*, etc.—its real importance to one's understanding of the poet's use of inherited material lies in its amalgamation of literary techniques—principally allegory, the dream-vision, symbolism, stanzaic structure—and it would be best to include a discussion of the sources of *Pearl* under that topic.

The poet's skill in adapting his inherited sources to fit his particular themes and dramatic effects reaches its height in *Sir Gawain and the*

Green Knight where, as noted, the outcome of the Beheading Game is made dependent upon the results of Gawain's temptation. To the sources of *Sir Gawain and the Green Knight*, however, the poet adds a great deal of original material in order to emphasize the themes of testing and obedience, which nearly all critics see at the center of the poem. Although scholars disagree about the origins of the various parts of the poem and about the way the basic plot motifs of the poem were combined, they are somewhat more in agreement concerning those items actually added by the English poet. First of all, the *Gawain*-poet may very well have added that plot which binds together the Beheading Game and the Temptation—the so-called Exchange of Winnings between Bercilak and Gawain, which, though it appears in the *Miles Gloriosus*, a twelfth-century Latin poem which borrows the Plautine character, is used uniquely in the Arthur romances by the *Gawain*-poet. Not only does the Exchange of Winnings form a bridge between the two major structural elements of the poem by suggesting the exchange of blows between Bercilak and Gawain and by climaxing each day's temptation, but it also foreshadows and motivates the final testing of Gawain by Bercilak at the Green Chapel.

Kittredge (1916:120–30) listed the following as "certainly added or greatly elaborated by the English author":

> the learned introductory stanza summarizing the fabulous settlements of Western Europe . . . ; the description of the Christmas festivities (i,3) and that of the Green Knight (i,7–9); the challenge (i,12–13) and the speech of Gawain (i,16); the highly poetical stanzas on the changing seasons (ii,1–2); the very elaborate description of the process of arming a knight (ii,4–6), with the allegorical account of the pentangle of virtues (ii,7); Gawain's itinerary—Logres, North Wales, Anglesea, Holyhead, the wilderness of Wirral (ii,9); the winter piece (ii,10); the justly celebrated account of the three hunts (ii,1ff.).

In these additions, certainly, the real greatness of the poem lies. For no matter what he may believe about the origins of the plot and characters, it is to these sections of the poem added by the English poet that the reader finds himself drawn. The initial clash of Bercilak and Gawain, the lovely description of the changing seasons, Gawain's wild journey to the North, the hunts—these are the great literary passages; and in these the original genius of the poet, as well as his most conspicuous use of the medieval literary traditions, is most apparent.

Nearly all the commentators have singled out this use of detail, whether drawn from subsidiary sources or from his own imagination, as the poet's most accomplished poetic technique. The extraordinary visual effectiveness of all four poems is accomplished not only by the poet's singular ability in the descriptive scenes to select and concentrate on those details which best typify the mood and character of the scene—Gawain's sleeping on the rocks in his armor, for example, during his journey through the Wirral—but also by his success in using these details to reinforce and give substance to the themes which everywhere occupy his attention.

LITERARY ART

Though they are markedly similar in theme, the four poems of the *Gawain*-poet involve such differences in literary art and technique that they cannot be discussed in terms of shared devices, even those which, like allegory or the conventions of romance, dominate medieval literature. They are thus best presented individually, each in terms of its own particular features.

The first two of the poems, judged chronologically, do however share to a degree a common structure. *Patience* and *Purity* are best seen as adaptations of the medieval sermon; both follow the homiletic pattern of theme, protheme, dilation, and exemplum. The two poems may very well also share a common verse form; the manuscript would seem to indicate that they were composed in stanzas and this edition so presents them.

But aside from these similarities in structure and common use of the Vulgate, they are quite different poems. *Patience* is extremely tightly constructed, seldom deviating from its narrative line, the biblical story of Jonah. This is not to say that the poet's descriptions are not graphic and his language vivid; they are. But the poem's proportions, its bones, are everywhere visible, and it would seem to be the work of a careful young craftsman.

Purity, by comparison, seems at times diffuse, even long-winded. The poet here has almost too much material to handle, and the kind of amplification which was rigorously controlled in *Patience* occasionally seems digressive in *Purity*. This is probably due to the complexity of the poem's structure, which for the first time exhibits the techniques of amalgamation and fusion which are employed so successfully in *Pearl* and in *Sir Gawain and the Green Knight*.

The exemplum section of the poem is composed of three elaborated Old Testament narratives—Noah's Flood, the Destruction of Sodom and Gomorrah, and Belshazzar's Feast—each of which is accompanied by two rather sparsely told Old Testament narratives closely joining the principal narrative in the scriptural source and illustrating a failure in "trawthe" (i.e., obedience or fidelity) in Lucifer and Adam, Sarah and Lot's wife, and Zedekiah and Nebuchadnezzar. It is clear, moreover, not only that the poet relates the groups of stories employed in the poem chronologically by treating them as parts of the same running narrative, but also that he has given them a thematic relationship by allowing the themes of impurity and disloyalty to overlap and complement each other.

On the simplest level, for example, the major narrative in each group of three contrasts with its two accompanying minor narratives by demonstrating that God's wrath upon the unclean is more dramatically severe than his punishment of the unfaithful. Lucifer and Adam are driven from God's presence for their lack of "trawthe," but all unclean men are horribly destroyed in Noah's Flood. Lot's wife is turned to salt and Sarah goes free of punishment, but Sodom and Gomorrah are razed. Zedekiah is led into captivity and Nebuchadnezzar driven mad, but Belshazzar and all his kingdom are destroyed. The poet makes this relationship amply clear when, at the end of the story of the fall of Lucifer, he asserts that the Lord was not made wrathful by Lucifer's treachery (230), only to assert later (249–50) that in destroying the world at the time of Noah God manifested His merciless wrath.

However, these two kinds of narratives are more than simple contrasts. The major narratives suggest that impurity results from disloyalty and disobedience. Only Noah among all men is faithful to God's commandments; only Lot welcomes God's messengers and protects them against the filthy Sodomites. Belshazzar, though the point is unsure here, neither regards the clear warning of God (1503–04) nor does he share the respect of Nebuchadnezzar for the Jewish God and for the temple vessels. In each case, once the sinner has cast away the bonds of loyalty that bind him to God, he sinks into the mire of his own "natural" impurity. In short, the poem does not deal simply with impurity and with disobedience, but with the impurity which stems from disobedience.

This is the poet's first attempt at thematic fusion, a technique which operates much more fully in *Pearl*, in which the elements joined are literary traditions—the elegy, the dream-vision, and the allegory—and in *Sir Gawain and the Green Knight*, in which they are folk motifs—the Beheading Game and the Temptation. But in all three poems the items linked by the poet, whether narratives, genres, or traditions, lead to a fusion of precisely the same two themes —purity and loyalty. In *Pearl*, the father's dream-vision of his lost daughter's symbolic purity leads him to "trawthe" and to a renewed obedience to God. Gawain's total test involves both fidelity to his word and to his host (the Beheading Game) and sexual purity (the Temptation).

Yet despite the fact that the poet makes this extremely complex use of nine biblical stories as examples, three of which are recounted at great length, and that his enthusiasm at times outruns his judgment in proportion, the overall structure of each poem is generally clearly defined. The poems' excesses are redeemed by the imagination and passion of the poet's exposition of the central themes of purity and obedience.

The poet in these two works shows not only a concern for structure, but also an awareness, unusual in medieval writers, of the effectiveness of imagery. The imagery of *Patience*, for example, constantly supports and advances the major theme of flight and judgment. The poem is filled with images of violent forces of nature—particularly the winds, the whale, and the worm—which are seen within the poem to act as the willing instruments of the Almighty and are so contrasted with the disobedient Jonah. The poet also employs a great many images of tricks, traps, and games which illustrate the devices used by God in subduing Jonah. There are also subsidiary images of sleeping and waking, of house and bower, and of clothing, winds, the sowing of seed, flight, and hiding. It has been suggested also that the image of the vessel, seen both as utensil and as man the vessel of God, serves as a controlling image throughout the poem. All these images unify the poem and give life and vitality to the narrative.

The principal image of the poem, as well as its greatest symbol, is of course the figure of Jonah himself, "all joyless and carping." He is presented as a negative image of what the poet calls "patience," by which he means something very close to "humility," the ready acceptance of God's mission for the individual, however unpleasant that mission may be. This is in itself a startling use of the familiar biblical character; for, although the Book of Jonah certainly contains the seeds of such an interpretation, it was seldom so read in the Middle Ages. Job, positively considered, was the usual Old Testament symbol of patience, not Jonah. Jonah, on the other hand, was almost universally considered by the schoolmen as a type of Christ, reborn from the tomb of the whale's belly.

Again in *Purity* the poet points up his principal themes by means of imagery. Throughout the poem, unpleasant sights and smells are associated with impurity, particularly in the Sodom and Gomorrah section, and pleasant objects with purity. The poet also makes extensive use of purification images, particularly those of washing, burnishing, and polishing, and of images of clean and unclean clothing. The pearl also appears (556) as a symbol of Christ and of the pure soul, a fact that obviously links *Purity* to *Pearl*, where the pearl symbol is similarly conceived. Natural forces, such as the flood, the rain of fire, and the earthquake, are, as in *Patience*, used by the poet as the swift and obedient instruments of God's vengeance.

Patience and *Purity* also make some slight use of another literary device which the poet uses to great effect in *Pearl*, that of the *persona*, the "I" narrator who is in name the poet and yet in character not he, the assumed mask, the fictive personality who tells the tale, Long Will in *Piers Plowman*, Chaucer the Pilgrim. Without entering into the debate of literary historians as to whether such a sophisticated technique of fiction could in fact have existed in the fourteenth century, it should be apparent that there is indeed an "I" present in both poems. In *Patience* the *persona* is the preacher and is actively present in the poem. The reader is from time to time made aware that he is listening not to an impersonal and omniscient author, but to a narrator who, although not strongly individualized, is nevertheless a man of firm opinion. "Patience is so appointed that it often displeases," the poem begins and ends. In between these two statements of the poem's moral lesson, the narrator-preacher argues from both authority and experience by asserting time after time both aphorisms and statements of personal experience.

In *Purity*, the device is not so evident. Yet the poem begins, as did *Patience*, with a firm statement of the theme of "clannesse," purity; and the poet's single point of view is everywhere evident.

Although on looking backward one can see the seeds of the literary artistry of the later poems in the earlier ones, to move to *Pearl* from these early homiletic poems is still quite a journey. Here the verse structure seems dramatically sophisticated even to an age like the present which expects sophistication in structure.

The verse itself reflects the poet's acquaintance with the usages not only of the explosive, dramatic alliterative verse of the Anglo-Saxons, but also of the stanza-linking techniques of the imported French forms. The poem consists of 101 twelve-line stanzas, arranged in nineteen groups of five stanzas each and in one group (the fifteenth) of six stanzas. The natural supposition is, of course, that one stanza of the fifteenth group, probably either Stanza 72 or 76, is either spurious or was not canceled by the poet. The stanza groups are held together internally by the linking together of each group of verses through the repetition of a concluding refrain and through a device known as concatenation, the repetition of the last word of each verse in the first line of the following stanza.

The poet uses both alliteration and rhyme throughout. The basic line is the familiar irregular four-stress accentual line of alliterative verse, but the twelve lines of the stanza consistently follow the rhyme scheme *a b a b a b a b b c b c*. This combination of styles of verse, along with the linking of stanzas, results in a metrical pattern of great complexity, perfectly suited to the mixture of formality and personal feeling, of objectivity and deep emotion demanded by elegy.

Pearl also makes use of an amalgamation of literary forms—the elegy, the dream-vision, and the allegory—in order to present under the guise of literary fiction (the dream-vision) the meaning (the allegory) of what may have been a personal experience (the elegy). This peculiar mixture of personal poet-narrator and allegorical subject matter is responsible for the most perplexing of the purely literary problems involved in *Pearl*. Is the poem in fact an elegy on the death of the poet-narrator's two-year-old daughter or is it, or even could it be, purely allegorical, with the death of the child having no referent in the life of the poet-narrator and thus functioning only as a literary device?

Space permits only a brief review of the critical storm which has raged over this problem. Basically, the elegiac interpretation depends upon a number of apparently personal references within the poem. The maiden refers to herself as having left the "world's woe" (761) at a "young and tender" age (412); the dreamer asserts that at her death the child was not yet two years old and that she had learned neither Paternoster nor Creed (483–85); upon seeing her, the dreamer recognizes her immediately (164) and asserts that she was "nearer than aunt or niece" to him (233). This interpretation was initiated by Morris in his edition in 1864 and has been supported by, among others, Gordon, Osgood, Gollancz, Coulton, Wellek, and Dorothy Everett.

The elegiac interpretation was first challenged in 1895 by Courthope, who saw the poem as "allegory made the vehicle of contemplation." Since that time, it has been questioned by Schofield, who saw the child as clean maidenhood, by Garrett as the Holy Eucharist, by Sister Mary Madelena as the lost sweetness of God, by Fletcher as lost innocence, by Greene as divine grace, by Sister M. V. Hillmann as the beauty of the soul, and by Marie Hamilton as the regenerate soul.

This tendency, initiated sixty years ago, to see the poem as allegory has perhaps reached its natural culmination in the work of those recent critics who specialize in applying the canons of exegetical criticism to *Pearl*. In working with *Pearl* these critics have used as a point of departure St. Thomas Aquinas's famous statement in *Summa Theologica* (later applied by both Dante and Boccaccio, among others, to secular literature) of the possible levels of meaning—literal, allegorical, moral, and anagogical—at which a passage of scripture might be read.

Thus one critic, viewing the poem as an allegory of the place of innocence in the scheme of things, maintains that on the literal level the pearl is simply a jewel; on the allegorical, the life of innocence in the New Jerusalem. Another critic, working from a slightly different interpretation of St. Thomas's categories, sees the child, literally and historically, as an unresolved question of identification; allegorically, as the loss of spiritual peace; morally, as the loss of faith; and, anagogically, as the loss of heaven.

A number of critics have abandoned both the elegiac and the allegorical approaches to the whole poem in order to stress the sym-

bolism and the imagery of its parts. Indeed, the poem is filled with
individual images and with image clusters of all kinds—of flowers
and growing things and of the harvest, of blood and water, of light,
of music and jewels, and of the cities of God and man. All of these
essentially point to the bounty of God and to the vast difference in
the poem between heavenly and earthly values; as a result, the imagery
promotes the moral purpose of the poem. It may be also, as Father
Blenkner has observed, that the three settings of the poem—the "erber"
wherein the narrator falls asleep, the dream landscape in which he
finds himself, and the New Jerusalem which he perceives in a vision
—are themselves images of "the external world of creation, the in-
ternal world of the psyche, and the superior world of God."

Of all the symbols with which the poem deals, the most prominent
and the most immediately effective is that of the pearl. Just as the
medieval bestiaries interpreted allegorically the characteristics of ani-
mals, medieval lapidaries interpreted the symbolic qualities of gems.
In these books the pearl, or "margarita," is continually cited as a
symbol of purity, presumably because of its whiteness. As such, the
pearl was often associated with virginity and with the Blessed Virgin,
and so came in time to form the basis of a cult which drew its mem-
bership from the ranks of courtly maidens and which took as its
patron the third-century St. Margaret of Antioch.

Thus the whole symbolic tradition of the pearl comes to bear upon
the poem. The pearl is here both the maiden, who might well have
been named Margery or Margarita, and the symbol of her spotless
body and soul. She is arrayed in pearls; she wears upon her breast
the "pearl of great price" and upon her head a crown of pearls. At
the height of her argument, she enjoins the dreamer to renounce the
foolish world and to search for his own spotless pearl. In this way,
the pearl, imbued with all the connotative symbolic richness of its
centuries of development, dominates the symbolism of the poem and
enriches the reader's perception of the place of the innocent in the
hierarchy of heaven.

Other students have found a key to the meaning of the poem

precisely in this question of hierarchy and in the long theological debate between narrator and maiden centering on the Church's view of salvation, whether by grace or merit. Nor can anyone doubt that the illumination of doctrine is one of the poet's purposes. In fact, it is impossible to come to grips with the poem without some understanding both of the doctrine argued and of the intensity of the argument.

The orthodoxy of the *Gawain*-poet's theology in the debate between maiden and dreamer went unquestioned until 1904, when an important article by Carleton F. Brown presented the poet as a learned ecclesiast whose theological opinions in the poem were clearly in opposition to the accepted doctrines of his time. The pearl-maiden's insistence in the poem that the "grace of God is great enough" for salvation and that there is equality among the saved in heaven is, according to Brown, in marked contradiction to the system of rewards for good deeds established by Saints Jerome, Augustine, and Gregory. The poem thus disregards patristic authority and tradition, relying instead on scripture and making salvation purely a matter of grace uninfluenced by merit. In Brown's view, the *Gawain*-poet is a forerunner of the sixteenth-century Protestant Reformation since he maintains, as does Luther, that salvation is by grace alone. But, although Brown's opinion did much to focus the attention of readers on the theology of the poem, few, if any, scholars have agreed with his conclusions or followed his lead.

Much of the confusion surrounding the theology of the poem can be dispelled if one recalls that the maiden's arguments are part of a dramatic situation within the poem. She is presented by the poet as arguing actively and at times vehemently with the narrator in an attempt to break through his stubborn earthliness and to force him to recognize the truth of the vision which he has been permitted to see. Thus it is natural that she should to some degree overstate her case and overemphasize in her eagerness certain aspects of the doctrines she is advocating.

It is evident also that the poem makes similar use of a number of other medieval traditions. The poem abounds in scriptural and patristical allusions, not only in those passages in which great scriptural scenes are extensively and creatively paraphrased—the parable of the vineyard (Matt. 20:1–16), the vision of the New Jerusalem (Rev. 21:10–22:7), and the procession of the 144,000 virgins (Rev. 14:1–5)—but in numerous scattered allusions and images connected with the description of the maiden, particularly in connection with her raiment, with her arguments, and with the miraculous landscape of the poem.

For example, the allegorical interpretation of the Song of Songs, widely prevalent in the Middle Ages, which saw in the marriage of Bridegroom and Bride the union of Christ and the Church, is reflected in the maiden's description of herself as the bride of Christ (763–64). The pearly crown that the maiden wears reflects a popular medieval hymn, and the river that separates dreamer and child is that which proceeds out of the throne of God (Rev. 22:1) as well as the barrier-river of the Other-World romances. In the use of these allusions the *Gawain*-poet follows the usual customs of medieval writers in adapting ancient customs and descriptions to his own time; thus, the New Jerusalem becomes a manor enclosed in a castle wall.

There are some indications also that *Pearl* reflects to a small degree the courtly tradition, a fact that links the poem to *Sir Gawain and the Green Knight*, in which that tradition is very strong. The dream-vision form itself is that of the *Roman de la Rose*, and the miraculous garden in which the dreamer finds himself is very like that of dozens of Other-World romances. The details of dress, particularly the fashionable wedding gown of the maiden, and of architecture reflect the same intimate knowledge of courtly life revealed in *Sir Gawain and the Green Knight*.

Even the tone of the dreamer's discussion with the pearl-maiden obviously relies upon an accepted code of manners, for it is marked by that peculiarly late medieval view of courtesy which could so blend the canons of secular and divine love as to make their terms almost interchangeable (as in "I Sing of a Maiden" and "Maiden in the Moor Lay," both of which can be read as either erotic or religious poems). Thus the Blessed Virgin, the "queen of Courtesy" (432), is in *Pearl* both matchless mother of God and perfection of the virginal courtly graces. And St. Paul's "grace," by which all are made members of Christ's body, becomes simply "cortaysye" (457).

Given *Patience, Purity,* and *Pearl* one would probably not have predicted *Sir Gawain and the Green Knight.* It is in *genre* a courtly romance, a form traditionally aristocratic and secular whose staple themes are courtly love and warfare. Although *Sir Gawain and the Green Knight* deals with the poet's central themes—purity and obedience—it is in subject matter and tone far removed from his earlier poems. It is almost as though Rossetti were discovered to have written "Gunga Din."

Like *Pearl, Sir Gawain and the Green Knight* is metrically innovative. In fact, a great deal of the effectiveness of *Sir Gawain and the Green Knight* lies in its complex and varied line and stanza structure. The 2,530 lines of the poem are arranged in 101 stanzas varying from twelve to thirty-eight lines in length, each of which concludes with a unique five-line, cross-rhyming "bob and wheel," the "bob" consisting of a single one-stress line and the "wheel" of four three-stress lines. As in *Patience, Purity,* and *Pearl,* the main body of the stanza is alliterative, and much of the metrical tension of the poem results from the play in each stanza between the short rhymed concluding lines and the long alliterative lines, just as refrain and concatenation add interest to *Pearl.*

Sir Gawain and the Green Knight exhibits also a flexibility in the use of the alliterative line unrivaled in Middle English verse. The lines of the poem, for example, are far richer in the number of alliterating syllables than are the usual verses of the period. Whereas the standard alliterative line of the period has three accented alliterative words, two in the first and one in the second half-line, the *Gawain*-poet many times exceeds this minimum by using three accents in the first half-line. He makes use also of a number of other elaborate variations of standard alliterative technique. He often uses two sets of alliterating syllables within a single line, he alliterates voiceless with voiced consonants ("f" and "v," "s" with "z"), and he allows the alliteration to fall on an unaccented syllable, such as a prefix or an unaccented preposition or the second element of a compound word. He sometimes even allows the unalliterated final word of a line to determine the alliterative pattern for the following line.

Such liberties provide the poem with a rhythm patterned and flexible, determined and free. Because of the added alliterating syllables in many lines, the poet is able to use a much longer line than is ordinarily possible. This permits him a greater freedom in the placement of accent and so adds interest and variation to the meter. The reader, however, is not cognizant of the artifices and poetic devices employed by the poet, only of the graceful, swinging quality of the verse.

Like the other works of the poet, *Sir Gawain and the Green Knight* exhibits a strongly defined structure, far tighter than that of the usual romance, which as a type is episodic and digressive.

Even so, the overall structure of the poem may have been misunderstood to some degree by modern critics. Sir Frederick Madden, who first edited the poem in modern times, divided the work into four great sections or "fits," the divisions occurring at lines 491, 1126, and 1998; and the poem has been so divided by every subsequent editor. However, as Laurita L. Hill has pointed out, the poem in the manuscript is itself divided internally by the use of capital initials of various sizes into *nine* divisions. Four of these divisions coincide with those marked by Madden; the others occur at lines 619, 763, 1421, 1893, and 2259.

It is clear, moreover, that in the other three poems of Cotton Nero A.x. similar capital letters are used with the obvious intent of dividing the poems into their natural divisions—in *Pearl*, to mark the famous five-verse divisions; in *Patience*, to separate the four chapters of Jonah with an introductory prologue; in *Purity*, both to correspond to chapters in the Vulgate and to mark other changes in source. It is therefore highly likely, as Miss Hill points out, that the poem is actually more intricately organized than its editors have indicated. Certainly the division created by the use of capitals within the poem emphasizes far more precisely than does the four-part division the stages of development of the action in that it clearly delineates as entities such sections of the poem as the passing of the year and the journey of Gawain.

No matter how one divides the poem, it is clear that the main incidents of the work are arranged in a perfectly defined and balanced pattern. The poem begins with three introductory elements—the reference to the fall of Troy, the account of the founding of Britain by the Trojan Brutus, and the setting of the scene in Arthur's court— elements which are almost verbally repeated in reverse order to round out and conclude the poem.

Each of the hunting scenes of Fit III is, moreover, developed in the same way. The account of the hunt is itself divided by the inter-view between Gawain and Bercilak's lady and is concluded by evening festivities. There is evidence also that the poet telescoped the third and fourth days of the Christmas celebrations at Bercilak's court in order to keep the symmetry of the three hunts and the three blows of Bercilak.

Even more strikingly the action of the hunts mirrors perfectly the temptations that Gawain undergoes in his bower. Like the deer, he is on the first day politic, adroit, and tactful in handling the overtures of the lady. On the second day, he, like the hunted boar, faces his pursuer directly and resists her advances actively. Finally, on the third day, to his shame he follows the duplicity of the fox.

The unity of structure is also assured by a number of parallel situations and images whose main function is to draw together the various parts and themes of the poem. In each fit there are festal meals and descriptions of the arming of knights, and many parallel incidents also serve to make connections backward and forward in the poem and so keep the major action of the work constantly before the reader. For example, the slaughtering of the captured animals suggests the beheading game; the exchange of gifts at the end of each day in the castle and the New Year's gift game at Arthur's court suggest the exchange of blows; each of Gawain's two journeys suggests the other by repetition of the description of the terrain. These, like the descriptions of arms and dress, serve both to maintain structural unity and to establish the background of pomp and splendor against which much of the action takes place.

Sir Gawain and the Green Knight, in its balanced and coherent structure, its skillful adaptation and functional use of its sources and traditional devices, its original use of meter and language, and its sharply defined scenes of courtly life, reveals in much fuller measure than his earlier poems the superlative talent of the *Gawain*-poet. And the poem makes it clear also that the poet's talent as it developed constantly sought after new forms of expression. In *Patience* and *Purity,* the poet used familiar biblical narratives as vehicles; in *Pearl,* he turned to the elegiac and to the dream-vision conventions. *Sir Gawain and the Green Knight* is a courtly romance in which both the narrative and the descriptions reach far back into Celtic myth.

Nor does this variety in source material in the four poems represent experimentation for its own sake. As noted, one of the distinctive marks of the *Gawain*-poet's method and talent has been his ability to use, sometimes in a highly original fashion, his basic sources for thematic purposes. The Jonah story as seen by the *Gawain*-poet is a parable of disobedience. The Old Testament narratives in *Purity* contain in themselves the seeds of the interpretation given to them by the poet. The elegiac and dream-vision traditions combine to form an effective medium for the themes of *Pearl.* A number of critics have thus attempted to find a key to the theme of the poem in the myths so carefully joined by the poet to make up the narrative structure of *Sir Gawain and the Green Knight.*

In general, however, these early myth-hunting critics were concerned only with the relationship of the folk elements in *Sir Gawain and the Green Knight* and not at all with the structures of meaning which these myths carried in themselves and thence contributed to the total meaning of the poem. Only with the rise of "myth criticism" in the 1940s and 1950s did such issues begin to occupy the attention of scholars and critics generally. It was inevitable that *Sir Gawain and the Green Knight*, in which the origins of the mythic sources of the poem had already been thoroughly classified and traced, should become a prime subject for investigation at that time.

The greatest single impetus to the investigation of myth in the poem came from an article published by the English critic John Speirs in 1949. Speirs argued that the poem was a "midwinter festival poem" in which "Gawain is seen in his traditional role as the hero, the agent who brought back the spring, restored the frozen life-processes, revived the god—or (in later versions) cured the king" (1957:220).

The importance of Speirs's article, however, lay not so much in its conclusions, which had already been suggested by other critics, but in its brash assertion that all previous attempts to trace the origins of the poem in Celtic tradition and French romance, in fact all investigative scholarship devoted to the poem, had been worthless or, worse still, misleading. The "only" way of approach to the poem, asserted Speirs, was through its "inner organizing, unifying and realizing principle of life and growth" (1957:218).

As might be expected, most scholars writing on the poem since 1949 do not share Speirs's thesis, not so much because of his specific conclusions about the poem, but because of his underlying assumption that the poem does not merely reflect the myth and ritual elements inherent in the sources, but rather that these myths and rituals are consciously invoked by the poet in order to contribute to the meaning of the poem. Thus Speirs's article, despite its great interest, has proved after all to be a false scent. Although students have continued to investigate the mythic and folklore sources of the poem, they have not generally accepted Speirs's assertion that the poet's use of myth is conscious nor have they followed his general identification of myth and poem. Instead, these readers have concentrated, as did the older generation of investigators, on the specific ways in which myth determines the structure and meaning of the poem.

For example, the mythic Morgan le Fay is surely the most controversial figure in the poem, and her ambiguous role has become the crux of the poem for a number of critics. It is of course puzzling that, although Morgan appears in the poem only once and is named only twice, with her influence on the action discussed in a single passage of but twenty-one lines, she is said by the poet to be the prime mover of the entire action. Certainly critical opinion has been divided on the role that Morgan plays in the poem. Kittredge, writing in 1916, asserted that Morgan's action stemmed from her traditional hatred of Guinevere and from a desire to warn the court of the queen's unfaithfulness. Kittredge concluded that the poet had through his use of Morgan supplied the medieval reader familiar with her general role in the Arthur legend with an entirely adequate explanation of Bercilak's motives. J. R. Hulbert, however, writing in the same year, saw Bercilak's explanation as inherently unreasonable and condemned it as a last-minute attempt by the poet to supply Bercilak with some sort of explanation for his actions.

A sampling reveals that more modern criticism has come no closer to agreement. While one critic has suggested that Morgan intended to purge Arthur's court of moral depravity and that her plan did in fact succeed in humiliating Arthur, another has answered his argument point by point and has asserted that Morgan is present in the poem solely as a foil to enhance the beauty of Gawain's temptress.

Mother Angela Carson has stated that Morgan le Fay, traditionally a shape-shifter, actually appears in the poem both as witch and temptress, as the old woman whom Gawain sees in Bercilak's chapel and also as Bercilak's fair wife. T. McAlindon forthrightly calls her a pagan goddess, and Dale Randall, an agent of Satan. Morton Bloomfield, on the other hand, feels that Morgan is simply playing a game with Arthur's court.

And perhaps the answer to the puzzling question of Morgan's influence on the action does indeed lie in her traditional character.

For, even though Albert Friedman, Mother Carson, and others reject the idea, the tradition of Morgan le Fay does include her role as healer and tester. It is perfectly in character, as Kittredge and Denver Baughan have demonstrated, for her to test the honor, fidelity, and morality of individuals. That the poem does involve the testing of Gawain no critic has doubted; and, although the precise qualities being tested have been debated, courage, fidelity, and chastity are certainly among them.

Critics, however, are divided as to the degree of success with which Gawain meets his test. One critic, for example, maintains that Gawain, in spite of his apparent failure to keep faith with Bercilak, is nevertheless a "splendid man" and that his actions demonstrate "what a perfect knight can do when he is forced to face the unknown" (Markman, 1957:575). Yet another critic maintains that the poem is concerned with the irony of Gawain's "muddled conscience" (Green, 1962:138). Still another holds that the poem is "a human and sympathetic presentation designed to reveal how human and imperfect is even a supposedly perfect knight such as the pentagonal Gawain" (Engelhardt, 1955:224–25). And various studies of the poem's several confession scenes, of the penitential doctrines reflected in the poem, and of the imagery of the Grail quest underlying the poem have emphasized the ethical and, specifically, the Christian nature of *Sir Gawain and the Green Knight*.

Yet, in spite of its obviously ethical and moral nature, the poem is a gay and happy affair, and a great number of recent studies reveal the comic nature of much of the action. Certainly the poem's comic touches—its extravagance in description and conversation, for example—serve to balance the sober ethical themes, just as in *Pearl* the poet uses the same counterbalance to avoid any taint of either bathos or sentimentality. One is faced with a poem which obviously does have room for variations in tone, for both "bliss and care"; and the impurities of comedy thus serve to temper Gawain's failure, though oddly enough also to make it human and understandable.

The foregoing account of the major areas of interest in the poem should reveal the principal barrier to any clear statement of the poem's central theme: the complexity of tone, idea, and form which the poem everywhere reveals. In the end it is well-nigh impossible to say with any degree of assurance *exactly* what *Sir Gawain and the Green Knight* is *only* about. The poem is certainly about society, both flourishing and decadent. But it involves not only the relationship between civilization and nature and the responsibility of the individual to society, but also the individual's responsibility to himself—to his own ideals of conduct and, ultimately, to his survival.

The poet's thoughts on these matters are complex; the poem is no simple rule book, but a remarkably rich commentary on life. Gawain is in his own eyes a failure, but in the eyes of his society he is an enormous success. Within the castle all is gaiety and warmth, yet outside horrible beasts and icy storms and godless men await even the best of knights on the most godly of errands. Bercilak's lady is lovely and charming; yet she is wanton and in the end lures Gawain into disgrace. Bercilak is both monster and courtier. Such paradoxes as these from the poem could be listed for some time without really coming any closer to the point.

Nor does further investigation of the mythic background or of the other traditions that make up the poem really serve to expose the poem's center or to define its appeal. The poem is a romance, to be sure, and, like the romances that precede it, contains certain more-or-less standard characteristics: feasts, hunts, tourneys, descriptions of arms, lonely quests, hairbreadth escapes, supernatural monsters—the lot. Yet *Sir Gawain and the Green Knight* is obviously no ordinary romance, and an analysis of the ways in which the poem conforms to its type leads only to the conclusion that its essence is not a mere combination of romantic devices.

Much the same point can be made about the use of courtly love in the poem. For, although the heyday of courtly love as a way of life (if, indeed, it ever were more than a literary convention) was long since past by the time of the *Gawain*-poet, its influence is certainly to be seen in the poem. The lady, like many a literary (if not real-life) heroine, obviously either is or pretends to be a devotee of courtly love, though an unusually aggressive one; and she is disappointed at Gawain's unwillingness to play the game. Yet while courtly love is presented as a snare and a temptation, Gawain successfully resists its lures, and it is clear that courtly love is only a part of the poem's interplay of theme and idea, not its core.

In short, no single approach to the poem can ever illuminate all of its many facets. The scores of studies of sources, symbols, poetic devices, and literary traditions have served to remove some of the shadows which time has cast over the poem. No one can doubt that future studies will clarify much that is now obscure and dark. But no matter how pointed and well-directed, such studies can never reduce to a single set of literary or moral principles the complex pattern of Gawain's search for knightly perfection.

GENERAL THEMES

So much has been said of theme in the course of the previous discussions that a brief resume should suffice here.

Patience, almost certainly the first of the poet's works, deals with the theme of disobedience, with Jonah's pride in fleeing from what he considers the injustice of life and the presumption of God. Only through the acquisition of spiritual "poverty" and patience, through humility, says the poet, can man escape the fate of "grouching" Jonah and be reconciled to the inevitability of pain and to the ways of God. Thus *Patience*, though it does not deal as do the other three poems with sexual purity, is certainly linked to the other poems through its concern with obedience to God's commandments.

Purity presents these two themes by the use of contrasting and, at times, overlapping biblical stories of impurity and unfaithfulness. *Pearl* contrasts the purity and obedience of the pearl-maiden with the restless "grouching" (a theme first developed in *Patience*) of the narrator-father. Sir Gawain is tested both for sexual purity and for obedience to his word. In all three cases, the qualities of purity and obedience are closely related. Failure in obedience to God, as seen in the Hebrews in *Purity*, leads to impurity and sacrilege. The spotless innocence of the pearl-maiden, on the other hand, seems almost to symbolize her unquestioning obedience to God's will, just as her father's inability to accept what seems to him the arbitrary nature of God's disposition of the saved souls in heaven reflects his essential worldliness. Gawain, although he passes Morgan's test for sexual purity, ultimately fails in resisting the temptation to save his life, even though saving it results in his breaking his given word.

All four poems thus involve failures in purity and/or obedience, and the difference between success and failure is generally treated by the poet in specifically Christian terms. The disobedience of Jonah and the ancient Hebrews in *Purity* is directly opposed to the commands of Jehovah. The grumbling failure of the narrator in *Pearl* to accept God's judgment is directly contrary to the will of God as stated by the maiden. And, in *Sir Gawain and the Green Knight*, Gawain fails in being obedient to his word in spite of the symbolic protection of his armor with its pentangle of Christian virtues and the personal guidance of the Blessed Virgin. The pure and constant values of heaven are, therefore, contrasted in all four poems with the tarnished and shifting standards of earth.

These religious failures lead the reader to a general vision of man in the *Gawain*-poet as fallen, degenerate, and incapable in himself of achieving salvation, of attaining true felicity, or even of maintaining a decent standard of conduct in life. The poet consistently sees society as corrupt; even the civilization of Arthur, that golden, chivalric court in its "first age," is essentially cowardly and frivolous. The man who wishes to live by God's standards is thus presented as being constantly in conflict with the values of society; his greatest temptation is to take the easy road away from the strictures of God. And the *Gawain*-poet is unyielding on this point: to accept God's appointed mission is to bring upon oneself the scorn and fury of the world. Jonah, the Old Testament heroes in *Purity*, the father in *Pearl*, and Sir Gawain do not avoid present trouble—though they may, as in

Purity, escape eternal damnation—by taking up their crosses to follow God. Jonah is far happier sleeping on the ship, falsely certain that he has escaped God, than he ever is preaching God's word. The father's discovery of the pearl-maiden's glorification in heaven brings him only confusion and unhappiness. Gawain would have, in a sense, been far better off at home in Arthur's gay court than lost in the frozen Wirral, attacked by outlaws and terrifying beasts.

Yet society in these poems—unless, like the Ninevites in *Patience*, it turns to God—is doomed, even as the Round Table is, by its own inherent, fallen sinfulness. Only a handful of heroes, set upon and despised, can hope for the mercy of God and for salvation in the orthodox Christian way, through the merits of Christ. Thus the father of the pearl-maiden and Gawain have in the end attained a measure of wisdom, though they are overcome by a sense of their own unworthiness and by a perception of the evil of the world in which they live. While the *Gawain*-poet may here have been described in terms more applicable to T. S. Eliot or to Graham Greene than to a medieval clerk, yet these comparisons do not seem inappropriate. All these writers are parts of the same Catholic tradition and share essentially the same moral vision, though expressed in vastly different terms, of man struggling for grace in a fallen world.

THE POET'S LANGUAGE

So numerous and rich are the discussions of the language of the *Gawain*-poet that it would seem profitless to replow a field in which the furrows are already well dug. Indeed one sometimes feels that editors edit old texts simply in order to write the detailed linguistic essays that preface them. Whatever their motives, the linguistic analyses of Mary S. Serjeantson (1940:xli–lxvi) and Norman Davis (1967:132–52), though directed principally to the forms of *Sir Gawain and the Green Knight,* taken together seem to cover thoroughly every possible aspect of the poet's language and the reader can be directed to them with confidence. For the general linguistic background of the period, historically surveyed, A. H. Markwardt's revision of Moore's *Historical Outlines of English Sounds and Inflections* is the standard text, and several good handbooks are in print.

However, for the benefit of those readers whose interests are not especially linguistic and who have already become acquainted with the "easiest" of the ME dialects, the East Midland of Chaucer, a brief analysis of the poet's dialect follows.

The language of Cotton Nero A.x. is basically a dialect of the Northwest Midlands, though the changing state of the language, both in form and vocabulary, in the late fourteenth century and the poet's use of a poetic diction passed down to him in the alliterative oral tradition make any exact placing impossible. The poems contain conspicuously Northern, even Scottish forms, e.g. the present participial ending *ande* and the *es* and *eʒ* verb endings, but there are also present structures that are clearly West Midland, such as the present indicative plural ending *en* and the *ho* form of the third person singular feminine pronoun. Though the poet presumably lived far from London, the number of French words he uses is high when compared to his Midland contemporaries, and the number of Scandinavian words, over 10 percent in *Sir Gawain and the Green Knight*, quite striking. In short, the poet's language, in form and diction, is probably very much his own.

The principal forms of that language, especially as they differ from those of Chaucer (with whose language some familiarity is assumed), may be simply presented. Orthographical variants (e.g. *y* and *i*) are ignored.

I. Accidence

1. Articles: Indefinite: *a*; *an* or *on* before vowels and *h*.
   Definite: *þe*; *þo*, *þose* in pl.

2. Demonstratives: Adjective: sing. *þat*, pl. *þose*.
   Pronoun: sing. *þis*, pl. *þis*, *þise*, *þese*.

3. Personal pronouns:

		SINGULAR			PLURAL
1st	nom.	I			we
	gen.	my, myn			oure
	dat. acc.	me			us
2nd	nom.	þou, þu			ȝe
	gen.	þy, þyn			ȝoure
	dat. acc.	þe, þu			yow

		Masculine	*Feminine*	*Neuter*	
3rd	nom.	he	ho, scho	hit	þay
	gen.	his	hir, her	his	her, hor, þayr
	dat. acc.	him	hir, her	hit	hom, hem, him

4. Indefinite pronouns: *mon, men, who, quo, what.*

5. Relative pronouns: *whom, wham, quom, þat.*

6. Nouns:

	SINGULAR	PLURAL
nom. acc.	e, —	(e)ȝ (e)s, esse, en, us, e, r
gen.	(e)s, (e)ȝ, e, —	(e)ȝ, (e)s, en

7. Adjectives: no case or gender; pl. in *e,* often dropped.

8. Verbs: Infinitive: *en, e, y.*

Participles: pres, *ande, yng*; past, *en, n, e* (strong verbs)
    d, t (weak verbs)

Pres. Ind.	SINGULAR	PLURAL
1st.	e, (e)ȝ, —.	(e)n, e, (e)ȝ, tȝ, —
2nd.	(e)ȝ,	
3rd.	ȝ, s, tȝ	

Past Ind. Strong verbs: sing. no ending; pl. *on, e, en.*

Weak verbs:	SINGULAR	PLURAL
1st.	de, te	(e)d, (e)t
2nd.	des, tes	
3rd.	de, te	

Imperative: *e*, -; pl. *eʒ, es*

The verb "to be":

Inf: ben, be

Present indicative

	SINGULAR	PLURAL
1st.	am	ar, arn, ben
2nd.	art	
3rd.	is	

Past indicative

	SINGULAR	PLURAL
1st.	watʒ	wer, weren, were, wern
2nd.	watʒ, were	
3rd.	watʒ	

II. Spelling and Phonology

In general, the scribe's spelling is perhaps better, that is to say more consistent, than that of his contemporaries, and his variations may very well represent the inconsistencies of his original as well as his own.

His use of the letter ʒ, however, needs explanation. It represents both the voiceless fricatives [x] as in *knyʒt* and *aʒt* and the voiced front spirant or semi-vowel [j] (Chaucer's *y*) as in *ʒere*. It represents also the sounds [w] and [u] medially after *a* or *o* plus *l* or *r* as in *sorʒe*. Moreover, ʒ could be voiceless [s] or [z] in a terminal position as in *frendeʒ* or *watʒ*.

Qu presumably has the phonetic value of *wh* [hw]. We thus find both *quyl* and *whyle*. *W* sometimes is [u] as in *nwe*, *v* and *w* are occasionally confused as in *awyse*, and *c* is sometimes used for *s* as in *falce*.

The poet's exact sounds are not always easy to determine. The leveling of unstressed vowels in the Middle English period reduces unstressed *a, o,* and *u* along with *e* to an indeterminate [ə]. And the problem of the pronunciation of final *e* in poetry is here, as in Chaucer, an unsolvable mystery, at least at present.

III. Vocabulary

The poet's vocabulary is a medley of English, French, and Scandinavian words. A "crude count" by Norman Davis reveals that of the 2,650 different words of *Sir Gawain and the Green Knight* some 1,000 "have no ancestors in Old English" and of these "some 250 are Scandinavian and about 750 French." The Scandinavian element is almost as pronounced in the other poems (a little over 9 percent in *Patience* and *Pearl* and 7½ percent in *Purity*), and the French element equally pronounced, an unusual mixture for a north-country poet, even allowing for the general dissemination of Norman French and the needs of alliterative verse.

The linguistic evidence, like the evidence of subject matter, thus points to a widely read, sophisticated poet. And there is linguistic evidence, too, of his poetic training in the ways of the old alliterative verse. Like the pre-invasion writers he depends upon formulaic phrases and varied synonyms for common objects, not only in the alliterative *Sir Gawain and the Green Knight,* but in the other three poems as well. "Man" thus becomes *burn, freke, gome, hathel, knyȝt, lede, mon, noble, prince, schalk, segge,* and *wyȝe.*

· Bibliography ·

GENERAL WORKS AND COLLECTED EDITIONS

Blanch, Robert J., ed. (1966), Sir Gawain and Pearl: Critical Essays. Bloomington.

Cawley, A. C., ed. (1962), Pearl and Sir Gawain and the Green Knight. Everyman's Library 346, London.

Chambers, E. K. (1945), English Literature at the Close of the Middle Ages. London.

Chapman, C. O. (1951), An Index of Names in Pearl, Patience, Purity and Sir Gawain. Ithaca.

Cuffe, Rev. Edwin (1951), An Interpretation of Patience, Cleanness, and Pearl from the Viewpoint of Imagery. Unpublished dissertation, Chapel Hill.

Gardner, John, tr. (1965), The Complete Works of the Gawain-Poet. Chicago.

Gollancz, Israel (1923), Pearl, Cleanness, Patience and Sir Gawain. Reproduced in facsimile from MS Cotton Nero A.x., EETS 162, London.

Hamilton, Marie P. (1970), The Pearl-Poet, A Manual of the Writings in Middle English. Ed. J. Burke Severs, Hamden, Conn. Vol. II: 339–53, 503–16. (Revision of Well's Manual. Includes Pearl, Purity and Patience. The section of the Manual on Sir Gawain and the Green Knight, prepared by Helaine Newstead, is included in Vol. I, pp. 54–57.)

Housman, A. E. (1961), The Application of Thought to Textual Criticism, Selected Prose, ed. John Carter. Cambridge.

Kottler, Barnet and Alan M. Markman (1966), A Concordance to Five Middle English Poems: Cleanness, St. Erkenwald, Sir Gawain and the Green Knight, Patience, and Pearl. Pittsburgh.

Moorman, Charles (1968), The Pearl-Poet. New York.

Morris, R., ed. (1864, rev. 1869), Early English Alliterative Poems in the West Midland Dialect of the Fourteenth Century. EETS 1, London. (Pearl, Purity, and Patience.)

Williams, Margaret, tr. (1966), The Pearl-Poet: His Complete Works. New York.

Willis, James (1972), Latin Textual Criticism. Urbana.

· BIBLIOGRAPHY ·

Zavadil, J. B. (1962), A Study of Meaning in Patience and Cleanness. Unpublished dissertation, Stanford.

THE PRINCIPAL EDITIONS—*Patience*

Patience, A West Midland Poem of the Fourteenth Century (1918), 2nd edn., ed. H. Bateson. Manchester. 1st edn., 1912.

Patience, An Alliterative Version of Jonah by the Poet of Pearl (1924), 2nd edn., ed. Sir I. Gollancz. London. 1st edn., 1913.

Patience (1969), ed. J. J. Anderson. Manchester.

THE PRINCIPAL EDITIONS—*Purity*

Purity, A ME Poem (1920), ed. R. J. Menner. New Haven.

Cleanness, An Alliterative Tripartite Poem (Part I, 1921, Part II, 1933), ed. Sir I. Gollancz. London.

THE PRINCIPAL EDITIONS—*Pearl*

Pearl, An English Poem of the Fourteenth Century (1921), new edn., ed. Sir I. Gollancz. London. 1st edn., 1891, revd., 1897.

The Pearl, A ME Poem (1906), ed. C. G. Osgood. Boston.

The Pearl (1932), ed. S. P. Chase and others. Boston.

Pearl (1953), ed. E. V. Gordon. Oxford.

The Pearl (1961), ed. Sister M. V. Hillmann. New York.

THE PRINCIPAL EDITIONS
Sir Gawain and the Green Knight

Syr Gawayne (1839), ed. Sir F. Madden, for the Bannatyne Club. London.

Sir Gawayne and the Green Knight (1897, 1912), revd. Sir I. Gollancz, ed. R. Morris, EETS 4. London. 1st edn., 1864.

Sir Gawain and the Green Knight (1967), 2nd edn. revd. Norman Davis; ed. J. R. R. Tolkien and E. V. Gordon. Oxford. 1st edn., 1925.

Sir Gawain and the Green Knight (1940), ed. Sir I. Gollancz with introductory essays by M. Day and M. S. Serjeantson. EETS 210, London.

Sir Gawain and the Green Knight (1970), ed. R. A. Waldron. York Medieval Texts, Evanston.

THE MANUSCRIPT

Bateson, H. (1918), The Text of Cleanness. MLR 13: 377–86.

Gollancz, I. (1919), The Text of Cleanness. MLR 14: 152–62.

Greg, W. W. (1932), A Bibliographical Paradox: Cotton Nero A.x. The Library 13: 188–91.

Hill, L. (1946), Madden's Divisions of Sir Gawain and the Large Initial Capitals of Cotton Nero A.x. Spec 21: 67–71.

Oakden, J. P. (1935), The Scribes of the Poems of the MS Cotton Nero A.x., Alliterative Poetry in Middle English. Manchester.

———— (1933), The Scribal Errors in MS Cotton Nero A.x. The Library 14: 353–58.

Tuttleton, James W. (1966), The Manuscript Divisions of Sir Gawain and the Green Knight. Spec 41: 304–10.

Vantuono, William (1972), The Question of Quatrains in Patience. Manuscripta 16: 24–30.

THE ALLITERATIVE REVIVAL

Day, M. (1931), Strophic Division in Middle English Alliterative Verse. EStn 66: 245–48.

Everett, D. (1955), Essays on Middle English Literature, ed. Patricia Kean. Oxford.

Greg, W. W. (1932), Continuity of the Alliterative Tradition. MLR 27: 453–54.

Hulbert, J. R. (1930–31), A Hypothesis Concerning the Alliterative Revival. MP 28: 405–22.

Moorman, Charles (1969), The Origins of the Alliterative Revival. SoQ 7: 345–71.

Oakden, J. P. (1930), Alliterative Poetry in Middle English, Vol. I. Manchester.

———— (1935), Alliterative Poetry in Middle English, Vol. II. Manchester.

Salter, Elizabeth (1966), The Alliterative Revival I. MP 64: 146–50.

———— (1967), The Alliterative Revival II. MP 64: 233–37.

Waldron, R. A. (1957), Oral-Formulaic Technique and Middle English Alliterative Poetry. Spec 32: 792–804.

AUTHORSHIP, DATE AND PLACE OF COMPOSITION

Brown, Carleton F. (1904a), The Author of The Pearl. Considered in the Light of His Theological Opinions. PMLA 19: 115–45.

———— (1904b), Note on the Question of Strode's Authorship of the Pearl. PMLA 19: 146–48.

Cargill, O. and M. Slauch (1928), The Pearl and Its Jeweller. PMLA 43: 105–23.

Chapman, C. O. (1931), Musical Training of the Pearl-Poet. PMLA 46: 177–81.

———— (1932), The Authorship of The Pearl. PMLA 47: 346–53.

———— (1945), Virgil and the Gawain-Poet. PMLA 60: 16–23.

· BIBLIOGRAPHY ·

———— (1953), Chaucer and the Gawain-Poet; a Conjecture. MLN 68: 521–24.

Clark, John W. (1949), Observations on Certain Differences in Vocabulary between Cleanness and Sir Gawain and the Green Knight. PQ 28: 261–73.

———— (1950a), The Gawain-Poet and the Substantival Adjective. JEGP 49: 60–66.

———— (1950b), Paraphrases for God in the Poems Attributed to The Gawain-Poet. MLN 65: 232–36.

———— (1951), On Certain Alliterative and Poetic Words in the Poems Attributed to the Gawain-Poet. MLQ 12: 387–98.

Ebbs, J. D. (1958), Stylistic Mannerisms of the Gawain-Poet. JEGP 57: 522–25.

Everett, D. and N. Hurnand (1947), Legal Phraseology in a Passage in Pearl. MÆ 16: 9–15.

Gerould, G. H. (1936), The Gawain-Poet and Dante: a Conjecture. PMLA 51: 31–36.

J., G. P. (1956), The Author of Sir Gawain and the Green Knight, N&Q 3: 53–54.

McCracken, H. N. (1910), Concerning Huchown. PMLA 25: 507–34.

Nelson, George (1902), Huchown of the Awle Ryale, The Alliterative Poet. Glasgow.

SOURCES AND ANALOGUES—*Patience* and *Purity*

Bradley, H. (January 14, 1888), The English Gawain-Poet and the Wars of Alexander. Academy 1888: 27.

Brown, C. F. (1904), Note on the Dependence of Cleanness on The Book of Mandeville. PMLA 19: 150–53.

Day, Mabel (1940), Connection with the Wars of Alexander. Sir Gawain and the Green Knight, ed. Gollancz. London. xiii–xviii.

Emerson, O. F. (1895), A Parallel between the Middle English Poem Patience and an Early Latin Poem Attributed to Tertullian. PMLA 10: 242–48.

———— (1919), Middle English Clannesse. PMLA 34: 494–522.

Hill, Ordelle G. (1967), The Late-Latin De Jona as a Source for Patience. JEGP 66: 21–25.

Kelly, Ellin M. (1966–67), Parallels between the Middle English Patience and Hymnus Ieiunantium of Prudentius. ELN 4: 244–47.

Vantuono, William (1972), The Structure and Sources of Patience. MS 34: 401–21.

SOURCES AND ANALOGUES—*Pearl*

Ackerman, R. W. (1964), The Pearl-Maiden and the Penny. RPh 17: 615–23.

Conley, J. (1955), Pearl and a Lost Tradition. JEGP 54: 332–47.

· BIBLIOGRAPHY ·

Luttrell, C. A. (1962), The Medieval Tradition of the Pearl Virginity. MÆ 31: 194–200.
Pilch, Herbert (1964), The Middle English Pearl: Its Relation to Roman de la Rose. NM 65: 427–46.
Watts, V. E. (1963), Pearl as a Consolatio. MÆ 32: 34–36.

SOURCES AND ANALOGUES
Sir Gawain and the Green Knight

Benson, L. D. (1961), Source of the Beheading Episode in Sir Gawain and the Green Knight. MP 59: 1–12.
Braddy, H. (1952), Sir Gawain and Ralph Holmes the Green Knight. MLN 67: 240–42.
Buchanan, A. (1932), The Irish Framework of Gawain and the Green Knight. PMLA 47: 315–38.
Colgrave, B. (1938), Gawain's Green Chapel. Ant 12: 351–53.
Coomaraswamy, Ananda (1944), Sir Gawain and the Green Knight: Indra and Namuci. Spec 19: 104–25.
Highfield, J. R. L. (1953), The Green Squire. MÆ 22: 18–23.
Hulbert, J. R. (1915–16). Syr Gawayn and the Grene Knyȝt. MP 13: 433–62, 689–730.
Jackson, Isaac (1913), Sir Gawain and the Green Knight Considered as a Garter Poem. Angl 37: 393–423.
Kittredge, G. L. (1916), A Study of Gawain and the Green Knight. Cambridge, Mass.
Krappe, H. H. (1938), Who Was the Green Knight? Spec 13: 206–15.
Loomis, Laura Hibbard (1959), Gawain and the Green Knight. Arthurian Literature in the Middle Ages. London. 528–40.
Loomis, R. S. (1927), Celtic Myth and Arthurian Romance. New York.
——— (1943), More Celtic Elements in Gawain and the Green Knight. JEGP 42: 149–84.
Nitze, W. A. (1935–36), Is the Green Knight Story a Vegetation Myth? MP 33: 351–66.
Randall, Dale B. J. (1960), Was the Green Knight a Fiend? SP 57: 479–91.
Savage, H. L. (1952), The Feast of Fools in Sir Gawain and the Green Knight. JEGP 51: 536–44.
Schaubert, Else von (1923), Der englische Ursprung von Syr Gawayn and the Green Knyght. EStn 57: 331–446.
Whiting, B. J. (1947), Gawain: His Reputation, His Courtesy, and His Appearance in Chaucer's Squire's Tale. MS 9: 189–234.

· BIBLIOGRAPHY ·

LITERARY ART—*Patience* and *Purity*

Anderson, J. J. (1965–66), The Prologue of Patience. MP 63: 283–87.

Hill, Ordelle G. (1968), The Audience of Patience. MP 66: 103–9.

Moorman, Charles (1963), The Role of the Narrator in Patience. MP 61: 90–95.

Morse, Charlotte C. (1971), The Image of the Vessel in Cleanness. UTQ 40: 202–16.

Schleusener, Joy (1971), History and Action in Patience. PMLA 86: 959–65.

Spearing, Anthony C. (1966), Patience and the Gawain-poet. Angl 84: 305–29.

Williams, Davis (1970), The Point of Patience. MP 68: 127–36.

LITERARY ART—*Pearl*

Bishop, I. (1957), The Significance of the Garlande Gay in the Allegory of Pearl. RES n.s. 8: 12–21.

——— (1968), Pearl in Its Setting: A Critical Study of the Structure and Meaning of the Middle English Poem. New York.

Blanch, Robert J. (1965), Precious Metal and Gem Symbolism in Pearl. The Lock Haven Review 7: 1–12.

Blenkner, Louis, O. S. B. (1968), The Theological Structure of Pearl. Trad 24: 43–75.

——— (1971), The Pattern of Traditional Images in Pearl. SP 68: 26–49.

Brewer, D. S. (1966), Courtesy and the Gawain-Poet: Patterns of Love and Courtesy, Essays in Memory of C. S. Lewis, ed. John Lawlor. London.

Chapman, C. O. (1939), Numerical Symbolism in Dante and the Pearl. MLN 54: 256–59.

Conley, John, comp. (1970), The Middle English Pearl: Critical Essays. Notre Dame.

Coulton, G. G. (1906), In Defence of Pearl. MLR 2: 39–43.

Elliott, R. W. V. (1951), Pearl and the Medieval Garden: Convention or Originality? LanM 45: 85–98.

Fletcher, J. B. (1921), The Allegory of The Pearl. JEGP 20: 1–21.

Greene, W. K. (1925), The Pearl: A New Interpretation. PMLA 40: 814–27.

Hamilton, Marie Padgett (1955), The Meaning of the Middle English Pearl. PMLA 70: 805–24.

Hart, Elizabeth (1927), The Heaven of Virgins. MLN 42: 113–16.

Heisermann, A. R. (1965), The Plot of Pearl. PMLA 80: 164–71.

Hieatt, Constance (1965), Pearl and the Dream-Vision Tradition. SN 37: 139–45.

Hillmann, Sister Mary Vincent (1941), Pearl: Inlyche and Rewarde. MLN 56: 457–58.

———— (1945), Some Debatable Words in Pearl and Its Theme. MLN 60: 241–48.

———— (1953), Pearl 382: Mare reȝmysse? MLN 68: 528–31.

Hoffman, Stanton De Voren (1960), The Pearl: Notes for an Interpretation. MP 58: 73–80.

Johnson, W. S. (1953), The Imagery and Diction of The Pearl: Towards an Interpretation. ELH 20: 161–80.

Kean, P. M. (1965), Numerical Composition in Pearl. N&Q 12: 49–51.

———— (1967), The Pearl: An Interpretation. London.

Knightly, William J. (1961), Pearl: The Hy Seysoun. MLN 26: 97–102.

Luttrell, C. A. (1962), The Medieval Tradition of the Pearl Virginity. MÆ 31: 194–200.

———— (1965), Symbolism in a Garden Setting. Neophil 49: 160–76.

Macrae-Gibson, O. D. (1968), Pearl: The Link Words and the Thematic Structure. Neophil 52: 54–64.

Madeleva, Sister Mary (1925), Pearl: A Study in Spiritual Dryness. New York.

McAndrew, Bruno (1957), The Pearl, A Catholic Paradise Lost. American Benedictine Review 8: 243–51.

McGilliard, John C (1969), Links, Language, and Style in The Pearl. Studies in Language, Literature, and Culture of the Middle Ages and Later, ed. E. Bagby Atwood and Archibald A. Hill. Austin. 279–99.

Medary, Margaret P. (1916), Stanza-linking in Middle English Verse. RR 7: 243–70.

Moorman, C. (1955), The Role of the Narrator in Pearl. MP 53: 73–81.

Northrup, C. S. (1897), A Study of the Metrical Structure of the Pearl. PMLA 12: 326–40.

Patch, Howard R. (1950), The Other World, According to Descriptions in Medieval Literature. Cambridge, Mass.

Robertson, D. W., Jr. (1950a), The Heresy of the Pearl. MLN 65: 152–55.

———— (1950b), The Pearl as a Symbol. MLN 65: 155–61.

Schofield, W. H. (1904), The Nature and Fabric of The Pearl. PMLA 19: 154–215.

———— (1909), Symbolism, Allegory, and Autobiography in The Pearl. PMLA 24: 585–675.

Spearing, A. C. (1962), Symbolic and Dramatic Development in Pearl. MP 60: 1–12.

Stern, M. R. (1955), An Approach to Pearl. JEGP 54: 684–92.

Vasta, Edward (1967), Pearl: Immortal Flowers and the Pearl's Decay. JEGP 66: 519–31.

· BIBLIOGRAPHY ·

Wellek, R. (1933), The Pearl: An Interpretation of the Middle English Poem. Studies in English, 4, Prague.

LITERARY ART
Sir Gawain and the Green Knight

Ackerman, R. W. (1958), Gawain's Shield: Penitential Doctrine. Angl 76: 254–65.

Barnet, S. (1956), A Note on the Structure of Sir Gawain and the Green Knight. MLN 71: 319.

Baughan, Denver E. (1950), The Role of Morgan le Fay in Sir Gawain and the Green Knight. ELH 17: 241–51.

Benson, L. D. (1965), Art and Tradition in Sir Gawain and the Green Knight. New Brunswick.

Bercovitch, S. (1965), Romance and Anti-Romance in Gawain and the Green Knight. PQ 44: 30–37.

Bloomfield, Morton W. (1958), Symbolism in Medieval Literature. MP 56: 73–81.

Borroff, M. (1962), Sir Gawain and the Green Knight: A Stylistic and Metrical Study. New Haven.

Bowers, R. H. (1963), Gawain and the Green Knight as Entertainment. MLQ 24: 333–41.

Brewer, D. S. (1967), The Gawain-Poet; a General Appreciation of Four Poems. EC 17: 130–42.

Burrow, J. (1959), The Two Confession Scenes in Sir Gawain and the Green Knight. MP 57: 73–79.

———— (1965), A Reading of Sir Gawain and the Green Knight. London.

Carson, Mother Angela (1962), Morgan la Fee as the Principle of Unity in Gawain and the Green Knight. MLQ 23: 3–16.

———— (1963), The Green Chapel: Its Meaning and Its Function. SP 60: 598–605.

Champion, Larry S. (1967), Grace Versus Merit in Sir Gawain and the Green Knight. MLQ 28: 413–25.

Clark, Cecily (1966), Sir Gawain and the Green Knight: Characterization by Syntax. EC 16: 361–74.

Cook, R. G. (1963), The Play-Element in Sir Gawain and the Green Knight. Tulane Studies in English XIII. New Orleans.

Delany, P. (1965), The Role of the Guide in GGK. Neophil 49: 250–55.

Engelhardt, G. J. (1955), The Predicament of Gawain. MLQ 16: 218–25.

Field, P. J. C. (1971), A Rereading of Sir Gawain and the Green Knight. SP 68: 255–69.

· BIBLIOGRAPHY ·

Friedman, Albert B. (1960), Morgan le Fay in Sir Gawain and the Green Knight. Spec 35: 260–74.

Goldhurst, W. (1958–59), The Green and the Gold: The Major Theme of Sir Gawain and the Green Knight. CE 20: 61–65.

Green, Richard Hamilton (1962), Gawain's Shield and the Quest for Perfection. ELH 29: 121–39.

Haines, V. Y. (1971), Morgan and the Missing Day in Sir Gawain and the Green Knight. MS 33: 354–59.

Halverson, John (1969), Template Criticism: Sir Gawain and the Green Knight. MP 67: 113–39.

Hieatt, A. Kent (1968), Sir Gawain: Pentangle, Luf-Lace, Numerical Structure. PLL 4: 339–50.

Hill, Laurita L. (1946), Madden's Divisions of Sir Gawain and the Large Initial Capitals of Cotton Nero A.x. Spec 21: 67–71.

Hills, D. F. (1963), Gawain's Fault in GGK. RES n.s. 14: 124–31.

Howard, Donald R. (1964), Structure and Symmetry in Sir Gawain. Spec. 39: 424–33.

Hughes, Derek W. (1971), The Problem of Reality in Sir Gawain and the Green Knight. UTQ 40: 217–35.

Hulbert, J. R. (1915–16), Syr Gawayn and the Grene Knyȝt. MP 13: 433–62, 689–730.

Jones, Edward T. (1969), The Sound of Laughter in Sir Gawain and the Green Knight. MS 31: 343–45.

Kiteley, John F. (1971), The Endless Knot: Magical Aspects of the Pentangle in Sir Gawain and the Green Knight. SLI 4: 41–50.

Lewis, John S. (1959–60), Gawain and the Green Knight. CE 21: 50–51.

Lucas, Peter J. (1968), Gawain's Anti-Feminism. N&Q 15: 324–25.

Manning, Stephen (1964), A Psychological Interpretation of Sir Gawain and the Green Knight. Criticism 6: 165–77.

Markman, Alan M. (1957), The Meaning of Sir Gawain and the Green Knight. PMLA 72: 574–86.

McAlindon, T. (1965), Magic, Fate, and Providence in Medieval Narrative and GGK. RES n.s. 16: 121–39.

Mills, D. (1968), An Analysis of the Temptation Scenes in GGK. JEGP 67: 612–30.

Moorman, C. (1956), Myth and Medieval Literature: Sir Gawain and the Green Knight. MS 18: 158–72.

Pearsall, D. A. (1955), Rhetorical Description in GGK. MLR 50: 129–34.

· BIBLIOGRAPHY ·

Randall, D. B. J. (1957), A Note on Structure in Sir Gawain and the Green Knight. MLN 72: 161–63.

Renoir, A. (1958), Descriptive Technique in Gawain and the Green Knight. Orbis Litterarum 13: 126–32.

———— (1960), Progressive Magnification: An Instance of Psychological Description in the Green Knight. MSpr 54: 245–53.

———— (1962), An Echo to the Sense: The Patterns of Sound in Gawain and the Green Knight. EM 13: 9–23.

Schnyder, Hans (1961), Sir Gawain and the Green Knight: An Essay in Interpretation. Cooper Monographs 6, Bern.

Shedd, G. M. (1967), Knight in Tarnished Armour: The Meaning of GGK. MLR 62: 3–13.

Silverstein, T. (1964), The Art of GGK. UTQ 33: 258–78.

Skinner, Veronica L. (1969), The Concept of Trawþe in Sir Gawain and the Green Knight. Mass. Studies in English 2: 49–58.

Smithers, G. V. (1963), What GGK is About. MÆ 32: 171–89.

Speirs, John (1957), Medieval English Poetry: The Non-Chaucerian Tradition. London.

Stevens, Martin (1972), Laughter and Game in Sir Gawain and the Green Knight. Spec 47: 65–78.

Taylor, P. B. (1969), Blysse and Blunder, Nature and Ritual in Sir Gawain and the Green Knight. ES 50: 165–75.

———— (1971), Commerce and Comedy in Sir Gawain. PQ 50: 1–15.

Watson, M. R. (1949), The Chronology of Sir Gawain and the Green Knight. MLN 64: 85–86.

Zimmer, H. (1948), The King and the Corpse. New York.

LANGUAGE

Bloomfield, Morton W. (1969), Some Notes on SGGK and Pearl. Studies in Language, Literature, and Culture of the Middle Ages and Later, ed. E. Bagby Atwood and Archibald A. Hill. Austin. 300–2.

Day, Mabel K. (1919), The Weak Verb in the Works of the Gawain-Poet. MLR 14: 413–15.

Hulbert, J. R. (1921), The West Midland of the Romances. MP 19: 1–16.

Luttrell, C. A. (1955), The Gawain-Group: Cruxes, Etymologies, Interpretations. Neophil 39: 207–17.

———— (1962), A Gawain-Group Miscellany. N&Q 9: 447–50.

McLaughlin, J. C. (1963), A Graphemic-Phonemic Study of a Middle English Manuscript (Cotton Nero A.x.). The Hague.

· BIBLIOGRAPHY ·

Menner, R. G. (1922), G.G.K. and the West Midland. PMLA 37: 503–26.

Mustanoja, T. G. (1960), A Middle English Syntax, Vol. I. Helsinki.

Serjeantson, M. S. (1927), The Dialects of the West Midlands in Middle English. RES 3: 54–67, 188–203, 319–31.

Wright, E. M. (1939), Notes on Pearl (erroneously entitled Additional Notes on Sir Gawain and the Green Knight). JEGP 38: 1–22.

—————— (1940), Additional Notes on Pearl. JEGP 39: 315–18.

· Frequently Cited Sources ·

PATIENCE

A   Patience (1969), ed., J. J. Anderson. Manchester: Manchester University Press.

B   Patience: A West Midland Poem of the Fourteenth Century (1918), ed., Hartley Bateson, 2nd edn. Manchester: Manchester University Press.

Ekwall   Ekwall, E. (1912), Some Notes on the Text of the Alliterative Poem Patience. EStn 44: 165–73.

———— (1913–14), Another Note on the Poem Patience. EStn 47: 313–16.

———— (1913), Review of Bateson's Patience. AngB 24: 133–36.

———— (1925), Review of Gollancz's Patience (2nd edn.). AngB 36: 267–70.

Emerson   Emerson, O. F. (1936), A Note on the Poem Patience. EStn 47: 125–31.

———— (1916), More Notes on Patience. MLN 31: 1–10.

———— (1913), Review of Bateson's Patience. MLN 28: 171–80.

———— (1919), Review of Bateson's Patience (2nd edn.). JEGP 18: 633–40.

Go   Patience (1924), ed. I. Gollancz, 2nd edn. London: Oxford University Press.

Grattan   Grattan, J. H. G. (1914), Review of Gollancz's Patience (1st edn.). MLN 9: 403–05.

PURITY

Bateson   Bateson, Hartley (1918), The Text of Cleanness. MLR 13: 377–86.

Emerson   Emerson, O. F. (1919), Middle English Clannesse. PMLA 34: 494–522.

Go   Cleanness (1921 and 1933), ed., I. Gollancz. Select Early English Poems VII, IX, XI. London: Oxford University Press.

Luttrell   Luttrell, C. A. (1955), The Gawain Group: Cruxes, Etymologies, Interpretations. Neophil 39: 207–17.

M   Early English Alliterative Poems in the West Midland Dialect (1864), ed., R. Morris. EETS, I. London: Oxford University Press.

· FREQUENTLY CITED SOURCES ·

M   Purity: A Middle English Poem (1920), ed., Robert J. Menner, Yale
Studies in English 61. New Haven: Yale University Press.

Skeat   Skeat, W. W. (1894), Specimens of Early English, Part II. London:
Oxford University Press.

Thomas   Thomas, P. G. (1922), Notes on Cleanness. MLR 17: 64–66.

PEARL

C   The Pearl (1932), ed., S. P. Chase and students of Bowdoin College.
Boston: Bruce Humphries, Inc.

Emerson   Emerson, O. F. (1922), Some Notes on The Pearl. PMLA 37:
52–93.

G¹   Pearl (1891), ed., I. Gollancz. London: David Nutt.

Go   Pearl, ed., I. Gollancz. London: Chatto and Windus.

Gn   Pearl (1953), ed., E. V. Gordon. Oxford: The Clarendon Press.

Hamilton   Hamilton, Marie P. (1955), Review of Pearl, ed. E. V. Gordon.
JEGP 54: 123–26.

H   The Pearl: Mediaeval Text with a Literal Translation and Interpretation
(1961), ed., Sister Mary Vincent Hillmann. New Jersey: College of Saint
Elizabeth Press.

Kean   Kean, P. M. (1967), The Pearl: An Interpretation. New York: Barnes
and Noble.

M   Early English Alliterative Poems in the West-Midland Dialect (1864),
ed., R. Morris. EETS, 1. London: Oxford University Press.

O   The Pearl: A Middle English Poem (1906), ed., Charles G. Osgood.
Boston: D. C. Heath.

Savage   Savage, H. L. (1956), Review of Pearl, ed. E. V. Gordon. MLN 71:
124–29.

Wright   Wright, Elizabeth M. (1939), Additional Notes on Sir Gawain
and the Green Knight. JEGP 38: 1–22. (Actually notes on Pearl).

SIR GAWAIN AND THE GREEN KNIGHT

Banks   Sir Gawain and the Green Knight (1929), tr., Theodore H. Banks.
New York: F. S. Crofts and Co.

Bloomfield   Bloomfield, Morton W. (1969), Some Notes on SGGK and
Pearl. Studies in Language, Literature, and Culture of the Middle Ages and
Later, ed. E. Bagby Atwood and Archibald A. Hill. Austin: University of
Texas Press, 300–02.

· FREQUENTLY CITED SOURCES ·

D Sir Gawain and the Green Knight (1967), ed J. R. R. Tolkien and E. V. Gordon, revd. Norman Davis. Oxford: The Clarendon Press.

Emerson Emerson, O. F. (1922), Notes on Sir Gawain and the Green Knight. JEGP 21: 363–410.

Go Sir Gawain and the Green Knight (1940), ed., Sir Israel Gollancz, with introductory essays by Mabel Day and May S. Serjeantson, EETS, 210. London: Oxford University Press.

Madden Syr Gawayne (1839), ed., Sir Frederick Madden for the Bannantyne Club. London.

Morris Sir Gawayne and the Green Knight (1864), ed., R. Morris, EETS, 4. London: Oxford University Press. Text revd. Sir Israel Gollancz, 1897, 1912.

Napier Napier, A. S. (1902), Notes on Sir Gawain and the Green Knight. MLN 17: 85–87.

Onions Onions, C. T. (1924), Notes on Sir Gawain and the Green Knight. N&Q 146: 203–04, 244–45, 285–86.

Savage Savage, H. L. (1931), Notes on Sir Gawain and the Green Knight. PMLA 46: 169–76.

——— (1944), Review of Gollancz's Edition. MLN 49: 342–50.

——— (1956), The Gawain-Poet: Studies in his Personality and Background. Chapel Hill: University of North Carolina Press.

TG Sir Gawain and the Green Knight (1925), ed., J. R. R. Tolkien and E. V. Gordon. London: Oxford University Press. Reprinted with corrections 1930, 1936, 1946.

W Sir Gawain and the Green Knight (1970), ed., R. A. Waldron. Evanston, Ill.: Northwestern University Press.

Wright Wright, Elizabeth M. (1906), Sir Gawain and the Green Knight. EStn 36: 209–27; (1935), JEGP 34: 157–79, 339–50; (1936), JEGP 35: 313–20; (1938), JEGP 37: 2–22.

JONAH CAST INTO THE SEA

· Patience ·

Pacience is apoynt þaȝ hit displese ofte   (f.83a)
When heuy herttes ben hurt wyth heþyng oþer elles
Suffraunce may aswagen hem & þe swelme leþe
4 For ho quelles°vche a qued°& quenches malyce   *subdues / evil*

For quoso suffer cowþe syt° sele° wolde folȝe *sorrow / happiness*
& quo for þro may noȝt þole þe þikker°he sufferes   *more*
Þen is better to abyde þe bur°vmbestoundes°   *blow / betimes*
8 Þen ay þrow forth° my þro þaȝ me þynk ylle   *give vent to*

1. apoynt: A a poynt; B a nobel poynt.
3. aswagen: MS aswagend.

1ff. It will be apparent that I am following here, as in *Purity*, the quatrain arrangement first used by Sir Israel Gollancz in his edition of *Patience* in 1913 and followed by J. J. Anderson. In general, Go's statement that "the poem was written in what may be described as alliterative quatrains, and that the original number of lines was either 528 or 532" (the present number is 531, though see 509ff.*n*) would seem to be correct, though some qualifications are needed. Certainly the division marks in the MS are not as "clear" or as regular as Go suggests, and O. F. Emerson believes that the "thought sequence" of the poem clearly falls into couplets rather than quatrains and that "printing as blank verse" the text of the poem is preferable. G. C. Macauley in reviewing Bateson's edition (MLR 8: 396–98) also denies the quatrain arrangement on the grounds that "after the first twelve lines the arrangement is distinctly in couplets to l. 28, and again from l. 49 to l. 60 the arrangement is entirely in groups of either two or three lines." Interestingly, even though B, in his "recast and partly rewritten" edition of 1918, calls the quatrain arrangement "the best suggestion ever made regarding this poem," he himself prints the text as

I herde on a halyday at a hyȝe masse
How Mathew melede°þat his mayster his meyny°
con teche   *said | followers*
Aȝt happes°he hem hyȝt & vche on a mede°   *beatitudes | reward*
12 Sunderlupes° for hit dissert vpon a ser wyse° *severally | variously*

Thay arn happen°þat han in hert pouerte   *blessed*
For hores is þe heuen-ryche°to holde for euer *kingdom of heaven*
Þay ar happen also þat haunte mekenesse
16 For þay schal welde þis worlde & alle her wylle haue

"blank verse." William Vantuono, also an editor of *Patience*, has recently re-opened the question (Manuscripta 16: 24–30) and concludes, contrary to A's view, that since the marginal double lines may be scribal rather than authorial, the matter may still be "open to debate" and that, in fact, since the "thought patterns do not group themselves into four-line stanzas, . . . it seems more likely that the poet, in composing for oral recitation, did not intend any stanzaic arrangement."

1. See *GGK* 1n.

1–4. I have decided to follow here the MS reading of *apoynt* rather than the "*a poynt*" or "*a [noble] poynt*" of other editions on the basis of what Emerson calls the "better sense which it supplies" (MLN 29:85). A rough translation of these first lines might thus be: "Patience is so appointed, even though it is often displeasing, that when hearts already heavy are wounded by scorn or otherwise, forbearance may (both) assuage them and calm their flames, since it (both) subdues every ill and quenches malice." These remarkably compact lines so

read thus impart to the virtue of patience two clearly distinguishable healing properties: (1) it can alleviate the cares of the world and (2) it can nullify the torments of the unthinking crowd.

There is no need to emend 1 in order to make it agree with 531, since the other poems of Cotton Nero A.x. do not show a literal repetition of the first line in the last.

1–60. For a general interpretation of this prologue, see C. Moorman, "The Role of the Narrator in *Patience*" (MP 61:90–95) and A, 7–9.

9. Emerson points out (PMLA 10:242–48) that the beatitudes here are introduced in a manner very similar to that used in Tertullian's *De Patientia* (see Introduction), though the *Gawain*-poet follows the order of the beatitudes in the Vulgate rather than that of Tertullian's treatise.

13. *pouerte*: Clearly the poet is referring here to spiritual poverty, the poverty *spiritu* of the Sermon on the Mount, the ability to entrust oneself completely to God's judgments, rather than, as has occasionally been claimed,

Thay ar happen also þat for her harme wepes
For þay schal comfort encroche° in kythes°
    ful mony   *obtain / regions*
Þay ar happen also þat hungeres after ryȝt°   *righteousness*
20 For þay schal frely be refete°ful of alle gode   *fed*

Thay ar happen also þat han in hert rauþe°   *pity*
For mercy in alle maneres her mede schal worþe
Þay ar happen also þat arn of hert clene
24 For þay her sauyour in sete schal se with her yȝen°   *eyes*

Thay ar happen also þat halden her pese
For þay þe gracious Godes sunes schal godly be called
Þay ar happen also þat con her hert stere°   *govern*
28 For hores is þe heuen-ryche as I er sayde

These arn þe happes alle aȝt þat vus bihyȝt° weren   *promised*
If we þyse ladyes wolde lof in lyknyng° of þewes° *copying / virtues*
Dame Pouert dame Pitee dame Penaunce þe þrydde   (f.83b)
32 Dame Mekenesse dame Mercy & miry Clannesse

& þenne dame Pes & Pacyence put in þerafter

24. with: *throughout the text,* ms *abreviates* Wᵗ; Go *expands to* wyth. *Where* ms *reads* with (*lines* 289 *and* 481) *and* wyth (*lines* 2, 48, 255, 300, *and* 518) *it is transcribed as written. The* Wᵗ *abbreviation also occurs in* withinne (*lines* 120, 208, 215, 260, 363, 387 *and* 523), withouten (*lines* 252 *and* 267), withheld (*line* 408), *and* þerwith (*line* 232).

to material poverty. Certainly material poverty is in no real sense a *play-fere* of patience nor does Jonah in any way suffer from poverty of goods, though he does of course lack the ability to trust completely God's will for him.

30. Mabel Day (MÆ 3:241) thinks this to be a variation of *Purity* 1057-68, where the poet, naming the *Ro-man de la Rose* as source, converts Jean de Meun's cynical statement of the successful lover's need to cater to his lady's taste to express the desire of the Christian to "conform to Christ."

31–33. Such personifications are common in medieval allegorical writing. Both Go's and B's notes supply examples.

He were happen þat hade one alle were þe better
Bot syn I am put to a poynt þat pouerte hatte°   *is called*
36 I schal me poruay°pacyence & play me with boþe   *provide*

For in þe tyxte þere þyse two arn in teme layde°   *coupled*
Hit arn fettled in on forme þe forme & þe laste
& by quest of her quoyntyse enquylen on mede
40 & als in myn vpynyoun hit arn of on kynde

For þeras pouert hir proferes ho nyl° be put vtter   *will not*
Bot lenge wheresoeuer hir lyst lyke oþer greme
& þereas pouert enpresses þaȝ mon pyne þynk
44 Much maugre his mun he mot nede suffer

35. syn: ᴍs fyn.

---

38. *forme*: Go explains this as the "formula '*quoniam*', etc." used in the Vulgate beatitudes. B glosses as "formula," without further explanation and translates the line "they are arrayed in one formula, the first and the last (terms in it)."

38–39. While 38 seems clear enough, *quest* and *quoyntyse* make 39 very difficult. Go sees in *quoyntyse* a personification of Christ and so translates the two lines: "They [poverty and patience] are put, fastened together, in one form (*i.e.* the formula '*quoniam*', etc. [used in the Vulgate beatitudes which the poet has just translated]); and by the judgment of their Wisdom, *i.e.* Christ, they receive one reward." This rendering of 39, though ingenious, hardly fits the context established by 38. B, Go, and A translate *quoyntyse* as "wisdom" and Morris as "device"; B and Morris see *quest* simply as "quest" and A as "judgment."

B, however, remarks that *quoyntyse* may "perhaps" be "acquaintance," a suggestion well worth following up. *NED* does indeed list such a meaning for the related form *quaintance*, and *quest* may have the meaning, now obsolete, of "bequest" (*NED*, sb.², obs). The line can thus be read: "And as a result of their acquaintance, they receive one reward," a rendering which fits perfectly the thought begun in the preceding line.

41–45. The two subordinate clauses beginning þeras seem to me to be in parallel construction. A rough translation would be: "For whereas Poverty presents herself and will not be put out, but lingers wheresoever she wishes to, like it or not; and whereas Poverty impresses much on a man that he finds harmful, but that he must, willy-nilly, endure; thus Poverty and Patience must needs be comrades."

Thus pouerte & pacyence are nedes play-feres
Syþen I am sette with hem samen° suffer me byhoues   *together*
Þenne is me lyȝtloker hit lyke & her lotes prayse
48 Þenne wyþer°wyth & be wroth & þe wers haue   *strive*

Ȝif me be dyȝt° a destyne due to haue   *appointed*
What dowes°me þe dedayn° oþer
    dispit° make   *avails | disdain | annoyance*
Oþer ȝif my lege lorde lyst on lyue me to bidde
52 Oþer to ryde oþer to renne to rome in his ernde

What grayþed° me þe grychchyng° bot
    grame° more seche   *would avail | complaining | trouble*
Much ȝif he ne me made maugref my chekes
& þenne þrat moste I þole & vnþonk to mede
56 Þe had bowed to his bode bongre my hyure

45. are: MS arn.
54. Much: Go & muth.
54. ne me made: MS, A me ne made; Go me mande.
55. & þenne: Go þenne.
56. Þe had: B Þet had.

---

47. "Then is it easier to like it (*i.e.* what befalls) and praise the portions (allotted by them)" (B).

51–52. *bidde*: Translated "bid" by Go, "bide" by Morris and B. To Ekwall, "*oþer to ryde*, etc. must be governed by *to bidde*"; *on lyue* Ekwall takes "to mean 'ever' (*i.e.* 'in my life')." Like Emerson, Ekwall believes *to rome* means "to Rome" and so translates the whole passage, "If my liege lord should ever choose to bid me either to ride or to run to Rome on an errand of his . . . ." A prints "*Rome*."

54–58. I am reproducing here the MS reading without any of the emendations of former editors. Go emended

54 to read "[&] *mu[t]h ȝif he me ma[n]de, maugre my chekes*" and translated "and, finally, if God commanded me to speak, I gainsaying, etc." B, following Morris, emended *þe* to *þe[t]* in 56, and translated: "If he did not make me great (much), notwithstanding my demur, and then I had to endure trouble and displeasure for a reward, who should have been obedient to his command according to the terms of my hiring, did not Jonah do such a foolish thing at one time in Judea? (Seeking) to place himself in safety, he incurs misfortune." Emerson, also accepting Morris's emendation, translated: "If he did not make me

Did not Jonas in Jude suche jape sumwhyle°   *once*
To sette hym to sewrte vnsounde he hym feches
Wyl ʒe tary a lyttel tyne & tent°me a whyle   *attend*
60 I schal wysse yow þerwyth as holy wryt telles

---

great, and then I who had been obedient to his command had to endure trouble and displeasure for a reward, did not Jonah in Judea do such a foolish thing at one time?" Ker, according to Grattan, thought *made* here to mean "caused a person to do," *much* to be an "elliptical ejaculation, apodosis to 'ʒif he ne me made'," and *bongre* to be a noun absolute. Ker thus translated: "Lucky if he did not make me (run his errand); and then must I endure rebuke, and disfavour for my guerdon, when I might have bowed to his bidding, with his good favour for my recompense." A substantially agrees with Ker.

In spite of what seems to the modern reader the awkwardness of the passage, some such very free translation as this is possible: "(For even) if he did not grant me much, in spite of my prayers, and (even if) then I had to endure vexations and have ingratitude as a reward when I had bowed to his wishes in accordance with my hire, did not Jonah in Judea once act the fool in such a way that in trying for safety he incurred disaster?"

It will be obvious that in so translating the passage I have differed from former editors in glossing (1) *made* (54) in the sense of "grant" or "provide" (*NED, s.v.* "make," v¹, I, 14), (2) *þe* (56) as the temporal adverb "when," (3) *jape* (57) as a verb, and (4) *suche* (57) as an adverb, (*NED,*

s.v. "the," particle, relative pron., 2.b), all of which usages being common in the period. The poet, we remember, has just finished making the point that no matter what tasks God imposes— *to bidde/ Oþer to ryde oþer to renne to rome in his ernde*—the wise man will comply rather than bring further misfortune on himself. Then he goes on to make a transition from that general statement to the story of Jonah which follows. Thus, in spite of the apparent dislocation between the two principal clauses of the transition sentence, the clear inference is that Jonah, who lost everything through disobedience, was a great deal more foolish than the narrator, who has managed to salvage at least some things through patience.

56. *bongre my hyure*: Go sees in this phrase a possible allusion to the parable of the vineyard, a parable used by the poet with great effect in *Pearl*. It is difficult to see, however, just how the meaning of the parable suits this context or how it reflects, as B thinks it does, "the reward promised in the Beatitudes." Surely in this passage the poet is simply remarking on his duty to God by means of a familiar figure of speech.

59. *a lyttel tyne*: As Go says, this is almost the earliest instance of this phrase, glossed by the *NED* as "a very little time."

59–60. See *GGK* 30–31n.

I

Hit bitydde sumtyme in þe termes of Jude
Jonas joyned°watz þerinne jentyle prophete   *appointed*
Goddes glam°to hym glod°þat hym vnglad made   *word | came*
64 With a roghlych rurd° rowned in his ere   *stern cry*

Rys radly he says & rayke°forth euen   *go*
Nym° þe way to Nynyue° wythouten oþer speche *take | Nineveh*
& in þat cete my saȝes°soghe alle aboute   *sayings* (f.84a)
68 Þat in þat place at þe poynt I put in þi hert

For iwysse hit arn so wykke þat in þat won dowelleȝ
& her malys is so much I may not abyde
Bot venge me on her vilanye & venym bilyue
72 Now sweȝe°me þider swyftly & say me þis
    arende°   *speed | message*

When þat steuen watz stynt° þat stowned°his
    mynde   *ceased |troubled*
Al he wrathed in his wyt & wyþerly°he þoȝt   *rebelliously*
If I bowe to his bode & bryng hem þis tale
76 & I be nummen° in Nuniue my nyes°begynes *taken | troubles*

He telles me þose traytoures arn typped schrewes
I com wyth þose tyþynges þay ta°me bylyue   *take*

---

73. stowned: MS stownod.
77. typped: B typpede.

---

77. *typped schrewes*: There are two major interpretations of *typped*: (1) "drunken" (Emerson) from English dialect *tip*, "a drink" and *tippled*, "drunk" and (2) "tipped" meaning "highly finished, complete, consummate" (Ekwall), a meaning derived from the "finishing" of certain objects (staves, shoes, etc.) by tipping them (Cf. Fr. *ferré*, Ger. *beschlagen*). Go's glossing "tip-top" from ON *typpi*, "apex," does not seem to fit the context. My own feeling is that "drunken," however questionable its etymology, certainly makes sense here.

78. Kluge (Mittelenglisches Lese-

Pyneȝ°me in a prysoun put me in stokkes   *shut up*
80 Wryþe°me in a warlok wrast out myn yȝen   *torture*

Þis is a meruayl message a man for to preche
Amonge enmyes so mony & mansed fendes°   *cursed wildoers*
Bot if my gaynlych°God such gref to me wolde   *gracious*
84 For desert of sum sake þat I slayn were

At alle peryles quoþ þe prophete I aproche hit no nerre
I wyl me sum oþer waye þat he ne wayte°after   *search*
I schal tee° into Tarce°& tary þere a whyle   *go / Tarshish*
88 & lyȝtly when I am lest° he letes me alone   *lost*

Þenne he ryses radly & raykes°bilyue   *goes*
Jonas toward port Japh ay janglande° for tene   *grumbling*
Þat he nolde þole for noþyng non of þose pynes
92 Þaȝ þe fader þat hym formed were fale of his hele

Oure syre syttes he says on sege° so hyȝe   *seat*

84. For: ms Fof.

---

buch 1912:105) places "If" at the be-
ginning of this line in order to enforce
the obvious subordination of the clause.
Emerson remarks, however, that Jonah
may well be pictured as being so ex-
cited that he here simply does not
bother to subordinate.

80. *warlok*: An instrument of tor-
ture glossed in *Promptorium Parvu-
lorum* (EETS, Extra Series 102) as a
"fetir lock: *sera pedicalis uel com-
pedalis*," apparently shackles fitted
with a padlock. The text would seem
to indicate also a device that can be
twisted.

81ff. Ekwall wishes "to connect
Bot if etc. [83] with the preceding
sentence and place a full stop at the

end of l. 84." A adopts Ekwall's punc-
tuation.

92. *fale of his hele*: There seem to
be at least four possible renderings of
this obscure phrase: (1) "friend of his
well-being," using a line in *Sir Ferum-
bras, stonde þan þer by þy fale,* as
authority for *fale* as "friend"; (2) Go's
suggestion that *fale* be derived from
on *falr*, "venal, to be sold" and the
line rendered "though the Father that
formed him made cheap of (set little
value on) his welfare"; (3) Emerson's
gloss of *fale* as "fell, hostile to" related
to of *fel*, "unmerciful"; and (4) A's
"unconcerned about his [Jonah's]
safety."

In his glowande glorye & gloumbes° ful lyttel   *scowls*

Þaȝ I be nummen° in Nunniue & naked dispoyled   *taken*

96 On rode rwly torent° with rybaudes°

    mony   *miserably torn to pieces / ruffians*

Þus he passes to þat port his passage to seche

Fyndes he a fayr schyp to þe fare redy

Maches hym with þe maryneres makes her paye

100 For to towe hym into Tarce as tyd° as þay myȝt   *quickly*

Then he tron on þo tres & þay her tramme ruchen

Cachen vp þe crossayl cables þay fasten

Wiȝt as þe wyndas weȝen her ankres   (f.84b)

94. glowande: MS g wande.

98ff. This passage on the launching of the ship is justly regarded as one of the great showpieces of the poem. It certainly bears witness to the same sense of vivid detail which the poet will exploit in his later poems.

The passage, however, has been the cause of a great deal of controversy stemming principally from the poet's use of the technical nautical terms of his time. My own feeling is that we must presume, as in the hunting scenes in *Sir Gawain and the Green Knight*, that the poet is absolutely accurate in his language and that the seeming difficulties of the passage stem from our ignorance rather than from his.

No one will dispute, however, that the poet's knowledge of the merchant ship of his time was greater than that of the illustrator of the MS. The ship in the illustration on folio 82a gives no clear conception of the vessel described by the poet, except to verify that the poet is not trying—and indeed it would never occur to a medieval poet even to consider trying—to describe accurately a ship of Jonah's time.

Emerson states that the vessel most familiar to the poet would be of the same rig and form as, though somewhat larger than, a present day Norwegian herring boat and proceeds to work out the nautical terms of the poem with such a vessel in mind. Certainly it was a "broadly-built, round-shaped ship" (B) with a single quadrangular sail and probably an elaborate, high-standing poop. A identifies the vessel as a "Cog," "common in northern waters from the thirteenth to the fifteenth centuries."

It is in this celebrated account of the storm at sea that a number of parallels with Tertullian's *De Jona* occur (see Introduction).

101ff. *tramme*: I think, following Emerson and B, that this is "mast,"

· 75 ·

104 Sprude spak to þe sprete þe spare bawelyne

Gederen to þe gyde ropes þe grete cloþ falles
Þay layden in on ladde borde & þe lofe wynnes
Þe blyþe breþe at her bak þe bosum he fyndes
108 He swenges me þys swete schip swefte fro þe hauen

Watȝ neuer so joyful a Jue as Jonas watȝ þenne
Þat þe daunger°of dryȝtyn so derfly°ascaped   *power / audaciously*
He wende wel þat þat wyȝ þat al þe world planted
112 Hade no maȝt° in þat mere°no man for to greue   *power / sea*

---

104. Sprude: MS *either* Sprude *or* Spynde; A Spynde.

---

though Go's suggestion of "gear, machinery" is tempting. Emerson derives the term from LG *traam*, "beam, shaft," B from ON *tramm*, "log," and Go from Norw. *traam*, "frame" and ME *tramme*, "machines." Ekwall disagrees with all these readings on etymological grounds and sees in the spellings *traime* and *traume* (*Wars of Alexander*) some reflection of French derivation. Ekwall's suggested translation, "ship," seems to me, as to others, too general for the context. Emerson suggests "gangplank" for *tres*, though B and A have "deck-boards."

B translates the passage, beginning half-way through 101: "They set up the mast, hoist up the mainyard, fasten the cables, weigh anchor, fasten the hawline (sparely [infrequently] used, and only in keeping the weather-edge of the sail taut), tug at the guide-ropes and the main-sail shakes down."

104. *spare bawelyne*: "The bowline was used to keep the weather-side of

the sail tight when sailing close to the wind" (B). I agree with Emerson, B, Go, and the *NED* that *spare* here means "kept in reserve for future use or to supply an emergency" (*NED*), rather than "slender" as Ekwall claims or "taut" as Grattan maintains. A's statement that "before the fifteenth century sailing ships had only one bowline" seems unrealistic. *Spak*, here and in 338, is surely "smartly" (Grattan).

For *Sprude*, A reads the MS here as *Spynde*, a "past tense plural form of *spennen* 'fasten'." It is difficult for me to see the letter following the *sp* ligature as "a truncated *y*" rather than as an *r*.

105. *Gederen to þe gyde ropes*: "tug at" (B); "gather at the guide ropes" (Emerson).

106–108. Emerson explains that "as the leeward edge of the sail is hauled round by the sailors, the windward edge catches the breeze first—'wins' in the modern sense—when the sail bellies out and the boat turns from the

Lo þe wytles°wrechche for he wolde noȝt suffer   *foolish*

Now hatȝ he put hym in plyt of peril wel more

Hit watȝ a wenyng°vnwar° þat welt in his mynde   *hope / foolish*

116 Þaȝ he were soȝt fro Samarye þat God seȝ no fyrre

Ȝise° he blusched°ful brode þat burde hym

     by sure   *truly / looked*

Þat ofte kyd°hym þe carpe° þat kyng sayde   *showed / discourse*

Dyngne° Dauid on des þat demed þis speche   *noble*

120 In a psalme þat he set þe sauter°withinne   *psalter*

O foleȝ in folk feleȝ oþer whyle

& vnderstondes vmbestounde° þaȝ ȝe be stape

     in fole   *occasionally*

Hope ȝe þat he heres not þat eres alle made

124 Hit may not be þat he is blynde þat bigged°vche yȝe   *formed*

---

114. peril: MS pil.

122. ȝe: MS he.

122. stape in fole: MS, A, B stape fole.

---

haven toward the sea." B, who generally agrees with Emerson's theory of the launching, translates *layden in on ladde borde* (106) as "they placed themselves . . . on the larboard (in order to manipulate for gaining the luff: partly thus steadying the vessel, and partly to put the helm on the starboard and fetch the ship's head into the wind)." The phrase *lofe wynnes* (106) certainly refers to the action of the sailors in turning the ship into the wind.

111. See *GGK* 2441–42n.

116. *soȝt*: Grattan says that Ker thought this meant "travelled" here and derived the form from ON *soekja*.

117. *þat burde hym by sure*: A takes *hym* to refer to Jonah and *þat* to be elliptical "with the value of 'of that, about that'." I take *hym* to refer to God and *by* to be an imperative: "it beseemed him, to be sure!"

122. *þaȝ ȝe be stape in fole*: MS *he . . . stape fole*. This is Go's emendation, agreed to by Ekwall, "though ye be advanced in folly" and A, "though you are quite mad." B suggests that the same meaning may be had without the insertion of *in*. B also suggests that *stupe-fole*, "stupid person" might be read as the poet's translation of the Vulgate's *stulti*. Ker, according to Grattan, wished to retain the *he* of the MS and translate it "any one of you."

    Bot he dredes no dynt þat dotes for elde°   *age*

    For he watʒ fer in þe flod foundande° to Tarce   *hastᶜning*

    Bot I trow ful tyd° ouertan þat he were   *swiftly*

128 So þat schomely° to schort he schote of his ame   *shamefully*

    For þe welder of wyt þat wot alle þynges

    Þat ay wakes & waytes at wylle hatʒ he slyʒtes°   *devices*

    He calde on þat ilk crafte he carf with his hondes

132 Þay wakened wel þe wroþeloker° for wroþely

        he cleped   *more worthy*

    Ewrus & Aquiloun þat on est sittes

    Blowes boþe at my bode vpon blo°watteres   *livid*

    Þenne watʒ no tom° þer bytwene his tale & her dede *delay*

136 So bayn° wer þay boþe two his bone° for to

        wyrk   *prompt / bidding*

    Anon out of þe norþest þe noys bigynes

    When boþe breþes con blowe vpon blo watteres

    Roʒ rakkes° þer ros with rudnyng

        anvnder   *rough storm clouds* (f.85a)

140 Þe see souʒed ful sore gret selly°to here   *a wonder*

    Þe wyndes on þe wonne°water so wrastel togeder   *dark*

    Þat þe wawes ful wode waltered so hiʒe

    & efte busched to þe abyme þat breed fysches

144 Durst nowhere for roʒ°arest° at þe bothem   *upheaval / remain*

---

129. See *GGK* 2331–32n.

137–56. This description of the storm at sea is generally regarded as a good example of the poet's great original descriptive powers, though there is a parallel passage in Tertullian (see Introduction).

137. *þe norþ est*: B notes that this would seem to point to the poet's familiarity with North Sea rather than Irish Sea storms since the latter are caused by southwest winds.

143. *breed fysches*: Probably "affrighted fishes," as in modern Lancashire *bree*, "frighten," as Go suggested on the authority of the *English Dialect Dictionary*. Certainly Kluge's suggestion (Mittelenglisches Lesebuch 1912: 105) and Emerson's that the two words form a compound *breedfysches* cannot be maintained nor can Morris's glossing of *breed* as a kind of fish.

When þe breth & þe brok & þe bote metten

Hit watȝ a ioyles gyn° þat Jonas watȝ inne — *craft*

For hit reled on roun vpon þe roȝe yþes° — *waves*

148 Þe bur ber to hit baft þat brast°alle her gere° — *shattered / rigging*

Þen hurled on a hepe þe helme & þe sterne

Furst tomurte° mony rop & þe mast after — *broke*

Þe sayl sweyed on þe see þenne suppe°bihoued — *drink*

152 Þe coge° of þe colde water & þenne þe cry ryses — *small boat*

Ȝet coruen°þay þe cordes & kest al þeroute — *cut*

Mony ladde þer forth lep to laue & to kest

Scopen out þe scaþel°water þat fayn scape wolde — *noxious*

156 For be monnes lode° neuer so luþer° þe lyf is ay swete — *path / bad*

Þer watȝ busy ouerborde bale to kest

Her bagges & her feþer beddes & her bryȝt wedes

Her kysttes° & her coferes her caraldes° alle — *chests / casks*

160 & al to lyȝten þat lome ȝif leþe°wolde schape° — *calm / take place*

Bot euer watȝ ilyche° loud þe lot of þe wyndes — *equally*

& euer wroþer þe water & wodder°þe stremes — *angrier*

Þen þo wery forwroȝt°wyst no bote — *overworked*

164 Bot vchon glewed° on his god þat gayned hym
　　beste — *cried aloud*

---

147. roun: B round.
152. colde: MS clolde.

---

143. *busched*: I agree with Ekwall, B, and Go that this verb means "rushed" or "dashed," not "hushed" as previous commentators understood it. *NED* lists *busch* as "to push" and the *English Dialect Dictionary* as "to toss," both related meanings.

148. *ber to*: "was carried to, rushed to" (B); "struck, hit" (Ekwall); "pressed against" (Go). Emerson thought *baft* in this line a substantive, rather than an adverb as the context would seem to demand.

154. *to laue & to kest*: "Probably nautical terms corresponding to the modern 'bale out' and 'pitch' " (B).

157. *busy*: This is surely, as Emerson, Ekwall, and Go agree, a substantive meaning "haste" or possibly "labour" (Go).

157. *bale*: Probably used, as Ekwall suggested, in a collective sense.

Summe to Vernagu þer vouched avowes solemne
Summe to Diana deuout & derf°Nepturne   *mighty*
To Mahoun & to Mergot þe mone & þe sunne
168 & vche lede as he loued & layde had his hert

Þenne bispeke þe spakest° dispayred wel nere   *cleverest*
I leue here be sum losynger° sum lawles wrech   *traitor*
Þat hatʒ greued his god & gotʒ here amonge vus
172 Lo al synkes in his synne & for his sake marres°   *perishes*

I lovue°þat we lay lotes on ledes vchone   *propose*
& whoso lympes°þe losse lay hym þeroute   *befalls*
& quen þe gulty is gon what may gome trawe   (f.85b)
176 Bot he þat rules þe rak may rwe on þose oþer

Þis watʒ sette in asent & sembled þay were
Herʒed° out of vche hyrne°to hent þat falles   *routed | corner*
A lodesmon° lyʒtly lep vnder hachches   *pilot*
180 For to layte°mo ledes & hem to lote bryng   *seek*

Bot hym fayled no freke þat he fynde myʒt
Saf Jonas þe Jwe þat jowked° in derne°   *slept | secret*
He watʒ flowen for ferde of þe
    flode lotes°   *the roaring of the waves*
184 Into þe boþem of þe bot & on a brede°lyggede   *board*

166. Nepturne: A Neptune.
173. lovue: MS *possibly* lovne.

---

165. *Vernagu*: A giant in the Old French romances.

167. *Mahoun &...Mergot*: Mohammed, here as nearly always in the Middle Ages, is a heathen deity, and Mergot (or Margot) is the Magog of Gog and Magog (see B's note). They are used here simply to suggest, along with Vernagu and Diana, the great range of gods worshipped by the heathen crew and so to prepare for their later conversion (237ff.).

Interestingly, Morris took the second part of 167, *þe mone & þe sunne*, as being in apposition with the first half and so identified Mahoun and Mergot as the moon and the sun.

Onhelde by þe hurrok for þe heuen wrache°   *vengeance*
Slypped vpon a sloumbe slepe & slomberande he routes
Þe freke hym frunt with his fot & bede hym ferk vp
188 Þer Ragnel in his rakentes°hym rere of his dremes   *chains*

186. sloumbe slepe: MS, Go, A sloumbe selepe.
186. slomberande: MS, B, Go, A sloberande.
188. Ragnel: B Raguel.

---

185. *Onhelde*: This may be two words (Onions, ES 47:316–17), one word (B, Ekwall), or a hyphenated word (Go). The meaning, however, is certainly "huddled, prostrate, stooping" or something of the kind.

185. *hurrok*: The best opinion (Ekwall, Go, B) is that this word is derived from OE *þurrock*, "the bottom part of a ship," the *þ* at the beginning of the word having been dropped through a confusion with the definite article, which indeed in ME often attached itself to words beginning with vowels (cf. *þacces* [325]).

There is considerable division, however, as to the precise meaning of the word here. Go feels that the *hurrok* was "some detachable part of the vessel, not an integral part of it, the 'Kannie' [a piece of wood between the helmsman's seat and the stern], and also the space under it." Onions (ES 47:316–17), who is generally in agreement with Go, quotes also the *NED*'s definition, "the part of a boat between the sternmost seat and the stern," as well as those of the *English Dialect Dictionary* and J. S. Angus's *Glossary of the Shetland Dialect*, and translates the line "huddled up in the stern sheets."

B, on the other hand, states that since we know Jonah to be asleep in the "bottom of the boat," these meanings hardly fit. B, placing heavy weight upon the dialect meaning, "drain," quotes from *Our Ladyes Mirroure* (via Tyrwhitt's commentary on *The Canterbury Tales*) that "there ys a place in the bottome of a shyppe wherin ys gathered all the fylthe that cometh into the shyppe—and it is called in some contre of thys londe a thorrocke." B thus regards the *hurrok* as the very bottom of the ship, the place where all the filth taken in through the limber-holes would find its way.

Emerson, who originally thought *hurrok* to be derived from the dialect *hurroch*, a "heap of stones," withdrew this opinion after attacks by Ekwall and Onions.

186. *sloumbe slepe & slomberande*: The adjective certainly indicates a "dull, sluggish" (Go) or "deep" (B) sleep. I have emended the MS's *sloberande* to *slomberande* upon the suggestion of Go (*Athenaeum* 1894: 646), who, interestingly enough, does not follow it himself and so translates the phrase "slobbering he snores." B's note reviews the possible meanings of *sloberande*.

188. *Ragnel*: The name of a demon in the Chester *Antichrist*. The MS,

Bi þe here haspede°he hentes hym þenne   *fastened*
& broȝt hym vp by þe brest & vpon borde sette
Arayned hym ful runyschly° what raysoun he hade   *fiercely*
192 In such slaȝtes of sorȝe° to slepe so faste   *dire onslaughts*

Sone haf þay her sortes sette & serelych deled
& ay þe lote vpon laste lymped on Jonas
Þenne ascryed þay hym sckete° & asked ful loude   *quickly*
196 What þe deuel hatȝ þou don doted wrech

What seches þou on see synful schrewe
With þy lastes° so luþer° to lose vus vchone   *vices / had*
Hatȝ þou gome no gouernour ne god on to calle
200 Þat þou þus slydes on slepe when þou slayn worþes

Of what londe art þou lent what laytes° þou here   *look for*
Whyder in worlde þat þou wylt & what is þyn arnde
Lo þy dom is þe dyȝt for þy dedes ille
204 Do gyf glory to þy godde er þou glyde hens

I am an Ebru quoþ he of Israyl borne
Þat wyȝe I worchyp iwysse þat wroȝt alle þynges

189. here hasped: ᴍꜱ, A haspede; B hater hasped; Go hayre hasped.
194. þe: ᴍꜱ þe þe.
196. doted: B dotede.

---

however, is not clear; the word may be, as B reads, *Raguel*, the angel of chastisement in the apocryphal book of *Enoch*. However, *Ragnel* seems better to suit the context: "The man kicked him and told him to hasten to [the place] where Ragnel in his chains would rouse him from his dreams." A notes a connection with Dame Ragnel's supernatural powers in *The Wedding of Sir Gawain and Dame Ragnell*.

189. *here*: Not in ᴍꜱ. Certainly this line requires an addition for reasons of both meter and sense, and *here*, "hair," fulfills the requirements of both. Go added *hayre*, "hair-cloth sacking"; B follows Ekwall's suggestion of *hater*, "garment, dress," on the supposition that "Jonah is brought up by the breast"; Emerson suggested *heved*, "head," *haspede* in his opinion modifying *hym*. All of these seem to me needlessly elaborate emendations.

206. See *GGK* 2441–42*n*.

Alle þe worlde with þe welkyn° þe wynde & þe sternes   *sky*
208 & alle þat woneʒ þer withinne at a worde one

Alle þis meschef for me is made at þys tyme
For I haf greued my God & gulty am founden
Forþy bereʒ me to þe borde & baþes° me þeroute   *plunge* (f.86a)
212 Er gete ʒe no happe I hope for soþe°   *truth*

He ossed°hym by vnnynges° þat þay
    vndernomen   *showed / signs*
Þat he watʒ flawen fro þe face of frelych° dryʒtyn   *noble*
Þenne such a ferde° on hem fel & flayed hem withinne   *fear*
216 Þat þay ruyt hym to rowwe & letten þe rynk one°   *the man alone*

Haþeles hyʒed in haste with ores ful longe
Syn her sayl watʒ hem aslypped on sydeʒ to rowe
Hef & hale vpon hyʒt to helpen hymseluen
220 Bot al watʒ nedles note þat nolde not bityde

In bluber° of þe blo flod bursten her ores   *foaming waves*
Þenne hade þay noʒt in her honde þat hem help myʒt
Þenne nas no coumfort to keuer° ne counsel non oþer   *obtain*
224 Bot Jonas into his juis° jugge bylyue°   *doom / at once*

Fyrst þay prayen to þe prynce þat prophetes seruen
Þat he gef hem þe grace to greuen hym neuer
Þat þay in baleleʒ° blod þer blenden her handeʒ   *innocent*
228 Þaʒ þat haþel wer his þat þay here quelled

211. baþes: ᴍꜱ baþeþes.
219. hale: B, Go haled.

---

216. *ruyt hym to rowwe*: Despite Go's "refrained from ill-treating him," the more obvious "hastened to row" seems preferable.

219. *Hef & hale*: I would sponsor here the view of Ker, as quoted in Grattan, and of Emerson that this is the traditional cry "Heave and haul."

The line thus means "Heave and haul [they cryed] on high to help themselves." B amends *hale* to *haled* and reads both it and *Hef* as preterite plural forms.

220. *nedles note*: "a useless task."

225. See *GGK* 2441–42n.

Tyd by top & bi to þay token hym synne
Into þat lodlych loȝe°þay luche hym sone   *loathsome water*
He watȝ no tytter outtulde þat tempest ne sessed
232 Þe se saȝtled þerwith as sone as ho moȝt

Þenne þaȝ her takel were torne þat totered on yþes°   *waves*
Styffe stremes & streȝt hem strayned a whyle
Þat drof hem dryȝlych adoun þe depe to serue
236 Tyl a swetter°ful swyþe hem sweȝed° to bonk   *sweeter one / sped*

Þer watȝ louyng on lofte when þay þe londe wonnen
To oure mercyable God on Moyses wyse
Wyth sacrafyse vpset & solempne vowes
240 & graunted hym on to be God & graythly non oþer

Þaȝ þay be jolef° for joye Jonas ȝet dredes   *glad*
Þaȝ he nolde suffer no sore his seele° is on
    anter°   *happiness / in danger*
For whatso worþed of þat wyȝe fro he in water dipped
244 Hit were a wonder to wene ȝif holy wryt nere°   *did not exist*

II

Now is Jonas þe Jwe jugged to drowne
Of þat schended° schyp men schowued hym sone   *ruined*

240. on: MS vn.
245. to: MS to to.

---

231. *ne*: The negative here is superlative and certainly unusual; it is probably, as Go explains, "idiomatically due to the preceding negative comparative." As B shows, there are only a few parallel constructions to be found in Middle English, and the negative had best be disregarded in translating the line.

235. *þe depe to serue*: "to give way to the sea" (B); "to keep the open sea" (Go); "to be the slave of the deep" (A).

235. *dryȝlych*: Perhaps "incessantly" (Wright, ES 36:209).

240. *graunted hym on to be God*: "Granted Him alone (or Himself) to be God." (B's translation, though the suggested translation of *on* originally was Emerson's).

A wylde walterande whal as wyrde°þen schaped   *fate* (f.86b)
248 Þat watȝ beten fro þe abyme bi þat bot flotte

& watȝ war of þat wyȝe þat þe water soȝte
& swyftely swenged hym to swepe & his swolȝ opened
Þe folk ȝet haldande his fete þe fysch hym tyd hentes
252 Withouten towche of any tothe he tult in his þrote

Thenne he swengeȝ & swayues to þe se boþem
Bi mony rokkeȝ ful roȝe & rydelande strondes
Wyth þe mon in his mawe malskred°in drede   *bewildered*
256 As lyttel wonder hit watȝ ȝif he wo dreȝed

For nade þe hyȝe heuen-kyng þurȝ his hond myȝt°   *power*
Warded þis wrech man in warlowes gutteȝ

---

250. *swolȝ*: As B points out, this word is "used of a pit, a gullet, the mouth of Hell" (see 258*n*.), as in *The Legend of Good Women* 1102.

252ff. It is interesting that in the poet's description of the swallowing of Jonah by the whale, there is very little (see 258*n*), if any, suggestion of the usual allegorical meaning attached by the church fathers to the story of Jonah, *i.e.*, the descent of Christ into hell, an interpretation of the Old Testament story which has, of course, our Lord's authority (Matt 12:40–41; Luke 11:29–32). This interpretation is often alluded to by the schoolmen and can frequently be seen in medieval iconography, *e.g.*, a 1471 German *Biblia Pauperum*, where triptych-like drawings portray the entombment of Christ flanked by portrayals of Jonah's being swallowed and by Joseph's descent into the well and the Resurrection by portrayals of Jonah's being coughed up

and by Samson's destruction of the temple. The book of Jonah was also, because of this interpretation, assigned for reading during Passion Week. It is thus unusual that the poet, who must have been aware of this allegorical reading, should choose to ignore it, though he might well have felt that its use here would somehow detract from his main theme, Jonah's lack of patience and spiritual poverty.

254. *rydelande*: M and Go relate this to late OE *hriddel*, "sieve" and gloss it "oozing, sifting." Go, however, suggests that it may come from OF *rideler*, "fall."

258. *warlowes gutteȝ*: Identified by Go as the mouth of Sheol, the fiend who, in Isaiah 5:14, "enlarged herself and opened her mouth without measure." The poet may thus be identifying the mouth of the whale with the "Mouth of Hell," often depicted as gaping animal jaws in popular art and on

What lede moȝt lyue bi lawe of any kynde
260 Þat any lyf myȝt be lent so longe hym withinne

Bot he watȝ sokored by þat syre þat syttes so hiȝe
Þaȝ were wanleȝ of wele in wombe of þat fissche
& also dryuen þurȝ þe depe & in derk waltereȝ
264 Lorde colde watȝ his cumfort and his care huge

For he knew vche a cace°& kark°þat hym
 lymped°   *misfortune / sorrow / befell*
How fro þe bot into þe blober°watȝ with a
 best lachched°   *seething water / seized*
& þrwe in at hit þrote withouten þret more
268 As mote in at a munster dor so mukel wern his chawleȝ° *jaws*

He glydes in by þe giles þurȝ glaymande glette° *filth*
Relande in by a rop a rode þat hym þoȝt
Ay hele ouer hed hourlande aboute
272 Til he blunt° in a blok as brod as a halle   *staggered*

---

259. lyue: Go leue.
262. wanleȝ: ms wauleȝ.
263. waltereȝ: ms *possibly* wattereȝ.
269. glaymande: B glaym ande.

---

the stage and so, by extension, suggesting an identification of Jonah and Christ (see 252*n*). "The reference is to the whale as an allegory of the grave—the way to resurrection; Jonah is unmarred by 'Warlowe', i.e. Sheol, Death, —the Fiend" (Go). A cites *Cursor Mundi* 27060–61 (Warlau) and *NED* (Warlock) and defines *Warlow* as "traitor, devil, the Devil, monster."

259. *lawe of any kynde*: "Natural order of things" (B) as contrasted with the miraculous or supernatural.

261. See *GGK* 2441–42*n*.

262. *were*: The personal pronoun is understood here: "Though he were hopeless of weal etc." *Wanleȝ* (ms *wauleȝ*) is M's emendation. Go is "strongly tempted to take 'were' as a noun," "man," though there is really no reason so to construe it.

269. *glaymande*: Emerson and B prefer *glaym ande*, but the adjectival construction works equally well here as it perhaps does not in 279. A retains *glaymande* since the "participial adjective is better attested in ME than the corresponding noun."

   & þer he festnes þe fete & fathmeʒ aboute
   & stod vp in his stomak þat stank as þe deuel
   Þer in saym°& in sorʒe° þat sauoured as helle   *fat / filth*
276 Þer watʒ bylded his bour þat wyl no bale suffer

   & þenne he lurkkes & laytes where watʒ le°best   *shelter*
   In vche a nok of his nauel° bot nowhere he fyndeʒ   *interior*
   No rest ne recouerer bot ramel ande myre
280 In wych gut so euer he gotʒ bot euer is God swete

   & þer he lenged at þe last & to þe lede called
   Now prynce of þy prophete pite þou haue
   Þaʒ I be fol & fykel & falce of my hert   *(f.87a)*
284 Dewoyde° now þy vengaunce þurʒ vertu of rauthe   *put away*

   Thaʒ I be gulty of gyle as gaule°of prophetes   *scum*
   Þou art God & alle gowdeʒ ar grayþely° þyn owen   *truly*
   Haf now mercy of þy man & his mysdedes
288 & preue þe lyʒtly a lorde in londe & in water

   With þat he hitte to a hyrne° & helde hym þerinne   *corner*
   Þer no defoule of no fylþe watʒ fest hym abute
   Þer he sete also sounde saf for merk°one   *darkness*
292 As in þe bulk of þe bote þer he byfore sleped

   So in a bouel of þat best he bideʒ on lyue°   *alive*
   Þre dayes & þre nyʒt ay þenkande on dryʒtyn

275. sorʒe: B saur.
279. ramel ande: MS ramelande.
279. recouerer: MS recouer.
283. *The first six words of the line appear on the foot of the preceding
page, possibly functioning as catchwords.*
294. þre (2nd): MS þe.

---

279. *ramel ande myre*: Here, un-like *glaymande* in 269, the participle-adjectival form simply does not fit the context, and there is no evidence of a verb corresponding to *ramel*. Em-erson, Go, and A agree in printing *ramel ande*, "refuse and." M thought *ramelande* to be "filthy."

289. *hitte to*: "hit upon" (Grattan).

His myȝt & his merci his mesure þenne
296 Now he knaweȝ hym in care þat couþe not in sele

Ande euer walteres þis whal bi wyldren° depe   *wilderness*
Þurȝ mony a regioun ful roȝe þurȝ ronk° of his wylle   *boldness*
For þat mote in his mawe mad hym I trowe
300 Þaȝ hit lyttel were hym wyth to wamel at his hert

Ande as sayled þe segge ay sykerly he herde
Þe bygge borne on his bak & bete on his sydes
Þen a prayer ful prest þe prophete þer maked
304 On þis wyse as I wene his wordeȝ were mony

III

Lorde to þe haf I cleped in careȝ ful stronge
Out of þe hole þou me herde of hellen wombe
I calde & þou knew myn vncler steuen
308 Þou dipteȝ me of þe depe se into þe dymme hert

301. as sayled: ᴍꜱ assayled.
302. &: Go þat.

---

300. As Go suggests, the "caesura makes it desirable to break the line at 'wyth'."

299–302. One of the most difficult passages of the poem, its chief crux being the form and meaning of *as sayled*, ᴍꜱ *assayled*, in 301. The reading I prefer is that of Go and of Emerson, who based the emendation on a parallel passage in Tertullian's *De Jona* where Jonah "sails along untouched by the floods without."

Emerson thus translates the whole passage: "For that mote in his maw (stomach) made him, I trowe, though it were little with him (in his estimation), to be sick at his heart; and as sailed the man, ever he heard truly (clearly) the big sea on his back and beating on his sides."

Ekwall, though he later came to agree with Emerson, originally thought *assayled* to mean "to cause to feel unwell." He noted, however, that *segge* (301) referred to the whale (Emerson presumably took the *segge* to be Jonah), *he* (301) to Jonah, and *borne* (302) to the ocean; thus "he heard the mighty ocean upon its (the whale's) back and [heard it] beat

Þe grete flem° of þy flod folded me vmbe   *onrush*

Alle þe goteȝ of þy guferes & groundeleȝ powleȝ°   *deep waters*

& þy stryuande° stremeȝ of stryndeȝ° so

     mony   *contending / currents*

312 In on daschande dam dryueȝ me ouer

& ȝet I sayde as I seet in þe se boþem

Careful am I kest out fro þy cler yȝen

& deseuered fro þy syȝt ȝet surely I hope

316 Efte to trede on þy temple & teme to° þyseluen   *belong to*

I am wrapped in water to my wostoundeȝ°   *pangs of woe*

Þe abyme byndes þe body þat I byde inne

Þe pure poplande hourle° playes on my

     heued   *bubbling whirlpool* (f.87b)

320 To laste mere of vche a mount man am I fallen

Þe barreȝ of vche a bonk ful bigly me haldes

Þat I may lachche no lont & þou my lyf weldes

Þou schal releue me renk whil þy ryȝt slepeȝ

324 Þurȝ myȝt of þy mercy þat mukel is to tryste°   *confide*

For when þ'acces of anguych watȝ hid in my sawle

---

313. sayde: MS say.
325. þ'acces: MS þacces.

---

against its sides." B and Go substantially agree with these readings.

308. *into þe dymme hert*: The Vulgate's *in corde maris*.

310. *goteȝ*: "whirlpools" (B).

310. *guferes*: M and Emerson thought *guteres*, "gutters, water courses."

313. *I sayde*: MS *I say*. Go's emendation, on the grounds that the poet meant to render the Vulgate's *et ego dixi*.

316. *teme*: "attend, minister" (B and Emerson); "belong to" (Ekwall and A); "approach" (Morris).

319. *pure*: "absolutely, fiercely" (B).

320. *man*: "Am I fallen, a mere mortal" (Grattan). This is certainly the sense of the line.

322. *& þou*: The use of "&, where we expect *but* is due to Vulgate" (B).

325. Skeat's emendation, *þ'acces*, is followed by Go, B, and A. The word *acces* was originally a medical term

Þenne I remembred me ryȝt of my rych lorde

Prayande him for pete°his prophete to here   *pity*

328 Þat into his holy hous myn orisoun°moȝt entre   *prayer*

I haf meled with þy maystres mony longe day

Bot now I wot wyterly þat þose vnwyse ledes

Þat affyen°hem in vanyte & in vayne þynges   *trust*

332 For þink þat mountes to noȝt her mercy forsaken

Bot I dewoutly awowe þat verray betȝ° halden   *will be*

Soberly to do þe sacrafyse when I schal saue worþe

& offer þe for my hele a ful hol gyfte

336 & halde goud þat þou me hetes° haf here my trauthe   *command*

Thenne oure fader to þe fysch ferslych°biddeȝ   *fiercely*

Þat he hym sput spakly vpon spare drye

Þe whal wendeȝ at his wylle & a warþe° fyndeȝ   *shore*

340 & þer he brakeȝ vp þe buyrne° as bede hym oure lorde   *man*

Þenne he swepe to þe sonde in sluchched° cloþes   *muddy*

Hit may wel be þat mester° were his mantyle to wasche   *need*

Þe bonk þat he blosched to & bode hym bisyde

344 Wern of þe regiounes ryȝt þat he renayed° hade   *renounced*

331. hem: MS, Go, A hym.
341. sluchched: B sluchchede.
344. Wern: A Watȝ.

---

used to refer to the outbreak or "attack" of an ague and in time became applied to any outburst, including one of emotion (see *NED*).

331. *hem*: MS *hym*. Morris's emendation, followed by B, though not by Go or A. Certainly the referent is *ledes* in 330.

338. *spak*: See 104*n*.

338. *vpon spare drye*: Since the poet is obviously here rendering the Vulgate's *in aridam*, we must take *drye*

as an adjective used as a substantive and render it "dry land." *Spare* would seem to mean "uncultivated" (B) or "bare" (Grattan).

342. As B points out, "all homilists insist that the penitent must wash his mantle."

343. *bonk*. Go emended to *bonkes* to agree with *wern* in 344. However, as Go says, *bonk* itself may well be a collective plural. A emends *wern* in 344 to *watȝ* to reach agreement.

JONAH PREACHING TO THE NINEVITES

Þenne a wynde of Goddeʒ worde efte þe wyʒe bruxleʒ°   *upbraids*
Nylt þou neuer to Nyniue bi no kynnes wayeʒ
ᴣisse lorde quoþ þe lede lene me þy grace
348 For to go at þi gre° me gayneʒ non oþer   *will*

Ris aproche þen to prech lo þe place here
Lo my lore is in þe loke lance hit þerinne
Þenne þe renk radly ros as he myʒt
352 & to Niniue þat naʒt he neʒed°ful euen   *approached*

Hit watʒ a cete ful syde° & selly°of brede   *extensive / marvelous*
On to þrenge þerþurʒe watʒ þre daye dede
Þat on journay ful joynt Jonas hym ʒede   *(f.88a)*
356 Er euer he warpped°any worde to wyʒe þat he mette   *uttered*

& þenne he cryed so cler þat kenne°myʒt alle   *know*
Þe trwe tenor of his teme he tolde on þis wyse
ᴣet schal forty dayeʒ fully fare to an ende
360 & þenne schal Niniue be nomen & to noʒt worþe

Truly þis ilk toun schal tylte to grounde
Vpsodoun schal ʒe dumpe depe to þe abyme
To be swolʒed swyftly wyth þe swart° erþe   *black*
364 & alle þat lyuyes hereinne lose þe swete

346. Nyniue: ᴍs nuniue *altered to* nyniue; B, Go, A Nuniue.
348. non: ᴍs mon.
350. loke: B loken.
350. lance: Go, A lauce.

---

350. *lance*: Go and A render this *lauce* and *lansed* in 489 *laused*, thus initiating a tendency on the part of Go to read *u* for *n*, which in his edition of *GGK* (1940) amounts almost to an eccentricity.

354. *On to þrenge þerþurʒe*: I agree with Go that *on* is here (like ᴏᴇ *an* at times) adverbial: "merely to pass therethrough."

355. *joynt*: "entire" (B); "continuously" (Go); "quickly" (A).

361. A similar phrasing occurs in *Purity* 9.

Þis speche sprang in þat space & spradde alle aboute
To borges°& to bacheleres þat in þat burȝ lenged   *citizens*
Such a hidor°hem hent & a hatel°drede   *fear / fierce*
368 Þat al chaunged her chere & chylled at þe hert

Þe segge sesed not ȝet bot sayde euer ilyche
Þe verray vengaunce of God schal voyde þis place
Þenne þe peple pitosly pleyned ful stylle
372 & for þe drede of dryȝtyn doured°in hert   *mourned*

Heter hayreȝ° þay hent þat asperly°
    bited   *rough hair shirts / sharply*
& þose þay bounden to her bak & to her bare sydeȝ
Dropped dust on her hede & dymly bisoȝten
376 Þat þat penaunce plesed him þat playneȝ on her wronge

& ay he cryes in þat kyth tyl þe kyng herde
& he radly vpros & ran fro his chayer
His ryche robe he to rof of his rigge° naked   *back*
380 & of a hep of askes he hitte in þe myddeȝ

He askeȝ heterly a hayre & hasped hym vmbe
Sewed a sekke þer abof and syked° ful colde   *sighed*
Þer he dased in þat duste with droppande teres
384 Wepande ful wonderly alle his wrange dedes

Þenne sayde he to his seriauntes samnes°yow bilyue   *assemble*
Do dryue out a decre demed of myseluen

371–94. Cited by Ellin M. Kelly (ELN 4:244–47) as evidence of the influence on the poet of the *Hymnus Ieiunantium* of Prudentius. Although both poems expand the Vulgate's account of the Ninevite's response to Jonah's warning, the differences in detail and emphasis between the two expansions would seem to outweigh the similarities.

375. *dymly*: "gloomily" (Go and Ker); "secretly" (Morris); "in hazy striving" (Grattan).

378. *chayer*: A seat of honor, as distinct from a bench.

380. *hitte*: "struck, fell, flung himself" (Grattan).

385. *seriauntes*: While Go renders

Þat alle þe bodyes þat ben withinne þis borȝ quyk°   *alive*
388 Boþe burnes & bestes burdeȝ & childer

Vch prynce vche prest & prelates alle
Alle faste frely for her falce werkes
Seseȝ childer of her sok soghe hem so neuer   (f.88b)
392 Ne best bite on no brom ne no bent° nauþer   *grass*

Passe to no pasture ne pike non erbes
Ne non oxe to no hay ne no horse to water
Al schal crye forclemmed° with alle oure clere strenþe   *starved*
396 Þe rurd° schal ryse to hym þat rawþe schal haue   *clamor*

What wote oþer wyte may ȝif þe wyȝe lykes
Þat is hende in þe hyȝt of his gentryse
I wot his myȝt is so much þaȝ he be myssepayed°   *displeased*
400 Þat in his mylde amesyng° he mercy may fynde   *moderation*

& if we leuen þe layk°of oure layth°synnes   *activity / loathsome*
& stylle steppen in þe styȝe°he styȝtleȝ°
        hymseluen   *path / ordains*
He wyl wende of his wodschip°& his wrath leue   *anger*
404 & forgif vus þis gult ȝif we hym God leuen

Þenne al leued on his lawe & laften her synnes
Parformed alle þe penaunce þat þe prynce radde
& God þurȝ his godnesse forgef as he sayde
408 Þaȝ he oþer bihyȝt withhelde his vengaunce

---

this simply as "officers," B identifies
the *seriauntes* as "men of law," one of
whose duties it was to "announce a de-
cree by the 'hue and cry'."

391. *soghe hem so neuer*: "let it
smart them never so much" (Go).

397–98. "What man who is gracious
to the very height of gentle conduct
knows or even may know if [his con-
duct] is pleasing to God." There is no
need to treat the *what wote* as a trans-
lation of the *quis scit* of Jonah 3:9
and render it, as does B, as an elliptical
colloquial expression.

IV

Muche sorȝe þenne satteled vpon segge Jonas
He wex as wroth as þe wynde towarde oure lorde
So hatȝ anger onhit his hert he calleȝ
412 A prayer to þe hyȝe prynce for pyne on þys wyse

I biseche þe syre now þouself iugge
Watȝ not þis ilk my worde þat worþen is nouþe°   *now*
Þat I kest in my cuntre when þou þy carp sendeȝ
416 Þat I schulde tee° to þys toun þi talent° to preche   *go / purpose*

Wel knew I þi cortaysye þy quoynt soffraunce
Þy bounte of debonerte° & þy bene grace   *goodness*
Þy longe abydyng wyth lur° þy late vengaunce   *loss*
420 & ay þy mercy is mete be mysse° neuer so huge   *offense*

I wyst wel when I hade worded quatsoeuer I cowþe
To manace alle þise mody men þat in þis mote dowelleȝ
Wyth a prayer & a pyne þay myȝt her pese gete
424 & þerfore I wolde haf flowen fer into Tarce

Now lorde lach out my lyf hit lastes to longe
Bed me bilyue my bale stour° & bryng me on ende   *death pang*
For me were swetter to swelt° as swyþe as me þynk   *die (f.89a)*
428 Þen lede lenger þi lore þat þus me les°makeȝ   *false*

Þe soun of oure souerayn þen swey in his ere
Þat vpbraydes þis burne vpon a breme wyse
Herk renk is þis ryȝt so ronkly° to wrath   *fiercely*
432 For any dede þat I haf don oþer demed þe ȝet

Jonas al joyles & janglande vpryses
& haldeȝ out on est half of þe hyȝe place

411. he: ᴍs þe.

& farandely° on a felde he fetteleȝ hym to bide   *comfortably*
436 For to wayte on þat won what schulde worþe after

Þer he busked hym a bour þe best þat he myȝt
Of hay & of euerferne° & erbeȝ a fewe   *ditch fern*
For hit watȝ playn in þat place for plyande greueȝ°   *thickets*
440 For to schylde fro þe schene oþer any schade keste

He bowed vnder his lyttel boþe° his bak to þe sunne   *booth*
& þer he swowed & slept sadly al nyȝt
Þe whyle God of his grace ded growe of þat soyle
444 Þe fayrest bynde°hym abof þat euer burne wyste   *bindweed*

When þe dawande day dryȝtyn con sende
Þenne wakened þe wyȝ vnder wodbynde
Loked alofte on þe lef þat lylled grene
448 Such a lefsel° of lof neuer lede hade   *bower*

For hit watȝ brod at þe boþem boȝted on lofte
Happed vpon ayþer half a hous as hit were
A nos on þe norþ syde & nowhere non elleȝ
452 Bot al schet in a schaȝe þat schaded ful cole

Þe gome glyȝt on þe grene graciouse leues
Þat euer wayued a wynde so wyþe & so cole
Þe schyre sunne hit vmbeschon þaȝ no schafte myȝt
456 Þe mountaunce of a lyttel mote vpon þat man schyne

---

441. *boþe*: Ekwall derives this from East Scan. *boþ*, B from ON *būþ*.

446. *wodbynde*: Almost certainly not used here to refer specifically to any of the plants such as convalvulus or honeysuckle which today bear the name, but to any trailing plant, perhaps even ivy (see *The Century Dictionary*). The word *schaȝe*, "a stalk with leaves," in 452 has almost the same neutral cast.

447. *lylled*: "hung down" (Grattan).

451. *nos*: "opening," from ON *ōs* (Go); "porch," from OE *nosu* (Grattan); "nose," from OE *nosu* (A). As B notes, the term is now employed in architecture to refer to a "cornice to throw off water."

452. *schaȝe*: See 446n.

454. *wyþe*: *weþe* (Grattan).

Þenne watȝ þe gome so glad of his gay logge
Lys loltrande þerinne lokande to toune
So blyþe of his wodbynde he balteres° þervnder   *tumbles about*
460 Þat of no diete þat day þedeuelhaf he roȝt

& euer he laȝed as he loked þe loge alle aboute
& wysched hit were in his kyth þer he wony schulde
On heȝe vpon Effraym oþer Ermonnes hilleȝ   (f.89b)
464 Iwysse a worþloker won to welde I neuer keped

& quen hit neȝed to naȝt nappe hym bihoued
He slydeȝ on a sloumbe slep sloghe vnder leues
Whil God wayned a worme þat wrot vpe þe rote
468 & wyddered watȝ þe wodbynde bi þat þe wyȝe wakned

& syþen he warneȝ þe west to waken ful softe
& sayeȝ vnte ȝeferus þat he syfle° warme   *blow*
Þat þer quikken no cloude bifore þe cler sunne
472 & ho schal busch vp ful brode & brenne° as a candel   *burn*

459. þervnder: MS þervnde.
460. þedeuelhaf: MS *corrects* de *to read* þe.
469. to waken: B waken.

458. *loltrande*: Both Go and B suggest that this may be an error for *loitrande*. B guesses that if *loltrande* is genuine it is a frequentative of the Yorkshire dialect *lolt*, "lounge." A related it to *loll*, "of uncertain origin."

460. A notably difficult line to translate, principally because of *þedeuelhaf*. In spite of Go's statement that the line is "perfectly idiomatic and intelligible," it has caused disagreement among the doctors. Go himself renders the line "that of any diet that day the devil a bit he cared," his construction of *haf* following Ekwall's reading and paralleling Scots dialect *Deil hae't* from whence comes *hate* in the sense of "morsel." B, acting on a suggestion from Professor Macauley, punctuates the phrase as an interjection, *þe-deuel-haf*! Emerson translated *haf he roȝt* as a phrase, "would he have cared," and explained that "the passage would thus mean, not that Jonah ate nothing that day, but that he was so happy, he might have gone without food." I am inclined to agree with B and so have printed *þedeuelhaf* as a substantive.

463. *Ermonnes hilleȝ*: Mount Hermon (Psalm 12:89).

Þen wakened þe wyȝe of his wyl dremes
& blusched to his wodbynde þat broþely watȝ marred
Al welwed°& wasted þo worþelych leues   *faded*
476 Þe schyre sunne hade hem schent er euer þe schalk° wyst   *man*

  & þen hef vp þe hete & heterly brenned
Þe warm wynde of þe weste wertes he swyþeȝ
Þe man marred on þe molde þat moȝt hym not hyde
480 His wodbynde watȝ away he weped for sorȝe

  With hatel anger & hot heterly he calleȝ
A þou maker of man what maystery þe þynkeȝ
Þus þy freke to forfare forbi°alle oþer   *destroy more than*
484 With alle meschef þat þou may neuer þou me spareȝ

  I keuered me a cumfort þat now is caȝt fro me
My wodbynde so wlonk° þat wered my heued   *lovely*
Bot now I se þou art sette my solace to reue°   *rob*
488 Why ne dyȝtteȝ þou me to diȝe I dure° to longe   *continue*

  Ȝet oure lorde to þe lede lansed a speche
Is þis ryȝtwys þou renk alle þy ronk noyse
So wroth for a wodbynde to wax so sone
492 Why art þou so waymot° wyȝe for so lyttel   *sad*

  Hit is not lyttel quoþ þe lede bot lykker to ryȝt
I wolde I were of þis worlde wrapped in moldeȝ
Þenne byþenk þe mon if þe forþynk sore
496 If I wolde help my hondewerk haf þou no wonder

479. þe (2nd): ᴍs þo.
483. þus þy: ᴍs þy þy.
489. lansed: A laused.

---

473. *wyl dremes*: "wild, wander-
ing dreams" (B); "delusive dreams"
(Go); "pleasant dreams" (Ekwall and
A).

474. *broþely*: "quickly" (Emerson).
494. *wrapped in moldeȝ*: Literally
"wrapped in earth," poetically "bur-
ied."

Þou art waxen so wroth for þy wodbynde
& trauayledeȝ neuer to tent hit þe tyme of an howre
Bot at a wap° hit here wax & away at an oþer   *stroke* (f.90a)
500 & ȝet lykeȝ þe so luþer° þi lyf woldeȝ þou tyne   *ill*

Þenne wyte not me for þe werk þat I hit wolde help
& rwe on þo redles°þat remen° for synne   *sufferers / cry out*
Fyrst I made hem myself of materes myn one
504 & syþen I loked hem ful longe & hem on lode hade

& if I my trauayl schulde tyne of termes so longe
& type doun ȝonder toun when hit turned were
Þe sor of such a swete place burde synk to my hert
508 So mony malicious mon as mourneȝ þerinne

& of þat soumme ȝet arn summe such sotteȝ°
  formadde   *simpletons*
As lyttel barneȝ on barme°þat neuer bale wroȝt   *breast*
& wymmen vnwytte þat wale ne couþe
512 Þat on hande fro þat oþer for alle þis hyȝe worlde

[Bitwene þe stele & þe stayre disserne noȝt cunen

512. for: MS fol.

---

503. *materes*: B notes that the use of this term "suggests the clerk."

509. *formadde*: B suggests that this is an idiomatic expression essentially meaning "as being mad" or "foolish" and cites a similar Yorkshire dialect usage. Emerson and Ekwall believe the proper form to be *for-madde*, a past participle.

509ff. Go thought the verse form of the poem defective in this section, his general theory being that 513–15, "paraphrasing the Vulgate," followed 509 in the first version of the poem, but were scrapped by the poet in favor of 510–12. The unknowing scribe, however, copied all six lines, thus causing the apparent intrusion into the text of 513–15. Certainly there is some dislocation here, and I have simply, like Go and A, bracketed the offending lines in order to facilitate reading, but have omitted them from the stanza arrangement, a device which permits the poem to have an even number of stanzas and also clarifies the point at which God's speech ends (see 524*n*).

513. "Between the side and the step of a ladder one cannot distinguish."

What rule renes in roun°bitwene þe ryȝt hande   *secret*
& his lyfte þaȝ her lyf schulde lost be þerfor]

516 & als þer ben doumbe besteȝ in þe burȝ mony
Þat may not synne in no syt hemseluen to greue
Why schulde I wrath wyth hem syþen wyȝeȝ wyl torne
& cum & cnawe me for kyng & my carpe leue

520 Wer I as hastif as þou heere were harme lumpen°   *befall*
Couþe I not þole bot as þou þer þryued ful fewe
I may not be so malicious & mylde be halden
For malyse is noȝt to mayntyne° boute mercy withinne   *practice*

524 Be noȝt so gryndel° god man bot go forth þy wayes   *angry*
Be preue & be pacient in payne & in joye
For he þat is to rakel° to renden his cloþeȝ   *hasty*
Mot efte sitte with more vnsounde to sewe hem togeder

528 Forþy when pouerte me enpreceȝ° & payneȝ innoȝe   *oppresses*
Ful softly with suffraunce saȝttel me bihoueȝ
For þy penaunce & payne to preue hit in syȝt
Þat pacience is a nobel poynt þaȝ hit displese ofte
    Amen

---

515. her: MS, B, Go his.
520. as (2nd): MS a.
522. malicious: MS malcious.
523. noȝt: MS, A noȝ.

---

515. *her lyf*: I agree with A that MS *his* makes "no sense."

523. "For it is an evil thing simply to practise malice without inward mercy." For *noȝt* as "evil," see *NED.* "naught," A sb., 2. *obs.*

524. There is some disagreement as to where God's speech ends and the narrator resumes speaking. Go ends the speech at 527 in order to keep the quatrains intact (see 509ff.*n*), and Morris at 524. It seems to me that the poet demonstrates through the exhortation to the listener-reader (*god man*) that the narrator has again begun to speak and to re-emphasize immediately the message of the opening sixty lines (see Introduction).

525. *preue*: "steadfast" (B); "valiant" (Go); "kind" (Ekwall).

· Purity ·

I

Clannesse whoso kyndly cowþe comende   (f.57a)
& rekken vp alle þe resounȝ þat ho by riȝt askeȝ
Fayre formeȝ myȝt he fynde in forþering his speche
4 & in þe contrare kark & combraunce huge

For wonder wroth is þe wyȝ þat wroȝt alle þinges
Wyth þe freke þat in fylþe folȝes hym after
As renkeȝ° of relygioun þat reden & syngen   *men*
8 & aprochen to hys presens & presteȝ arn called

Thay teen vnto his temmple & temen° to hymseluen   *turn to*
Reken wyth reuerence þay rechen his auter°   *altar*
Þay hondel þer his aune body & vsen hit boþe
12 If þay in clannes be clos þay cleche° gret mede   *obtain*

3. forþering: MS forering.
10. Reken: Go Rekenly.
10. rechen: MS r..hen.

---

1. I have printed here, as in *Patience*, the quatrain arrangement first suggested by Gollancz in *CHEL* (1:361) on the basis that, while the poem seems to contain four five-line stanzas and two of six lines, the normal pattern of verse and sense in the poem is the quatrain. (Lines 1591–92 and 1791–92, designated by Menner [MLN 37:355–62] as two-line stanzas, appear to me to be parts of larger groups.)

One should remember that Pope, who was surely more conscious of metrical regularity than was our poet, occasionally used the triplet.

1. See *GGK* 1*n*.

1–4. M translates "He who could fittingly commend Purity, and recount all the arguments (in her praise) that are justly due her, might find fair themes to aid his discourse, but in (undertaking) the contrary (*i.e.* the

Bot if þay conterfete crafte & cortaysye wont

As be honest vtwyth° & inwith alle fylþeȝ — *outwardly*

Þen ar þay synful hemself & sulped altogeder

16 Loþe God & his gere & hym to greme cachen° — *drive*

He is so clene in his courte þe kyng þat al weldeȝ

& honeste in his housholde & hagherlych° serued — *fitly*

With angeleȝ enourled° in alle þat is clene — *surrounded*

20 Boþe wythinne & wythouten in wedeȝ° ful

bryȝt — *clothes*

Nif° he nere scoymus° & skyg° & non

scaþe° louied — *unless / particular / fastidious / sin*

Hit were a meruayl to much hit moȝt not falle

Kyrst kydde°hit hymself in a carp°

oneȝ — *made known / discourse*

24 Þer as he heuened aȝt happeȝ° & hyȝt° hem

her medeȝ — *blessings / promised*

Me myneȝ° on one amonge oþer as Maþew recordeȝ — *thinks*

Þat þus of clannesse vncloseȝ a ful cler speche

15. sulped: Go sulpen.
16. Loþe: MS, Go boþe.

---

praise of Impurity) he would find great difficulty and trouble."

7–16. M notes that "this is the only passage in all the poet's works where he alludes to the vices of the clergy," but that this criticism is tempered by his praise of the righteous priests.

9. A similar phrasing occurs in *Patience* 316.

16. Loþe: I am adopting here M's reading rather than the *boþe* of the MS reprinted by both Morris and Go, since the passage otherwise lacks a verb. P. G. Thomas, however, states that *hemself* in 15 suggests a contrast and so omits the comma after *altogeder* and retains *boþe*, translating the passage "Then are they sinful themselves, and both God and his vessels [are] altogeder defiled."

25ff. As in *Patience*, the poet quotes the appropriate beatitude to introduce his theme—the place of purity in the Beatific Vision—which, as Osgood points out (see *Pearl* 675*n*.), is central to the poet's work.

Þe haþel clene of his hert hapeneȝ ful fayre
28 For he schal loke on oure lorde wyth a bone chere°   *joyfully*

As so saytȝ to þat syȝt seche schal be neuer
Þat any vnclannesse hatȝ on auwhere abowte
For he þat flemus° vch fylþe fer fro his hert   *drives out*
32 May not byde þat burne þat hit his body neȝen

Forþy hyȝ not to heuen in haetereȝ° totorne°   *clothes / torn*
Ne in þe harlateȝ°hod and handeȝ unwaschen   *beggars*
For what vrþly haþel þat hyȝ honour haldeȝ
36 Wolde lyke if a ladde com lyþerly attyred

When he were sette solempnely in a sete ryche   (f.57b)
Abof dukeȝ on dece wyth dayntys serued

28. bone: Go leue.
32. burne: MS bur. e; Go burre.
32. neȝen: Go neȝe.
35. honour: MS *abbreviates* honō; *I have expanded to* honour *here and
similarly throughout the text in other words such as* court (*e.g., line* 70),
torment-toureȝ (*e.g., line* 154), sauiour (*e.g., line* 176), tourneȝ (*e.g., line*
192), mourkne (*e.g., line* 407), fourferde (*e.g., line* 560), honoureȝ (*e.g.,
line* 594), your (*e.g., line* 618), four (*line* 756), wourchyp (*e.g., line*
1127), pourtrayed (*e.g., line* 1271), conquerour (*e.g., line* 1322), Em-
perour (*e.g., line* 1323), honoured (*e.g., line* 1340), bourȝ (*e.g., line*
1377), *and* Mourkenes (*e.g., line* 1760).

32. *burne*: Morris in his 1869 edition
emended to *burre* on the basis of what
is best taken as simply a badly formed
letter in the MS. M is perfectly correct
in reading the second *þat* as a relative
pronoun which taken with *his* may
be rendered "whose" and in supplying
an auxiliary verb with *neȝen*. Thus the
passage reads "For he [M thinks
Christ] who drives every filthy thing
from his heart cannot endure that man
whose body filth comes near."
33–48. The poet's transition by
means of a homely example to the
parable of the wedding feast.
35ff. A long and involved period.
In spite of the punctuation of previous
editors, the sense of the passage is best
taken: "For what earthly man . . .
would like it if a lad came wretchedly
dressed when he was sitting majesti-
cally on a throne . . . [and] then the
wretch came to his table . . . . For any
one of all these [offences], he should
be . . . given a great whack. . . ."

Þen þe harlot wyth haste helded to þe table
40 Wyth rent cokreȝ°at þe kne and his clutte°
        trascheȝ   *stockings / patched*

    & his tabarde° totorne & his toteȝ oute   *upper garment*
    Oþer ani on of alle þyse he schulde be halden vtter
    With mony blame ful bygge a boffet peraunter
44 Hurled to þe halle dore & harde þeroute schowued

    & be forboden þat borȝe to bowe þider neuer
    On payne of enprysonment & puttyng in stokkeȝ
    & þus schal he be schent° for his schrowde feble   *disgraced*
48 Þaȝ neuer in talle°ne in tuch° he trespas more   *words / deed*

    & if vnwelcum he were to a wordlych prynce
    Ȝet hym is þe hyȝe kyng harder in heuen
    As Maþew meleȝ in his masse of þat man ryche
52 Þat made þe mukel mangerye° to marie   *great feast / heir*
        his here° dere

40. clutte trascheȝ: Go clutteȝ trasched.
49. wordlych: MS worþlych; Go werdlych.
50. heuen: MS her euen.

---

40. *trascheȝ*: Skeat is doubtless correct in seeing this as the plural of *trash*, "rags." Morris had thought "trousers" and the *NED* "worn-out shoes."

41. *toteȝ*: Almost certainly derived from Low G. *tote*, "peak," as Skeat proposed. M wisely suggests that these "peaks" are his elbows protruding from his *tabarde totorne* rather than his toes as earlier editors thought.

50. *in heuen*: M's reading of the MS *in her euen*.

51–160. Carleton Brown (PMLA 19:121) says that the marriage feast passage is a "skillful weaving together of the versions of the parable found in Matthew and in Luke," a statement reflecting Brown's general argument that the poet was an ecclesiastic and generally followed Scripture rather than paraphrases.

Those details given only in Luke's account include the excuses of the invited guests, the lord's second command to gather in the wayfarers, and the description of the wayfarers. On the other hand, the lord's statement that the invited guests were not worthy of an invitation and the incident

& sende his sonde° þen to say þat þay
    samme° schulde   *messenger / assemble*
& in comly quoyntis°to com to his feste   *fine dress*
For my boles & my boreʒ arn bayted°& slayne   *fattened*
56 & my fedde fouleʒ fatted wyth sclaʒt°   *slaughter*

My polyle° þat is penne-fed & partrykeʒ boþe   *poultry*
Wyth scheldeʒ° of wylde swyn swaneʒ
    & croneʒ°   *flanks / cranes*
Al is roþeled° & rosted ryʒt to þe sete°   *prepared / appetizingly*
60 Comeʒ cof°to my corte er hit colde worþe   *quickly*

When þay knewen his cal þat þider com schulde
Alle excused him by þe skyly he scape by moʒt
On hade boʒt hym a borʒ° he sayde by hys trawþe   *estate*
64 Now turne I þeder als tyd° þe toun to byholde   *at once*

Anoþer nayed also & nurned° þis cawse   *declared*
I haf ʒerned° & ʒat ʒokkeʒ of oxen   *desired*
& for my hyʒeʒ° hem boʒt to bowe haf
    I mester°   *servants / need*
68 To see hem pulle in þe plow aproche me byhoueʒ

And I haf wedded a wyf so wer hym þe þryd
Excuse me at þe court I may not com þere
Þus þay droʒ hem adreʒ° wyth daunger vch one   *away*
72 Þat non passed to þe place þaʒ he prayed were

64. turne: MS tne.
72. place: MS plate.

of the guest without a wedding gar-
ment are found only in Matthew.

  62. *skyly*: See note to 529. Here a
substantive, the word means "excuse"

or possibly "private matter."

  69. *wer*: The preterite 3rd singular
form, "so the third one defended him-
self."

Thenne þe ludych°lorde lyked ful ille   *of the people* (f.58a)
& hade dedayn of þat dede ful dryȝly° he carpeȝ   *angrily*
He saytȝ now for her owne sorȝe þay for forsaken habbeȝ
76 More to wyte is her wrange þen any wylle gentyl

Þenne gotȝ forth my gomeȝ to þe grete streeteȝ
& forsetteȝ on vche a syde þe cete aboute
Þe wayferande frekeȝ on fote & on hors
80 Boþe burneȝ & burdeȝ þe better & þe wers

Laþeȝ° hem alle luflyly° to lenge at my fest   *invite / courteously*
& bryngeȝ hem blyþly to borȝe as barouneȝ þay were
So þat my palays plat° ful be pyȝt°
    al aboute   *entirely / arrayed*
84 Þise oþer wrecheȝ iwysse worþy noȝt wern

Þen þay cayred & com þat þe cost° waked°   *coast / guarded*
Broȝten bachlereȝ°hem wyth þat þay by
    bonkeȝ metten   *young knights*
Swyereȝ° þat swyftly swyed° on
    blonkeȝ   *squires / follow*
88 & also fele vpon fote of fre & of bonde°   *serf*

When þay com to þe courte keppte°wern þay fayre   *entertained*
Styȝtled°wyth þe stewarde stad in þe halle   *arranged*
Ful manerly wyth marchal mad for to sitte
92 As he watȝ dere of degre dressed his seete

---

76. Morris thought *wylle* to be an adjective and *gentyl* a noun and paraphrased "More to blame is their fault, than any forlorn gentile." However, both M and P. G. Thomas take *wylle* to be the noun and *gentyl* an adjective. M thus reads "their wrong is more to blame than any heathen rage," and Thomas, taking *gentyl* in a more usual sense, translates "their ill-will is more apparent than any well-bred intention."

85. *caryed and com*: "went back and forth, hither and thither."

92. *dere of degree*: This phrase along with the statement in 114 that the guests were seated *ay þe best byfore* led Osgood (*Pearl* xl) to feel that the doctrine of the inequality of reward in heaven is here implied and

Þenne seggeʒ to þe souerayn sayden þerafter
Lo lorde wyth your leue at your lege heste
& at þi banne°we haf broʒt as þou beden habbeʒ   *proclamation*
96 Mony renischche° renkeʒ & ʒet in roum more   *strange*

Sayde þe lorde to þo ledeʒ layteʒ° ʒet ferre   *seek*
Ferre out in þe felde & fecheʒ mo gesteʒ
Wayteʒ forsteʒ°& greueʒ if ani gomeʒ lyggeʒ   *search moors*
100 What kyn folk so þer fare fecheʒ hem hider

Be þay fers be þay feble forloteʒ none
Be þay hol be þay halt be þay on-yʒed
& þaʒ þay ben boþe blynde & balterande° cruppeleʒ   *stumbling*
104 Þat my hous may holly by halkeʒ°by fylled   *recesses*

For certeʒ þyse ilk renkeʒ þat me renayed habbe
& denounced me noʒt now at þis tyme
Schul neuer sitte in my sale my soper to fele
108 Ne suppe on sope of my seve þaʒ þay swelt° schulde   *perish*

Thenne þe sergaunteʒ° at þat sawe°
    swengen° þeroute   *servants / command / rushed* (f.58b)
& diden þe dede þat is demed as he deuised hade

98. Ferre: Go Ferkeʒ.
101. forloteʒ: Go for-leteʒ.
108. þaʒ: MS þaʒ þaʒ.

---

that hence the idea of equality expounded in *Pearl* is a later development of the poet's thought. Such a view seems mistaken, however, since (a) the poet makes nothing of the fact of the unequal seating arrangement, (b) he would naturally envision any such courtly lord to seat his guests in this fashion (see *GGK* 73 and 1006), and (c) one might by the same process find the opposing doctrine implied in 113–14 and 120. Recent criticism has also sharply debated the exact state of the doctrine in *Pearl* (see Introduction).

101. *forloteʒ*: Morris's note suggests and Go reads *forleteʒ*, "forsake." It is probably derived from ON *lāta* and is correctly glossed "omits."

105–107. "For certainly these men who have refused me and not acknowledged me at this time shall never sit in my hall to taste my feast."

    & wyth peple of alle plyteȝ þe palays þay fyllen
112 Hit weren not alle on wyueȝ suneȝ wonen°wyth on
      fader   *beget*

    Wheþer þay wern worþy oþer wers wel wern þay stowed
    Ay þe best byfore & bryȝtest atyred
    Þe derrest at þe hyȝe dese þat dubbed wer fayrest
116 & syþen on lenþe bilooghe ledeȝ inogh

    & ay a segge soerly semed by her wedeȝ
    So with marschal at her mete mensked° þay were   *honored*
    Clene men in compaynye forknowen° wern lyte   *recognized*
120 & ȝet þe symplest in þat sale watȝ serued to þe fulle

    Boþe with menske° & wyth mete & mynstrasy°
      noble   *dignity / minstrelsy*
    & alle þe laykeȝ° þat a lorde aȝt in londe schewe   *amusements*
    & þay bigonne to be glad þat god drink haden
124 & vch mon wyth his mach made hym at ese

II

    Now inmyddeȝ þe mete þe mayster hym biþoȝt
    Þat he wolde se þe semble þat samned° was þere   *together*

           110. is: *Not in* MS; Go watȝ.
           117. a segge soerly: Go as segges seerly.

---

114. See 92*n*.

115–17. Emerson (JEGP 20:229–41) believes that a comma should follow 115 and a semicolon 116. Go places a period after *inogh* in 116, presumably to round out the four-line stanza.

117. *soerly*: The MS reading, followed by M, emends to *soberly*, even though an adjective is needed. Emerson (PMLA 34:494–522) suggested *serly*, "individually," and Go revised the line to read & ay as segges seerly semed by her wedeȝ. I agree with M that the word is an adjective derived from ON *saurligr*, "unclean" and that emendation is unnecessary. M's note on this line contains a very full explication of the use of *sauerly*, almost certainly the same form, in *Pearl* 226.

 & rehayte rekenly°þe riche & þe poueren   *cheer courteously*
128 & cherisch hem alle wyth his cher & chaufen° her joye *increase*

 Þen he boweʒ fro his bour into þe brode halle
 & to þe best on þe bench & bede hym° be myry   *them*
 Solased hem wyth semblaunt° & syled°fyrre   *welcome* / *went*
132 Tron°fro table to table & talkede ay myrþe   *stepped*

 Bot as he ferked° ouer þe flor he fande wyth
  his yʒe   *moved quickly*
 Hit watʒ not for a halyday honestly arayed
 A þral þryʒt° in þe þrong vnþryuandely°
  cloþed   *serf crowded* / *poorly*
136 Ne no festiual frok bot fyled°with werkkeʒ   *soiled*

 Þe gome watʒ vngarnyst° wyth god men to
  dele   *not properly dressed*
 & gremed°þerwyth þe grete lord & greue hym
  he þoʒt   *became angry*
 Say me frende quoþ þe freke wyth a felle chere
140 Hov wan þou into þis won in wedeʒ so fowle

 Þe abyt þat þou hatʒ vpon no halyday hit menskeʒ° *honored*
 Þou burne for no brydale° art busked in wedeʒ *wedding-feast*
 How watʒ þou hardy þis hous for þyn vnhap to neʒe° *approach*
144 In on so ratted a robe & rent at þe sydeʒ

127. poueren: MS pouener.
136. Ne no: Go Ne in no.
138. lord: MS *has black smudge at end of word.*
139. quoþ: MS *abbreviates* Qᵗ; M *expands to* quod *throughout text.*
143. to: *Not in* MS.

---

 136. Go supplies *in* between *Ne* and   144. *on so ratted a robe*: A combi-
no to complete the sense of the line. nation of two ME constructions, *one*
M suggests that one supply "something + *so* + adj. and *so* + *a* + adj.
like 'did he have on'."

Þow art a gome vngoderly in þat goun febele   (f.59a)
Þou praysed me & my place ful pouer°
    & ful gnede°   *poorly / in a beggarly manner*
Þat watȝ so prest to aproche my presens hereinne
148 Hopeȝ þou I be a harlot þi erigaut° to prayse   *a kind of cloak*

Þat oþer burne watȝ abayst of his broþe° wordeȝ   *angry*
& hurkeleȝ doun with his hede þe vrþe he biholdeȝ
He watȝ so scoumfit° of his scylle° lest he
    skaþe° hent   *discomfited / reason / injury*
152 Þat he ne wyst on worde what he warp° schulde   *utter*

Þen þe lorde wonder loude laled° & cryed   *spoke*
& talkeȝ to his tormenttoureȝ takeȝ hym he biddeȝ
Byndeȝ byhynde at his bak boþe two his handeȝ
156 & felle fettereȝ to his fete festeneȝ bylyue

Stik hym stifly in stokeȝ & stekeȝ hym þerafter
Depe in my doungoun þer doel euer dwelleȝ
Greuing & gretyng° & gryspyng° harde   *weeping / gnashing*
160 Of teþe tenfully° togeder to teche hym be
    quoynt°   *sorrowfully / well-dressed*

Thus comparisuneȝ kryst þe kyndom of heuen
To þis frelych° feste þat fele arn to called   *noble*

146. gnede: ᴍꜱ nede.
159. gryspyng: Go gryspytyng.

---

146. *gnede*: Morris's emendation of
ᴍꜱ *nede* is followed by all later editors.
146ff. Go claimed that here, in 697–
708, and in 1129–48 the poet was
influenced by the French version of
*The Book of the Knight of La Tour
Landry,* composed in 1371. Go's closest
parallel depends upon his reading of
erigaut (148) not as a shabby garment,
but as one "ultra-fashionable" and
hence suspect, in short a "particular
type of coat-hardy." Luttrell (MÆ
29:188), however, like M thinks all
Go's parallels too general and notes
that the subject in 148 is torn and
dirty clothing.

For alle arn laþed° luflyly þe luþer° &
    þe better   *invited / wicked*
164 Þat ever wern fulȝed° in font þat fest to haue   *baptized*

    Bot war þe wel if þou wylt þy wedeȝ ben clene
    & honest for þe halyday lest þou harme lache
    For aproch þou to þat prynce of parage noble
168 He hates helle no more þen hem þat ar sowle°   *unclean*

    Wich arn þenne þy wedeȝ þou wrappeȝ þe inne
    Þat schal schewe hem so schene schrowde of þe best
    Hit arn þy werkeȝ wyterly° þat þou wroȝt haueȝ   *clearly*
172 & lyued wyth þe lykyng þat lyȝe in þyn hert

    Þat þo be frely° & fresch° fonde in þy lyue   *fair / bright*
    & fetyse° of a fayr forme to fote & to honde   *well-proportioned*
    & syþen alle þyn oþer lymeȝ lapped° ful clene   *clothed*
176 Þenne may þou se þy sauiour & his sete ryche

    For fele° fauteȝ may a freke forfete his blysse   *many*
    Þat he þe souerayn ne se þen for slauþe one

---

164. Thomas suggests a comma after *font* in order to relate the closing phrase to *laþed* (163).

167. *For aproch þou*: M suggests that "we should expect something like 'when you approach'." However, *aproch* could well be a use, relatively rare in late ME, of the infinitive without *to*, in which case the phrase could be rendered "in order to approach."

169–76. The poet here interprets the wedding garments as the works of the suppliant rather than as *caritas* (St. Augustine). His authority would seem to be St. Jerome, who described the garments as both as *praecepta . . . Domini* and as *opera quae complentur ex lege et Evangelio* (the full passage is quoted in M). There thus seems to be no basis for arguing here the relative merits of works and faith, a topic fully debated by the poet in *Pearl*.

170. Thomas suggests a comma after *schene*: "What are thy garments in which thou wrappest thyself, that should appear so bright, garments of the best?" It seems best to me, however, in spite of the awkwardness in rendering *of þe best* to allow *schene* to modify *schrowde* directly.

As for bobaunce° & bost & bolnande° pryde   *boasting / swelling*
180 Þroly° into þe deueleȝ þrote man þryngeȝ°
    bylyue   *violently / rushes*

For couetyse & colwarde° & croked dedeȝ   (f.59b) *villainous*
For mon-sworne° & men-sclaȝt° & to much
    drynk   *perjury / manslaughter*
For þefte & for þrepyng° vnþonk° may mon haue *strife / harm*
184 For roborrye & riboudrye & resouneȝ° vntrwe   *words*

& dysheriete & depryue dowrie of wydoeȝ
For marryng of maryageȝ & mayntnaunce of
    schreweȝ°   *wicked people*
For traysoun & trichcherye & tyrauntyre boþe
188 & for fals famacions° & fayned laweȝ   *reports*

Man may mysse þe myrþe þat much is to prayse
For such vnþeweȝ° as þise & þole° much payne *vices / suffer*
& in þe creatores cort com neuer more
192 Ne neuer see hym with syȝt for such sour tourneȝ° *deeds*

III

Bot I haue herkned & herde of mony hyȝe clerkeȝ° *scholars*
& als in resouneȝ° of ryȝt red hit myseluen   *statements*
Þat þat ilk proper prynce þat paradys weldeȝ
196 Is displesed at vch a poynt þat plyes° to scaþe   *tends*

179. pryde: ms, Go priyde.
181. For: ms ffor. (*Also at begining of lines* 182, 186, 205, 257, 545, 549,
553, 657, 673, 1161, 1229, 1609, *and* 1653.)

187. *boþe*: Morris suggests *loth*. If,   192. *sour*: Both Go and M derive
however, as Go suggested, *boþe* is   from on *saurr*. Luttrell, however, de-
rendered "also," the idiom is perfectly   rives from oe *súr* and translates *sour*
understandable.   *tourneȝ* as "disgusting practises."

Bot neuer ȝet in no boke breued° I herde — *written down*
Þat euer he wrek° so wyþerly° on werk
    þat he made — *took vengeance / fiercely*
Ne venged for no vilte°of vice ne synne — *vileness*
200 Ne so hastyfly watȝ hot for hatel° of his wylle — *anger*

Ne neuer so sodenly soȝt vnsoundely to weng° — *take vengeance*
As for fylþe of þe flesch þat foles han vsed
For as I fynde þer he forȝet° alle his fre
    þeweȝ° — *abandoned / customs*
204 & wex wod to þe wrache° for wrath
    at his hert — *vengeance*

For þe fyrste felonye þe falce fende wroȝt
Whyl he watȝ hyȝe in þe heuen houen vpon lofte
Of alle þyse aþel aungeleȝ attled° þe fayrest — *ordained*
208 & he vnkyndely as a karle° kydde a reward — *base fellow*

He seȝ noȝt bot hymself how semly he were
Bot his souerayn he forsoke & sade þyse wordeȝ
I schal telde° up my trone in þe tramountayne — *raise up*
212 & by lyke to þat lorde þat þe lyft° made — *heavens*

With þis worde þat he warp þe wrake on hym lyȝt
Dryȝtyn wyth his dere dom° hym drof to þe abyme — *decree*

---

201. weng: M wenge.

---

201. Bateson proposed the line be read *Ne never so sodenly soȝt un, soundely to weng.* However, Go's rendering of *vnsoundely* as "dangerous, mortally" makes emendation unnecessary.

204ff. As M states, the narratives of Lucifer, Adam, and the flood which follow demonstrate that God's full wrath falls only upon those sinners who violate the canons of chastity.

211. *tramountayne*: From *transmontana stella*, "the pale star," the word should be translated "North." The popular tradition that Lucifer inhabited the northern part of heaven derives ultimately from Isa. 14:13, "I will sit also upon the mount of the congregation, in the sides of the north."

In þe mesure of his mode his metȝ neuer þe lasse
216 Bot þer he tynt° þe type dool° of his tour ryche   *lost / tenth part*

Þaȝ þe feloun were so fers for his fayre wedeȝ   (f.60a)
& his glorious glem þat glent so bryȝt
As sone as dryȝtyneȝ dome drof to hymseluen
220 Þikke þowsandeȝ þro þrwen° þeroute   *thrown violently*

Fellen fro þe fyrmament fendeȝ ful blake°   *black*
Sweued° at þe fyrst swap° as þe snaw
    þikke   *whirled / blow*
Hurled into helle-hole as þe hyue swarmeȝ
224 Fylter° fenden folk forty dayeȝ lencþe   *huddle together*

Er þat styngande storme stynt° ne myȝt   *to cease*
Bot as smylt° mele vnder smal siue° smokeȝ
    forþikke   *strained / sieve*
So fro heuen to helle þat hatel schor laste
228 On vche syde of þe worlde aywhere ilyche°   *equally*

Þis hit watȝ a brem° brest & a byge wrache   *raging*
& ȝet wrathed not þe wyȝ ne þe wrech saȝtled°   *became reconciled*

224. Fylter: ᴍs fy. .er.
225. Er: ᴍs *first letter is illegible.*
229. Þis: Go ȝisse.

---

215. *metȝ*: Probably a scribal error for *meth*. Morris and Go (MLR 14: 152–62) believe the intended word to be a form of *mese*, "pity."

222. *Sweued*: Go maintained the initial *S* "can still be read," M that he "cannot distinguish" it. Though illegible in Go's facsimile, the letter in the ᴍs itself seems to me to be clearly intended.

224. *forty dayeȝ*: As M remarks, the length of the fall seems more to be determined by the alliteration than by any known tradition. Milton's nine days is probably taken from Hesiod's description (*Theog.* 664–735) of the fall of the Titans.

230. M is almost certainly right in taking *wyȝ* as a reference to God and *wrech* to Satan. M sees in the line the poet's reiteration of the idea, central to the poem, that God's complete ire was not provoked by Satan, since his sin was not a violation of chastity. For earlier theories, see M's note.

Ne neuer wolde for wylfulnes his worþy God knawe
232 Ne pray hym for no pite so proud watʒ his wylle

Forþy þaʒ þe rape° were rank° þe rawþe watʒ
    lyttel   *blow | severe*
Þaʒ he be kest into kare he kepes no better
Bot þat oþer wrake þat wex on wyʒeʒ hit lyʒt
236 Þurʒ þe faut of a freke þat fayled in trawþe

Adam inobedyent ordaynt to blysse
Þer pryuely in paradys his place watʒ devised
To lyue þer in lykyng° þe lenþe of a terme   *pleasure*
240 & þenne enherite þat home þat aungeleʒ forgart° *forfeited*

Bot þurʒ þe eggyng of eue he ete of an apple
Þat enpoysened alle pepleʒ þat parted fro hem boþe
For a defence° þat watʒ dyʒt of dryʒtyn selven *prohibition*
244 & a payne þeron put & pertly° halden   *openly*

Þe defence watʒ þe fryt° þat þe freke towched   *fruit*
& þe dom is þe deþe þat dreþeʒ° vus alle   *destroys*
Al in mesure & meþe° watʒ and mad þe vengiaunce *moderation*
248 & efte amended wyth a mayden þat make° had neuer *equal*

IV

Bot in þe þryd watʒ forþrast° al þat þryue schuld *shattered*
Þer watʒ malys mercyles & mawgre°
    much scheued   *displeasure*

231. wylfulnes: MS, Go wylnesful.
233. lyttel: MS lyttlel.
247. vengiaunce: M vengaunce.

---

231. *wylfulnes*: The MS *wylnesful* is almost certainly a scribal error, though Go suggests a possible derivation from ME *wilnen* or from OE *wilnian*.

235. *þat oþer wrake*: The punishment of Adam's sin.

242. *enpoysened alle pepleʒ*: A similar phrasing—*mony a plyʒtles pepul has poysoned foreuer*—occurs in *St. Erkenwald* 296.

249. *þryd*: God's third act of vengeance, this time against Noah.

Þat watʒ for fylþe vpon folde þat þe folk vsed
252 Þat þen wonyed° in þe worlde wythouten any
    maysterʒ   *dwelled*

Hit wern þe fayrest of forme & of face als   (f.60b)
Þe most & þe myriest þat maked wern euer
Þe styfest þe stalworþest þat stod euer on fete
256 & lengest lyf in hem lent of ledeʒ alle oþer

For hit was þe forme-foster° þat þe folde bred   *first offspring*
Þe aþel aunctereʒ suneʒ þat Adam watʒ called
To wham God hade geuen alle þat gayn were
260 Alle þe blysse boute blame þat bodi myʒt haue

& þose lykkest to þe lede þat lyued next after
Forþy so semly to see syþen wern none
Þer watʒ no law to hem layd bot loke to kynde
264 & kepe to hit & alle hit cors clanly fulfylle

& þenne founden þay fylþe in fleschlych dedeʒ
& controeued agayn kynde° contrare werkeʒ   *nature*
& vsed hem vnþryftyly°vch on on oþer   *vilely*
268 & als with oþer wylsfully vpon a wrange wyse

So ferly fowled her flesch þat þe fende loked
How þe deʒter of þe douþe° wern derelych°
    fayre   *men / beautifully*
& fallen in felaʒschyp° wyth hem on folken wyse   *intercourse*
272 & engendered on hem ieaunteʒ° wyth her
    japeʒ°ille   *giants / tricks*

265ff. Emerson (PMLA 21:901) maintains that in the light of medieval legends the *fende* of 269 are the descendants of Seth and the *deʒter of* þe douþe (270) the daughters of Cain, from whose union sprang the *ieaunteʒ* (272).

Þose wern men meþeleȝ° & maȝty on vrþe   *extraordinary*
Þat for her lodlych laykeȝ alosed° þay
   were   *hateful devices famed*
  He watȝ famed for fre þat feȝt° loued best   *fighting*
276 & ay þe bigest in bale þe best watȝ halden

  & þenne eueleȝ on erþe ernestly grewen
  & multyplyed monyfolde inmongeȝ mankynde
  For þat þe maȝty on molde so marre þise oþer
280 Þat þe wyȝe þat al wroȝt ful wroþly bygynneȝ

  When he knew vche contre coruppte in hitseluen
  & vch freke forloyned fro þe ryȝt wayeȝ
  Felle temptande° tene towched his hert   *distressing*
284 As wyȝe wo hym withinne werp to hymseluen

  Me forþynkeȝ° ful much þat euer I mon made   *regret*
  Bot I schal delyuer° & do away þat doten° on
   þis molde   *destroy / do folly*
  & fleme° out of þe folde al þat flesch wereȝ   *banish*
288 Fro þe burne to þe best fro bryddeȝ° to fyscheȝ   *birds*

  Al schal doun & be ded & dryuen out of erþe   *(f.61a)*
  Þat euer I sette saule° inne & sore hit he rweȝ°   *soul / repents*
  Þat euer I made hem myself bot if I may herafter
292 I schal wayte to be war her wrencheȝ° to
   kepe°   *deceitful deeds / guard against*

---

279. marre: Go marred.

---

279. *marre*: Go, following Skeat, emends to *marred*. Gordon and Onions (MÆ 1:126ff.), however, claim that *marre*, like *deȝyre* (1648) and *sware* (1415), is a weak preterite with *d* omitted.

284. *as wyȝe*: This phrase, which is alien to the medieval idea that God does not grieve as do men over sin, seems added deliberately by the poet as (1) a rendering of the Vulgate and as (2) a means of intensifying God's greater concern with man's corruption than with his disobedience.

Þenne in worlde watȝ a wyȝe wonyande° on
    lyue°   *dwelling / alive*
Ful redy & ful ryȝtwys & rewled hym°
    fayre   *conducted himself*
In þe drede of dryȝtyn his dayeȝ he vseȝ
296 & ay glydande°wyth his God his grace watȝ
    þe more   *going (quietly)*

Hym watȝ þe nome Noe as is innoghe knawen
He had þre þryuen° suneȝ & þay þre wyueȝ   *grown-up*
Sem soþly° þat on þat oþer hyȝt Cam   *truly*
300 & þe jolef° Japheth watȝ gendered þe þryd   *fair*

Now God in nwy° to Noe con speke   *woe*
Wylde wrakful° wordeȝ in his wylle greued   *bitter*
Þe ende of alle kyneȝ flesch þat on vrþe meueȝ
304 Is fallen forþ wyth my face & forþer hit I þenk

Wyth her vnworþelych werk me wlateȝ°
    wythinne   *causes loathing*
Þe gore þerof me hatȝ greued & þe glette nwyed°   *filth vexed*
I schal strenkle my distresse & strye al togeder
308 Boþe ledeȝ & londe & alle þat lyf habbeȝ

Bot make to þe a mancioun & þat is my wylle
A cofer° closed of tres clanlych planed   *ark*
Wyrk woneȝ þerinne for wylde & for tame
312 & þenne cleme° hit wyth clay comly wythinne   *plaster*

---

312. wythinne: ᴍꜱ wythinme.

---

304. *forþ wyth*: Go reads *forþwyth.*
M's explanation that the verb *fallen*
forþ is a translation of *venit* in *venit*
coram me (Gen. 6:13) seems more

reasonable.

307. "I shall put aside my grief
[that referred to in 302] and destroy
everything."

& alle þe endentur dryuen daube° wythouten   *plaster*
& þus of lenþe & of large þat lome° þou make   *vessel*
Þre hundred of cupydez þou holde to þe lenþe
316 Of fyfty fayre ouerþwert° forme þe brede°   *crosswise / breadth*

& loke euen þat þyn ark haue of heʒþe þrette°   *thirty*
& a wyndow wyd vpon wroʒt vpon lofte
In þe compas of a cubit kyndely sware°   *square*
320 A wel dutande° dor don on þe syde   *closing*

Haf hallez þerinne & halkez°ful mony   *recesses*
Boþe boskez & bourez & wel bounden penez
For I schal waken vp a water to wasch alle þe worlde
324 & quelle alle þat is quik° wyth quauende°   *living / overwhelming*
   flodez

Alle þat glydez & gotz & gost of lyf habbez   (f.61b)
I schal wast° with my wrath þat wons vpon vrþe   *destroy*
Bot my forwarde° wyth þe I festen on þis wyse   *promise*
328 For þou in reysoun° hatz rengned & ryʒtwys ben euer   *wisdom*

Þou schal enter þis ark wyth þyn aþel barnez
& þy wedded wyf with þe þou take
Þe makez° of þy myry sunez þis meyny of aʒte   *wives*
332 I schal saue of monnez saulez & swelt° þose oþer   *destroy*

Of vche best þat berez lyf busk° þe a cupple   *prepare*
Of vche clene comly kynde enclose seuen makez

318. vpon: Go vponande.
318. lofte: ᴍs loste.
322. boskez: Go boskenz.

---

318. *vpon* (1st): Go emends to *vponande* in order to make the clause parallel with *wel dutande dor* (320). It is far simpler to take *vpon* as "open" as in 453 and 882.
 322. *boskez*: "bushes" rather than *boskenz*, "the divisions of a cow-house," suggested by Go, the etymology and use of which are hazy. The phrase "bushes and stalls and fens" describes perfectly the animals' quarters on the ark.

Of vche horwed° in ark halde bot a payre   *unclean*
336 For to saue me þe sede of alle ser°kyndeʒ   *various*

& ay þou meng wyth þe maleʒ þe mete
      ho-besteʒ°   *female animals*
Vche payre by payre to plese ayþer oþer
Wyth alle þe fode þat may be founde frette° þy cofer   *furnish*
340 For sustnaunce to yowself & also þose oþer

Ful grayþely gotʒ þis god man & dos Godeʒ hestes
In dryʒ° dred & daunger þat durst do non oþer   *great*
Wen hit watʒ fettled & forged & to þe fulle grayþed
344 Þenn con dryʒttyn hym dele dryʒly þyse wordeʒ

V

Now Noe quoþ oure lorde art þou al redy
Hatʒ þou closed þy kyst° wyth clay alle aboute   *coffer*
Ʒe lorde wyth þy leue sayde þe lede þenne
348 Al is wroʒt at þi worde as þou me wyt lanteʒ

Enter in þenn quoþ he & haf þi wyf wyth þe
Þy þre suneʒ wythouten þrep° & her þre wyueʒ   *contradiction*
Besteʒ as I bedene haue bosk þerinne als
352 & when ʒe arn staued styfly stekeʒ yow þerinne

Fro seuen dayeʒ ben seyed° I sende out bylyue   *passed*
Such a rowtande ryge° þat rayne schal swyþe   *rushing storm*
Þat schal wasch alle þe worlde of werkeʒ of fylþe
356 Schal no flesch vpon folde by founden on lyue

Outtaken° yow aʒt in þis ark staued   *except*
& sed þat I wyl saue of þyse ser besteʒ

---

348. Koch (Angl 22:368) maintains that since God has already given Noah directions, the second part of the line should be translated "as far as thou hast given me power to understand."

Now Noe neuer stynteȝ þat nyȝt he bygynneȝ
360 Er al wer stawed & stoken as þe steuen wolde

Thenne sone com þe seuenþe day when samned wern
   alle   (f.62a)
& alle woned in þe whichche° þe wylde & þe tame *ark*
Þen bolned þe abyme & bonkeȝ con ryse
364 Walteȝ° out vch welle-heued in ful wode stremeȝ *overflows*

Watȝ no brymme þat abod vnbrosten° bylyue *unbroken*
Þe mukel lauande loghe° to þe lyfte rered *pouring sea*
Mony clustered clowde clef alle in clowteȝ° *shreds*
368 Torent vch a rayn-ryfte & rusched to þe vrþe

Fon neuer in forty dayeȝ & þen þe flod ryses
Ouerwalteȝ vche a wod & þe wyde feldeȝ
For when þe water of þe welkyn° wyth þe worlde mette *sky*
372 Alle þat deth moȝt dryȝe drowned þerinne

Þer watȝ moon for to make when meschef was cnowen
Þat noȝt dowed° bot þe deth in þe depe stremeȝ *availed*
Water wylger ay wax woneȝ þat stryede
376 Hurled into vch hous hent þat þer dowelled

359. Now: MS ..w.
359. stynteȝ: MS stysteȝ.
359. nyȝt: MS myȝ.
364. welle-heued: MS, Go walle-heued.
369. Fon: MS ffon.

361ff. The picture of the flood here is very like the description of the storm in *Patience* 137–56 in its use of vivid details not found in the source.

364. *welle-heued*: M's emendation of the MS's *walle-heued*, adopted for consistency with 428. Go takes *walle-heued* to be the proper form, deriving it from OE *weall*.

375. *wylger*: Skeat believed this to be an error for *wylder*. Ker (MLR 24:323) thought "wilgern [wylger] = 'raving' or the like."

NOAH AND HIS FAMILY

Fyrst feng° to þe flyȝt alle þat fle myȝt   *took*

Vuche burde wyth her barne þe byggyng° þay leueȝ   *dwelling*

& bowed to þe hyȝ bonk þer brentest° hit wern   *highest*

380 & heterly° to þe hyȝe hylleȝ þay aled on faste   *quickly*

Bot al watȝ nedleȝ her note for neuer cowþe stynt

Þe roȝe raynande ryg þe raykande waweȝ°   *flowing waves*

Er vch boþom° watȝ brurdful° to þe bonkeȝ

    eggeȝ°   *valley / brimful / brinks*

384 & vche a dale so depe þat demmed at þe brynkeȝ

Þe moste mountayneȝ on mor° þenne watȝ no more

    dryȝe   *earth*

& þeron flokked þe folke for ferde of þe wrake

Syþen þe wylde of þe wode on þe water flette

388 Summe swymmed þeron þat saue hemself trawed°   *hoped*

Summe styȝe to a stud° and stared to þe heuen   *high place*

Rwly° wyth a loud rurd rored for drede   *pitifully*

Hareȝ hertteȝ also to þe hyȝe runnen

392 Bukkeȝ bauseneȝ° & buleȝ to þe bonkkeȝ hyȝed   *badgers*

377. Fyrst: MS ffyrst.
379. wern: M were.
380. aled: Go haled.
382. þe (2nd): Go ne þe.
385. watȝ no more: Go on more.

---

379. *bonk*: As in *Patience* 343, a curious use of the singular form of this noun with a plural verb.

380. *aled*: Morris and Skeat emend to *haled*, though the MS form is perfectly acceptable.

382. Morris unnecessarily inserted &, and Go *ne*, after *ryg*. The line properly read, however, makes perfect sense.

385. Go emends to þe moste mountayneȝ on mor þenne on more dryȝe, "then alone were dry," and conjectures that the scribe changed *on more* to *no more* and added *watȝ* to make sense of the construction. However, the line can easily be interpreted "the people ran to the high ground even as they became flooded" and hence needs no emendation.

& alle cryed for care to þe kyng of heuen
Recouerer of þe creator þay cryed vch one
Þat amounted þe mase his mercy watȝ passed
396 & alle his pyte departed fro peple þat he hated

Bi þat þe flod to her fete floȝed & waxed   (f.62b)
Þen vche a segge seȝ wel þat synk hym byhoued
Frendeȝ fellen in fere & faþmed° togeder   *embraced*
400 To dryȝ her delful° deystyne & dyȝen alle samen   *sorrowful*

Luf lokeȝ to luf & his leue takeȝ
For to ende alle at oneȝ & for euer twynne°   *part*
By forty dayeȝ wern faren on folde no flesch styryed
404 Þat þe flod nade al freten° wyth feȝtande waȝeȝ   *devoured*

For hit clam vche a clyffe cubites fyftene
Ouer þe hyȝest hylle þat hurkled on erþe
Þenne mourkne° in þe mudde most
    ful nede°   *rot / of adversity*
408 Alle þat spyrakle inspranc° no sprawlyng
    awayled°   *breath leaped into / availed*

Saue þe haþel vnder hach & his here straunge
Noe þat ofte neuened þe name of oure lorde
Hym aȝtsum° in þat ark as aþel God lyked   *one of eight*
412 Þer alle ledeȝ in lome lenged druye

Þe arc houen watȝ on hyȝe wyth hurlande goteȝ°   *streams*
Kest to kytheȝ°vncouþe° þe clowdeȝ ful nere *regions / foreign*
Hit waltered on þe wylde flod went as hit lyste
416 Drof vpon þe depe dam° in daunger hit semed   *water*

Withouten mast oþer myke° oþer myry bawelyne   *support*
Kable oþer capstan to clyppe to her ankreȝ

395. þe mase: ᴍs þe masse þe mase.

---

395. *Þat amounted þe mase*: "so that the confusion increased."

Hurrok° oþer hande-helme hasped° on
    roþer°   *stern / fastened / rudder*
420 Oþer any sweande° sayl to seche after hauen   *swelling*

Bot flote forthe wyth þe flyt of þe felle wyndeȝ
Whederwarde° so þe water wafte hit rebounde   *whithersoever*
Ofte hit roled on rounde & rered on ende
424 Nyf oure lorde hade ben her lodeȝmon° hem had
    lumpen harde   *guide*

Of þe lenþe of Noe lyf to lay a lel° date   *true*
Þe sex hundreth of his age & none odde ȝereȝ
Of secounde monyth þe seuenteþe day ryȝteȝ
428 Towalten° alle þyse welle-hedeȝ & þe water flowed *burst forth*

& þryeȝ fyfty þe flod of folwande dayeȝ
Vche hille watȝ þer hidde wyth yþeȝ° ful graye   *waves*
Al watȝ wasted þat þer wonyed þe worlde wythinne
432 Þer euer flote oþer flwe oþer on fote ȝede

That roȝly watȝ þe remnaunt þat þe rac° dryueȝ   *storm* (f.63a)
Þat alle gendreȝ so joyst° wern joyned wythinne   *lodged*

427. seuenteþe: ᴍꜱ, M seuenþe.
430. yþeȝ: ᴍꜱ yreȝ.
431. þat þer: Go þat.
432. Þer: Go Þat.

---

427. *seuenteþe*: ᴍꜱ reads *seuenþe*.
I am adopting Go's emendation to
seuenteþe, "seventeenth," as being in
accord with Genesis.

433. *that*: A rare spelling.

433–34. A number of interpreta-
tions of these difficult lines have been
proposed. Skeat thought *roȝly* (fr.
Swed *rolig*) to mean "glad" and para-
phrased: "that the remnant that the
rack drives were glad that all kinds of
animals, so well lodged, were safely
kept inside." Bateson took *roȝly* to be
"rough" and read the lines: "So that
the relic (from the flood) that the rack
drives about, within which all kinds
thus lodged were assembled together,
was in dire straits." Go thought: "It
was jolly lucky for the remnant that
the rack drives,/ That all species so
well lodged, had been enjoined (*i.e.*
commanded) within the ark," thus

Bot quen þe lorde of þe lyfte lyked hymseluen
436 For to mynne° on his mon his meth° þat
    abydeȝ   *remember | moderation*

Þen he wakened a wynde on watereȝ to blowe
Þenne lasned°þe llak þat large watȝ are   *subsided*
Þen he stac vp þe stangeȝ° stoped þe welleȝ   *pools*
440 Bed blynne° of þe rayn hit batede as fast   *cease*

Þenne lasned þe loȝ lowkande° togeder   *sea closing*
After harde dayeȝ wern out on hundreth & fyfte
As þat lyftande lome luged aboute
444 Where þe wynde & þe weder warpen hit wolde

Hit saȝtled on a softe day synkande to grounde
On a rasse° of a rok hit rest at þe laste   *top*
On þe mounte of Mararach of Armene hilles
448 Þat oþerwayeȝ on Ebru hit hat þe Thanes

Bot þaȝ þe kyste in þe crageȝ were closed to byde
Ȝet fyned° not þe flod ne fel to þe boþemeȝ   *ceased*

441. lasned: Go lausned.
449. were: MS wern.

---

making *þe remnaunt* dative and agreeing with Skeat that *roȝly* here means something like "mild." Emerson suggests that *joyst* is a past participle of ME *joissen* "rejoiced" and interprets 434 as "within which all species so happy were joined together." Emerson also agreed with Skeat as to the meaning of *roȝly*.

It seems possible to me also that, following Thomas, *roȝly* here may be, with the *rwly* of 390, translated by some adjective such as "sorrowful." The lines may thus be read: "So that it was pitiful for the ark that the storm drives and within which the animals were so happily lodged." Thomas suggests the *"remnaunt* refers, at one and the same time, to the vessel and to its inmates."

441. *lasned*: Go emended to *lausned* and related it to ON *losna*; *lausned* thus becomes "became loosened, parted."

447. *Mararach*: The form in the French version of Mandeville's *Travels* is Ararach. Go suggests very sensibly that the scribe may have miscopied the poet's M. Ararach, "Mount Ararach."

448. *Thanes*: A detail from the French Mandeville.

Bot þe hyȝest of þe eggeȝ vnhuled° wern a lyttel   *uncovered*
452 Þat þe burne bynne° borde byhelde þe bare erþe   *within*

Þenne wafte he vpon his wyndowe & wysed° þeroute   *sent*
A message fro þat meyny hem moldeȝ° to seche   *lands*
Þat watȝ þe rauen so ronk þat rebel watȝ euer
456 He watȝ colored as þe cole corbyal° vntrwe   *raven*

& he fongeȝ to þe flyȝt & fanneȝ on þe wyndeȝ
Houeȝ hyȝe vpon hyȝt to herken tyþyngeȝ
He croukeȝ for comfort when carayne he fyndeȝ
460 Kast vp on a clyffe þer costese lay drye

He hade þe smelle of þe smach° & smoltes°
    þeder sone   *scent / starts off*
Falleȝ on þe foule flesch & fylleȝ his wombe
& sone ȝederly° forȝete ȝisterday steuen   *entirely*
464 How þe cheuetayn hym charged þat þe kyst ȝemed

Þe rauen raykeȝ hym forth þat reches° ful lyttel   *cares*
How alle fodeȝ þer fare elleȝ he fynde mete
Bot þe burne bynne borde þat bod to hys come
468 Banned°hym ful bytterly wyth bestes alle samen   *cursed*

He secheȝ anoþer sondeȝmon° & setteȝ on þe
    douue   *messenger* (f.63b)

456. corbyal: Go corby al.
458. Houeȝ: MS *illegible*; Go Haleȝ.
464. kyst: Go chyst.
469. douue: MS doune.

---

459. *carayne he fyndeȝ*: M's note contains a full account of the development of this traditional explanation of the raven's failure to return to the ark.

469. *douue*: The MS reading is clearly *doune*, on the basis of which Morris proposed a feminine form **dovene* on the analogy of *vixen* and OE *wulvene*. It is easier, however, to assume that *doune* is a scribal error and that *doveue* (481) and *dowue* (485) represent other forms of the correct noun.

Bryngeȝ þat bryȝt vpon borde blessed & sayde
Wende worþelych wyȝt vus woneȝ to seche
472 Dryf ouer þis dymme water if þou druye fyndeȝ

Bryng bodworde°to bot blysse to vus alle   *message*
Þaȝ þat fowle be false fre be þou euer
Ho wyrle out on þe weder on wyngeȝ ful scharpe
476 Dreȝly alle alonge day þat dorst neuer lyȝt

& when ho fyndeȝ no folde her fote on to pyche
Ho vmbekesteȝ° þe coste & þe kyst secheȝ   *circles about*
Ho hitteȝ on þe euentyde & on þe ark sitteȝ
480 Noe nymmes° hir anon & naytly° hir staueȝ   *takes / properly*

Noe on anoþer day nymmeȝ efte þe dowve
& byddeȝ hir bowe ouer þe borne efte bonkeȝ to seche
& ho skyrmeȝ vnder skwe° & skowteȝ aboute   *cloud*
484 Tyl hit watȝ nyȝe at þe naȝt & Noe þen secheȝ

475. wyrle: Go wyrled.
481. dowve: ms, Go doveue.

---

470. *blessed*: M takes this to be a participle modifying *borde* and so places the comma after it. It seems more reasonable, however, to interpret *blessed* either (a) as the 3rd person preterite, even though such a reading involves a shift in tense, or (b) as a participle modifying *bryȝt*, "having blessed that bright one."

473. M insists that *blysse to vus alle* and *bodworde* cannot be in apposition "since the apposition of an abstract with a concrete noun, although not uncommon in Old English poetry, would be altogether anomalous here" and so reads *to bot* not as "to boot," *i.e.*, "for our good," but as standing for *to bode*, "to announce." However, Thomas notes that *gryndellayk, greme*, and *grete wordes* are set in apposition in just this way in *GGK* 312, and indeed there seems no good reason not to assume that such a construction could be used here.

475. *wyrle*: Go reads *wyrled*. The form may, however, be a weak preterite.

484. *hit watȝ nyȝe at þe naȝt*: Troutman (*Über. Verf.* 28) compares *GGK* 929, *hit watȝ neȝ at þe niȝt*, in demonstration of common authorship since the phrasing is peculiar to these poems.

VI

On ark on an euentyde houeȝ þe dowue
On stamyn° ho stod & stylle hym abydeȝ   *prow*
What ho broȝt in hir beke a bronch of olyue
488 Gracyously vmbegrouen° al wyth grene leueȝ   *covered*

Þat watȝ þe syngne° of sauyte þat sende hem oure lorde   *sign*
& þe saȝtlyng° of hymself wyth þo sely°
    besteȝ   *reconciliation / harmless*
Þen watȝ þer joy in þat gyn where jumpred er dryȝed
492 & much comfort in þat cofer þat watȝ clay-daubed

Myryly on a fayr morn monyth þe fyrst
Þat falleȝ formast in þe ȝer & þe fyrst day
Ledeȝ loȝen in þat lome & loked þeroute
496 How þat wattereȝ wern woned & þe worlde dryed

Vch on loued oure lorde bot lenged ay stylle
Tyl þay had tyþyng fro þe tolke° þat tyned°
    hem þerinne   *man / enclosed*
Þen Godeȝ glam° to hem glod° þat gladed
    hem alle   *message / came*
500 Bede hem drawe to þe dor delyuer hem he wolde

Þen went þay to þe wykket hit walt vpon sone
Boþe þe burne & his barneȝ bowed þeroute

491. where: Go where watȝ.
491. dryȝed: Go dryȝe.

491. Go emends to *where watȝ jumpred er dryȝe*, "where was riveted before for many a long year," on the assumption that *jumpred* is a hitherto unidentified early use of "jumper," "to drill by means of a jumper," and that *dryȝe* is the adverb "long, patiently." However, *dryȝed* is clearly a verb and *jumpred*, though an unusual form, a noun derived from ME *jumpre*, "to jumble." The line might thus be read, "then was there joy in that Ark where confusion [had] long been endured."

Her wyueȝ walkeȝ hem wyth & þe wylde after

504 Þroly þrublande° in þronge þrowen ful þykke   *crowding*

Bot Noe of vche honest kynde nem out an odde   (f.64a)

& heuened vp an auter & halȝed° hit fayre   *consecrated*

& sette a sakerfyse þeron of vch a ser kynde

508 Þat watȝ comly & clene God kepeȝ non oþer

When bremly brened° þose besteȝ & þe

breþe° rysed   *fiercely burned / smell*

Þe sauour of his sacrafyse soȝt to hym euen

Þat al spedeȝ° & spylleȝ° he spekes wyth þat ilke   *prospers / kills*

512 In comly comfort ful clos & cortays° wordeȝ   *gracious*

Now Noe no more nel I neuer wary°   *condemn*

Alle þe mukel mayny on molde for no manneȝ synneȝ

For I se wel þat hit is sothe þat alle manneȝ wytteȝ

516 To vnþryfte°arn alle þrawen wyth þoȝt of

her hertteȝ   *wickedness*

& ay hatȝ ben & wyl be ȝet fro her barnage

Al is þe mynde of þe man to malyce enclyned

Forþy schal I neuer schende so schortly at ones

520 As dysstrye al for maneȝ synne dayeȝ of þis erþe

514. on: *Not in* MS.
515. manneȝ: Go seggeȝ.
520. maneȝ synne: MS *inserts* synne *above the line following* maneȝ; Go
þe douþe; M manez dedes.

504. Cf. 879 where *þrobled, þrong,* and *þrwe* again appear in combination.

514. *on*: Inserted by Morris, Skeat, and M. Emerson and Go would preserve the MS reading, taking *mayny* to be an adjective modifying *molde* as in *mainland,* "the wide earth."

515. *manneȝ*: Go emends to *seggeȝ* for the sake of the alliteration, taking *manneȝ* to be a copying error from 514.

520. *synne*: Inserted above the line following *maneȝ*. Go emends to *þe douþe* and M to *dedes* in order to preserve the alliteration.

Bot waxeʒ now & wendeʒ forth & worþeʒ to monye
Multyplyeʒ on þis molde & menske yow bytyde
Sesouneʒ schal yow neuer sese of sede ne of heruest
524 Ne hete ne no harde forst vmbre°   ne droʒþe   *darkness*

Ne þe swetnesse of somer ne þe sadde wynter
Ne þe nyʒt ne þe day ne þe newe ʒereʒ
Bot euer renne restleʒ rengneʒ ʒe þerinne
528 Þerwyth he blesseʒ vch a best & bytaʒt°   hem þis
       erþe   *delivered*

Þen watʒ a skylly skyualde quen scaped alle þe wylde
Vche fowle to þe flyʒt þat fyþereʒ myʒt serue
Vche fysch to þe flod þat fynne couþe nayte°   *use*
532 Vche beste to þe bent þat bytes on erbeʒ

Wylde wormeʒ°   to her won wryþeʒ in þe erþe   *serpents*
Þe fox & þe folmarde°   to þe fryth wyndeʒ   *polecat*
Herttes to hyʒe heþe hareʒ to gorsteʒ
536 & lyouneʒ & lebardeʒ to þe lake-ryftes°   *cavernous dens*

Herneʒ°   & hauekeʒ to þe hyʒe rocheʒ   *eagles*
Þe hole-foted°   fowle to þe flod hyʒeʒ   *web-footed*
& vche best at a brayde°   þer hym best lykeʒ   *sudden movement*
540 Þe fowre frekeʒ of þe folde fongeʒ þe empyre

529. skyualde: Go skylnade.
532. þat: MS þat þat.

---

529. *skylly skyualde*: The MS *skyu-
alde* seems to me perfectly clear, al-
though Go reads *skynalde*. Luttrell
says "either (a) *skylly* is a noun and
skyvalde a past participle, or (b) *skylly*
is an adjective and *skyvalde* a noun."
Morris thought (a), Skeat (b), M (a),
and Go (b). Go resolves the issue by
reading *skylnade* (fr. ON *skilnaðr*),

"a separation."
    Luttrell sees *skylly* as an adjective re-
lated to ON *skilligr*, hence meaning
"distinct" or "divergent"; *skyvalde* he
reconstructs, using the *sk* initial conso-
nantism and the *olde* suffix, as a noun
meaning a "rushing away" or "bolt-
ing off." The animals are thus seen
"rushing away in all directions."

Lo suche a wrakful wo for wlatsum° dedeȝ   *detestable* (f.64b)
Parformed þe hyȝe fader on folke þat he made
Þat he chysly° hade cherisched he chastysed ful harde   *carefully*
544 In devoydynge° þe vylanye þat venkquyst
     his þeweȝ°   *destroying / ordinances*

Forþy war þe now wyȝe þat worschyp desyres
In his comlych courte þat kyng is of blysse
In þe fylþe of þe flesch þat þou be founden neuer
548 Tyl any water in þe worlde to wasche þe fayly

For is no segge vnder sunne so seme of his crafteȝ
If he be sulped in synne þat sytteȝ vnclene
On spec of a spote may spede° to mysse   *cause*
552 Of þe syȝte of þe souerayn þat sytteȝ so hyȝe

For þat schewe me schale in þo schyre howseȝ
As þe beryl bornyst byhoueȝ be clene
Þat is sounde° on vche a syde & no
     sem° habes   *perfect / blemish*
556 Wythouten maskle° oþer mote as margerye-perle   *spot*

543. harde: ms, Go hardee.

549–51. M explains these troublesome lines as an anacoluthon: "The poet says: 'For there is no man under the sun so goodly in his deeds, if he is soiled by unclean sin'—and intended to continue 'that he can attain the kingdom of heaven'; but, he breaks off, as he wishes to emphasize the fact that a very little may keep a man from the bliss of heaven, and declares 'a speck of a spot may cause [such a man] to miss the sight of our Lord'."

553–54. Bateson, like Go, takes þat to refer to *spec of a spote* (551) and translates "For that (spot) shall expose me in those bright mansions." M thinks that 553 has no true subject and reads "In order that I may appear in those bright dwellings, I must be clean as a burnished beryl." Thomas, however, very sensibly states that "*þat* = that which, as in l. 580, while *me* simply records the interest of the writer in the event" and so reads "For that which shall appear in those bright houses must needs be pure as the burnished beryl."

VII

Syþen þe souerayn in sete so sore forþoȝt
Þat euer he man vpon molde merked° to lyuy   *placed*
For he in fylþe watȝ fallen felly° he uenged   *fiercely*
560 Quen fourferde° alle þe flesch þat he formed hade   *perished*

Hym rwed þat he hem vprerde & raȝt hem
     lyflode°   *means of living*
& efte þat he hem vndyd° hard hit hym þoȝt   *destroyed*
For quen þe swemande° sorȝe soȝt to his hert   *afflicting*
564 He knyt° a couenaunde cortaysly wyth
     monkynde þere   *established*

In þe mesure of his mode & meþe of his wylle
Þat he schulde neuer for no syt° smyte al at oneȝ   *vexation*
As to quelle alle quykeȝ for qued° þat myȝt falle   *evil*
568 Whyl of þe lenþe of þe londe lasteȝ þe terme

Þat ilke skyl for no scaþe ascaped hym neuer
Wheder wonderly he wrak on wykked men after
Ful felly for þat ilk faute forferde a kyth ryche
572 In þe anger of his ire þat arȝed°mony   *frightened*

& al watȝ for þis ilk euel þat vnhappen° glette   *wicked*
Þe venym & þe vylanye & þe vycios fylþe
Þat bysulpeȝ° manneȝ saule in vnsounde hert   *defiles*
576 Þat he his saueour ne see wyth syȝt of his yȝen

Alle illeȝ° he hates as helle þat stynkkeȝ   *evils* (f.65a)
Bot non nuyeȝ hym on naȝt ne neuer vpon dayeȝ

577. Alle: ᴍꜱ, M Þat alle.

569–70. M reads: "This promise (that God would never again destroy *all* flesh) never escaped him, i.e., he never forgot, because of any wickedness (however great). Nevertheless he did take terrible vengeance on wicked men afterwards."

577. It seems impossible to treat the

As harlottrye°vnhonest heþyng° of seluen   *obscenity / contempt*
580 Þat schameʒ° for no schrewedschyp° schent
      mot he worþe   *feels shame / wickedness*

Bot sauor mon in þyself þaʒ þou a sotte° lyuie   *fool*
Þaʒ þou bere þyself babel° byþenk þe sumtyme   *foolishly*
Wheþer he þat stykked vche a stare°in vche
      steppe° yʒe   *power of sight / bright*
584 ʒif hymself be bore blynde hit is a brod wonder

& he þat fetly°in face fettled alle eres   *neatly*
If he hatʒ losed þe lysten°hit
      lyfteʒ meruayle°   *sense of hearing / is more than strange*
Trave°þou neuer þat tale vntrwe þou hit fyndeʒ   *believe*
588 Þer is no dede so derne° þat ditteʒ° his yʒen   *secret / closes*

Þer is no wyʒe in his werk so war ne so stylle
Þat hit ne þraweʒ° to hym þro er he hit þoʒt haue   *rushes*
For he is þe gropande°God þe grounde of alle dedeʒ   *searching*
592 Rypande° of vche a ring°þe reynyeʒ°
      & hert   *scrutinizing / man / reins*

& þere he fyndeʒ al fayre a freke wythinne
Þat hert honest & hol þat haþel he honoureʒ

581. sauor: MS, Go sauyour.
584. hymself: MS hymsele.
586. he: MS he he.
590. þro: MS þre.
594. Þat (1st): Go Wyth.

þat clauses in 575–77 in parallel fash-
ion as M's punctuation suggests. I am
therefore adopting Go's suggestion
that the þat of 577 be omitted as a re-
copying of the same word in 576.

581. *Sauor*: M's emendation. MS,
Morris, and Go read *sauyour*. How-
ever, Go notes that *sauyour* is prob-
ably a form of *saueour* or *sauour* mean-

ing "apprehend." The Vulgate source
reads "*Intelligite, insipientes in popu-
lo; et stulti, aliquando sapite*"; *sauor*
would thus seem to translate the two
verbs.

581–82. Here the phrase *þaʒ þou
a sotte lyuie* translates *insipientes*
and *babel* translates *stulti*. (See note
above).

Sendeȝ hym a sad syȝt to se his auen face
596 & harde honyseȝ° þise oþer & of his erde° flemeȝ   *ruins / land*

Bot of þe dome of þe douþe for dedeȝ of schame
He is so skoymos° of þat skaþe he scarreȝ bylyue   *particular*
He may not dryȝe to draw allyt bot drepeȝ in hast
600 & þat watȝ schewed schortly by a scaþe° oneȝ   *dire punishment*

VIII

Olde Abraham in erde oneȝ he syttez
Euen byfore his hous dore vnder an oke grene
Bryȝt blykked þe bem of þe brode heuen
604 In þe hyȝe hete þerof Abraham bideȝ

He watȝ schunt° to þe schadow vnder schyre
  leueȝ   *gone aside*
Þenne watȝ he war on þe waye of wlonk wyȝeȝ þrynne
If þay wer farande°& fre & fayre to beholde   *handsome*
608 Hit is eþe to leue by þe last ende

For þe lede þat þer laye þe leueȝ anvnder
When he hade of hem syȝt he hyȝeȝ bylyue
& as to God þe good mon gos hem agayneȝ
612 & haylsed° hem in onhede° & sayde hende lorde   *greeted / unity*

600. scaþe: Go schaþe.

---

598. *scarreȝ*: *NED* lists this instance as the first use in English of the verb meaning "to take fright," and Go also derives the verb from ON *skirra*, "to shrink from." M, however, asserts that the meaning of the line can hardly be that God is frightened. He thus sees *scarreȝ* as a cognate of *skair*, listed in *NED* as "to scatter." Luttrell seems to solve the dilemma by asserting that the verb, although derived from Nynorsk *skjerra*, "to shun," probably here means "to be provoked, react fiercely."

599. *draw allyt*: As M and Bateson explain, *allyt* is not *a lyte*, "a little," but a form of *on lyte*, "with delay."

606. *þenne*: Relative temporal adverb; see *NED* "then."

Ȝif euer þy mon vpon molde merit disserued (f.65b)
Lenge a lyttel with þy lede I loȝly biseche
Passe neuer fro þi pouere° ȝif I hit pray durst   *poor servant*
616 Er þou haf biden with þi burne & vnder boȝe° restted   *bough*

&I schal wynne yow wyȝt° of water a lyttel   *quickly*
& fast aboute schal I fare your fette wer waschene
Restteȝ here on þis rote & I schal rachche after
620 & brynge a morsel of bred to baume your hertte

Fare forthe quoþ þe frekeȝ & fech as þou seggeȝ
By bole° of þis brode tre we byde þe here   *trunk*
Þenne orppedly° into his hous he hyȝed to Sare   *quickly*
624 Comaunded hir to be cof & quyk at þis oneȝ

Þre metteȝ° of mele menge° & ma kakeȝ   *measures | mix*
Vnder askeȝ ful hote happe° hem byliue   *cover*
Quyl I fete sumquat fat þou þe fyr bete
628 Prestly at þis ilke poynte sum polment° to make   *pottage*

He cached to his covhous & a calf bryngeȝ
Þat watȝ tender & not toȝe bed tyrue° of þe hyde   *strip*
& sayde to his seruaunt þat he hit seþe faste
632 & he deruely°at his dome dyȝt hit bylyue   *quickly*

Þe burne to be bare-heued buskeȝ hym þenne
Clecheȝ°to a clene cloþe & kesteȝ on þe grene   *grasps*
Þrwe þryftyly°þeron þo
    þre þerue° kakeȝ   *in a becoming manner | unleavened*
636 & bryngeȝ butter wythal & by þe bred setteȝ

620. baume: ᴍs, M banne.
621. Fare: ᴍs ffare.

620. *baume*: ᴍs *banne*, connected by Morris and by Go (*Athenaeum*, 1894, 2.646), though Go later changed his mind, with Scotch *bawne*, "fortification," really does not fit the context. Since, however, the scribe's *u*'s and *n*'s are notoriously indistinguishable, *baume*, translating the Vulgate's *confortate*, probably represents the scribe's intention.

Mete messeʒ°of mylke he merkkeʒ bytwene   *portions*
Syþen potage & polment in plater honest
As sewer° in a god assyse° he serued hem fayre   *servant | fashion*
640 Wyth sadde semblaunt° & swete of such as he
     hade   *dignified demeanor*

& God as a glad gest mad god chere
Þat watʒ fayn of his frende & his fest praysed
Abraham al hodleʒ wyth armeʒ vpfolden
644 Mynystred°mete byfore þo men þat myʒtes al weldeʒ   *served*

Þenne þay sayden as þay sete samen alle þrynne
When þe mete watʒ remued & þay of mensk speken
I schal efte here away Abram þay sayden
648 ʒet er þy lyueʒ lyʒt leþe°vpon erþe   *cease*

& þenne schal Sare consayue & a sun bere   (f.66a)
Þat schal be Abrahameʒ ayre & after hym wynne
Wyth wele & wyth worschyp þe worþely peple
652 Þat schal halde in heritage þat I haf men ʒarked°   *prepared*

Þenne þe burde byhynde þe dor for busmar° laʒed   *scorn*
& sayde sotyly to hirself Sare þe madde
May þou traw for tykle þat þou teme moʒteʒ
656 & I so hyʒe out of age & also my lorde

---

652. men ʒarked: ᴍꜱ men ʒark; Go hem ʒarked.
654. sotyly: ᴍꜱ, M sothly.
655. teme: ᴍꜱ, Go tonne.

---

637. *mete*: The adjective "meet, fitting," here modifying *messeʒ*.

652. *ʒarked*: It is impossible to read ᴍꜱ's *ʒark* as an adjective as did M. Go also emends *men* in this line to *hem* for the sake of the alliteration.

654. *sotyly*: I am adopting here Go's emendation of the ᴍꜱ's *sothly* since this word better translates the Vulgate's *occulte* (King James "within herself"). Go notes that the direct address, *þou*, in the next line probably derives from a commentary used by the poet which pictured Sarah as "addressing her body."

655. *teme*: I am following here the

For soþely as says þe wryt he wern of sadde elde°   *grave age*
Boþe þe wyȝe & his wyf such werk watȝ hem fayled
Fro mony a brod day byfore ho barayn ay bydene
660 Þat selue Sare wythouten sede into þat same tyme

Þenne sayde oure syre þer he sete se so Sare laȝes
Not trawande þe tale þat I þe to schewed
Hopeȝ ho oȝt° may be harde my hondeȝ to work   *anything*
664 & ȝet I avow verayly þe avaunt°þat I made   *promise*

I schal ȝeply° aȝayn & ȝelde þat I hyȝt   *quickly*
& sothely sende to Sare a soun & an hayre
Þenne swenged forth Sare & swer by hir trawþe
668 Þat for lot° þat þay lansed ho laȝed neuer   *speech*

Now innoghe hit is not so þenne nurned°þe dryȝtyn   *said*
For þou laȝed aloȝ bot let we hit one
With þat þay ros vp radly as þay rayke schulde
672 & setten toward Sodamas her syȝt alle at oneȝ

For þat cite þerbysyde watȝ sette in a vale
No myleȝ fro Mambre mo þen tweyne
Whereso wonyed þis ilke wyȝ þat wendeȝ wyth oure lorde
676 For to tent°hym wyth tale & teche hym þe gate   *attend*

---

659. bydene: ᴍs by ene; M bene.

---

substitution of *teme* for the ᴍs *tonne* as suggested by Emerson and M. Go makes a case for the ᴍs *tonne* as a verb connected with *tun*, listed in *NED* and *EDD* as meaning "to be big with child." Thomas suggested including *Sare þe madde* in quotation marks to read "She said to herself, 'Sarah, the mad, canst thou believe for wantonness that thou mayst conceive, while I am so advanced in age and also my lord?' " Ker, in a letter to Thomas (MLR, 14: 323–24) suggested that "*toune* = *towen* = you think [me] wanton whom you might [know to be] well behould."

659. bydene: "continuously." This is Go's emendation of the ᴍs *by ene*. M's *bene* is grammatically unsatisfactory.

Þen glydeȝ forth God þe god mon hym folȝeȝ
Abraham heldeȝ°hem wyth hem to conueye   *proceeds*
In towarde þe cety of Sodamas þat synned had þenne
680 In þe faute of þis fylþe þe fader hem þretes

   & sayde þus to þe segg þat sued hym after
How myȝt I hyde myn hert fro Habraham þe trwe
Þat I ne dyscouered to his corse my counsayl so dere
684 Syþen he is chosen to be chef chyldryn fader

   Þat so folk schal falle fro to flete° alle þe worlde   *fill* (f.66b)
& vche blod in þat burne blessed schal worþe
Me bos° telle to þat tolk þe tene of my wylle   *is necessary*
686 & alle myn atlyng° to Abraham
       vnhaspe°bilyue   *purpose / reveal*

IX

The grete soun of Sodamas synkkeȝ in myn ereȝ
& þe gult of Gomorre gareȝ°me to wrath   *drives*
I schal lyȝt into þat led°& loke myseluen   *nation*
692 If þay haf don as þe dyne° dryueȝ on lofte   *din*

   Þay han lerned a lyst þat lykeȝ me ille
Þat þay han founden in her flesch of fauteȝ þe werst
Vch male matȝ his mach a man as hymseluen
696 & fylter folyly in fere on femmaleȝ wyse

   I compast° hem a kynde crafte & kende°
       hit hem derne°   *devised / taught / secretly*
& amed°hit in myn ordenaunce oddely°
       dere   *esteemed / singularly*

685. folk: Go fele folk.
692. If: MS if.

---

683. *to his corse*: "to him."
685. Go adds *fele* after *so* in order to reflect the Vulgate's *in gentem mag-*
num.
696. "join unchastely together."
697–708. See note to 146ff.

    & dyȝt drwry° þerinne doole° alþerswettest   *love / intercourse*
700 & þe play of paramoreȝ°I portrayed°myseluen   *lovers / devised*

    & made þerto a maner myriest of oþer
    When two true togeder had tyȝed hemseluen
    Bytwene a male & his make such merþe schulde come
704 Wel nyȝe pure paradys moȝt preue no better

    Elleȝ þay moȝt honestly ayþer oþer welde
    At a stylle stollen steuen, vnstered wyth syȝt
    Luf-lowe°hem bytwene lasched°so hote   *flame of love / burned*
708 Þat alle þe meschefeȝ on mold moȝt hit not sleke°   *quench*

    Now haf þay skyfted°my skyl & scorned natwre   *disobeyed*
    & hentteȝ hem in heþyng an vsage vnclene
    Hem to smyte for þat smod° smartly I þenk   *filth*
712 Þat wyȝeȝ schal be by hem war worlde wythouten ende

    Þenne arȝed° Abraham & alle his mod chaunged   *was afraid*
    For hope of þe harde hate þat hyȝt hatȝ oure lorde
    Al sykande°he sayde sir wyth yor leue   *sighing*
716 Schal synful & sakleȝ° suffer al on payne   *innocent*

    Weþer euer hit lyke my lorde to lyfte such domeȝ
    Þat þe wykked & þe worþy schal on wrake suffer
    & weye vpon þe worre°half þat wrathed þe neuer   *smaller*
720 Þat watȝ neuer þy won þat wroȝteȝ vus alle

    Now fyfty fyn frendeȝ wer founde in ȝonde toune   (f.67a)
    In þe cety of Sodamas & also Gomorre
    Þat neuer lakked þy laue bot loued ay trauþe
724 & reȝtful wern & resounable & redy þe to serue

703. come: ᴍꜱ conne.
713. chaunged: ᴍꜱ chaunge.

---

    702. Translate: "[that] when two   gether."
true [lovers] had tied themselves to-

Schal þay falle in þe faute þat oþer frekeȝ wroȝt
& joyne to her juggement her juise°to haue   *judgment*
Þat nas neuer þyn note vnneuened hit worþe
728 Þat art so gaynly a God & of goste mylde

Nay for fyfty quoþ þe fader & þy fayre speche
& þay be founden in þat folk of her fylþe clene
I schal forgyue alle þe gylt þurȝ my grace one
732 & let hem smolt° al vnsmyten smoþely° at
     oneȝ   *escape / peaceably*

Aa blessed be þow quoþ þe burne so boner°
     & þewed°   *compassionate / gracious*
& al haldeȝ in þy honde þe heuen & þe erþe
Bot for I haf þis talke tatȝ to non ille
736 Ȝif I mele a lyttel more þat mul° am & askeȝ   *dust*

What if fyue faylen of fyfty þe noumbre
& þe remnaunt be reken how restes þy wylle
& fyue wont of fyfty quoþ God I schal forȝete alle
740 & wythhalde my honde for hortyng°on lede   *harming*

& quat if faurty be fre & fauty þyse oþer
Schalt þow schortly al schende & schape°non oþer   *decree*
Nay þaȝ faurty forfete ȝet fryst I a whyle
744 & voyde away my vengaunce þaȝ me vyl þynk

Þen Abraham obeched° hym & loȝly him
     þonkkeȝ   *did obeisance to*
Now sayned° be þou sauiour so symple in þy wrath   *blessed*

745. Abraham: Go þe burne.
745. & loȝly: Go & boȝsomly; M and hyȝly.

---

743. *forfete*: Best read as equivalent to the *be fre* of 741.

745. Go emends this line to *þen þe burne obeched hym & boȝsomly him þonkkeȝ* on the grounds that, *obeched* being the alliterating word, "a scribe has substituted 'Abraham' for 'þe burne' . . ." and that MS *loȝly* "must then be an error for a word beginning with *b*," Go's choice being

I am bot erþe ful euel & vsle° so blake   *ashes*
748 For to mele wyth such a mayster as myȝteȝ hatȝ alle

Bot I haue bygonnen wyth my God & he hit gayn þynkeȝ
Ȝif I forloyne as a fol þy fraunchyse° may serue   *liberality*
What if þretty þryuande°be þrad in ȝon touneȝ   *worthy*
752 What schal I leue of my lorde if he hem leþe wolde

Þenne þe godlych God gef hym onsware
Ȝet for þretty in þrong I schal my þro steke
& spare spakly°of spyt° in space of my þeweȝ   *promptly / wrath*
756 & my rankor refrayne four þy reken wordeȝ

What for twenty quoþ þe tolke vntwyneȝ° þou
    hem þenne   *destroy* (f.67b)
Nay ȝif þou ȝerneȝ hit ȝet ȝark°I hem grace   *grant*
If þat twenty be trwe I tene hem no more
760 Bot relece alle þat regioun of her ronk werkkeȝ

Now aþel lorde quoþ Abraham oneȝ a speche
& I schal schape°no more þo schalkkeȝ° to
    helpe   *endeavor / men*
If ten trysty in toune be tan in þi werkkeȝ
764 Wylt þou mese° þy mode & menddyng abyde   *moderate*

I graunt quoþ þe grete God graunt mercy þat oþer
& þenne arest þe renk & raȝt no fyrre
& Godde glydeȝ his gate by þose grene wayeȝ
768 & he conueyen hym con wyth cast of his yȝe

752. of: ᴍs if.
752. if: Go nif.

---

boȝsomly from dialect *bowly*, "curved, bent," here meaning "meekly." M, on the basis of *GGK* 773, emends *loȝly* to *hyȝly*. However, the alliteration aside, there seems to me no good reason for emending the ᴍs here.

751. *þrad*: Thomas notes that "*þrad* may be related to ᴏᴇ *þrægan*, 'to proceed in a course.'" Luttrell (NQ 184:447–50) thinks the meaning to be "affected, punished," the reading favored by M.

& as he loked along þere as oure lorde passed

ȝet he cryed hym after wyth careful steuen°   *voice*

Meke mayster on þy mon to mynne° if þe lyked   *remember*

772 Loth lengeȝ in ȝon leede þat is my lef° broþer   *dear*

He sytteȝ þer in Sodomis þy seruaunt so pouere

Among þe mansed° men þat han þe much greued   *cursed*

ȝif þou tyneȝ°þat toun tempre þyn yre   *destroy*

776 As þy mersy may malte° þy meke to spare   *soften*

Þen he wendeȝ his way wepande for care

Towarde þe mere of Mambre wepande for sorȝe

& þere in longyng al nyȝt he lengeȝ in wones

780 Whyl þe souerayn to Sodamas sende to spye

X

His sondes into Sodomas watȝ sende in þat tyme

In þat ilk euentyde by aungels tweyne

Meuande mekely togeder as myry men ȝonge

784 As Loot in a loge-dor lened hym alone

In a porche of þat place pyȝt to þe ȝates

Þat watȝ ryal & ryche so watȝ þe renkes seluen

As he stared into þe strete þer stout men played

788 He sayȝe þer swey° in asent swete men tweyne   *come*

777. wendeȝ: ᴍꜱ wendeȝ wendeȝ.
778. wepande: Go murnande; M mornande.
778. sorȝe: ᴍꜱ, Go sorewe.
781. sondes: Go sonde.
783. Meuande: ᴍꜱ meuande meuande.

---

785. *pyȝt to*: Thomas states that *pyȝt to* is a "compound particle [pyȝt-to] in an absolute construction and needs a preceding comma." How- ever, there seems no good reason not to take *pyȝt* as a simple participle and *to* as a preposition of respect.

Bolde burneȝ wer þay boþe wyth berdles chynneȝ
Royl rollande fax°to raw sylk lyke   hair
Of ble° as þe brere-flour° where so þe bare
    schewed   color | briar-rose
792 Ful clene watȝ þe countenaunce of her cler yȝen

Wlonk whit watȝ her wede & wel hit hem semed   (f.68a)
Of alle fetureȝ ful fyn & fautleȝ boþe
Watȝ non aucly° in ouþer for aungels hit wern   awry
796 & þat þe ȝep vnderȝede°þat in þe ȝate
    sytteȝ   alert one perceived

He ros vp ful radly & ran hem to mete
& loȝe he louteȝ°hem to Loth to þe grounde   bows
& syþen soberly° syreȝ I yow byseche   humbly
800 Þat ȝe wolde lyȝt at my loge & lenge þerinne

Comeȝ to your knaueȝ kote° I craue at þis oneȝ   cottage
I schal fette° yow a fatte° your fette forto wasche   fetch | vat
I norne° yow bot for on nyȝt neȝe me to lenge   entreat
804 & in þe myry mornyng ȝe may your waye take

& þay nay þat þay nolde neȝ no howseȝ
Bot stylly þer in þe strete as þay stadde wern
Þay wolde lenge þe long naȝt & logge þeroute
808 Hit watȝ hous innoȝe to hem þe heuen vpon lofte

Loth laþed so longe wyth luflych wordeȝ
Þat þay hym graunted to go & gruȝt no lenger

789. wer: M were.
790. Royl: Go Ryol.
791. schewed: MS, Go scheweed.
801. knaueȝ: Go knaues.

---

795. *aucly*: My own reading here   reads *aucly* rather than *autly* as M
confirms Go's impression that the MS   maintained.

Þe bolde to his byggyng bryngeȝ hem bylyue
812 Þat ryally arayed for he watȝ ryche euer

Þe wyȝeȝ wern welcom as þe wyf couþe
His two dere doȝtereȝ deuoutly hem haylsed
Þat wer maydeneȝ ful meke maryed not ȝet
816 & þay wer semly & swete & swyþe wel arayed

Loth þenne ful lyȝtly lokeȝ hym aboute
& his men amonestes° mete for to dyȝt   *admonishes*
Bot þenkkeȝ on hit be þrefte° what þynk so ȝe
    make   *unleavened*
820 For wyth no sour ne no salt serueȝ hym neuer

Bot ȝet I wene þat þe wyf hit wroth to dyspyt°   *anger*
& sayde softely to hirself þis vnsauere
    hyne°   *disagreeable fellows*
Loueȝ no salt in her sauce ȝet hit no skyl° were *sense*
824 Þat oþer burne be boute þaȝ boþe be nyse

Þenne ho sauereȝ wyth salt her seueȝ vch one
Agayne þe bone of þe burne þat hit forboden hade
& als ho scelt° hem in scorne þat wel her skyl°
    knewen   *served / mind*
828 Why watȝ ho wrech so wod ho wrathed oure lorde

Þenne seten þay at þe soper wern serued bylyue   (f.68b)
Þe gestes gay & ful glad of glam° debonere   *speech*

812. Þat: Go, M Þat watȝ.
822. vnsauere: ᴍs unfauere.

819–28. The tradition that Lot's wife was turned into a pillar of salt because she deliberately disobeyed Lot's command and served salt to the heavenly visitors is probably of Hebraic origin and may indicate, as Emerson suggests (MLR 10:373–75), that the poet was working here from Hebrew commentaries rather than from the standard medieval commentaries in which the tradition does not appear.

Welawynnely° wlonk tyl þay waschen hade   *joyfully*
832 Þe trestes tylt°to þe woȝe°& þe table
    boþe   *trestles pushed | walls*

Fro þe seggeȝ haden souped & seten bot a whyle
Er euer þay bosked to bedde þe borȝ watȝ al vp
Alle þat weppen myȝt welde þe wakker & þe stronger
836 To vmbelyȝe Lotheȝ hous þe ledeȝ to take

In grete flokkeȝ of folk þay fallen to his ȝateȝ
As a scowte-wach scarred so þe asscry rysed
Wyth kene clobbeȝ of þat clos þay clatȝ° on þe woweȝ   *beat*
840 & wyth a schrylle scharp schout þay schewe þyse worde

If þou louyeȝ þy lyf Loth in þyse wones
Ȝete vus out þose ȝong men þat ȝorewhyle° here
    entred   *a short time ago*
Þat we may lere°hym of lof as oure lyst biddeȝ   *teach*
844 As is þe asyse of Sodomas to seggeȝ þat passen

Whatt þay sputen & speken of so spitous° fylþe   *abominable*
What þay ȝeȝed°& ȝolped°of ȝestande°
    sorȝe   *cried | boasted | frothing*
Þat ȝet þe wynd & þe weder & þe worlde stynkes
848 Of þe brych þat vpbraydeȝ þose broþelych wordeȝ

Þe god man glyfte wyth þat glam & gloped for noyse
So scharpe schame to hym schot he schrank at þe hert

833. Fro: ᴍs ffro.
839. clatȝ: Go clatereȝ.
840. worde: Go wordeȝ.

848. *brych*: Clearly from ᴏᴇ *bryce*, though as Go says, *brych* may be related to ᴏᴇ *bræc*, a "flowing" or "rheum," and so here may very well mean "spew" and thus relate to the literal meaning of *vpbraydeȝ*, "throw up, cast up." The line may thus be read as Go suggests: "The spew that those wild words cast up."

For he knew þe costoum þat kyþed° þose wrecheʒ   *practiced*
852 He doted° neuer for no doel so depe in his mynde   *was dazed*

Allas sayd hym þenne Loth & lyʒtly he ryseʒ
& boweʒ forth fro þe bench into þe brode ʒates
What he wonded°no woþe° of wekked knaueʒ   *feared / danger*
856 Þat he ne passed þe port þe peril to abide

He went forthe at þe wyket & waft° hit hym after   *shut*
Þat a clyket hit cleʒt clos hym byhynde
Þenne he meled to þo men mesurable wordeʒ
860 For harloteʒ wyth his hendelayk° he hoped to chast   *courtesy*

Oo my frendeʒ so fre your fare is to strange
Dotʒ away your derf dyn & dereʒ°neuer my gestes   *harm*
Avoy hit is your vylaynye ʒe vylen yourseluen
864 & ʒe ar jolyf gentylmen your japeʒ ar ille

Bot I schal kenne yow by kynde a crafte þat is better   *(f.69a)*
I haf a tresor in my telde° of tow my fayre deʒter   *house*
Þat ar maydeneʒ vnmard°for alle men ʒette   *virgin*
868 In Sodamas þaʒ I hit say non semloker° burdes   *fairer*

Hit arn ronk° hit arn rype & redy to manne   *full-grown*
To samen wyth þo semly þe solace is better
I schal biteche° yow þo two þat tayt° arn &
     quoynt°   *deliver / lively / dainty*
872 & laykeʒ° wyth hem as yow lyst & leteʒ my gestes one   *play*

Þenne þe rebaudeʒ° so ronk° rerd such a
     noyse   *dissolute men / vile*
Þat aʒly°hurled in his ereʒ her harloteʒ speche   *fearfully*
Wost þou not wel þat þou woneʒ here a wyʒe strange
876 An outcomlyng° a carle we kylle° of
     þyn heued°   *stranger / strike / head*

856. peril: MS pil.

Who joyned þe be jostyse° oure japeȝ to blame   *judge*
Þat com a boy to þis borȝ þaȝ þou be burne ryche
Þus þay þrobled°& þrong & þrwe vmbe his ereȝ   *crowded*
880 & distresed hym wonder strayt wyth strenkþe in þe prece

Bot þat þe ȝonge men so ȝepe° ȝornen° þeroute   *bold / ran*
Wapped vpon° þe wyket & wonnen hem tylle   *flung open*
& by þe hondeȝ hym hent & horyed hym wythinne
884 & steken þe ȝates ston-harde wyth stalworth barreȝ

Þay blwe a boffet in blande° þat
    banned° peple   *together / brought a curse upon*
Þat þay blustered° as blynde as Bayard watȝ euer   *strayed about*
Þay lest of Loteȝ logging any lysoun° to fynde   *trace*
888 Bot nyteled°þer alle þe nyȝt for noȝt at þe last   *struggled*

Þenne vch tolke tyȝt° hem þat hade of tayt°
    fayled   *betook himself / pleasure*
& vch on roþeled to þe rest þat he reche moȝt
Bot þay wern wakned al wrank þat þer in won lenged
892 Of on þe vglokest vnhap þat euer on erd suffred

XI

Ruddon°of þe day-rawe ros vpon vȝten°   *redness / early morning*
When merk of þe mydnyȝt moȝt no more last
Ful erly þose aungeleȝ þis haþel þay ruþen°   *arouse*
896 & glopnedly° on Godeȝ halue gart° hym
    vpryse   *fearfully / make*

892. vnhap þat: Go vnhap.

---

886. *blynde as Bayard*: NED states that "'Bayard' [was] taken as the type of blindness or blind recklessness" in the Middle Ages.

890. *roþeled*: M suggests that the use of the word here strongly suggests a derivation from ON *þroða*, "to huddle up." This meaning, however, would not explain the *roþeled* of 59 where, as Go suggests, it may be "a dialect variant of 'rozzle,' to heat, warm, or scorch."

Fast þe freke ferkeʒ vp ful ferd at his hert
Þay comaunded hym cof to cach þat he hade
Wyth þy wyf & þy wyʒeʒ & þy wlonc deʒtters
900 For we laþe þe Sir Loth þat þou þy lyf haue

Cayre tid of þis kythe er combred° þou
      worþe   *overwhelmed* (f.69b)
With alle þi here vpon haste tyl þou a hil fynde
Foundeʒ°faste on your fete bifore your face lokes   *set out*
904 Bot bes neuer so bolde to blusch° yow bihynde   *look*

& loke ʒe stemme° no stepe bot strecheʒ on faste   *delay*
Til ʒe reche to a reset° rest ʒe neuer   *refuge*
For we schal tyne þis toun & trayþely° disstrye   *quickly*
908 Wyth alle þise wyʒeʒ so wykke wyʒtly devoyde

& alle þe londe wyth þise ledeʒ we losen° at oneʒ   *destroy*
Sodomas schal ful sodenly synk into grounde
& þe grounde of Gomorre gorde into helle
912 & vche a koste of þis kyth clater vpon hepes

Þen laled Loth lorde what is best
If I me fele vpon fote þat I fle moʒt
Hov schulde I huyde me fro hem þat hatʒ his hate
      kynned°   *aroused*
916 In þe brath°of his breth þat brenneʒ alle þinkeʒ   *violence*

To crepe fro my creatour & know not wheder
Ne wheþer his fooschip° me folʒeʒ bifore oþer bihynde   *enmity*
Þe freke sayde no foschip oure fader hatʒ þe schewed
920 Bot hiʒly heuened þi hele° fro hem þat arn combred   *welfare*

Nov wale þe a wonnyng° þat þe warisch°
      myʒt   *dwelling | protect*
& he schal saue hit for þy sake þat hatʒ vus sende hider

912. kyth: Go kythe.
915. hem: Go hym.
917. &: Go I.

For þou art oddely þyn one° out of þis
    fylþe   *entirely alone*
924 & als Abraham þyn em° hit at himself asked   *uncle*

Lorde loued he worþe quoþ Loth vpon erþe
Þer is a cite herbisyde þat Segor hit hatte
Here vtter on a rounde hil hit houeȝ hit one
928 I wolde if his wylle wore to þat won scape

Þenn fare forth quoþ þat fre & fyne þou neuer
Wyth þose ilk þat þow wylt þat þrenge þe after
& ay goande on your gate wythouten agayntote°   *looking back*
932 For alle þis londe schal be lorne° longe er þe sonne
    rise   *destroyed*

Þe wyȝe wakened his wyf & his wlonk deȝteres
& oþer two myri men þo maydeneȝ schulde wedde
& þay token hit as tayt & tented hit lyttel
936 Þaȝ fast laþed hem Loth þay leȝen ful stylle

Þe aungeleȝ hasted þise oþer & aȝly hem þratten   (f.70a)
& enforsed alle fawre forth at þe ȝateȝ
Þo wern Loth & his lef his luflyche deȝter
940 Þer soȝt no mo to sauement° of cities aþel fyue   *safety*

<hr>

924. þyn em: ᴍꜱ þy broþer; Go þyn eme.
926. Þer: ᴍꜱ Þen.
935. tayt: ᴍꜱ, Go tyt.

<hr>

924. *Abraham þyn em*: The second scribe has here superimposed *broþer* over the *n* of *þyn* and what looks like *em* or *eme*. As M notes, "the corrector . . . was probably thinking of 772, where Abraham speaks of Lot as 'my lef broþer' (Vulgate *frater*)." This use of "brother" as "kinsman" is Hebraic.

935. *token hit as tayt*: Go prints the ᴍꜱ *tyt*, which he interprets as "mere tittle-tattle." M is probably right in assuming that "the scribe, thinking of the common phrase *as tyt*, 'at once,' . . . wrote *tyt* for *tayt*, 'play, sport, game'."

Þise aungeleȝ hade hem by hande out at þe ȝateȝ
Prechande hem þe perile & beden hem passe fast
Lest ȝe be taken in þe teche of tyrauvteȝ° here   *villains*
944 Loke ȝe bowe now bi bot boweȝ fast hence

  & þay kayre ne con & kenely° flowen   *hastily*
Erly er any heuen-glem þay to a hil comen
Þe grete God in his greme bygynneȝ on lofte
948 To wakan wedereȝ so wylde þe wyndeȝ he calleȝ

  & þay wroþely vpwafte° & wrastled togeder   *rose up*
Fro fawre half of þe folde flytande° loude   *striving*
Clowdeȝ clustered bytwene kesten vp torres°   *peak-like shapes*
952 Þat þe þik þunder-þrast þirled° hem ofte   *pierced*

  Þe rayn rueled adoun ridlande° þikke   *falling*
Of felle flaunkes of fyr & flakes of soufre°   *sulphur*
Al in smolderande smoke smachande° ful ille   *smelling*
956 Swe° aboute Sodames & hit sydeȝ alle   *rushed*

  Gorde to Gomorra þat þe grounde laused°   *split open*
Abdama & Syboym þise ceteis alle faure
Al birolled wyth þe rayn rostted & brenned
960 & ferly flayed°þat folk þat in þose feeȝ° lenged   *terrified / cities*

  For when þat þe helle herde þe houndeȝ of heuen
He watȝ ferlyly° fayn vnfolded bylyue   *wonderfully*

944. boweȝ: Go boskeȝ.
948. wakan: Go waken.

---

961. *houndeȝ of heuen*: The exact origin of this interesting image is obscure. It may have perhaps arisen in contrast with the "hounds of hell," a phrase common in the Middle Ages. Its most famous literary uses are those of Dante in *Inferno* I: 101–102, *infin* *che il Veltro verra*, sometimes taken as an allusion to Christ, and, of course, of Francis Thompson. I have little faith in Go's explanation that the poet is thinking here of the "Gabriel hounds" of Lancashire, whose cry signaled the coming of death.

Þe grete barreȝ of þe abyme he barst vp at oneȝ
964 Þat alle þe regioun torof in riftes ful grete

   & clouen alle in lyttel cloutes þe clyffeȝ aywhere
   As lance° leueȝ of þe boke þat lepes in twynne   *spring forth*
   Þe brethe of þe brynston bi þat hit blende° were   *ceased*
968 Al þo citees & her sydes sunkken to helle

   Rydelles° wern þo grete rowtes° of renkkes
     wythinne   *in dismay / bands*
   When þay wern war of þe wrake þat no wyȝe achaped
   Such a ȝomerly ȝarm° of ȝellyng þer rysed   *lamentable outcry*
972 Þerof clatered þe cloudes þat Kryst myȝt haf rawþe

   Þe segge herde þat soun to Segor þat ȝede   (f.70b)
   & þe wenches hym wyth þat by þe way folȝed
   Ferly ferde watȝ her flesch þat flowen ay ilyche
976 Trynande° ay a hyȝe trot þat torne neuer dorsten   *stepping*

   Loth & þo luly-whit his lefly two deȝter
   Ay folȝed here face bifore her boþe yȝen
   Bot þe balleful° burde þat neuer bode keped   *wretched*
980 Blusched byhynden her bak þat bale for
     to herkken°   *give heed to*

   Hit watȝ lusty Lothes wyf þat ouer her lyfte schulder
   Ones ho bluschet to þe burȝe bot bod ho no lenger

984. Al so: M Also. *Also line 1045.*

---

980. *bale*: M glosses "fire, blaze," Go "evil mischief." Luttrell claims, rightly I think, that *bale* is used "here with an extension of the meaning 'woe, misery'," and adds that "it is the sound of human distress that caused Lot's wife to turn round."

681–82. Bateson (Folk-Lore 34:241) identifies *ouer her lyfte schulder* with a number of traditions associating the left shoulder with evil omens and glosses the phrase "with a sinister look, ominously, perversely."

Þat ho nas stadde a stiffe ston a stalworth image
984 Al so salt as ani se & so ho ȝet standeȝ

Þay slypped bi & syȝe hir not þat wern hir
    samenferes°   *fellow-travellers*
Tyl þay in Segor wern sette & sayned our lorde
Wyth lyȝt loueȝ vplyfte þay loued hym swyþe
988 Þat so his seruauntes wolde see & saue of such woþe

Al watȝ dampped° & don & drowned by þenne   *doomed*
Þe ledeȝ of þat lyttel toun wern lopen° out for drede   *rushed*
Into þat malscrande° mere marred°
    bylyue   *bewildering / destroyed*
992 Þat noȝt saued watȝ bot Segor þat sat on a lawe

Þe þre ledeȝ þerin Loth & his deȝter
For his make watȝ myst þat on þe mount lenged
In a stonen statue þat salt sauor habbes
996 For two fautes þat þe fol watȝ founde in
    mistrauþe°   *unfaithfulness*

On ho serued at þe soper salt bifore dryȝtyn
& syþen ho blusched hir bihynde þaȝ hir forboden were
For on ho standes a ston & salt for þat oþer
1000 & alle lyst on hir lik þat arn on launde bestes

Abraham ful erly watȝ vp on þe morne
Þat alle naȝt much niye° hade nomen in his hert   *anxiety*

---

984. Al so: M Also. *Also line 1045.*
993. þerin: Go lent þer-in.
1002. nomen: MS no mon.

992–93. Go places a period after 992 and adds *lent* after *ledeȝ* in the following line.

1002. *nomen*: Go, M, and Emerson think the MS *no mon* to be a scribal error. Thus "þat, referring back to Abraham, would be the subject of the relative clause, and *leyen* would be parallel to *nomen*, the *hade* which precedes *nomen* being understood for *leyen*" (M).

Al in longing for Loth leyen in a wache

1004 Þer he lafte hade oure lorde he is on lofte wonnen

He sende toward Sodomas þe syȝt of his yȝen

Þat euer hade ben an erde of erþe þe swettest

As aparaunt° to paradis þat plantted þe dryȝtyn   *dependency*

1008 Nov is hit plunged in a pit like of pich fylled

Suche a roþun°of a reche ros fro þe blake   *rotten (f.71a)*

Askeȝ vpe in þe ayre & vselleȝ° þer flowen   *ashes*

As a fornes° ful of flot° þat vpon fyr boyles   *cauldron / grease*

1012 When bryȝt brennande brondeȝ° ar bet° þer

     anvnder   *brands / kindled*

Þis watȝ a uengaunce violent þat voyded þise places

Þat foundered hatȝ so fayr a folk & þe folde sonkken

Þer fyue citees wern set nov is a see called

1016 Þat ay is drouy° & dym & ded in hit kynde   *turbid*

Blo° blubrande° & blak vnblyþe° to

     neȝe   *livid / surging / dismal*

As a stynkande stanc° þat stryed synne   *pool*

1015. Þer fyue: ᴍꜱ, M Þer faure; Go Þer þe fyue.

1015. *fyue citees*: I am here follow-
ing Go in printing *fyve* rather than
faure as does M. The manuscript here
is difficult to decipher, *þer faure* ap-
parently being an emendation of the
second scribe. Since Mandeville, whom
the poet follows closely here, mentions
five cities, it is probable that he wrote
fyue and that the second scribe altered
the line to make the number agree
with that of Gen. 19, in which Zoar,
the fifth city, is not destroyed along
with the other four. However, the
scribe may well have been attempting
to follow the poet's original intention,
since in 992 Zoar (Segor) is men-
tioned as being spared by God.

1015–48. Carleton Brown was, I be-
lieve, the first to suggest that this entire
passage is based on the French edition
of Mandeville's *Travels* (PMLA 19:
149). The relevant lines from Mande-
ville are quoted in M's notes. Since, as
Brown conjectures, the *Voyage d'Outre
Mer* was probably not known in
England before 1371, this date pro-
vides a *terminus a quo* for the poem.

Þat euer of smelle & of smach smart° is to fele   *bitter*
1020 Forþy þe derk Dede See hit is demed euermore

For hit dedeȝ of deþe duren þere ȝet
For hit is brod & boþemleȝ & bitter as þe galle
& noȝt may lenge in þat lake þat any lyf bereȝ
1024 & alle þe costeȝ of kynde hit combreȝ vch one

For lay þeron a lump of led & hit on loft fleteȝ
& folde þeron a lyȝt fyþer & hit to founs° synkkeȝ   *bottom*
& þer water may walter°to wete any erþe   *roll*
1028 Schal neuer grene þeron growe gresse ne wod nawþer

If any schalke to be schent wer schowued þerinne
Þaȝ he bode in þat boþem broþely a monyth
He most ay lyue in þat loȝe in losyng° euermore   *perdition*
1032 & neuer dryȝe no dethe to dayes of ende

& as hit is corsed of kynde & hit coosteȝ als
Þe clay þat clenges þerby arn corsyes° strong   *corrosives*
As alum & alkaran° þat angre° arn boþe   *mineral pitch / bitter*
1036 Soufre sour & saundyuer & oþer such mony

& þer walteȝ°of þat water in waxlokes°
    grete   *bubbles out / waxen lumps*
Þe spumande aspaltoun° þat spysereȝ°
    sellen   *foaming asphalt / dealers*
& suche is alle þe soyle by þat se halues°   *shore*
1040 Þat fel fretes þe flesch & festres bones

1019. smelle: ms synne.
1038. spumande: ms *has five strokes between* sp *and* ande, *and the last
of these strokes is an* i *as stroke above shows.*
1040. þe: Go &.
1040. festres: ms, Go festred.

1019. *smelle:* I am here following
both Go and M in printing *smelle*
rather than the ms *synne,* a word prob-

ably picked up by the poet from the
preceding line.
1040. Go reconstructs this line *Þat*

    & þer ar tres by þat terne° of traytoures   *lake*

    & þay borgounez° & beres blomez ful fayre   *bud*

    & þe fayrest fryt þat may on folde growe

1044 As orenge & oþer fryt & apple garnade°   *pomegranate*

    Al so red & so ripe & rychely hwed   (f.71b)

    As any dom°myȝt deuice of dayntyez oute   *mind*

    Bot quen hit is brused oþer broken oþer byten in twynne

1048 No worldez goud hit wythinne bot

        wyndowande° askes   *scattering in the wind*

XII

    Alle þyse ar teches & tokenes to trow vpon ȝet

    & wittnesse of þat wykked werk & þe wrake after

    Þat oure fader forferde for fylþe of þose ledes

1052 Þenne vch wyȝe may wel wyt þat he þe wlonk louies

    & if he louyes clene layk° þat is oure lorde ryche   *behavior*

    & to be couþe in his courte þou coueytes þenne

    To se þat semly° in sete & his swete face   *seemly one*

1056 Clerrer counseyl con I non bot þat þou clene worþe

    For Clopyngnel in þe compas of his clene

        Rose°   Roman de la Rose

1041. traytoures: Go traytoures kynde.
1051. forferde: Go forþerde.
1056. counseyl: ᴍѕ counseyl counsayl; Go counsayl.
1057. For: Go For so.

---

fel fretes [&] *flesch* & *festred bones,*
i.e., "so that fell and flesh and festered
bones are eaten away." I am, however,
following M in emending *festred* to
the 3rd singular form *festres.*

  1057–66. As the poet himself says,
this passage is a paraphrase of that
portion of the *Roman de la Rose* writ-
ten by Jean Clopinel (Jean de Meun).
The original, contained in M's notes,
is a part of a speech by the Lover's
Friend advising the Lover to win the
favor of the Lady by deliberately
catering to her standards of conduct.

Þer he expouneʒ a speche to hym þat spede° wolde   *succeed*
Of a lady to be loued loke to hir sone
1060 Of wich beryng þat ho be & wych ho best louyes

   & be ryʒt such in vch a borʒe of body & of dedes
   & folʒ þe fet of þat fere þat þou fre haldes
   & if þou wyrkkes on þis wyse þaʒ ho wyk were
1064 Hir schal lyke þat layk þat lyknes° hir tylle   *is like*

   If þou wyl dele drwrye wyth° dryʒtyn þenne   *have love of*
   & lelly° louy þy lorde & his leef° worþe   *faithfully / precious*
   Þenne confourme þe to Kryst & þe clene make
1068 Þat euer is polyced° als playn as þe perle seluen   *polished*

   For loke fro fyrst þat he lyʒt wythinne þe lel° mayden   *fair*
   By how comly a kest he watʒ clos þere
   When venkkyst° watʒ no vergynyte ne vyolence
      maked   *destroyed*
1072 Bot much clener watʒ hir corse° God kynned°
      þerinne   *body / conceived*

   & efte when he borne watʒ in Beþelen þe ryche
   In wych puryte þay departed þaʒ þay pouer were
   Watʒ neuer so blysful a bour as watʒ a bos° þenne   *cow-stall*
1076 Ne no schroude-hous° so schene as a schepon°
      þare   *shelter-house / cattle-shed*

The poet, however, in 1165ff. applies the Friend's advice to the pursuit of chastity by advising his reader to *confourme . . . to Kryst and þe clene make*.

1068. The frequent use of the pearl in medieval literature as a symbol of Christ stems from the Fathers' interpretation of the pearl of great price of Matt. 13:45–56.

1075–80. This lovely passage reflects the same obvious veneration for the Virgin observed in *Pearl* 423ff. and 453ff. and *GGK* 647ff. The reference to Mary's painless delivery (1077) is commonly found in medieval hymns listing the Five Joys of Mary.

Ne non so glad vnder God as ho þat grone schulde

For þer watȝ seknesse al sounde° þat sarrest° is
halden   *well / most painful*

& þer watȝ rose reflayr° where rote° hatȝ ben euer   *scent / decay*

1080 & þer watȝ solace & songe wher sorȝ hatȝ ay cryed

For aungelles wyth instrumentes of organes & pypes   (f.72a)

& rial ryngande rotes & þe reken fyþel°   *merry violin*

& alle hende þat honestly moȝt an hert glade

1084 Aboutte my lady watȝ lent quen ho delyuer were

Þenne watȝ her blyþe barne burnyst so clene

Þat boþe þe ox & þe asse hym hered at ones

Þay knewe hym by his clannes for kyng of nature

1088 For non so clene of such a clos com neuer er þenne

& ȝif clanly he þenne com ful cortays þerafter

Þat alle þat longed to luþer° ful lodly° he
hated   *evil / with abhorrence*

By nobleye of his norture he nolde neuer towche

1092 Oȝt þat watȝ vngoderly oþer ordure° watȝ inne   *filth*

Ȝet comen lodly to þat lede as laȝares° monye   *diseased beggars*

Summe lepre summe lome & lomerande° blynde   *hobbling*

Poysened & parlatyk° & pyned° in
fyres°   *paralytic / consumed / fevers*

1096 Drye folk & ydropike° & dede at þe laste   *dropsical*

Alle called on þat cortayse & claymed his grace

He heled hem wyth hynde° speche of þat þay ask after   *gracious*

For whatso he towched also tyd tourned to hele

1100 Wel clanner þen any crafte cowþe devyse

1080–84. See *GGK* 118*n*.   adoration of the animals at the birth
1086. By the time of the poem, the   of Christ had become traditional.

So clene watȝ his hondelyng vche ordure hit schonied
    & þe gropyng°so goud of God & man boþe   *handling*
    Þat for fetys° of his fyngeres fonded°he neuer   *skill / tried*
1104 Nauþer to cout ne to kerue wyth knyf ne wyth egge

Forþy brek he þe bred blades wythouten
    For hit ferde freloker° in fete in his fayre honde   *more fairly*
    Displayed more pryuyly° when he hit part schulde   *skillfully*
1108 Þenne alle þe toles of Tolowse moȝt tyȝt hit to kerue

Þus is he kyryous° & clene þat þou his cort askes   *curious*
    Hov schulde þou com to his kyth bot if þou clene were
    Now ar we sore & synful & sovly° vch one   *vile*
1112 How schulde we se þen may we say þat syre vpon throne

ȝis þat mayster is mercyable þaȝ þou be man fenny°   *dirty*
    & al tomarred° in myre whyl þou on molde lyuyes   *ruined*
    Þou may schyne þurȝ schryfte þaȝ þou haf schome serued
1116 & pure þe with penaunce tyl þou a perle worþe

Perle praysed is prys þer perre° is schewed   *jewelry* (f.72b)
    Þaȝ hym not derrest be demed to dele for penies
    Quat may þe cause be called bot for hir clene hwes
1120 Þat wynnes worschyp abof alle whyte stones

1101. clene: Go hende.
1107. pryuyly: Go prystyly.
1111. Now: Go Nov; M Nou.
1114. whyl: Go whyle.
1118. hym: Go hit.

1103–108. Christ's clean breaking of the bread, mentioned also in the Towneley *Thomas of India,* would seem to be a medieval interpretation of Luke 24:35, in which the disciples are said to have recognized the risen Christ "in breaking of bread."

1118. *hym*: Although Go emends to *hit* used "idiomatically for 'ho'," M's explanation that *hym* is here a dative used for the nominative seems justified. "It may be that we have a case of attraction, the pronoun, which should be the subject of *þe demed*, being somehow thought of as the object of *to dele*" (M).

For ho schynes so schyr þat is of schap rounde
Wythouten faut oþer fylþe ȝif ho fyn were
& wax euer in þe worlde in weryng so olde
1124 ȝet þe perle payres° not whyle ho in pyese lasttes   *deteriorates*

& if hit cheue°þe chaunce vncheryst ho worþe   *happen*
Þat ho blyndes° of ble in bour þer ho lygges   *becomes dim*
No-bot° wasch hir wyth wourchyp in wyn as ho askes   *only*
1128 Ho by kynde schal becom clerer þen are

So if folk be defowled° by vnfre° chaunce   *defiled / shameful*
Þat he be sulped in sawle seche to schryfte°   *penance*
& he may polyce hym at þe prest by penaunce taken
1132 Wel bryȝter þen þe beryl oþer browden° perles   *woven*

Bot war þe wel if þou be waschen wyth water of schryfte
& polysed als playn as parchmen schauen
Sulp no more þenne in synne þy saule þerafter
1136 For þenne þou dryȝtyn dyspleses wyth dedes ful sore

& entyses hym to tene more trayþly þen euer
& wel hatter to hate þen hade þou not waschen
For when a sawele is saȝtled & sakred to dryȝtyn
1140 He holly haldes hit his & haue hit he wolde

1123. wax: Go wax ho.

1122–23. Go reads *ȝif ho fyn were*; & *wax* [*ho*] *euer in þe worlde* etc. and M agrees that *ho* is perhaps needed. However, *ȝif ho fyn were* may be taken as parenthetical if 1122–23 is considered a part of the question which begins with 1119 and concludes with 1124: "What may be considered the cause except her clean hue that wins her honor above all white stones, for she shines so brightly . . . ."

1124. *in pyese*: Go suggests that this is a variant of ME *o pece*, "still, yet." However, M's suggestion that the word may have originally been *pryse* is a more attractive theory.

1129–48. Cf. 146ff.*n.*

Þenne efte lastes°hit likkes he loses hit ille   *sins*

As hit were rafte° wyth vnryȝt & robbed wyth þewes   *robbed*

War þe þenne for þe wrake his wrath is achaufed°   *kindled*

1144 For þat þat ones watȝ his schulde efte be vnclene

Þaȝ hit be bot a bassyn a bolle oþer a scole

A dysche oþer a dobler° þat dryȝtyn oneȝ serued   *large plate*

To defowle hit euer vpon folde fast he forbedes

1148 So is he scoymus of scaþe° þat scylful° is

    euer   *repelled by sin / righteousness*

& þat watȝ bared in Babyloyn in Baltaȝar tyme

Hov harde vnhap þer hym hent & hastyly sone

For he þe vesselles avyled° þat vayled° in þe

    temple   *defiled / were of service*

1152 In seruyse of þe souerayn sumtyme byfore

Ȝif ȝe wolde tyȝt°me a tom° telle hit I

    wolde   *give / opportunity* (f.73a)

Hov charged more watȝ his chaunce þat hem cherych nolde

Þen his fader forloyne þat feched hem wyth strenþe

1156 & robbed þe relygioun of relykes alle

XIII

Danyel in his dialokeȝ deuysed sumtyme

As ȝet is proued expresse in his profecies

1143. is: Go hatz.

1141. Thomas glosses *loses* as "praises" and *wyth þewes* (1142) as "in respect of its qualities."

1153. See *GGK* 30–31*n*.

1155. Thomas states that "*fader* is singular and *forloyne* an example of the dropping of final -d, as in *l*.

1165." See also Mabel Day (MLR 14:413).

1157ff. The poet's version of the destruction of Jerusalem comes in the main from Jer. 52:1–26 and 2 Kings 24:18–25:17, though he adds details from other biblical passages.

Hov þe gentryse of Juise & Jherusalem þe ryche
1160 Watʒ disstryed wyth distres° & drawen to þe erþe   *violence*

For þat folke in her fayth watʒ founden vntrwe
Þat haden hyʒt þe hyʒe God to halde of hym euer
& he hem halʒed for his & help at her nede
1164 In mukel meschefes mony þat meruayl is to here

& þay forloyne her fayth & folʒed oþer goddes
& þat wakned his wrath & wrast hit so hyʒe
Þat he fylsened° þe faythful in þe falce lawe   *aided*
1168 To forfare þe falce in þe faythe trwe

Hit watʒ sen in þat syþe þat ʒedechyas rengned
In Juda þat justised þe Juyne kynges
He sete on Salamones solie° on solemne wyse   *throne*
1172 Bot of leaute° he watʒ lat° to his lorde
          hende   *fidelity / unmindful*

He vsed abominaciones of idolatrye
& lette lyʒt bi þe lawe þat he watʒ lege tylle
Forþi oure fader vpon folde a foman° hym wakned   *foe*
1176 Nabigo de Noʒar nuyed hym swyþe

He pursued into Palastyn wyth proude men mony
& þer he wast wyth werre þe wones of þorpes°   *towns*
He herʒed° vp alle Israel & hent of þe beste   *ravaged*
1180 & þe gentylest of Judee in Jerusalem biseged

1164. meruayl is: ᴍꜱ meruayl; Go is meruayl.
1169. ʒedechyas: ᴍꜱ ʒedethyas.
1176. Nabigo de Noʒar: M Nabigodenoʒar. (*Occurs throughout the text.*)
1178. wyth: ᴍꜱ wyth with.

1172–73. Zedekiah's idolatry is taken from 2 Chron. 36:12–14.
1176. *Nabigo de Noʒar*: Nebuchadnezzar. The ᴍꜱ form of *Nabigo* (or *Nabugo*) *de Noʒar* derives from the French custom of dividing the name. In 1226 and 1233 note that he uses only Nabugo.

Umbewalt° alle þe walles wyth wyȝes ful stronge   *surrounded*

At vche a dor a doȝty° duk & dutte hem wythinne   **brave**

For þe borȝ watȝ so bygge batayled°

   alofte   *fortified with battlements*

1184 & stoffed wythinne wyth stout men to stalle hem þeroute

Þenne watȝ þe sege sette þe cete aboute

Skete skarmoch skelt,° much skaþe

   lached   *A lively skirmish spread*

At vch brugge a berfray° on basteles°

   wyse   *movable tower / towers on wheels*

1188 Þat seuen syþe vch a day asayled þe ȝates   (f.73b)

Trwe tulkkes in toures teueled wythinne

In bigge brutage° of borde bulde on

   þe walles   *temporary parapet*

Þay feȝt & þay fende of & fylter° togeder   *joined in battle*

1192 Til two ȝer ouertorned ȝet tok þay hit neuer

At þe laste vpon longe þo ledes wythinne

Faste fayled hem þe fode enfaminied monie

Þe hote° hunger wythinne hert hem wel sarre   *biting*

1196 Þen any dunt° of þat douthe° þat dowelled

   þeroute   *blow / army*

Þenne wern þo rowtes redles° in þo ryche

   wones   *without counsel*

Fro þat mete watȝ myst megre° þay wexen   *lean*

& þay stoken so strayt þat þay ne stray myȝt

1200 A fote fro þat forselet° to forray no goudes   *fortress*

1183. batayled: MS baytayled.
1194. enfaminied: Go enfamined.

1189. *teueled*: Wright (Engl Stud 36:233–34) connects this with *teuelyng* in *GGK* 1514 and with dialectal *tevel*, "to confuse" and also with *tave*, "to strive, toil."

Þenne þe kyng of þe kyth a counsayl hym takes
Wyth þe best of his burnes a blench° for to make   *plan*
Þay stel out on a stylle nyȝt er any steuen rysed
1204 & harde hurles þurȝ þe oste° er enmies hit wyste   *host*

Bot er þay atwappe° ne moȝt þe wach wythoute   *escape*
Hiȝe skelt watȝ þe askry þe skewes anvnder
Loude alarom vpon launde lulted° watȝ þenne   *sounded*
1208 Ryche ruþed of her rest ran to her wedes

Hard hattes þay hent & on hors lepes
Cler claryoun crak° cryed on lofte   *blast*
By þat watȝ alle on a hepe hurlande swyþe
1212 Folȝande þat oþer flote° & fonde hem bilyue   *host*

Ouertok hem as tyd tult hem of sadeles
Tyl vche prynce hade his per° put to þe grounde   *rival*
& þer watȝ þe kyng kaȝt wyth Calde prynces
1216 & alle hise gentyle forjusted° on Ierico
           playnes   *overthrown in jousting*

& presented wern as presoneres to þe prynce rychest
Nabigo de Noȝar noble in his chayer
& he þe faynest freke þat he his fo hade
1220 & speke spitously hem to & spylt þerafter

Þe kynges sunnes in his syȝt he slow°euervch one   *slew*
& holkked° out his auen yȝen heterly boþe   *dug*
& bede þe burne to be broȝt to Babyloyn þe ryche
1224 & þere in doungoun be don to dreȝe°þer his
           wyrdes°   *suffer / fate* (f.74a)

1211. swyþe: ᴍꜱ, Go swyþee.
1220. spylt: Go spylt hem.

1203. *rysed*: Go reads the ᴍꜱ as   M, I see *rysed* in the ᴍꜱ.
rysod here, but emends to *rysed*. Like   1210. See *GGK* 118*n*.

Now se so þe souerayn set hatȝ his wrake
Nas hit not for Nabugo ne his noble nauþer
Þat oþer depryued watȝ of pryde with paynes stronge
1228 Bot for his beryng so badde agayn his blyþe lorde

For hade þe fader ben his frende þat hym bifore keped
Ne neuer trespast to him in teche of mysseleue°   *misbelief*
To colde wer alle Calde & kythes of Ynde
1232 ȝet take Torkye hem wyth her tene hade ben little

ȝet nolde neuer Nabugo þis ilke note leue
Er he hade tyrued þis toun & torne hit to grounde
He joyned vnto Jerusalem a gentyle duc þenne
1236 His name watȝ Nabuȝardan to noye þe Jues

1225. souerayn: MS soueray.
1231. To colde wer alle Calde: MS to Colde wer alle Calde; M To Calde wer alle calde.
1234. tyrued: MS tuyred.

1225–28. Thomas thinks these lines should "run on continuously, *that* being understood before *Nas*."

1229–32. M's punctuation treats 1231–32 as an apodosis, the protasis of which is 1229–30.

1230. The understood subject of *trespast* would certainly seem to be Zedekiah.

1231. *To colde wer alle calde*: The MS reading, *to Colde wer alle Calde*, is best explained by the scribe's confusion of *Colde* and *Calde*, both of which he capitalized. Go read *To colde wer alle Calde* without explanation. Thomas adopted the same reading and paraphrased "For if the Father had still been his friend and Zedekiah had not turned against him, neither Chaldea, nor India, nor even Turkey would have had the energy to attack him—their indignation would have been too slight." M emended 1231 to *To Calde wer alle calde*, placed a dash after *Ynde*, and read 1231–32 as "all (Nebuchadnezzar's hosts) would have been called away to Chaldea and the countries of India—and they would have had little trouble taking Turkey by the way."

My own reading follows Go's and Thomas's emendation of *Colde* to *colde*, and I am in agreement with Thomas as to the meaning of the lines, though, like him, I cannot translate them literally.

He watȝ mayster of his men & myȝty himseluen
Þe chef of his cheualrye his chekkes° to make   *attacks*
He brek þe bareres as bylyue & þe burȝ after
1240 & enteres in ful ernestly° in yre of his hert   *wrathfully*

What þe maysterry° watȝ mene° þe men wern
    away   *force | inferior*
Þe best boȝed wyth þe burne þat þe borȝ ȝemed
& þo þat byden wer so biten with þe bale hunger
1244 Þat on wyf hade ben worþe þe welgest° fourre   *strongest*

Nabiȝardan noȝt forþy nolde not spare
Bot bede al to þe bronde° vnder bare egge   *sword*
Þay slowen of swettest semlych burdes
1248 Baþed barnes in blod & her brayn spylled

Prestes & prelates þay presed to deþe
Wyues & wenches her wombes tocoruen°   *cut up*
Þat her boweles outborst aboute þe diches
1252 & al watȝ carfully kylde þat þay cach myȝt

& alle þat swypped° vnswolȝed° of þe sworde
    kene   *escaped | unharmed*
Þay wer cagged°& kaȝt on capeles° al bare   *fastened | horses*
Festned fettres to her fete vnder fole wombes
1256 & broþely broȝt to Babyloyn þer bale to suffer

So sytte in seruage & syte° þat sumtyme wer gentyle   *sorrow*
Now ar chaunged to chorles° & charged wyth werkkes   *serfs*
Boþe to cayre at þe kart & þe kuy mylke
1260 Þat sumtyme sete in her sale syres & burdes   (f.74b)

1243. so: MS fo.
1253. þat: *Not in* MS.
1257. So: Go To.

1257. *So*: Morris and Go read MS   *to*, but like M I see the word as *so*.

    & ȝet Nabuȝardan nyl neuer stynt
    Er he to þe temppple tee wyth his tulkkes alle
    Betes on þe barers brestes° vp þe ȝates   *bursts*
1264 Slouen alle at a slyp° þat serued þerinne   *stroke*

    Pulden prestes bi þe polle° & plat° of her hedes   *head / struck*
    Diȝten° dekenes to deþe dungen° doun
        clerkkes°   *put / struck / priests*
    & alle þe maydenes of þe munster° maȝtyly hokyllen *church*
1268 Wyth þe swayf° of þe sworde þat swolȝed hem
        alle   *swinging blow*

    Þenne ran þay to þe relykes as robbors wylde
    & pyled° alle þe apparement° þat pented°
        to þe kyrke   *pillaged / ornaments / belonged*
    Þe pure pyleres of bras pourtrayd in golde
1272 & þe chef chaundeler charged with þe lyȝt

    Þat ber þe lamp vpon lofte þat lemed euermore
    Bifore þe sancta sanctorum þer selcouth° watȝ ofte *wonder*
    Þay caȝt away þat condelstik & þe crowne als
1276 Þat þe auter hade vpon of aþel° golde ryche   *excellent*

    Þe gredirne & þe goblotes garnyst of syluer
    Þe bases of þe bryȝt postes & bassynes so schyre
    Dere disches of golde & dubleres fayre
1280 Þe vyoles & þe vesselment of vertuous° stones   *precious*

    Now hatȝ Nabuȝardan nomen alle þyse noble þynges
    & pyled þat precious place & pakked þose godes

          1267. hokyllen: M he kyllen.
          1271. of: o *is blotted in* MS.
          1274. þe sancta: MS þsancta.

    1267. *hokyllen*: As Go suggests,   *hockle*, "to cut up stubble." M emends
this is probably an unnoted form of   to *he kyllen*.

Þe golde of þe gaȝafylace to swyþe gret noumbre
1284 Wyth alle þe vrnmentes of þat hous he hamppred°
    togeder   *packed*

Alle he spoyled spitously in a sped whyle
Þat Salomon so mony a sadde ȝer soȝt to make
Wythe alle þe coyntyse° þat he cowþe clene to wyrke   *wisdom*
1288 Deuised he þe vesselment þe vestures clene

Wyth slyȝt° of his ciences his souerayn to loue   *skill*
Þe hous & þe anournementes he hyȝtled togedere
Now hatȝ Nabuȝardan nummen hit al samen
1292 & syþen bet doun þe burȝ & brend hit in askes

Þenne wyth legiounes of ledes ouer londes he rydes
Herȝeȝ of Israel þe hyrne° aboute   *corners*
Wyth charged chariotes þe cheftayn he fyndeȝ
1296 Bikennes° þe catel° to þe kyng þat he caȝt
    hade   *delivers* / *property* (f.75a)

Presented him þe presoneres in pray þat þay token
Moni a worþly wyȝe whil her worlde laste
Moni semly syre soun & swyþe rych maydenes
1300 Þe pruddest° of þe prouince & prophetes
    childer°   *proudest* / *children*

As Ananie & Aȝarie & als Miȝael
& dere Daniel also þat watȝ deuine noble
With moni a modey° moder chylde mo þen innoghe   *brave*
1304 & Nabugo de Noȝar makes much joye

1291. nummen: ᴍs nūnēd.
1294. hyrne: Go hyrneȝ.
1295. fyndeȝ: ᴍs fynde.

1283. *gaȝafylace*: Box in which offerings to the Temple were received.

Nov he þe kyng hatȝ conquest & þe kyth wunnen
& dreped alle þe doȝtyest & derrest in armes
& þe lederes of her lawe layd to þe grounde
1308 & þe pryce° of þe profecie° presoners
     maked   *most eminent | prophets*

Bot þe joy of þe juelrye so gentyle & ryche
When hit watȝ schewed hym so schene scharp watȝ
     his wonder
Of such vessel auayed° þat vayled°
     so huge   *informed | was worth*
1312 Neuer ȝet nas Nabugo de Noȝar er þenne

He sesed hem wyth solemnete° þe souerayn he
     praysed   *ceremoniously*
Þat watȝ aþel ouer alle Israel dryȝtyn
Such god such gomes such gay vesselles
1316 Comen neuer out of kyth to Caldee reames

He trussed° hem in his tresorye in a tryed°
     place   *stowed away | chosen*
Rekenly wyth reuerens as he ryȝt hade
& þer he wroȝt as þe wyse as ȝe may wyt hereafter
1320 For hade he let of hem lyȝt hym moȝt haf lumpen worse

Þat ryche in gret rialte rengned his lyue
As conquerour of vche a cost he cayser° watȝ hatte   *emperor*
Emperour of alle þe erþe & also þe saudan°   *sultan*
1324 & als þe god of þe grounde watȝ grauen° his name   *written*

1315. god: Go godes.
1315. gomes: Go gounes.

1317–20. The poet is careful to explain that Nebuchadnezzar escapes God's wrath by reverently storing the sacred vessels, while Belshazzar is punished for his sacrilege in the irreverent use of them; unlike Nebuchadnezzar he *let of hem lyȝt* (1320). Cf. 1357ff.

& al þurʒ dome of Daniel fro he deuised hade
Þat alle goudes com of God & gef hit hym bi
 samples°   *illustrative stories*
Þat he ful clanly bicnv° his carp bi þe laste *acknowledged*
1328 & ofte hit mekned° his mynde his masterful werkkes *humbled*

Bot al drawes to dyʒe° wyth doel vpon ende   *die*
Bi a haþel neuer so hyʒe he heldes to grounde
& so Nabugo de Noʒar as he nedes moste
1332 For alle his empire so hiʒe in erþe is he grauen° *buried* (f.75b)

Bot þenn þe bolde Baltaʒar þat watʒ his barn aldest
He watʒ stalled° in his stud & stabled°
 þe rengne   *enthroned / established*
In þe burʒ of Babiloyne þe biggest he trawed
1336 Þat nauþer in heuen ne on erþe hade no pere° *equal*

For he bigan in alle þe glori þat hym þe gome lafte
Nabugo de Noʒar þat watʒ his noble fader
So kene a kyng in Caldee com neuer er þenne
1340 Bot honoured he not hym þat in heuen wonies

Bot fals fantummes of fendes formed with handes
Wyth tool out of harde tre & telded on lofte
& of stokkes & stones he stoute goddes callʒ
1344 When þay are gilde al with golde & gered° wyth syluer *adorned*

& þere he kneles & calleʒ & clepes° after help *cries*
& þay reden° him ryʒt rewarde he hem hetes *counsel*

1329. vpon: MS vpn.
1336. on: MS no.
1336. hade: Go hade he.

1334–36. Both Go and M place a tuation after *Babiloyne*.
semicolon after *rengne* and no punc-

& if þay gruchen him his grace to gremen his hert
1348 He cleches to a gret klubbe & knokkes hem to peces

Þus in pryde & olipraunce his empyre he haldes
In lust & in lecherye & loþelych° werkkes   *hateful*
& hade a wyf for to welde a worþelych quene
1352 & mony a lemman° neuer þe later° þat ladis
   wer called   *mistress / nevertheless*

In þe clernes° of his concubines & curious°
   wedeȝ   *splendor / exquisite*
In notyng° of nwe metes & of nice gettes° *using / fashions*
Al watȝ þe mynde of þat man on misschapen° þinges *wicked*
1356 Til þe lorde of þe lyfte liste hit abate

XIV

Thenne þis bolde Baltaȝar biþenkkes hym ones
To vouche° on avayment° of his vayneglorie *resolve / exhibition*
Hit is not innoghe to þe nice° al noȝty þink vse *wanton*
1360 Bot if alle þe worlde wyt his wykked dedes

Baltaȝar þurȝ Babiloyn his banne gart crye° *proclaim*
& þurȝ þe cuntre of Caldee his callyng con spryng
Þat alle þe grete vpon grounde schulde geder hem samen
1364 & assemble at a set day at þe saudans fest

Such a mangerie to make þe man watȝ auised° *determined*
Þat vche a kythyn kyng schuld com þider

   1347. him his: Go him.
   1358. vayneglorie: ᴍs vayne gorie.

1349. *olipraunce*: Here, as in Robert Mannyng's *Handling Synne* 4581, the word clearly means "vanity, pretension." Go derives it from the name of Olibrius, the persecutor of St. Margaret, whose "name became a byword for ostentatious flaunting."

Vche duk wyth his duthe° & oþer dere lordes   *nobility*
1368 Schulde com to his court to kyþe° hym for
    lege   *acknowledge* (f.76a)

   & to reche° hym reuerens & his reuel herkken°   *render / attend*
To loke on his lemanes & ladis hem calle
To rose° hym in his rialty rych men soȝtten   *praise*
1372 & mony a baroun ful bolde to Babyloyn þe noble

Þer bowed toward Babiloyn burnes so mony
Kynges cayseres ful kene to þe court wonnen
Mony ludisch lordes þat ladies broȝten
1376 Þat to neuen þe noumbre to much nye were

For þe bourȝ watȝ so brod & so bigge alce
Stalled° in þe fayrest stud þe sterreȝ anvnder   *placed*
Prudly on a plat° playn plek° alþerfayrest   *flat / spot*
1380 Vmbesweyed° on vch a syde wyth seuen
    grete wateres   *encircled*

Wyth a wonder wroȝt walle wruxeled° ful hiȝe   *adorned*
Wyth koynt carneles° aboue coruen ful
    clene   *skillfully made battlements*
Troched toures bitwene twenty spere lenþe
1384 & þiker þrowen vmbeþour wyth ouerþwert°
    palle   *placed crosswise*

Þe place þat plyed þe pursaunt wythinne
Watȝ longe & ful large & euer ilych sware

1375–76. See *GGK* 165–56*n*.

1383. *troched toures*: As Skeat noted, *troched* originally referred to the small tines at the tip of a stag's horns and by extension became the architectural term "pinnacled."

1384. *vmbeþour*: Go derives from on *þori*, "the main part," thus "all about, generally."

1385. *pursaunt*: Used also in *Pearl* 1035, *Vch pane of þat place had þere ȝates/ So twelue in poursent I can asspye.* The example from *Pearl* is listed in *NED* under *purcinct*. Go

& vch a syde vpon soyle helde seuen myle
1388 & þe saudans sete sette in þe myddes

Þat watȝ a palayce of pryde passande alle oþer
Boþe of werk & of wunder & walle al aboute
Heȝe houses wythinne þe halle to hit med
1392 So brod bilde in a bay þat blonkkes myȝt renne

When þe terme° of þe tyde° watȝ towched of
    þe feste   *appointed date / time*
Dere droȝen þerto & vpon des° metten   *dais*
& Baltaȝar vpon bench was busked to sete
1396 Stepe stayred° stones of his stoute throne   *brightly shone*

Þenne watȝ alle þe halle-flor hiled wyth knyȝtes
& barounes at þe sidebordes bounet° aywhere   *went*
For non watȝ dressed vpon dece bot þe dere seluen
1400 & his clere concubynes in cloþes ful bryȝt

When alle segges were þet set þen seruyse bygynnes
Sturnen° trumpen strake steuen in halle   *loud*
Aywhere by þe wowes wrasten° krakkes   *blow*
1404 & brode baneres þerbi blusnande° of gold   *gleaming* (f.76b)

1390. walle: Go walled.
1391. med: M mad.
1393. þe (3rd): *Indistinct in* MS.
1398. aywhere: y *indistinct in* MS.
1402. Sturnen: Go Sturne.

glosses *place* here as "place," rather than as "palace," which seems here, as in the passage in *Pearl*, to be the obvious reading.

1390. *walle*: Go emends to *walled*, but if *walle* is taken along with *wunder* as the object of *of*, the construction seems clear.

1391. *med*: The MS reading is here defensible since *med* is clearly a form of *met*, from OE *gemet*, "measure," and *hit* is possessive. M emends to *mad*. Emerson glosses *to hit med* as "in their middle or midst."

Burnes berande þe bredes° vpon brode
    skeles°   *roast meats / platters*
Þat were of sylueren syȝt & served þerwyth
Lyfte logges þerouer & on lofte coruen
1408 Pared out of paper & poynted of golde

Broþe baboynes° abof besttes anvnder   *baboons*
Foles in foler flakerande° bitwene   *fluttering*
& al in asure & ynde° enaumayld ryche   *deep blue*
1412 & al on blonkken bak bere hit on honde

& ay þe nakeryn° noyse notes of pipes   *kettle-drums*
Tymbres & tabornes tulket° among   *sounded*
Symbales & soneteȝ sware° þe
    noyse   *musical instruments answer*
1416 & bougounȝ busch° batered so þikke   *striking*

1405. þe: MS þe þe.
1406. sylueren syȝt: Go syluer in suyt.
1406. served: MS seved *with a flourish apparently over* v;   Go seves.
1408. golde: MS glolde.
1414. tulket: Go tukket.

1408. *pared out of paper*: Cf. *GGK* 802, *pared out of papure*. Morris thought this to be a reference to table "subtleties," elaborate ornamental confections made chiefly of sugar. However, as R. W. Ackerman has pointed out (JEGP 61:410–17), these subtleties were mainly used in the fifteenth and sixteenth centuries and the reference here may be to actual paper ornaments "perched on a dish of food, a roast or stew."

1401ff. The description of Belshazzar's feast here is very like that of Arthur in *GGK* 114–24.

1410. *foler*: Although the etymology of this word is unknown, it could easily stem, as M notes, from a lost OF word **folier*, itself a derivative from late Latin **foliarum*. The word itself clearly means "foliage."

1413–16. See *GGK* 118n.

1414. *tulket*: Although *tukket*, in reference to the trumpet fanfares, is certainly a more attractive reading here, *tulket* is defensible. Though, as Go points out, *lk* and *kk* are often indistinguishable in script, here as in the MS generally *lk* is quite clear.

1415. *sware*: See 279n.

1416. *bougounȝ busch*: Brett (MLR 10:188–89) glosses *bougounȝ* as

So watȝ serued fele syþe þe sale alle aboute
Wyth solace at þe sere course bifore þe self lorde
Per þe lede & alle his loue lenged at þe table
1420 So faste þay weȝed to him wyne hit warmed his hert

& breyþed° vppe into his brayn & blemyst his mynde   *rushed*
& al waykned his wyt & wel neȝe he foles°   *becomes mad*
For he wayteȝ° on wyde his wenches he byholdes   *looks*
1424 & his bolde baronage aboute bi þe woȝes

Penne a dotage° ful depe drof to his hert   *folly*
& a caytif° counsayl he caȝt bi hymseluen   *wicked*
Maynly his marschal þe mayster vþon calles
1428 & comaundes hym cofly coferes to lance

& fech forþe vessel þat his fader broȝt
Nabugo de Noȝar noble in his strenþe
Conquerd with his knyȝtes & of kyrk rafte
1432 In Jude in Jerusalem in gentyle wyse

Bryng hem now to my borde of beuerage hem fylles
Let þise ladyes of hem lape° I luf hem in hert   *drink*
Pat schal I cortaysly kyþe & þay schin knawe sone
1436 Per is no bounte in burne lyk Baltaȝar þewes

Penne towchede to þe tresour þis tale watȝ sone
& he wyth keyes vncloses kystes ful mony
Mony burþen ful bryȝt watȝ broȝt into halle
1440 & couered mony a cupborde with cloþes ful quite°   *white* (f.77a)

1419. loue: Go leue.
1423. wenches he: Go wenches.
1429. forþe: Go forþ þe.

"drumsticks" from OF *bougon* which denotes, among other things, an "instrument with a rounded, swollen extremity."

1419. *loue*: Go emends to *leue*, but this removes the specific connotation of "concubines," who are said in 1400 to be at the high table.

Þe jueles out of Jerusalem wyth gemmes ful bryȝt
Bi þe syde of þe sale were semely arayed
Þe aþel auter of brasse watȝ hade into place
1444 Þe gay coroun of golde gered on lofte

Þat hade ben blessed bifore wyth bischopes hondes
& wyth besten blod busily° anoynted   *carefully*
In þe solempne sacrefyce þat goud sauor hade
1448 Bifore þe lorde of þe lyfte in louyng hymseluen

Now is sette for to serue Satanas þe blake
Bifore þe bolde Baltaȝar wyth bost & wyth pryde
Houen vpon þis auter watȝ aþel vessel
1452 Þat wyth so curious a crafte coruen watȝ wyly°   *cunningly*

Salamon sete him seuen ȝere & a syþe more
Wyth alle þe syence° þat hym sende þe souerayn lorde   *skill*
For to compas° & kest to haf hem clene wroȝt   *plan*
1456 For þer wer bassynes ful bryȝt of brende°
        golde clere   *burnished*

Enaumaylde wyth aȝer & eweres of sute°   *pitchers to match*
Couered cowpes foul° clene as casteles arayed   *cups very*
Enbaned vnder batelment wyth bantelles quoynt
1460 & fyled out of fygures of ferlyle° schappes   *marvellous*

1452. so: ᴍs fo.
1453. seuen: ᴍs *illegible.*
1460. ferlyle: M ferlyche.

1459. enbaned . . . bantelles: According to Skeat (*Trans. Phil. Soc.,* 1903–1906, 359), the phrase means "provided, beneath battlements, with fair outworks." Skeat derives *enbaned* from ᴏғ *bane,* "horn," and *bantel* from ᴏғ **banetel,* a double diminutive of *bane.* "We may conclude," says Skeat, "that an *embanamen* was made with a kind of horn-work, an outwork with angles, including a space like three sides of a square beyond the main-wall; and such a horn-work may well have been called a *bantel.*"

Þe coperounes° of þe couacles þat on þe cuppe reres   *tops*
Wer fetysely° formed out in fylyoles° longe   *skillfully / turrets*
Pinacles pyȝt þer apert þat profert bitwene
1464 & al bolled°abof wyth braunches & leues   *embossed*

Pyes° & papejayes° purtrayed withinne   *magpies / parrots*
As þay prudly hade piked of pomgarnades
For alle þe blomes of þe boȝes wer blyknande° perles   *shining*
1468 & alle þe fruyt in þo formes of flaumbeande° gemmes   *glowing*

Ande safyres & sardiners° & semely topace   *precious stones*
Alabaundarynes & amaraunȝ & amaffised° stones   *amethystine*
Casydoynes° & crysolytes & clere rubies   *chalcedonies*
1472 Penitotes° & pynkardines° ay perles
          bitwene   *peridots / precious stones*

So trayled & tryfled a-trauerce wer alle
Bi vche bekyr ande bolle þe brurdes al vmbe

1461. couacles: MS canacles.
1461. cuppe reres: Go cuppes rere.
1470. Alabaundarynes: MS *illegible*.
1474. bekyr ande bolle: MS bekyrande þe bolde.

1461. *couacles*: The same word is used in 1515. In *Partonope of Blois* (See Bödtker, MLN 26:127), as here, it means "cover." M believes that "the scribe undoubtedly thought the word was *conacle* (*canacle*), mistaking *ou* for *on*, and he would naturally write *con-* or *can-* indifferently."

1464ff. A number of the details in this passage are taken from Mandeville's description of the palace of the Great Chan, particularly the ornamental candlesticks of 1484–86 and the *fruyt in þo formes of flaumbeande gemmes* of 1468. The relevant passages from the French version of Man-

deville are contained in M's note.

1470. *Alabaundrynes*: The letters following *d* are smudged in the MS, though they may have been retraced. The reference is almost certainly to the alabandine or almandine which takes its name from Alabanda, a city of Caria. This exotic stone, like the *peridot* (1472), is mentioned by Mandeville.

1472. *Penitotes*: As Go notes, this is a form of OF *peritot*, "pen(n)y" for "perry" being a "characteristic English modification."

1473. "So decorated with a trailing pattern and ornamented with trefoils,

Þe gobelotes of golde grauen aboute

1476 & fyoles° fretted wyth flores & fleeȝ of golde   *cups* (f.77b)

Vpon þat avter watȝ al aliche dresset

Þe candelstik bi a cost watȝ cayred þider sone

Vpon þe pyleres apyked° þat praysed hit mony   *adorned*

1480 Vpon hit baseȝ of brasse þat ber vp þe werkes

Þe boȝes bryȝt þer abof brayden of golde

Braunches bredande° þeron & bryddes þer seten   *growing*

Of mony curious kyndes of fele-kyn° hues   *many kinds*

1484 As þay wyth wynge vpon wynde hade waged° her   *waved*
     fyþeres

Inmong þe leues of þe launces° lampes wer grayþed   *branches*

& oþer louflych lyȝt þat lemed ful fayre

As mony morteres° of wax merkked wythoute   *candlesticks*

1488 Wyth mony a borlych° best al of brende golde   *noble*

Hit watȝ not wonte in þat wone to wast no serges°   *wax candles*

Bot in temple of þe trauþe trwly to stonde

Bifore þe sancta sanctorum þer soþefast° dryȝtyn   *true*

1492 Expouned his speche spyrytually to special prophetes

1479. Vpon: ᴍꜱ pon.
1483. curious: *Not in* ᴍꜱ; Go cler.
1485. launces: *Not in* ᴍꜱ; Go lefsel.
1491. þer: *Not in* ᴍꜱ.
1492. spyrytually: Go spiritually.

---

crosswise were they all." *Tryfled* is almost certainly a form earlier than those mentioned by *NED* of *trefoiled*.

1474. *bekyr ande bolle*: Go, Emerson, and M so emend the ᴍꜱ *bekyrande þe bolde*. The phrase indicates that the bowls were decorated with a cross-work pattern.

1483. *curious*: An addition is clearly called for here. Following M, I have added *curious*. Go adds *cler*.

1485. *launces*: I am again following M in supplying *launces* before *lampes*. Go adds *lefsel*, "bower of leaves," which seems overly fanciful.

1491. *þer*: This addition is suggested by Go, M, and Emerson.

Leue þou wel þat þe lorde þat þe lyfte ʒemes
Displesed much at þat play in þat plyt° stronge   *sin*
Þat his jueles so gent° wyth jaueles° wer
    fouled   *exquisite / low fellows*
1496 Þat presyous in his presens wer proued sumwhyle°   *formerly*

Soberly in his sacrafyce summe wer anoynted
Þurʒ þe somones of himselfe þat syttes so hyʒe
Now a boster on benche bibbes° þerof   *drinks*
1500 Tyl he be dronkken as þe devel & dotes° þer he
    syttes   *acts foolishly*

So þe worcher° of þis worlde wlates°
    þerwyth   *creator / feels horror*
Þat in þe poynt of her play he poruayes° a mynde   *settles on*
Bot er harme hem he wolde in haste of his yre
1504 He wayned° hem a warnyng þat wonder hem þoʒt   *sent*

Nov is alle þis guere° geten glotounes to serue   *apparatus*
Stad in a ryche stal & stared ful bryʒte
Baltaʒar in a brayd bede bus° þerof   *drink*
1508 Weʒe wyn in þis won wassayl° he cryes   *your health*

Swyfte swaynes ful swyþe swepen þertylle°   *thither*
Kyppe° kowpes in honde kyngeʒ to serue   *seize*
In bryʒt bolleʒ ful bayn birlen° þise oþer   *readily pour drink*
1512 & vche mon for his mayster machches° alone   *attends* (f.78a)

1494. stronge: Go strange.
1506. bryʒte: MS bryʒtʒ.
1507. bus: MS, Go vus.

1494. *stronge*: Go emends to
strange, but *stronge* in the sense of
"great" is equally appropriate.
    1502. *a mynde*: Thomas prefers

amynde, in which case "the closing
phrase means 'to settle on reparation'."
    1507. *bus*: In spite of Go's objection,
this seems a necessary emendation.

Þer watȝ rynging on ryȝt of ryche metalles
Quen renkkes in þat ryche rok rennen hit to cache
Clatering of couacleȝ þat kesten þo burdes
1516 As sonet° out of sauteray° songe als
     myry   *music / stringed instrument*

Þen þe dotel° on dece drank þat myȝt   *fool*
& þenne arn dressed dukeȝ & prynces
Concubines & knyȝtes bi cause of þat merthe
1520 As vch on hade hym inhelde° he haled°
     of þe cuppe   *poured in / took drink of*

So long likked þise lordes þise lykores swete
& gloryed on her falce goddes & her grace calles
Þat were of stokkes & stones stille euermore
1524 Neuer steuen hem astel° so stoken is hor tonge   *escaped from*

Alle þe goude golden goddes þe gauleȝ° ȝet neuenen   *wretches*
Belfagor & Belyal & Belssabub als

> 1516. sauteray: MS saueray.
> 1518. þenne: Go þenne þat derrest; M þenne drinkez.
> 1518. dressed: M dressed to.
> 1524. is: MS īs.

1514. *hit*: Refers to the *wyn* of 1508.

1514. *rok*: Although M, Go, and Bateson derived this from Scot. *rok* (*NED s.v. ruck*) and defined it "crowd, throng," M more sensibly connects it with ME *rok(ke)*, here in its figurative sense, frequent in OF literature, of "castle."

1518. Although perfectly clear in the MS, the line is too short metrically. For this reason all previous editors have suggested additions. Go reads *þenne þat derrest arn dressed* and M *drynkeȝ arn dressed to* (other emendations are given in M's notes).

However, since the line makes perfect sense as it stands, I am unwilling to tamper with it. As Go points out, the wassail ceremony is here outlined. After the king calls out "Wassail" (1508), he drinks as deeply as he can (1517) and the cup is then passed among the nobles (1518–20). Lines 1518–19 can thus be translated "and then are addressed the dukes and princes, the concubines and knights, because of the festivity."

Heyred° hem as hyȝly as heuen wer þayres   *worshipped*
1528 Bot hym þat alle goudes giues þat God þay forȝeten

For þer a ferly bifel þat fele folk seȝen
Fyrst knew hit þe kyng & alle þe cort after
In þe palays pryncipale vpon þe playn wowe°   *wall*
1532 In contrary of° þe candelstik þat clerest hit schyned   *opposite*

Þer apered a paume° wyth poyntel°
   in fyngres   *hand / a pointed instrument for writing*
Þat watȝ grysly & gret & grymly he wrytes
Non oþer forme bot a fust faylande° þe wryste   *lacking*
1536 Pared on þe parget° purtrayed lettres   *plaster of the walls*

When þat bolde Baltaȝar blusched to þat neue
Such a dasande° drede dusched° to his hert   *dazing / rushed*
þat al falewed° his face & fayled þe chere   *became pale*
1540 Þe stronge strok of þe stonde° strayned his joyntes   *blow*

His cnes cachches to close & cluchches his hommes°   *bend of knee*
& he wyth plattyng° his paumes displayes his
   lers°   *striking / features*
& romyes° as a rad ryth° þat roreȝ for
   drede   *roars / frightened bull*
1544 Ay biholdand þe honde til hit hade al grauen
& rasked on þe roȝ woȝe runisch saueȝ.

1527. Heyred: Go Heryed.
1529. For þer: Go For-þy.
1532. þat: Go þer.
1541. &: Go & he.
1542. & he: Go &.
1542. lers: ᴍs lers; Go lerus.

1542. *lers*: Go emends to *lerus*, to suggest that in his terror Belshaz-
which he derives from ᴏᴇ *lira*, "calves zar claps his hands to his face, thus
of the legs." The line seems, however, distorting his features.

When hit þe scrypture hade scraped wyth a scrof° penne   *rough*
As a coltour in clay cerues þo forȝes°   *furrows*
1548 Þenne hit vanist verayly & voyded of syȝt   (f.78b)
Bot þe lettres bileued ful large vpon plaster

Sone so þe kynge for his care carping myȝt wynne
He bede his burnes boȝ to þat wer bok-lered°   *learned in books*
1552 To wayte° þe wryt þat hit wolde & wyter° hym
      to say   *examine / clearly*
For al hit frayes° my flesche þe fyngres so grymme   *frightens*

Scoleres skelten° þeratte þe skyl° for to
      fynde   *applied themselves / significance*
Bot þer watȝ neuer on so wyse couþe on worde rede
1556 Ne what ledisch lore ne langage nauþer
What typyng ne tale tokened þo draȝtes°   *marks*

Þenne þe bolde Baltaȝar bred ner wode
& bede þe cete to seche segges þurȝout
1560 Þat wer wyse of wychecrafte & warlaȝes oþer
Þat con dele wyth demerlayk° & deuine° lettres *magic / interpret*

Calle hem alle to my cort þo Calde clerkkes
Vnfolde hem alle þis ferly þat is bifallen here
1564 & calle wyth a hiȝe cry he þat þe kyng wysses°   *instructs*
In expounyng of speche þat spredes in þise lettres

& make þe mater to malt° my mynde wythinne   *filter in*
Þat I may wyterly wyt what þat wryt menes

1546. scrof: MS strof.
1547. þo: Go þe.
1559. bede: MS ede; Go eþede.
1566. make: Go makes.

1566. *make*: As Thomas suggests,   emends to *makes*.
this is probably a subjunctive. Go

1568 He schal be gered ful gaye in gounes of porpre°   *purple*
    & a coler of cler golde clos vmbe his þrote

He schal be prymate & prynce of pure clergye
& of my þreuenest° lordeȝ þe þrydde he schal   *most honorable*
1572 & of my reme þe rychest to ryde wyth myseluen
Outtaken bare two & þenne he þe þrydde

Þis cry watȝ vp caste & þer comen mony
Clerkes out of Caldye þat kennest wer knauen
1576 As þe sage sathrapas þat sorsory couþe
Wycheȝ & walkyries wonnen to þat sale

Deuinores of demorlaykes þat dremes cowþe rede
Sorsers & exorsismus & fele such clerkes
1580 & alle þat loked on þat letter as lewed þay were
As þay had loked in þe leþer of my lyft bote

Þenne cryes þe kyng & kerues° his wedes   *tears*
What he corsed his clerkes & calde hem chorles
1584 To henge° þe harlotes he heȝed ful ofte   *hang* (f.79a)
So watȝ þe wyȝe wytles he wed wel ner

Ho herde hym chyde to þe chambre þat watȝ þe chef quene
When ho watȝ wytered° bi wyȝes what watȝ þe cause *informed*

1571. schal: Go schal be.
1579. Sorsers &: Go Sorsers of.

1576. *sathrapas*: The term "satrap" came in the Middle Ages to mean "wise man" or "sorcerer."

1577. *walkyries*: An interesting, because very late, reference to the warrior maidens of Teutonic myth. As Go points out, the word had by late Anglo-Saxon times already become synonymous with either "witch" or "wizard," the specific gender of the original having been lost. Its true meaning was not re-introduced into the language until the Romantic revival of interest in Nordic mythology.

1584. *heȝed*: Go states that this means "shouted, called aloud, not 'hied' (*i.e.* hastened)," but there are no other evidences in ME that such a verb existed.

1588 Suche a chaungande chaunce in þe chef halle
Þe lady to lauce° þat los° þat þe lorde hade   *solve / quandary*
Glydes doun by þe grece & gos to þe kyng

Ho kneles on þe colde erþe & carpes to hymseluen
1592 Wordes of worchyp wyth a wys speche
Kene kyng quoþ þe quene kayser of vrþe
Euer laste þy lyf in lenþe of dayes

Why hatȝ þou rended þy robe forredles°
   hereinne   *without counsel*
1596 Þaȝ þose ledes ben lewed lettres to rede
& hatȝ a haþel in þy holde as I haf herde ofte
Þat hatȝ þe gostes of God þat gyes° alle soþes   *governs*

His sawle is ful of syence saȝes to schawe
1600 To open vch a hide° þyng of aunteres°
   vncowþe   *hidden / marvels*
Þat is he þat ful ofte hatȝ heuened þy fader
Of mony anger ful hote wyth his holy speche

When Nabugo de Noȝar watȝ nyed in
   stoundes°   *at different times*
1604 He devysed his dremes to þe dere trawþe
He keuered° hym wyth his counsayl of caytyf wyrdes   *cured*
Alle þat he spured° hym in space° he expowned
   clene   *asked / soon*

Þurȝ þe sped° of þe spyryt þat sprad hym wythinne   *aid*
1608 Of þe godelest° goddeȝ þat gaynes°
   aywhere   *most gracious / avail*

1595. forredles: MS, Go for redles.
1598. gostes: Go gost.
1608. godelest: Go godeliest.

1598. *gostes of God*: Translates the   5:14).
Vulgate's *spiritum deorum* (Dan.

For his depe diuinite & his dere sawes
Þy bolde fader Baltaȝar bede by his name

Þat now is demed Danyel of derne coninges°　　　　*learnings*
1612 Þat caȝt watȝ in þe captyuide in cuntre of Jues
Nabuȝardan hym nome & now is he here
A prophete of þat prouince of pryce° of þe worlde　　*chief*

Sende into þe cete to seche hym bylyue
1616 & wynne hym wyth þe worchyp to wayne° þe bote　　*give*
& paȝ þe mater be merk° þat merked°
　　　is ȝender°　　　　*obscure / written / yonder*
He schal declar hit also as hit on clay stande

Þat gode counseyl at þe quene watȝ cached as swyþe
1620 Þe burne byfore Baltaȝar watȝ broȝt in a whyle　　(f.79b)
When he com bifore þe kyng & clanly had halsed
Baltaȝar vmbebrayde° hym & leue sir he sayde　　　*accosted*

Hit is tolde me bi tulkes þat þou trwe were
1624 Profete of þat þrouynce þat prayed my fader
Ande þat þou hatȝ in þy hert holy connyng
Of sapyence° þi sawle ful soþes to schawe　　　*wisdom*

Goddes gost is þe geuen þat gyes alle þynges
1628 & þou vnhyles° vch hidde þat heuenkyng
　　　myntes°　　　　*uncover / purposes*
& here is a ferly byfallen & I fayn wolde
Wyt þe wytte° of þe wryt þat on þe wowe clyues　　*meaning*

For alle Calde clerkes han cowwardely° fayled　　*miserably*
1632 If þou wyth quayntyse° conquere hit I quyte° þe
　　　þy mede　　　　*wisdom / repay*

1616. þe (1st): Go þi.
1618. also: Go also cler.
1618. stande: Go standeȝ.
1619. as: MS as as.
1622. leue: Go beue.

For if þou redes hit by ryȝt & hit to resoun brynges
Fyrst telle me þe tyxte of þe tede° lettres   *joined together*

& syþen þe mater of þe mode mene° me þerafter   *explain*
1636 & I schal halde þe þe hest° þat I þe hyȝt haue   *promise*
Apyke þe in porpre cloþe palle° alþerfynest   *fine cloth*
& þe byȝe° of bryȝt golde abowte þyn nekke   *necklace*

& þe þryd þryuenest° þat þrynges me after   *most honorably*
1640 Þou schal be baroun vpon benche bede I þe no lasse
Derfly þenne Danyel deles þyse wordes
Ryche kyng of þis rengne rede þe oure lorde

Hit is surely soth þe souerayn of heuen
1644 Fylsened° euer þy fader & vpon folde cheryched   *supported*
Gart hym grattest to be of gouernores alle
& alle þe worlde in his wylle welde as hym lykes

Whoso wolde wel do wel hym bityde
1648 & quos deth so he deȝyre he dreped als fast
Whoso hym lyked to lyft on lofte watȝ he sone
& quoso hym lyked to lay watȝ loȝed bylyue

So watȝ noted þe note of Nabugo de Noȝar
1652 Styfly stabled þe rengne bi þe stronge dryȝtyn
For of þe hyȝest he hade a hope in his hert
Þat vche pouer past out of þat prynce euen

1646. lykes: Go lyked.
1648. deȝyre: Go deȝyred.

1634. *tede lettres*: *tede* translates the Vulgate *ligita*. Cf. *GGK* 35, *lel letteres loken*.

1635. *mode*: Go takes this to stand for *mote*, "stamp, mark," a word derived from ON *motā* or OE *metan* and not found elsewhere in English. However, *mode* may well mean "thought, idea," a meaning which fits perfectly the context here.

1648. See 279n.

& whyle þat watʒ cleʒt clos in his hert
1656 Þere watʒ no mon vpon molde of myʒt as hymseluen
Til hit bitide on a tyme towched hym pryde   (f.80a)
For his lordeschyp so large & his lyf ryche

He hade so huge an insyʒt° to his aune dedes   *opinion*
1660 Þat þe power of þe hyʒe prynce he purely forʒetes
Þenne blynnes he not of blasfemy on to blame þe dryʒtyn
His myʒt mete to Goddes he made wyth his wordes

I am god of þe grounde to gye as me lykes
1664 As he þat hyʒe is in heuen his aungeles þat weldes
If he hatʒ formed þe folde & folk þervpone
I haf bigged° Babiloyne burʒ alþerrychest°   *built / richest*
Stabled þerinne vche a ston in strenkþe of myn armes
1668 Moʒt neuer myʒt bot myn make such anoþer

Watʒ not þis ilke worde wonnen of his mowþe
Er þenne þe souerayn saʒe souned in his eres
Now Nabugo de Noʒar innoʒe hatʒ spoken
1672 Now is alle þy pryncipalte past at ones

& þou remued fro monnes sunes on mor most abide
& in wasturne° walk & wyth þe wylde dowelle   *wilderness*
As best byte on þe bent of braken & erbes
1676 Wyth wroþe° wolfes to won & wyth wylde asses   *fierce*

1655. þat: Go þat coyntise.
1663. god: M God.
1669. worde wonnen of his mowþe: MS worde wonnen of his mowþe
one; Go worde one wonnen of his mowþe. (*In the* MS, one *is written
at the end of the line in a smaller and different hand*).

1655. Various editors have added a word following þat, Bulbring using connynge or counseyl, Go coyntise. However, since þat refers so clearly to the idea of the two preceding lines —Nebuchadnezzar's belief in God— an addition seems unnecessary.

Inmydde þe poynt of his pryde departed he þere
Fro þe soly° of his solempnete his solace he leues   *seat*
& carfully is outkast to contre vnknawen
1680 Fer into a fyr fryth þere frekes neuer comen

His hert heldet vnhole he hoped non oþer
Bot a best þat he be a bol oþer an oxe
He fares forth on alle faure fogge° watȝ his mete   *grass*
1684 & ete ay as a horce when erbes were fallen

Þus he countes hym a kow þat watȝ a kyng ryche
Quyle seuen syþeȝ were ouerseyed° someres I trawe   *passed by*
By þat mony þik thyȝe þryȝt vmbe his lyre
1688 Þat alle watȝ dubbed & dryȝt in þe dew of heuen

Faxe fyltered° & felt flosed°
   hym vmbe   *became tangled / matted hair was shaggy*
Þat schad fro his schulderes to his schere-wykes°   *groin*

1687. thyȝe: Go theȝe.
1689. Faxe: ᴍs ffaxe.
1690. schere-wykes: ᴍs schyre wykes.

1684. *ay*: Thomas took this as a "variant of *fogge*" (1683) meaning "hay."

1686. Go places a comma after *ouerseyed*.

1687. M's interpretation of this difficult line seems to me essentially correct. Go emends *thyȝe* to *theȝe*, "thews," although no use of "thews" in the sense of "sinews" is recorded this early. Thomas renders the line "By that time many thick thighs crowded around his flesh" and explains that Nebuchadnezzar then possessed "many (*i.e.* fair) thick thighs because he had degenerated into what the poet describes alternately as a 'horse' or a 'cow'." Ker (MLR 24:323-34) read *thyfel* or *thyvel*, "bush," for *thyȝe* and took *lyre* to mean "face."

M, on the other hand, takes *thyȝe* to be a verb, the preterite 3rd plural of ᴍᴇ *the*, "to grow, increase," *þryȝt* to be a past participle used as an adjective, and *mony þik* to be a substantive meaning "many thick hairs or tufts of hairs." The line as it stands in the ᴍs could thus be rendered "By that time many thick (tufts of hair) were growing about his flesh."

&twentyfolde twynande hit to his tos raȝt
1692 Þer mony clyuy as clyde° hit clyȝt° togeder   *plaster / stuck*

His berde ibrad° alle his brest to þe bare vrþe   *covered*
His browes bresed° as breres° aboute his
     brode chekes   *bristled / briars* (f.80b)
Holȝe° were his yȝen & vnder campe
     hores°   *hollow / shaggy hairs*
1696 & al watȝ gray as þe glede° wyth ful grymme clawres   *kite*

Þat were croked & kene as þe kyte paune°   *claws*
Erne-hwed° he watȝ & al
     ouerbrawden°   *eagle-colored / covered over*
Til he wyst ful wel who wroȝt alle myȝtes
1700 & cowþe vche kyndam tokerue° & keuer° when
     hym lyked   *divide / restore*

Þenne he wayned hym his wyt þat hade wo soffered
Þat he com to knawlach & kenned hymseluen
Þenne he loued þat lorde & leued in trawþe
1704 Hit watȝ non oþer þen he þat hade al in honde

Þenne sone watȝ he sende agayn his sete restored
His barounes boȝed hym to blyþe of his come
Haȝerly° in his aune hwe his heued watȝ couered   *fitly*
1708 & so ȝeply watȝ ȝarked & ȝolden° his state   *restored*

Bot þou Baltaȝar his barne & his bolde ayre
Seȝ þese syngnes wyth syȝt & set hem at lyttel

1697. paune: Go pauue.
1703. loued: MS laued.

1694. *bresed*: Clearly here a verb, not an adjective as listed in *NED*.
   1697. *paune*: Go reads *pauue*, "paw." However, *paune* could be read as the plural of *pau*, as M notes.

Bot ay hatʒ hofen þy hert agaynes þe hyʒe dryʒtyn
1712 Wyth bobaunce & wyth blasfamye bost at hym kest

& now his vessayles avyled in vanyte vnclene
Þat in his hows hym to honour were heuened of fyrst
Bifore þe barounʒ hatʒ hom broʒt & byrled°
     þerinne   *poured drink*
1716 Wale wyne to þy wenches in waryed° stoundes   *cursed*

Bifore þy borde hatʒ þou broʒt beuerage in þede
Þat blyþely were fyrst blest wyth bischopes hondes
Louande þeron lese goddeʒ þat lyf haden neuer
1720 Made of stokkes & stoneʒ þat neuer styry° moʒt   *stir*

& for þat froþande° fylþe þe fader of heuen   *frothing*
Hatʒ sende into þis sale þise syʒtes vncowþe
Þe fyste wyth þe fyngeres þat flayed þi hert
1724 Þat rasped renyschly° þe woʒe wyth þe roʒ penne   *strangely*

Þise ar þe wordes here wryten wythoute werk more
By vch fygure as I fynde as oure fader lykes
Mane techal phares merked in þrynne
1728 Þat þretes þe of þyn vnþryfte vpon þre wyse

Now expowne þe þis speche spedly I þenk
Mane menes als much as maynful° Gode   *mighty* (f.81a)
Hatʒ counted þy kyndam bi a clene noumbre
1732 & fulfylled hit in fayth to þe fyrre ende

1711. dryʒtyn: ᴍꜱ dryʒtn.
1717. þede: Go þ'ydres.
1722. Hatʒ sende: ᴍꜱ Hatʒ sende hatʒ sende.

1717. *þede*: Go emends to *þ'ydres*
from ᴏᴇ *ydre*, "a water vessel." How-
ever, even though *þede* is literally a
brewer's strainer, the term may here
be used generally to designate a drink-
ing vessel.
    1727. Go places a colon after *phares*
and a comma at the end of the line.

DANIEL EXPOUNDING THE WALL WRITING

To teche þe of techal þat terme þus menes
Þy wale rengne is walt° in weȝtes to heng   *adjudged*
& is funde ful fewe of hit fayth-dedes
1736 & phares folȝes for þose fawtes to frayst° þe trawþe   *examine*

In phares fynde I forsoþe þise felle saȝes
Departed is þy pryncipalte depryved þou worþes
Þy rengne rafte is þe fro & raȝt is þe Perses
1740 Þe Medes schal be maysteres here & þou of menske
    schowued°   *ejected*

Þe kyng comaunded anon to clepe° þat wyse   *dress*
In frokkes of fyn cloþ as forward hit asked
Þenne sone watȝ Danyel dubbed in ful dere porpor
1744 & a coler of cler golde kest vmbe his swyre°   *neck*

Þen watȝ demed a decre bi þe duk seluen
Bolde Baltaȝar bed þat hym bowe schulde
Þe comynes° al of Calde þat to þe kyng longed   *common people*
1748 As to þe prynce pryuyest° preued þe þrydde   *most intimate*

Heȝest of alle oþer saf onelych° tweyne   *only*
To boȝ after Baltaȝar in borȝe & in felde
Þys watȝ cryed & knawen in cort als fast
1752 & alle þe folk þerof fayn þat folȝed hym tylle

Bot howso Danyel watȝ dyȝt þat day ouerȝede°   *passed*
Nyȝt neȝed ryȝt now wyth nyes fol mony
For daȝed° neuer anoþer day þat ilk derk after   *dawned*
1756 Er dalt° were þat ilk dome þat Danyel deuysed   *delivered*

Þe solace of þe solempnete in þat sale dured
Of þat farand°fest tyl fayled þe sunne   *joyous*
Þenne blykned þe ble of þe bryȝt skwes
1760 Mourkenes° þe mery weder & þe myst dryues   *grows dark*
Þorȝ þe lyst of þe lyfte bi þe loȝ medoes

1744. coler: MS cloler.
1746. Baltaȝar: MS baltaȝa.

Vche haþel to his home hyȝes ful fast
Seten at her soper & songen þerafter
1764 Þen foundeȝ vch a felaȝschyp° fyrre at
       forþ naȝtes°   *company / late at night*
Baltaȝar to his bedd with blysse watȝ caryed
Reche þe rest as hym lyst he ros neuer þerafter   (f.81b)

For his foes in þe felde in flokkes ful grete
1768 Þat longe hade layted° þat lede his londes to strye   *sought*
Now ar þay sodenly assembled at þe self tyme
Of hem wyst no wyȝe þat in þat won dowelled

Hit watȝ þe dere Daryus þe duk of þise Medes
1772 Þe prowde prynce of Perce & Porros of Ynde
Wyth mony a legioun ful large wyth ledes of armes
Þat now hatȝ spyed a space to spoyle Caldeeȝ

Þay þrongen þeder in þe þester° on þrawen hepes   *darkness*
1776 Asscaped ouer þe skyre° watteres & scaled þe walles   *clear*
Lyfte laddres ful longe & vpon lofte wonen
Stelen stylly þe toun er any steuen rysed

Wythinne an oure of þe nyȝt an entre þay hade
1780 Ȝet afrayed þay no freke fyrre þay passen
& to þe palays pryncipal þay aproched ful stylle
Þenne ran þay in on a res° on rowtes ful grete   *rush*

1766. þer: MS, M þe.
1776. scaled: MS scaþed; Go scayled.
1779. nyȝt: MS myȝt.

1766. *þer*: Like Go, I have so emended the MS *þe*: "Let him rest there as best he can."

1772. Although Porus of India is non-scriptural, he was a familiar character to the poet's audience through the Alexander romances.

1776. *scaled*: The MS *scaþed* is almost certainly an error.

Blastes out of bryȝt brasse brestes so hyȝe
1784 Ascry scarred on þe scue° þat
      scomfyted° mony   *sky | threw into confusion*
Segges slepande were slayne er þay slyppe myȝt
Vche hous heyred° watȝ wythinne a
      hondewhyle°   *pillaged | moment*

Baltaȝar in his bed watȝ beten to deþe
1788 Þat boþe his blod & his brayn blende on þe cloþes
The kyng in his cortyn watȝ kaȝt bi þe heles
Feryed out bi þe fete & fowle dispysed
Þat watȝ so doȝty þat day & drank of þe vessayl
1792 Now is a dogge also dere þat in a dych lygges

For þe mayster of þyse Medes on þe morne ryses
Dere Daryous þat day dyȝt vpon trone
Þat cete seses ful sounde & saȝtlyng makes
1796 Wyth alle þe barounȝ þeraboute þat bowed hym after

& þus watȝ þat londe lost for þe lordes synne
& þe fylþe of þe freke þat defowled hade
Þe ornementes of Goddeȝ hous þat holy were maked
1800 He watȝ corsed for his vnclannes & cached þerinne

Done doun of his dyngnete for dedeȝ vnfayre
& of þyse worldes worchyp wrast out for euer   (f.82a)
& ȝet of lykynges on lofte letted° I trowe   *deprived*
1804 To loke on oure lofly lorde late bitydes

Þus vpon þrynne wyses I haf yow þro schewed
Þat vnclannes tocleues° in corage° dere   *is cleft asunder | heart*

1786. heyred: Go heryed.
1804. bitydes: Go betydes.

1783. See *GGK* 118*n*.

Of þat wynnelych° lorde þat wonyes in heuen   *gracious*
1808 Entyses hym to be tene teldes vp his wrake

    Ande clannes in his comfort & coyntyse he louyes
    & þose þat seme° arn & swete schyn se his face   *seemly*
    Þat we gon gay in oure gere° þat grace he vus sende   *apparel*
1812 Þat we may serue in his syȝt þer solace neuer blynneȝ
                         Amen

1808. teldes: ᴍs, Go telled.
1811. þat (2nd): Go his.

1808. *teldes*: M's emendation of ᴍs *telled*, which Go takes to be a participle, "his vengeance being raised up."

THE DREAMER ASLEEP

· Pearl ·

1

Perle plesaunte to prynces paye°   *pleasure* (f.39a)
To clanly clos in golde so clere
Oute of Oryent I hardyly saye

---

1. *Perle*: For general views of the pearl and of the whole poem, see Introduction. These opening lines have of course been variously interpreted in order to fit the commentator's general reading of the poem.

A note on the verse form is appropriate here. The stanza form used in *Pearl* in general consists of twelve four-stress alliterative lines rhyming *ababababbcbc*, though there are of course minor irregularities in meter (see E. V. Gordon: 89–91). This stanza is by no means uncommon in Middle English verse and was apparently a part of the "West Midland tradition" (Gn:87). However, as Dorothy Everett says (*Essays on Middle English Literature*: 88), "nowhere else is there anything like this complex scheme, nor is the stanza handled with such mastery." The poem consists of twenty groups, each consisting of five such stanzas except for group XV which has six stanzas, of which either 72 (C. G. Osgood) or 76 (Gn) is likely to have been accidentally included.

C. O. Chapman's argument (MLN 54:256) that the extra stanza was deliberately added to bring the total number of stanzas to ninety-nine, the last two stanzas in the poem being in Chapman's eyes superfluous, seems hardly credible. Each group of five stanzas is set apart by a refrain which varies only slightly from stanza to stanza within the group. Each stanza, moreover, is linked to that following it by a device called *concatenatio* in which the last word in a given stanza appears in the first line of the next. The refrain and *concatenatio* taken together thus "produce an effect of both pause and continuity between stanzas" (O). O also feels that "each group [of stanzas] is by itself a complete lyric of five stanzas, each of which in turn possesses characteristics of the individual lyric." Kean (NQ 210:49–51) suggests that "the extra stanza makes a deliberate break in the system of 5, 20 and 100" since it brings the line total to 1212 which is "obviously appropriate to a poem which celebrates the twelve times twelve thousand Virgins who follow the Lamb,

Ne proued I neuer her precios pere
5 So rounde so reken° in vche araye°   *fresh / each setting*
So smal so smoþe her sydeʒ were
Queresoeuer I jugged gemmeʒ gaye

---

and the architecture, with its basis of 12 x 12, of the Heavenly Jerusalem."

It is clear that the beginning of the poem demonstrates the poet's rhetorical as well as his metrical skill. Kean, for example, traces carefully a number of rhetorical formulae—*propositio, descriptio, exclamatio, expolitio, circumlocutio,* and *amplificatio*—through the first twenty sections (the proem) of the poem in order to show how the poet introduces his principal themes of growth, death, and regeneration through a structure of biblical allusion.

See also *GGK* 1*n.*

1. *prynces:* Contrary to O's judgment, the primary meaning here seem to be a prince of this world and only secondarily Christ (Gn, M. V. Hillmann), though of course the echoing phrase in the refrain of the last stanza clearly refers directly to Christ. The phrase here simply means "fit for a prince."

2. *To clanly clos:* A difficult phrase. Gollancz took *clos* to be an adjective and *to* to be "too," thus rendering the phrase as "too chastely set in gold" for earthly existence. O, following the same general construction, took *to* to modify *clos* and translated "too fast (though decently) enclosed for my present happiness." Both these constructions seem strained, and I should prefer to follow those editors who read

the phrase as a split infinitive, "to set fairly in gold" (Gn) or "to set without flaw" or "neatly" (H). O's comment that the line "may contain also a secondary allusion to the maiden's tomb" is pushing the elegiac interpretation into passages where it does not logically fit.

3. *Oute of Oryent:* The best pearls were from oriental waters.

4. *her:* Needless to say, the elegiac critics render this "her" and the allegorical critics "its." There is no doubt (1) that the feminine form of the pronoun is grammatically appropriate to *perle,* (2) that, as Go says, "the feminine pronoun would not strike a medieval reader as in modern English," and (3) that the poet also "frequently uses the indefinite 'hit,' *e.g.* ll. 10, 41, etc." to refer to the pearl (see 10*n*). However, in view of the obviously feminine characteristics attributed to the pearl in 6—*so smal so smoþe her sydeʒ were*—one seems justified in supposing that a human figure is being described. *Smal* and *smoþe* were both used to describe ladies in the romances, *e.g., Hyr syde longe, hyr myddyll small (Erle of Toulous,* 352). It is not strange, moreover, to find a child so described in this context; there is in the poem a very definite strain of courtly imagery linking the child with an idealized courtly heroine and with

I sette hyr sengeley in synglere°   *apart as unique*
Allas I leste hyr in on erbere
10 Þurȝ gresse to grounde hit fro me yot
I dewyne fordolked of luf-daungere
Of þat pryuy° perle wythouten spot   *my own*

8. synglere: ᴍꜱ, H synglure; O, Go, syngulere.
11. fordolked: Go for-dokked.

---

the Blessed Virgin, the "Quen of Cortaysye."

Despite H's objection that *rounde* is "applicable to a pearl, but scarcely to an exquisitely beautiful child" (77), I find it here and in 738 (*endeleȝ rounde*) glossed as "well-shaped" (*NED, round*, a.1, 3.b.) at least as appropriate as *so smal so smoþe her sydeȝ were*. The roundness of the pearl contributes to its symbolism; "because of its roundness, and its lack of facets, the pearl, like the egg, is a symbol of perfection, of wholeness, and of eternity" (Kean: 141).

Passages such as this are of course capable of a variety of interpretations, and the reader should realize that indeed these lines may have been intended to describe several things simultaneously—a pearl, a child, the soul, etc.—without contradiction or strain.

8. *in synglere*: ᴍꜱ *synglure* is preserved only by H. Go and O read *syngulere*. The phrase points to the unique importance of the gem in the poet's life.

9. *erbere*: Certainly not an "arbor" in the modern sense of a vine-covered latticework, but neither, as Go sug-

gests, an "herb-garden." The *NED* notion of a "garden lawn or 'green'" is probably what the poet has in mind. And while I certainly do not concur with Go that a graveyard is here suggested, I cannot agree at the opposite extreme with H's remark that it would not be "strange" for a professional jeweller to lose a valuable pearl "in such a place."

Reacting against R. W. V. Elliott's notion (LanM 45:85–92) that the *erbere* is quite literally an "arbor," "a shady bower tucked away in a corner of a garden," C. A. Luttrell (Neophil 49:160–76) maintains that *erbere* in the poet's time might still refer to a flower and herb garden and that one of the chief features of the *erbere* was a "raised piece of turf, square, flowery and pleasant," the *huyle* of 41. Luttrell's interpretation of *erbere* and *huyle* becomes the basis of an allegorical reading of the poem in which "on one level . . . he [the narrator] was in a garden and on a turfed mound; on another, the mound was on the *erber* of the initial allegory; on a third, he was in a Garden of Remembrance."

Kean's analysis of the various contexts of *erbere* in Scripture and medi-

2

Syþen°in þat spote hit fro me sprange   *since*
Ofte haf I wayted wyschande°þat
    wele°   *wishing for / precious thing*

---

eval literature links the poem to both the Song of Songs and to the *Roman de la Rose.*

10. *hit*: The reference is, of course, to the pearl. O's explanation for the change from *her* to *hit* (see note to 4 above), that it "indicates an imperfect identification of the symbol with the object symbolized," is inadequate in the face of the poet's usual care in such matters. Nor do I accept Schofield's statement (PMLA 24:595), approved by H, that the poet makes indiscriminate use of *her*, the grammatically correct form, and *hit*, the "more natural" form.

Gn's suggestion, however, that the nominative form of the pronoun in ME usage was "much more definite in its indication of sex or gender" seems consistently to fit the poet's practice in the poem. Thus while the poet "tends to use the feminine form in the genitive or accusative, he always uses the neuter in the nominative, where the feminine *ho* would suggest a female figure and over-emphasize the personal symbolism."

10. *yot*: The form of the word here has caused some difficulty as to its meaning. C. F. Emerson related *yot* to OE *geat*, "flawed," Go to OE *gretan*, "get," and O and H to ME *gon*, OE *gan*, "go." Hamilton relates *yot* in meaning to *schede* in 411 and claims

that both *gēoton* and *sceadan* were used to render Latin *fundere*, "to pour or spill." Figuratively in the poem then, continues Hamilton, both *yot* and *schede* seem "to have been used chiefly, if not solely, for the effusion of grace or the pouring out of love, heart, 'soul,' or the spirit of God" and so refer directly to that "which the pearl symbolizes," in Hamilton's view, the soul.

11. *dewyne*: Apparently a weak preterite without -d, "pined." See Mabel Day (MLR 14:413–15).

11. *fordolked*: Go read *for-dokked*, "robbed," and *NED fordulled*, "stupefied." No emendation, however, seems necessary.

11. *luf-daungere*: Simply the power of love, and not necessarily, as H maintains, any "inordinate" affection. Everett (*Essays on Middle English Literature*), however, points out rightly that the term does evoke "memories" of the separation of lovers and of the love-longing "so often described by poets of the *Roman de la Rose* tradition" (90). Although, as noted in 4*n* above, there is a minor strain of courtly love imagery throughout the poem, it would be a mistake to try to make any firm identification of the narrator's situation with that of a courtly lover, though of course the grief and sense of loss are similar. Simi-

15 Þat wont watȝ whyle deuoyde my wrange
   & heuen my happe & al my hele
   Þat dotȝ bot þrych my hert þrange
   My breste in bale°bot bolne & bele   *sorrow*
   ȝet þoȝt me neuer so swete a sange
20 As stylle stounde let to me stele

17. hert: Go herte.

---

larly, it would be a mistake to attempt to equate the *erbere* with the Garden of Love. Kean relates *luf-daungere* also to Song of Songs 2:5 and 5:7–8.

15–16. *deuoyde my wrange*: Emerson took *deuoyde*, translated by him and by H as "sin," to be a participial adjective with *wrange* as its object, and *heuen* to be a noun. He thus translated: "wishing that weal/ That was wont when lacking my sin,/ And heaven (was) my chance and all my salvation." *Deuoyde* is now, however, generally accepted to be an infinitive, and *heuen* is presumably the infinitive of the verb meaning "to exalt."

17. *Þat*: I take this to refer to *wele* in 14 rather than to the "action of 14" as Go claims. The sense of the line is thus "that (wealth now, however,) does but crush my heart oppressively."

18. *bele*: Luttrell (Neophil 39:207–17) took this to be "the verb in the *NED* s.v. *beal*, 'to swell with moisture or morbid matter, suppurate',," the derivation being from Old Swedish *bulin, bolin,* "swollen," which "presumes a lost Scandinavian verb *bela.*" The usual interpretation is "burn" from ON *bela.*

19–21. I would recommend here the punctuation of Kean who translates: "And yet I thought I had never heard such a sweet sound as a momentary stillness allowed to steal over me —truly, many (such sounds) reach me."

19. *sange*: O thought the word alluded to "this poem, or at least the poet's first conception of it," a judgment agreed to by Gn and Wright, who called this line the "first whisper of things to come."

Interestingly enough, Gn's note on this passage and on 17 have aroused some controversy. In both notes Gn refers rather casually to the "grave" beside which the poet is ostensibly sitting, a natural assumption to anyone of the elegiac persuasion. This mention of a grave was strongly objected to by Hamilton, who pointed out, quite correctly though somewhat starchily, that the poet did not at any time allude to a grave. H. L. Savage defended Gn on this point, only to find himself under attack by Hamilton. Needless to say, there is justice on both sides, and one's general theory of the poem tends to dictate one's interpretation of these lines.

Forsoþe þer fleten° to me fele   *floated*
To þenke hir color so clad in clot°   *clay*
O moul° þou marreʒ a myry iuele   *earth*
My priuy perle wythouten spotte

3

25 Þat spot of spyseʒ mot° nedeʒ sprede°   *must / be covered*
Þer° such rycheʒ to rot is runne   *where*
Blomeʒ blayke° & blwe & rede   *yellow*
Þer schyneʒ ful schyr°agayn þe sunne   *brightly*

23. iuele: Go mele.
25. mot: MS *illegible except for* t.
26. runne: MS runnen.

---

21. *fele*: Many such songs.

23. *iuele*: Emended by Go, following Morris's suggestion, to *mele*, the phrase *myry mele*, "merry mele," *i.e.* a "joyous thing," being not uncommon in the period. However, the long open *e* of *iuele* is necessary for the rhyme and *iuele* does fit both sense and image pattern.

25–36. In an article devoted to this puzzling stanza (JEGP 66:519–31) Edward Vasta points out that the poet here seems to contradict himself. Vasta notes that in 25–28 the poet states that the Pearl has "run to rot" and so produced lovely flowers, yet in 33–36 he expresses the hope "that the Pearl might not fail [at some time in the future] to produce growing spices." Vasta reconciles the contradiction by taking *fede* (29) as "fed" from OE *fedan* and consequently *may* (29) as expressing permission; thus the narrator "expresses his desire that flower and fruit may not be permitted to feed on his Pearl."

C. A. Luttrell (Neophil, 49:160–76) believes that if *schyneʒ* (28) "were *schyne*, the infinitive, dependent like *sprede* (25) on *mot*, and a comma, instead of a semi-colon, supplied after the second line, the stanza would be argument from beginning to end, with the narrator saying that spices, flowers, and fruit *ought* to spring from the pearl." But *schyneʒ* is not *schyne*, and the lines make perfect sense as written.

For a full discussion of the flower and garden imagery of the poem see Kean.

25. *mot*: Morris and Go both read *myʒt* here, the MS being almost illegibile. The more positive *mot*, however, seems better to suit the narrator's point.

26. *rot*: I cannot agree with H that this word is inappropriate when "used by a loving father in regard to the body of his dead child." The statement is,

Flor & fryte may not be fede
30 Þer hit doun drof° in moldeʒ dunne°   *sank / brown earth*
For vch gresse mot grow of grayneʒ dede
No whete were elleʒ to woneʒ wonne
Of goud vche goude is ay bygonne
So semly a sede moʒt fayly°not   *fail*
35 Þat spryngande spyceʒ vp ne sponne°   *would not spring up*
Of þat precios perle wythouten spotte

4

To þat spot þat I in speche expoun   (f.39b)
I entred in þat erber grene
In Auguste in a hyʒ seysoun

35. spryngande: MS sprygande; H spryg ande.

I think, bitter and unreconciled in tone, and the harsh language is perfectly in keeping with this kind of grief (see Kean: 23).

H's note here, by the way, opens up the whole question of point of view in *Pearl* (see Introduction). Having said that "the jeweller well knows that the acid action of earth . . . will soon result in the decomposition of its [the pearl's] delicate organic layers," she immediately states that the "poet goes on to liken the lost pearl to a seed buried in the earth." Obviously, the two are not in H's eyes the same person, since jeweller and poet here express diametrically opposed sentiments, the one still grieving his material loss, the other prophesying a spiritual gain.

29. *fede*: Almost certainly the adjective *fade*, "faded," though the spelling is difficult to account for. It is not, I am certain, derived from ON *feyja*

as Go suggested, since "decayed" is in context almost contradictory to the poet's intended meaning. See, however, 25–36*n*.

32. *woneʒ*: Emerson thought "pleasure" from *OE *wunne*, parallel to OHG *wunna*, GMC *wonne*.

35. *spryngande*: H emends to *spryg ande*, "sprig and," without explanation. The line, however, like the manuscript, is perfectly intelligible, and *spryg ande spyceʒ* makes for an awkward confusion in number.

37–38. The poet is very careful here. He entered *in*, "into," the *erber* and advanced *to* the spot where the pearl was lost, in Go's terms, "where the child is buried." *Erber* is thus not, as O states, in opposition with *spot*.

39. *hyʒ seysoun*: There are three defensible theories as to this "high season" in August. Go, supported by Gn, claimed that it was Lammastide,

40 Quen corne is coruen wyth crokeȝ kene
   On huyle þer perle hit trendeled° doun   *rolled*
   Schadowed þis worteȝ° ful schyre & schene   *plants*
   Gilofre gyngure & gromylyoun
   & pyonys powdered ay bytwene
45 Ȝif hit watȝ semly on to sene°   *look*
   A fayr reflayr°ȝet fro hit flot°   *fragrance | flowed*

August 1, at which time "loaves were consecrated from the first ripe corn." O, supported by H, thought it to be the Feast of the Assumption, August 15, the "highest feast" of August. W. J. Knightly (MLN 76:97–102) has recently suggested the Feast of the Transfiguration, August 6, since the significance of that feast "agrees closely with that of the other images in the herber as a type and a symbol of the glory of the resurrection." Could, however, *hyȝ* be simply an unlisted alternative spelling of (or possibly a scribal error for) *híȝ* or *héȝ*, "hay," and the phrase read quite naturally as the "hay season when the grain is cut with sharp sickles"?

41. *huyle*: Glossed by Go and O as "mound" and frankly identified as "the grave-mound" by Gn. Go, acting upon a suggestion in Gn, goes on to conjecture that *huyle* as used here "must be distinguished from *hyl* or *hylle*, the usual forms of 'hill' in this MS." *Hyule*, on the other hand, represents the Lancashire dialect *hile*, "a thick cluster of plants," origin unknown. The poet, Gn continues, may thus be thinking of the "grave-mound overgrown with flowers," and the reference to the same mound as a *hylle*

in 1172 may be an error, possibly that of a copyist. Hamilton is opposed to Gn's theory on the grounds that *hil* always renders the Vulgate *mons*, a statement opposed by Savage. H, strangely enough, finds herself agreeing with Gn on the grounds that a thick cluster of plants would be an ideal spot to lose an actual pearl. See also 9*n*.

43. *worteȝ*: The description of these plants, all of which are spices, is perhaps derived from the description of the spices growing in the garden of Deduit in the *Roman de la Rose*. But as Gn points out, spice gardens were not unusual in medieval literature. The list itself, though not the particular spices, may be, as Kean notes, reminiscent of the Song of Songs, 4.

More interesting is the fact pointed out by M. R. Stern (JEGP 54:684–92) that the spices here mentioned are "earthly manifestations of heaven's beneficence": the gilliflower in medieval times was considered a "healing clove"; the ginger was considered an "energizing anti-irritant." The gromwell, on the other hand, produced nutlets "very much like pearls," and peonies, as Go points out, were thought to have a "medicinal effect."

Þer wonys þat worþyly I wot & wene
My precious perle wythouten spot

5

Bifore þat spot my honde I spenned°   *clasped*
50 For care ful colde þat to me caȝt
A deuely dele in my hert denned
Þaȝ° resoun sette myseluen saȝt°   *though | at rest*
I playned my perle þat þer watȝ spenned
Wyth fyrce skylleȝ þat faste faȝt
55 Þaȝ kynde of Kryst me comfort kenned
My wreched wylle in wo ay wraȝte

49. spenned: MS spennd.
51. deuely: O deruely.
53. spenned: Go penned.
54. fyrce: MS, O, H fyrte.

47. "There dwells that precious one I know and think."

51. *deuely*: "desolating" (Gn), "benumbing" (Wright), reflected in modern dialect *deavely, davely* in northern England (*NED* and *EDD*, s.v. *deavely*), a word usually applied to a lonely path or road. While the derivation is quite vague, there seems no need to connect the word with ME *deuel*, "devil," as does H, and therefore to render it awkwardly as "wicked."

51. *denned*: "made tumult" (O), "resounded" (Go), both from OE *dynian*, properly *dynnan*, an etymology agreed to by Wright and Savage. However, Hulbert (MP 25:18), Gn, and H all derive *denned* from some form of OE *denn*, "lair," and render it "lurked, to be hidden."

53. *spenned*: Usually derived from ON *spenna* (Gn, H, O, Go) and trans-lated "clasped, locked, imprisoned." Hamilton, however, thinks this may be the past participle of *spenden* (OE *spendan*), "to disperse, dissipate," and translates the line "I mourned for my pearl that was lost there."

54: *fyrce*: MS *fyrte*. In spite of the MS and of H, who sees this as a noun governed by *wyth*, I prefer to see it as an adjective modifying *skylleȝ*. The sense of 53–54 is grasped once it is noted that 55–56 are in opposition: "With fierce arguments that locked in battle I mourned my pearl that there (in the earth) was imprisoned: (on the one hand) the nature of Christ taught me comfort; (but on the other hand) my wretched will ever writhed in woe."

56. *wraȝte*: Emerson thought this to be active voice, "he tormented," from OE *wrecian*, "rouse, excite."

I felle vpon þat floury flaȝt°   *turf*
Suche odour to my herneȝ° schot   *brains*
I slode vpon a slepyng-slaȝte
60 On þat precios perle wythouten spot

II/6

Fro spot my spyryt þer sprang in space
My body on balke°þer bod in sweuen°   *a mound / dreams*
My goste is gon in Godeȝ grace
In auenture þer meruayleȝ meuen°   *take place*
65 I ne wyste in þis worlde quere þat hit wace
Bot I knew me keste þer klyfeȝ cleuen
Towarde a foreste I bere°þe face   *turned*
Where rych rokkeȝ wer to dyscreuen°   *be discerned*
Þe lyȝt of hem myȝt no mon leuen°   *believe*
70 Þe glemande° glory þat of hem glent   *gleaming*
For wern neuer webbeȝ°þat wyȝeȝ weuen°   *fabrics/ men wove*
Of half so dere adubbemente°   *glorious adornment*

7

Dubbed wern alle þo downeȝ sydeȝ°   *those hillsides* (f.40a)
Wyth crystal klyffeȝ so cler of kynde°   *nature*

60. precios: MS precos.
64. meruayleȝ: H meruayles.
68. rych: Go ryche.
72. adubbemente: MS, H adubmente.

59. *slepyng-slaȝte*: "attack of sleep."
Slaȝt generally means a "blow."
61. *in space*: "after a time," not, as
H suggests, "at once." Morton Bloom-
field, however, argues that *space* here
means "space" and reflects the theory
that in sleep the soul travels "in space."
65ff. As Patch pointed out (*The*
Other World), the account of the gar-
den, while "highly original" (190),
boasts many of the features of the
"otherworld reminiscence." Kean (89–
133) discusses at great length the pos-
sible sources of these descriptive stan-
zas.
66. *cleuen*: "abide, stand" (O),

75 Holtewodeʒ°bryʒt aboute hem bydeʒ° *woods | them stand*
 Of bolleʒ°as blwe as ble of Ynde°   *trunks | indigo*
 As bornyst° syluer þe lef onslydeʒ° *burnished | unfolds*
 Þat þike con trylle° on vch a tynde° *quivers | each branch*
 Quen glem of glodeʒ° agaynʒ hem glydeʒ *bright patches of sky*
80 Wyth schymeryng schene ful schrylle° þay
  schynde°   *dazzlingly | shone*
 Þe grauayl þat on grounde con grynde
 Wern precious perleʒ of oryente
 Þe sunnebemeʒ bot blo & blynde° *are only dark and dim*
 In respecte of þat adubbement

8

85 The adubbemente of þo downeʒ dere
 Garten°my goste al greffe forʒete° *made | grief forget*
 So frech flauoreʒ° of fryteʒ°were *fragrances | fruits*
 As fode hit con° me fayre refete°   *did | revive*
 Fowleʒ þer flowen in fryth in fere° *woods together*
90 Of flaumbande hweʒ boþe smale & grete
 Bot sytole-stryng & gyternere°   *cithern–player*
 Her reken° myrþe moʒt not retrete° *ready | imitate*
 For quen þose bryddeʒ her wyngeʒ bete
 Þay songen wyth a swete asent°   *harmony*

81. þat: Go þat I.

"rise" (Go)—both from OE *clifian*, *cleofian*, "to adhere"; Emerson, Wright, Gn, H, and Savage all derive from OE *clēofan* "to split" and render it variously as "cleave, separate, splinter," etc. Gn seems correct in designating its form here as past tense.

77. *onslydeʒ*: The image is that of the leaves slipping in and out of the light.

86. *Garten*: Plural, though with a singular subject, *adubbemente* (85). Go and Gn feel that *garten* was "attracted from agreement" by *downeʒ*, though H calls this construction "not unusual in ME" and points to other examples in *Pearl*.

95 So gracios gle couþe no mon gete
  As here & se her adubbement

9

So al watȝ dubbet on dere asyse°   *fashion*
Þat fryth þer° fortwne forth me fereȝ°   *wood where | leads*
Þe derþe° þerof for to deuyse   *glory*
100 Nis no wyȝ worþe þat tonge bereȝ
  I welke ay°forth in wely wyse°   *walked ever | a blissful manner*
  No bonk so byg þat did me dereȝ°   *harm*
  Þe fyrre° in þe fryth þe feier con ryse   *farther*
  Þe playn þe plontteȝ þe spyse þe pereȝ
105 & raweȝ & randeȝ & rych reuereȝ
  As fyldor° fyn her bonkes brent°   *gold thread | steep*
  I wan to a water by schore þat schereȝ
  Lorde dere watȝ hit adubbement

95. gracios: MS gracos.
103. feier: O, Go, H feirer.
106. bonkes: o *imperfect in* MS.

---

95. *gle*: Wright thought this to refer only to entertainments, not to internal joys. She thus translates "such beneficent (or, delightful) glee no man could make (or, compass, devise)."

95. *gete*: O and Gn render "get, obtain," Gn "procure," H "attain"—all from ON *geta*. Emerson, Savage, and Wright, however, all derive from ON *geta*, "watch, heed," a difficult meaning to fit into context.

96. *& se*: "while seeing" (Bloomfield).

103. *feier*: Most editors emend to the clearer form *feirer*. However, as Gn points out, *feier* might well be a form of *feierre*, as might *fayr* in 46.

105. "And hedgerows and borders and rich river banks."

107. *a water*: This stream is later identified (1055–60) as the stream, mentioned in Rev. 22:1–2, that flows "out of the throne of God and of the Lamb."

107. *schereȝ*: The etymology and meaning of this word are uncertain. Go and Emerson derived it from OE *sceran* and felt that the "water cut along the shore" (Go). H (MLN 59: 43) suggests "swerves" or "sheers off," and Gn, perhaps in the best suggestion to date, relates the verb to *sheer* (*NED*, v²), "to swerve, alter course," and so translates the phrase "meanders along by the shore."

10

The dubbemente of þo derworth
    depe°   *those splendid depths* (f.40b)
110 Wern bonkeȝ bene of beryl bryȝt
Swangeande°swete þe water con swepe   *swirling*
Wyth a rownande rourde raykande aryȝt
In þe founce°þer stonden stoneȝ stepe   *bottom*
As glente° þurȝ glas þat glowed & glyȝt°   *light / shone*
115 As stremande sterneȝ° quen stroþe-men slepe   *streaming stars*
Staren°in welkyn° in wynter nyȝt   *shine / sky*
For vche a pobbel in pole° þer pyȝt°   *stream / set*
Watȝ emerad saffer oþer gemme gente
Þat alle þe loȝe lemed°of lyȝt   *pool gleamed*
120 So dere watȝ hit adubbement

115. As: MS a.
119. alle: H all.

109ff. Milton R. Stern (JEGP 54: 684–92) notes that the "jewels of the stream-bed are considered as gem-stones of virtue." Thus "the soul must 'walk' on virtue in crossing the barrier between earth and heaven."

110. *bene*: Emerson connects this with Scandinavian *beinn*, "hospitable," though it is generally felt to be of un-certain origin.

110. *beryl*: According to Stern (JEGP 54:684–92), symbolic of the Resurrection. The other gems men-tioned also have an appropriate sym-bolism. The emerald represents chas-tity, faith, and good works, and the sapphire hope and salvation by Christ. See 997n.

111. *Swangeande*: Emerson thought this to be two words "slow and."

112. "With a whispering murmur flowing straight on."

113. *stonden*: C. Revard (NQ, 207: 9–10) translates this "shone" rather than "stood" and cites parallel uses of *standan* in OE literature (cf. *NED, stand*, v. 33). Cf 740n.

115. *stroþe-men*: Go identified *stroþe* with Scottish *strath*, "a valley through which a river runs," hence *stroþe-men* are "dalesmen." O, com-paring this passage with *GGK* 1710, glossed "close, secure," while Wright (ES 34:223) thought "strong." The most reasonable suggestion is again Gn's, that the word is derived from a probable OE *stroð*, "marshy land," and that *stroþe-men* may mean "men of the low earth," hence "mortals."

THE DREAMER STANDING BY THE STREAM

III/11

The dubbement dere of doun & daleȝ
Of wod & water & wlonk°playneȝ   *splendid*
Bylde° in me blys abated my baleȝ   *aroused*
Fordidden° my stresse dystryed my payneȝ   *did away with*
125 Doun after a strem þat dryȝly haleȝ°   *steadily flows*
I bowed°in blys bredful°my brayneȝ   *went / brimful*
Þe fyrre I folȝed þose floty valeȝ
Þe more strenghþe of ioye myn herte strayneȝ°   *stirs*
As fortune fares þeras ho frayneȝ°   *she makes trial*
130 Wheþer solace ho sende oþer elleȝ sore
Þe wyȝ to wham her wylle ho wayneȝ°   *grants*
Hytteȝ°to haue ay more & more   *chances*

122. wlonk: Go wlonke.

---

124. *forbidden*: Like *Garten* (86) a plural attracted from its singular subject, *dubbement* in 121.

127. *floty*: O and Go both translated "watery," deriving from oe *flot*, *flotian* + *y*, Go comparing of *pré flotis*. Emerson translated "flat, level," on the basis of Scandinavian *flatr*. Gn, using O's etymology, suggested "well-supplied with streams." H, however, using the same etymology, glosses as "waving, undulating," which seems to best fit the context.

129. *fortune*: Inherited from pagan times, the blind goddess of chance comes to fulfill a unique place in Christian thought as the servant of God entrusted with bestowing the fruits of this world upon man. She is best symbolized by the wheel which she turns, now elevating, now destroying the fortunes of the men attached to it. She is seen in this passage in her typical role, dispensing either *solace* or *sore*. In the usual Christian interpretation of the figure, the gifts—good or bad—of Fortune are to be regarded as a test (cf. *frayneȝ* in 129). Even though her gifts remain constant (*hytteȝ to haue ay more & more*) for long periods—a "run" of luck, either good or bad—they are bound to change as the wheel turns, and we must be prepared for a change of Fortune. It is for this reason that Boethius and many other writers constantly enjoined man to seek true, heavenly felicity, which is sure and constant, rather than false, earthly pleasures and power, which Fortune may sweep away as quickly as she brought them.

12

More of wele watȝ in þat wyse
Þen I cowþe telle þaȝ I tom°hade   *leisure*
135 For vrþely herte myȝt not suffyse
To þe tenþe dole°of þo gladneȝ glade   *part*
Forþy°I þoȝt þat paradyse   *therefore*
Watȝ þer ouer gayn°þo bonkeȝ brade°   *against | broad slopes*
I hoped þe water were a deuyse
140 Bytwene myrþeȝ by mereȝ made

134. I tom: Go tom I.
138. ouer: ᴍs, H oþer.
140. myrþeȝ . . . mereȝ: Go mereȝ . . . Myrþe.

133–36. See *GGK*, 165–66*n*.

136. *gladneȝ*: Emerson sees this as the nominative plural of *gladen*, "a ᴍᴇ and North of England word meaning 'open shore, glade'."

140. A line made difficult by *myrþeȝ* and *mereȝ* and by *deuyse* in the preceding line, none of which really requires emendation. Morris (Acad 39:603) read *myrcheȝ* as "borders." Go emended the whole line to read *By-twene mereȝ by Myrþe made* with the ingenious explanation that the poet or more probably the scribe, who was thinking of the garden of Deduit in the *Roman de la Rose*, transposed *mereȝ* and *myrþe* and "having transposed them, naturally wrote 'myrþeȝ' for 'myrþe.'" O agreed with Go's emendation, though he doubted that the poet would use the description of so secular a garden as that of Mirth in his own description of Paradise. Gn, while restoring the manuscript reading, agrees that the passage derives from the *Roman de la Rose*, but, acting upon a suggestion of O's, glosses *myrþeȝ* as "pleasure gardens." In general, however, *myrþeȝ* is taken as "delights, joys" and the whole passage as derived from the *Roman de la Rose*.

Mereȝ offers similar problems. Go derived it from ᴏᴇ *mere* and glossed it "stream," a reading followed by Gn. However, O, Emerson, and H derive it from ᴏᴇ *maare*, "boundaries," referring, as H says, to the natural divisions between "states of beatitude."

Deuyse was glossed by Go as "device" and by O and H as "division," all from ᴏꜰ *devise*. Gn, however, while glossing "division," suggests that the word might also designate "an artificial conduit such as was cut between the fountains in the garden of Deduit."

David C. Fowler has recently suggested (MLQ 21:27–29) that *deuyse* is the key word in the passage and that the passage contains no reference to

Byӡonde þe broke by slente oþer slade°   *slope or valley*
I hope þat mote merked wore
Bot þe water watӡ depe I dorst not wade
& euer me longed a more & more

13

145 More & more & ӡet wel mare
 Me lyste° to se þe broke byӡonde   *I wished* (f.41a)
 For if hit watӡ fayr þer I con fare
 Wel loueloker° watӡ þe fyrre londe   *lovelier*
 Abowte me con I stote°& stare   *I did halt*
150 To fynde a forþe°faste con I fonde°   *ford / I tried*
 Bot woþeӡ mo° iwysse þer ware   *dangers more*
 Þe fyrre I stalked by þe stronde
 & euer me þoӡt I schulde not wonde°   *flinch*
 For wo þer weleӡ so wynne wore
155 Þenne nwe note° me com on honde   *matter*
 Þat meued my mynde ay more & more

142. hope: Go, Gn hoped.
144. a: Go, Gn ay.
154. wo þer: Go woþe.

---

the *Roman de la Rose*. Glossing *deuyse* as a "deception," a "trick of the eye," Fowler translates the passage: "I thought the water was a deception/ Made by meres among the delights," meaning that "although the water seemed to be continuous and impassible, the dreamer thought that this was only an appearance caused by the abundance of pools among the splendors of the landscape; if he were to walk along the shore for a while, he would surely find an opening, and would be able to thread his way past the pools to the other side." Putting all these interpretations to-gether, the possibility emerges that the poet might be exploiting the natural ambiguities and overlappings of meaning inherent in *deuyse* and *mereӡ* and that some such reading as this might best express the poet's intent: "I thought the stream to be a dividing-device/ Made by boundary-pools between the delights."

142. *merked*: H derives this from OE *mercian* and translates "reached."

154. "From danger where delights so joyful were."

155. *on honde*: Savage translates "speedily," H "came to my attention."

14

More meruayle con my dom adaunt°   *subdued my judgment*

I seȝ byȝonde þat myry mere°   *pleasant pool*

A crystal clyffe ful relusaunt°   *shining*

160 Mony ryal ray con fro hit rere°   *rose from it*

At þe fote þerof þer sete°a faunt°   *sat / child*

A mayden of menske ful debonere

Blysnande°whyt watȝ hyr bleaunt°   *gleaming / mantle*

I knew hyr wel I hade sen hyr ere

165 As glysnande golde þat man con schere

So schon þat schene anvnder schore°   *fair one under the hill*

On lenghe I loked to°hyr þere   *at*

Þe lenger I knew hyr more & more

15

The more I frayste°hyr fayre face   *scanned*

170 Her fygure fyn quen I had fonte°   *noticed*

Suche gladande°glory con to me

     glace°   *gladdening / gilded to me*

As lyttel° byfore þerto watȝ wente°   *seldom / accustomed*

To calle hyr lyste con me enchace

Bot baysment gef°myn hert a brunt°   *amazement gave / blow*

175 I seȝ hyr in so strange a place

166. schore: Gn shore.

157ff. Kean relates the narrator's meeting with the Pearl to Dante's meetings with Matilda and Beatrice in the Earthly Paradise.

162. *menske*: "Rank" is the best reading, although other suggestions are "honor" (Morris); "grace, dignity" (Go); "decorous bearing" (O); and "courtesy" (Gn).

165. *schere*: Go, taking this to be "in close connection" with *schorne* in 213, claimed both to be part of a verb *schere* meaning "to purify" and related it to Old Swedish *skæra* and ᴏɴ *skærr*. The more general opinion, however, is that the verb *schere* means "to cut" and that the poet is thinking of *fil d'or*.

167. *on lenghe*: Emerson thought "during the time."

173. "Desire urged me to call her."

Such a burre myȝt°make myn herte
    blunt°   *shock could / stunned*
Þenne vereȝ ho°vp her fayre frount°   *she lifts / forehead*
Hyr vysayge whyt as playn yuore
Þat stonge myn hert ful stray atount°   *stunned*
180 & euer þe lenger þe more & more

IV/16

More þen me lyste°my drede aros   *I wished* (f.41b)
I stod ful stylle & dorste not calle
Wyth yȝen open & mouth ful clos
I stod as hende° as hawk in halle   *quiet*
185 I hope° þat gostly°watȝ þat porpose   *supposed / spiritual*
I dred onende° quat schulde byfalle   *concerning*
Lest ho me eschaped þat I þer chos°   *saw*
Er I at steuen hir moȝt stalle
Þat gracios gay° wythouten galle°   *fair one / flaw*
190 So smoþe so smal so seme slyȝt°   *seemly slim*
Ryseȝ vp in hir araye ryalle
A precios pyece in perleȝ pyȝt°   *adorned*

17

Perleȝ pyȝte of ryal prys
Þere moȝt mon°by grace haf sene   *could one*
195 Quen þat frech as flor-de-lys

179. atount: Go astount.
185. hope: Go, Gn hoped.
192. precios: MS precos.

---

188. *at steuen*: Emerson thought "with voice."

189ff. The fourth group of stanzas is devoted mainly to a description of the maiden's costume. The reader is directed to Gn's note to 228 for an excellent summary of that description.

Kean (138ff.) provides a useful account of the development of the symbolism of the pearl and its association in the poem with other symbols of perfection, notably the crown, the rose, and the color gold.

Doun þe bonke con boȝe bydene°   *slope came straightway*
Al blysnande whyt watȝ hir beau biys
Vpon°at sydeȝ & bounden bene°   *open / bordered well*
Wyth þe myryeste margarys at my deuyse
200 Þat euer I seȝ ȝet with myn yzen
Wyth lappeȝ° large I wot & I wene   *sleeves*
Dubbed with double perle & dyȝte°   *adorned*
Her cortel of self sute schene
Wyth precios perleȝ al vmbepyȝte°   *adorned around*

18

205 A pyȝt coroune° ȝet wer° þat gyrle   *adorned crown / wore*
Of mariorys°& non oþer ston   *pearls*
Hiȝe pynakled of cler quyt perle
Wyth flurted°flowreȝ perfet°vpon   *figured / perfect*

197. beau biys: ᴍꜱ beauuiys, *possibly* beauuiys;
      O bleaunt of biys; Go beau mys; H beaumys.
200. yȝen: Go, Gn ene.
208. flowreȝ: H flowereȝ.

---

197. *beau biys*: ᴍꜱ *beauuiys* or, more probably, *beaumys*. Go took *mys* to be *amys*, "amice," used to mean "upper garment." O emended the line to read *bleaunt of biys* on the grounds that the ecclesiastical "amice" certainly would not be worn by a fourteenth-century child and that a *bleaunt* or *surcot* was the proper garment. H, however, has come to O's defense by quoting the *Catholic Encyclopedia* (s.v. *Amictus*) to the effect that the amice was at one time identified with *anagolagium*, "a sort of linen wrap used by women to throw over their shoulders."
The form adopted here, *beau biys*, while not that of the manuscript, has a firm basis in Scripture. Rev. 19:8 describes the bride of the Lamb as "arrayed in fine linen, clean and white" (*byssinum splendens, candidum*), rendered almost exactly as *al blysnande whyt watȝ hir beau biys*.

199. *at my deuyse*: Rendered "opinion" by all editors except Gn, who, noting an alternate meaning (*NED*, 3) "desire, will" (also noted by Wright), translates "as many (as fine) as one (I) could (wish to) think of" and Bloomfield "that I could imagine."

203. "her kirtle of the same fair style."

To hed hade ho non oþer werle
210 Her here leke al hyr vmbegon
Her semblaunt sade for doc oþer erle
Her ble more blaȝt°þen whalleȝ bon   *white*
As schorne°golde schyr her fax° þenne schon   *cut | hair*
On schyldereȝ° þat leghe vnlapped
      lyȝte°   *shoulders | lay unbound lightly*
215 Her depe colour ȝet wonted non
Of precios perle in porfyl pyȝte

209. werle: O herle.
210. here leke: ms, H lere leke;
    Go here heke.

---

209. *werle*: A nonce word, this almost certainly refers to some sort of circlet or circular ornament worn by the child round her head. Gn compares OE *hwirfling*, "something round, orb." Emerson, however, derived it from the Scandinavian *huirfill*, "circle, ring," and translated it "twist of hair." Bradley in the *MED* glossed it as "garland," and O emended the word to *herle*, a "twist" or "fillet." The sense of the line, though, is perfectly clear: "She wore no other circlet (than the *pyȝt coroune*) upon her head."

210. *here leke*: ms *lere leke*. Go read *here-heke* and translated, assuming a missing finite verb, " 'Her hair, too, all about her,' *i.e.* 'hanging loose,' . . . as became a bride." O emended, as here, to *here-leke*, "locks of hair," but took *vmbegon* to be 3rd person plural with *hyr* as object. Emerson thought *leke* to be a past tense of *laiken*, "hang down," while Mabel Day (MÆ 3:241–42) thought it a strong preterite form of OE *lācon*, "to float."

All these it will be noted assume that the phrase refers to the child's hair. H, however, has kept the ms reading of *lere leke* which she renders "face-radiance," the "radiance of her countenance," *lere* being derived from ON *hleor*, "cheek," and *leke* from OE *lacan*, "to flash." H argues that the poet does not discuss the maiden's hair until 213–14 and that 210–11 are devoted to a description of her face— "Her face-radiance all 'round her beamed."

The weight of critical opinion and the syntax of the passage, which almost demands that *leke* be a finite verb with *semblaunt* and *ble* as objects, lead me to agree with Gn that *leke* is probably related to OE *lūcan*, "to enclose" and *vmbegon*, in spite of O's objections, is probably a past participle. Thus, "Her hair, lying all about her, framed her face, grave enough for duke or earl, (and her) countenance, whiter than whale's bone."

211. *sade*: "steadfast, beyond the

19

Pyȝt watȝ poyned°& vche a°hemme — *wristband / each* (f.42a)
At honde at sydeȝ at ouerture° — *opening*
Wyth whyte perle & non oþer gemme
220 & bornyste quyte watȝ hyr uesture
Bot a wonder° perle wythouten wemme° — *wonderful / flaw*
Inmyddeȝ hyr breste watȝ sette so sure
A manneȝ dom moȝt dryȝly demme
Er mynde moȝt malte°in hit mesure° — *comprehend / value*
225 I hope° no tong moȝt endure° — *suppose / suffice*
No sauerly saghe say° of þat syȝt — *fitting word to say*
So watȝ hit clene & cler & pure
Þat precios perle þer hit watȝ pyȝt

20

Pyȝt in perle þat precios pyece
230 On wyþer half°water com doun þe schore — *the opposite side*
No gladder gome heþen into Grece
Þen I quen ho on brymme wore° — *bank was*

217. watȝ poyned &: O & poyned watȝ.
225. tong: Go tonge.
229. pyece: ᴍꜱ pyse.

---

changes of earthly emotion" (Kean).
215. *colour*: The major dispute here is between "color" and "collar." Cf. A. S. Cook (MP 6:197) and H. However, those editors who gloss "color" cannot agree whether in regard to the maiden's countenance the word denotes a "ruddy hue" (O), an intense whiteness (Gn), simply great beauty (Go), or a "vital radiance" (Wright). The context (cf. 212 above) and the use of *colour* to mean whiteness in 753 (*by colour passeȝ þe flour-de-lys*) sug-

gest that whiteness is meant here: "Her intense whiteness lacked nothing (of the luster) of the precious pearls set in her embroidery."
223. "Man's reason might be thwarted."
231. "No gayer man from here to Greece." See also the similar line in *GGK*, 2023. As Gn points out, the usual phrase seemed to involve Constantinople (cf. O's note) and the *Gawain*-poet may have chosen Greece for alliterating purposes.

Ho watʒ me nerre þen aunte or nece
My joy forþy° watʒ much þe more   *therefore*
235 Ho profered me speche þat special spece°   *excellent person*
Enclynande° lowe in wommon lore°   *bowing / womanly manner*
Caʒte of° her coroun of grete tresore   *took off*
& haylsed° me wyth a lote lyʒte°   *greeted / joyous word*
Wel watʒ me þat euer I watʒ bore
240 To sware° þat swete in perleʒ pyʒte   *answer*

V/21

O perle quoþ I in perleʒ pyʒt
Art þou my perle þat I haf playned
Regretted by myn one on° nyʒte   *myself alone at*
Much longeyng haf I for þe layned°   *concealed*
245 Syþen into gresse þou me aglyʒte
Pensyf payred° I am forpayned°   *broken / tormented*
& þou in a lyf of lykyng° lyʒte   *pleasure*
In Paradys erde° of stryf vnstrayned°   *land / untroubled*

235. profered: ᴍꜱ pfered.
235. spece: ᴍꜱ spyce.
241. quoþ: O, Gn, H *always expand as* quod.

---

233. *nerre þen aunte or nece*: A great comfort to the elegiac school, this line is variously interpreted by the allegorists. For example, Gn says that *nerre* "can in the language of the time only mean here 'nearer in blood-relationship,'" while Dorothy Everett (*Essays on Middle English Literature*) insists that this line "need not imply blood-relationship." O claims that the phrase admits "of no allegorical interpretation," while H states that if taken to refer to relationship, lines 233–34 "are simply ludicrous" and that *nerre* refers only to "position, lo-cality."

My own feeling is that this line, taken along with a number of other lines (see Introduction), certainly supports the elegiac view, though it does not necessarily negate the allegorical view.

245. *aglyʒte*: Of uncertain etymology, glossed as "slipped away" by Go, O and Gn, and as "glittered away" from ᴏɴ *glīa*, "to shine," by H, who sees this as another proof of the poet's concern with an actual pearl.

247. &: "While."

What wyrde° hatȝ hyder my iuel vayned°   *fate / sent*
250 & don°me in þys del° & gret daunger°   *put / sorrow / subjection*
Fro we in twynne wern towen & twayned
I haf ben a joyleȝ iuelere

22

That iuel þenne in gemmeȝ gente
Vered° vp her vyse° wyth yȝen graye   *raised / face* (f.42b)
255 Set on hyr coroun of perle orient
& soberly after þenne con ho say
Sir ȝe haf your tale mysetente°   *misstated*
To say your perle is al awaye
Þat is in cofer so comly clente°   *beautifully enclosed*
260 As in þis gardyn gracios gaye
Hereinne to lenge for euer & play
Þer mys nee mornyng° com neuer nere   *loss nor mourning*
Her were a forser for þe in faye
If þou were a gentyl° iueler   *noble*

262. nere: MS, H here.

---

250. *don me in þys del*: Northrup (PMLA 12:326–40) proposed *m'in* and Emerson the deletion of *in* to improve the meter.

251. "Since we were drawn apart and separated."

252. *iuelere*: Needless to say, this reference to the narrator as a jeweller is H's chief proof of her theory that the narrator is an actual jeweller who has lost an actual pearl. Other critics, however, see in this reference an allusion to the jeweller in the parable of the pearl of great price (see 734 and Matt. 13:45–46).

254. *yȝen graye*: Gray is the usual color of the eyes of heroines of romance in the Middle Ages. See Introduction and Skeat's note to 152 of the General Prologue to *The Canterbury Tales* which lists a great number of gray-eyed heroines. F. N. Robinson's note to the same line suggests that the term probably included "blue (sky-blue) as well as the shades verging on green or yellow which it would now suggest."

262. *nere*: The MS *here* is kept only by H, who punctuates the passage to read, "Since neither loss nor mourning exists here in Heaven, here indeed would be your true treasure chest."

23

265 Bot jueler gente if þou schal lose
   Þy ioy for a gemme þat þe watȝ lef°   *dear*
   Me þynk þe put in a mad porpose
   & busyeȝ þe aboute a raysoun bref
   For þat° þou lesteȝ° watȝ bot a rose   *what / lost*
270 Þat flowred & fayled as kynde hyt gef
   Now þurȝ kynde of þe kyste þat hyt con close
   To a perle of prys hit is put in pref
   & þou hatȝ called þy wyrde° a þef   *fate*
   Þat oȝt of noȝt° hatȝ mad þe
      cler°   *something from nothing / clearly*
275 Þou blameȝ þe bote of° þy meschef   *cure for*
   Þou art no kynde° jueler   *gentle*

---

266. See *Purity* 117n.

269–72. Gn, like the earlier editors, interprets this passage to mean that the narrator's loss, like a rose, "bloomed and faded as roses do, but through the nature of the casket which encloses it, it has now become a pearl of price." Both Hamilton and H, however, follow Emerson's suggestion that *is put in pref* means "put to the test" not "proved to be." Hamilton thus translates 271–72, "now through the nature of the chest which encloses (enclosed) it [the dreamer's lost gem], it is (being) assayed for a pearl of price." H, in a puzzling comment, maintains that the "missing material pearl . . . is proved to be no pearl of price through the very character of the chest, i.e., the earth . . . , in which it is enclosed."

A. C. Spearing (MP 60:1–12) sees in 270 a reference to the rose of the garden of courtly love and a turning point in the narrator's view of his loss. To Spearing, the pearl is "a single symbol, with a single though complex meaning, which is . . . evolved" slowly in the mind of the narrator to whom the pearl is progressively seen as a child, as the rose of courtly love, as the biblical pearl of great price, and finally as the Lamb of God.

272. "It has proved to be a precious pearl."

277–78. H. R. Ruff (MLN 70:558–59) has suggested a double reading of 277–78 based on the fact that *geste* may be not only "guest" but "story, tale." Thus: the lines might be read: "A jewel (pearl) to me then was this guest (the pearl-maiden) or tale (pearl) and jewels (pearls) her gentle words (pearls)." The poet may also have had in mind Matt. 7:6, "Neither cast your pearls before swine," the dreamer tacitly identifying himself with the swine.

24

A juel to me þen watȝ þys geste
& iueleȝ wern hyr gentyl saweȝ
Iwyse quoþ I my blysfol beste°   *noblest one*
280 My grete dystresse þou al todraweȝ°   *draw away*
To be excused I make requeste
I trawed° my perle don out of daweȝ°   *believed / days*
Now haf I fonde hyt I schal ma feste
& wony°wyth hyt in schyr wodschaweȝ°   *dwell / bright groves*
285 & loue°my lorde an al his laweȝ   *praise*
Þat hatȝ me broȝ þys blys ner
Now were I at° yow byȝonde þise waweȝ°   *with / waves*
I were a ioyfol jueler

25

Jueler sayde þat gemme clene   (f.43a)
290 Wy borde°ȝe men so madde ȝe be   *jest*
Þre wordeȝ hatȝ þou spoken at ene°   *one time*
Vnavysed for soþe° wern alle þre   *ill-advised indeed*
Þou ne woste°in worlde quat on dotȝ mene° *know / one means*
Þy worde byfore þy wytte con fle
295 Þou says þou traweȝ°me in þis dene°   *believe/ valley*
Bycawse þou may wyth yȝen°me se
Anoþer þou says in þys countre
Þyself schal won wyth me ryȝt here

286. broȝ: O, Go, Gn, broȝt.
286. blys: Go blysse.
288. ioyfol: Gn ioyful.

---

283. *feste*: Emerson reads this as
"to make a fast" rather than "to feast"
and Savage to "make [it] fast."

307. *westernays*: This nonce word
is usually glossed as "reversed, awry"

on the supposition that it is an al-
tered form of *besternays*, or *bestorneis*.
H, however, suggested the reading
west ernays, an "empty pledge."

Þe þrydde to passe þys water fre°   *noble*
300 Þat may no ioyfol jueler

VI/26

I halde þat iueler lyttel to prayse
Þat leueȝ°wel þat he seȝ wyth yȝe   *believes*
& much to blame & vncortayse°   *discourteous*
Þat leueȝ oure lorde wolde make a lyȝe°   *lie*
305 Þat lelly hyȝte°your lyf to rayse *faithfully promised*
Þaȝ fortune dyd your flesch to dyȝe°   *die*
Ȝe setten hys wordeȝ ful westernays
Þat leueȝ noþynk bot°ȝe hit syȝe°   *unless | see*
& þat is a poynt o sorquydryȝe°   *of pride*
310 Þat vche god mon may euel byseme°   *ill befit*
To leue no tale be true to tryȝe°   *test*
Bot þat hys one skyl may dem

27

Deme now þyself if þou con dayly
As man to God wordeȝ schulde heue°   *lift*
315 Þou saytȝ þou schal won in þis bayly

302. leueȝ: MS, O loueȝ.
303. vncortayse: MS, H vncortoyse.
307. westernays: O besternays; H west ernays.
308. leueȝ: MS loueȝ.
309. is: MS īs.
312. dem: Go deme.

312. "But that which his reason alone may judge."

313–15. A difficulty here is raised by the fact that *dayly* and *bayly* rhyme with *fayle* and *counsayle* and thus may be derived either from OF *baillie*, "domain," and OF *dalier*, "to dally," or from OF *baille*, "castle," and ON *deila* "contend," or even possibly from a combination of these since, as O says, "-ly in derivations from French words in -li- may be either silent or uttered." It would seem here that "domain" and "talk courteously" (both from *dalier*—see Luttrell [NQ 207:447–59]) are better in context, though Savage, Emerson, and Wright feel that "complain, contend" would better translate *dayly*.

Me þynk þe burde°fyrst aske leue   *should*

& ʒet of graunt°þou myʒteʒ fayle   *permission*

Þou wylneʒ°ouer þys water to weue°   *wish | go*

Er moste þou ceuer°to oþer counsayl°   *attain | plan*

320 Þy corse in clot mot calder keue°   *in clay must colder sink*

For hit watʒ forgarte° at paradys greue°   *ruined | grove*

Oure ʒorefader hit con mysseʒeme°   *neglected*

Þurʒ drwry°deth boʒ°vch man dreue°   *cruel | it behooves | to pass*

Er ouer þys dam°hym dryʒtyn

deme°   *stream | the Lord may allow*

28

325 Demeʒ þou°me quoþ I my swete   *if you condemn* (f.43b)

To dol°agayn þenne I dowyne°   *sorrow | pine away*

Now haf I fonte þat°I forlete°   *found what | lost*

Schal I efte forgo hit er euer I fyne°   *die*

Why schal I hit boþe mysse & mete°   *lose and find*

330 My precios perle dotʒ me gret pyne°   *sorrow*

What serueʒ tresor bot gareʒ°men grete°   *makes | cry*

When he hit schal efte°wyth teneʒ tyne°   *later | pains lose*

Now rech°I neuer for to declyne   *care*

Ne how fer of folde°þat man me

fleme°   *far from earth | may drive me*

335 When I am partleʒ°of perle myne   *deprived*

Bot durande doel°what may men deme°   *lasting sorrow | call it*

29

Thow demeʒ noʒt bot°doel-dystresse   *of only*

Þenne sayde þat wyʒt why dotʒ þou so

319. counsayl: Go, Gn counsayle.
323. man: MS, Go, H ma.
331. gareʒ: Go gare.
335. perle: MS perleʒ.

---

333. *declyne*: Variously translated,   perity seems intended.
the idea of a fall from material pros-

For dyne of doel of lureʒ lesse
340 Ofte mony°mon forgos þe mo°   *many a / greater*
Þe oʒte better þyseluen blesse
& loue ay God & wele & wo
For anger gayneʒ þe not a cresse°   *watercress*
Who nedeʒ schal þole° be not so þro°   *must suffer / bold*
345 For þoʒ þou daunce as any do°   *doe*
Braundysch°& bray þy braþeʒ breme°   *toss about / agonies fierce*
When þou no fyrre may° to ne°fro   *farther can / or*
Þou moste abyde þat he schal deme

30

Deme dryʒtyn euer hym adyte
350 Of þe way a fote ne wyl he wryþe
Þy mendeʒ mounteʒ not a myte
Þaʒ þou for sorʒe be neuer blyþe
Stynst of þy strot & fyne to flyte
& sech hys blyþe°ful swefte & swyþe°   *seek his mercy / quickly*
355 Þy prayer may hys pyte byte°   *move*

342. & wele: Go, Gn in wele.
353. Stynst: Go, Gn Stynt.

---

339. "For sound of lamentations of lesser woes."

342. *& wele & wo*: Go and Gn emend to *in wele & wo*. The idea, however, of loving all God's creation and of accepting all experience, good and bad, is so much a part of the *Gawain*-poet's creed (cf. *Patience*, 7–8) that the line had best not be emended.

349–50. *adyte*: Surely Emerson and Gn are right in deriving this from OF *aditer*, "to accuse," rather than, as Go and O, from OE *adihtan*, "dispose." Thus, "Judge God, ever accuse Him,

from his path not one foot will He turn" (see Ps. 50:6) is the sense of the stanza.

351. *mendeʒ*: H must surely be right in seeing this as a plural form of *mynde* rather than as a derivative of OF *amende*, "recompense," as do the older editors. The point here is, of course, that the dreamer's opinions of God's values "do not amount to a mite," not that the recompenses of the contrite are meaningless.

353. *stynst*: There is little need to emend to *stynt* as do Gn and Go since,

Þat mercy schal hyr crafteȝ kyþe°   *powers show*
Hys comforte may þy langour lyþe°   *grief assuage*
& þy lureȝ of lyȝtly fleme
For marre oþer madde morne & myþe
360 Al lys in hym to dyȝt & deme

VII/31

Thenne demed° I to þat damyselle   *said* (f.44a)
Ne worþe° no wrathþe vnto my lorde   *let there be*

358. &: Go þat alle.
358. fleme: ms, Go, O, H leme.
359. marre: O, Go marred.

---

as Savage points out, *stynst* is the "correct form of imperative singular." Translate "Cease your arguing and put an end to chiding."

358. *fleme*: ms *leme* is followed by the other editors though with various explanations of derivation and meaning. Go, like Emerson, associated it with oe *lēoma*, "light," though he translated *leme of* as "glance off." O derived it from on *lemja* and translated it "beat, drive with blows," though *lemja*, strictly speaking, means "to lame," not to "beat off." Wright attempted a derivation from the northern English dialect *leam*, "to separate nuts from the husk." All in all, Gn's emendation to *fleme* from oe *flēman* (cf. 34), which together with *of* will give "banish," seems best.

359-60. "For whether you lament or rage, or mourn secretly, it lies with God to ordain and judge." See Gn's note for argument supporting *marre oþer madde* as "lament or rage."

361–420. *blysse*: The word *blysse*

which appears in the refrain of section VII refers, according to Hamilton, *only* to "eternal blessedness." Thus, she argues, if the pearl were a child, the dreamer "would have been liable to ecclesiastical censure for asserting that the blessed condition of his child in heaven, or of any other creature, was the foundation of all of his bliss, the highway to his own beatitude." Therefore, she continues, the poet must be addressing his own soul, if these statements are not "rank impiety" or "naive heresy." Needless to say. Hamilton's analysis of the poet's use of *blysse* in the poem is clearly tailored to her interpretation of the poem.

Incidentally the *NED* lists uses of "bliss" denoting secular joy centuries before the poet's time. As Morton Bloomfield remarks, "even if *blysse* were only religious, anyone could use it in a slightly different sense." As to ecclesiastical censure, Bloomfield notes that "more freedom was allowed Catholics before Trent" than after.

If rapely°I raue spornande in spelle° *rashly / stumbling in speech*
My herte watȝ al wyth mysse remorde°   *loss tormented*
365 As wallande water gotȝ out of welle
I do me°ay in hys myserecorde°   *put myself / mercy*
Rebuke me neuer wyth wordeȝ felle°   *cruel*
Þaȝ I forloyne° my dere endorde°   *lose / adored one*
Bot lyþeȝ°me kyndely your coumforde   *show*
370 Pytosly þenkande vpon þysse
Of care & me ȝe made acorde
Þat er watȝ grounde of alle my blysse

32

My blysse my bale ȝe han ben boþe
Bot much þe bygger ȝet watȝ my mon°   *grief*
375 Fro þou watȝ wroken fro vch a woþe
I wyste neuer quere my perle watȝ gon
Now I hit se now leþeȝ°my loþe°   *abates / woe*
& quen we departed we wern at on
God forbede we be now wroþe

363. I: *not in* MS.
369. lyþeȝ: Go, Gn kyþeȝ.
369. kyndely your: O kyndely with your.

364–65. These lines are clearly reminiscent of the Psalmist's *Sicut aqua effusus sum* and are part of the poet's constant appeal to Scripture for both argument and imagery.

365. gotȝ: Gn feels that *gotȝ out of welle* is a "contact clause" to be translated "like rushing water that runs from a fountain." Hamilton thinks that *gotȝ*, like *yot* in 10, is derived from OE *gēotan*.

375. woþe: O and Gn derive from ON *váði*, "peril, danger," and Sisam

and Tolkien translate "From the time when you were removed from every peril." Go, Wright, Savage, and H all derive from OE *waþ*, "path." *Fro vch a woþe* may thus mean "from every path" (Go), "from (my) daily life" (Savage and Wright), or "from every search" (H).

378–80. Translate: "And (since) when we separated we were in accord, God forbid we should be angry; we meet so seldom anywhere (by tree or stone)."

380 We meten so selden by stok oþer ston
    Þaȝ cortaysly ȝe carp con°   *can speak*
    I am bot mol and mariereȝ mysse
    Bot Crystes mersy & Mary & Jon
    Þise arn þe grounde of alle my blisse

33

385 In blysse I se þe blyþely blent°   *placed*
    & I a man al mornyf mate°   *mournful and sad*
    Ȝe take þeron ful lyttel tente°   *attention*
    Þaȝ I hente°ofte harmeȝ hate   *get*
    Bot now I am here in your presente
390 I wolde bysech wythouten debate
    Ȝe wolde me say in sobre asente
    What lyf ȝe lede erly & late
    For I am ful fayn°þat your astate   *glad*

381. carp: G carpe.
382. mariereȝ: MS, O marereȝ; H mare reȝ;
    Go, Gn manereȝ.

---

382. *mariereȝ mysse*: This phrase has been variously emended and interpreted. Go and Gn read *I . . . manereȝ mysse* ("I . . . lack manners"), although "manners" in this sense is not listed by *NED* until the late sixteenth century. H reads *I . . . mare reȝ mysse* ("I . . . lack great eloquence"). O kept *marereȝ mysse* and glossed the phrase a "botcher's blunder," a reading upheld by C. Hugh Holman (MLN 66: 33–36) on the grounds that it reflects Jer. 18:1–6, and rejected by H on the grounds that the "application of the term 'botcher' to God, the Creator, would constitute a blasphemy."

The best suggestion may well be that of Schofield (PMLA 24:603), who suggests that *mariereȝ*, "pearls," may have been intended. Upholding this reading, Hamilton says "contrasting himself with her, splendid in pearls, he might well say, 'I am but dust, and lack(ing) in pearls [virtue].' "

383: *mersy*: Not, of course, that of Mary and John, but of Christ only. The poet is thinking here either of the familiar grouping of the Crucifixion scene, observed on the rood screen of innumerable parish churches or, as Hamilton suggests, of Mary and John as mediators of the Last Judgment.

388. *harmeȝ hate*: "burning wrongs" (H).

Is worþen to worschyp & wele iwysse
395 Of alle my joy þe hyȝe gate°   road
Hit is in grounde of alle my blysse

34

Now blysse burne° mot þe bytyde°   man / befall (f.44b)
Þen sayde þat lufsoum° of lyth & lere°   lovely / limb and face
& welcum here to walk & byde
400 For now þy speche is to me dere
Maysterful mod°& hyȝe pryde   lordly spirit
I hete° þe arn heterly° hated here   assure / bitterly
My lorde ne loueȝ not for to chyde
For meke arn alle þat woneȝ hym nere
405 & when in hys place þou schal apere
Be dep deuote in hol°mekenesse   all
My lorde þe lamb loueȝ ay such chere°   expression
Þat is þe grounde of alle my blysse

35

A blysful lyf þou says I lede
410 Þou woldeȝ knaw þerof þe stage°   state
Þow wost°wel when þy perle con schede°   know / fell
I watȝ ful ȝong & tender of age
Bot my lorde þe lombe þurȝ hys godhede
He toke myself to hys maryage
415 Corounde me quene in blysse to brede°   flourish
In lenghe of dayeȝ þat euer schal wage°   endure
& sesed in°alle hys herytage   put in possession of
Hys lef°is I am holy hysse   beloved

---

394. "Has become one of honor and
prosperity indeed."
396. *in grounde of*: "at the founda-
tion of" (Gn).
417. *herytage*: As "heirs of God,

and joint heirs with Christ" (Rom.
8:16–17). The poem is, in fact, full
of legal and feudal language. (See
Kean, 185ff.)

Hys prese° hys prys & hys parage°   *worth / high rank*
Is rote & grounde of alle my blysse

VIII/36

Blysful quoþ I may þys be trwe
Dyspleseȝ not if I speke errour
Art þou þe quene of heueneȝ blwe
Þat al þys worlde schal do honour
425 We leuen on°Marye þat grace of grewe *believe in*
Þat ber a barne of vyrgyn flour
Þe croune fro hyr quo moȝt remwe°   *could remove*
Bot ho hir passed in sum fauour
Now for synglerty o°hyr dousour° *uniqueness of / sweetness*
430 We calle hyr fenyx of Arraby
Þat ferles fleze of°hyr fasor°   *flew from / creator*
Lyk to þe quen of cortaysye

431. ferles: MS freles.

---

425. *þat grace of grewe*: H is doubtless right in seeing in *grace* a personification of Christ and in glossing the phrase "from whom sprang Grace." The Blessed Virgin is never regarded as a source of grace, though she may be, as indeed may any saint, a channel of grace.

426. *of vyrgyn flour*: Hoxie Fairchild (*TLS*, March 5, 1931), answering a query by M. Whitely (*TLS*, Jan. 15, 1931), suggested that this phrase means simply "flower of the Virgin" and refers to Christ, who "is often regarded as the blossom of 'the rose that bare Jhesu'." Whitely had suggested "out of a spotless virginity," "with unstained virginity," and "a child of purest excellence," none of which seems really appropriate in context.

430. *Fenyx of Arraby*: Here used as a symbol of Mary's unique position as Mother of God in the hierarchy of heaven and earth and of the singularity of her sweetness (429). I have thus followed Hamilton's suggestion, supported by C. A. Luttrell (NQ 207: 447–52), in emending MS *freles* (431) to *ferles*, "peerless, without equal, unique" [*fēre* + *les* from OE *fēra*] as better fitting the comparison to the Phoenix and as paralleling the *makeleȝ moder* of 435. Granted that *freles*, "flawless," does have special relevance here to the Immaculate Conception, there still exists (in spite of H's references to the Phoenix Homily) no evidence that the Phoenix was so conceived and thus no real parallel to the Blessed Virgin. On the other hand, there does exist a comparison based on uniqueness in Albertus Magnus, *De*

37

Cortayse quen þenne sayde þat gaye° *fair one* (f.45a)
Knelande to grounde folde vp hyr face
435 Makeleȝ° moder & myryest may° *matchless / fairest maiden*
Blessed bygyner of vch a grace
Þenne ros ho vp & con restay° *paused*
& speke me towarde in þat space° *time*
Sir fele here porchaseȝ & fongeȝ pray
440 Bot supplantoreȝ°none wythinne þys place *usurpers*
Þat emperise al heuenȝ hatȝ
& vrþe & helle in her bayly° *rule*
Of erytage° ȝet non wyl ho chace *from heritage*
For ho is quen of cortaysye

38

445 The court of þe kyndom of God alyue
Hatȝ a property in hytself beyng
Alle þat may þerinne aryue
Of alle þe reme°is quen oþer kyng *realm*
& neuer oþer ȝet schal depryue
450 Bot vchon fayn°of oþereȝ hafyng° *each one glad / possession*

433. sayde: MS syde.
436. bygyner: MS bȳgyner.
441. heuenȝ: O, H heueneȝ.

Laudibus Beatae Mariae Virginis, in which Mary, "*singularis* in beauty and virtue . . . [is] compared with the phoenix *quae est unica avis sine patre*" (Gn).

432. *quen of cortaysye: regina gratiae*. See Introduction and 4*n*.

434. *folde*: I am inclined to agree with Go, O, and H that the pearl-maiden here covers her face in a gesture of horror at the narrator's blas-phemy in suggesting (423) that she may be the *quene of heueneȝ blwe*. Gn, however, suggests, in his glossary, that she "upturns" her face, presumably to invoke the Blessed Virgin or possibly "in devotion."

439. The editors agree that this line is deliberately rhetorical and contains no theological subtleties. "Many here win the prize they seek."

    & wolde her corouneȝ wern worþe þo fyue°   *five of them*

    If possyble were her mendyng°   *improvement*

    Bot my lady of quom Jesu con spryng

    Ho haldeȝ þe empyre ouer vus ful hyȝe

455 & þat dyspleseȝ non of oure gyng°   *company*

    For ho is quene of cortaysye

39

    Of courtaysye as saytȝ Saynt Poule

    Al arn we membreȝ of Jesu Kryst

    As heued & arme & legg & naule   *head*

460 Temen°to hys body ful trwe & tryste° *are joined* / *faithfully*

    Ryȝt° so is vch a Krysten sawle   *just*

    A longande lym°to þe mayster of myste *limb belonging*

    Þenne loke what hate oþer any gawle°   *bitterness*

    Is tached oþer tyȝed°þy lymmeȝ

       bytwyste°   *attached or tied* / *between*

465 Þy heued hatȝ nauþer greme ne gryste° *anger nor spite*

    On arme oþer fynger þaȝ þou ber byȝe° *wear a ring*

    So fare we alle wyth luf & lyste°   *joy*

    To kyng & quene by cortaysye

457. Poule: O, Go Paule.
460. tryste: ᴍѕ, O tyste.
461. sawle: ᴍѕ sawhe.

---

459. *naule*: Almost certainly "navel." We must remember that the navel in medieval times had none of the "modern associations of indelicacy" (Go). The stanza follows St. Paul's explication of the body of the church in 1 Cor. 12:12–31.

460. *tryste*: ᴍѕ *tyste*. An emendation first made by Go and followed by subsequent editors, with the exception of O, who takes *tyste* to be a variant of *tyȝte*, "thus spelled for the sake of rime." *Trwe and tryste* is, however, a common alliterative phrase.

462. *myste*: Like Gn and H, I believe this not to be a form of *myȝte*, "might," but, as the *NED* states, a noun meaning "spiritual mysteries." See Gn's note for instances. Wright derives from ᴏꜰ *miste* and translates "graciousness, courtesy."

40

Cortayse quoþ I I leue°   *believe* (f.45b)
470 & charyte grete be yow among
Bot my speche þat yow ne greue°   *may not grieve you*

. . . .

Þyself in heuen ouer hyȝ þou heue°   *raise*
To make þe quen þat watȝ so ȝonge
475 What more honour moȝte he acheue
Þat hade endured in worlde stronge°   *firmly*
& lyued in penaunce hys lyueȝ longe
Wyth bodyly bale°hym blysse to byye°   *harm / buy*
What more worschyp moȝt he fonge°   *get*
480 Þen corounde be kyng by cortayse

IX/41

That cortayse is to fre°of dede   *lavish*
ȝyf hyt be soth þat þou coneȝ saye
Þou lyfed not two ȝer in oure þede°   *land*
Þou cowþeȝ°neuer God nauþer plese ne pray   *could*
485 Ne neuer nawþer° Pater ne Crede   *nor ever knew either*

479. he: MS ho.

---

472. Sense and the usual occurrence of twelve lines per stanza (not MS spacing) indicate a missing line. Go supplies *Me þynk þou spekeȝ now ful wronge.*

483–85. Like 411–12 and the passages listed in the Introduction these lines with their references to the child's age and lack of education strongly support the elegiac theory. It is therefore interesting to watch the allegorists at work here. H, for example, maintains that the pearl was imported into England from the Orient only two years before its loss; thus, somehow confusing the actual material pearl with the maiden standing before him, the narrator rebukes a pagan jewel for not having learned Christian prayers and teaching.

485. *Pater ne Crede*: As O says, "from Bede's time down the English clergy were instructed to see that the people, *particularly the children,* should know at least the Pater Noster and the Creed" (italics mine).

& quen mad on þe fyrst day
I may not traw° so God me spede   *cannot believe*
Þat God wolde wryþe° so wrange° away   *turn / wrong*
Of countes damysel par ma fay
490 Wer° fayr in heuen to halde asstate   *it would be*
Oþer elleʒ a lady of lasse aray°   *lesser position*
Bot a quene hit is to dere a date

42

Þer is no date of hys godnesse
Þen sayde to me þat worþy wyʒte
495 For al is trawþe þat he con dresse°   *established*
& he may do noþynk bot ryʒt
As Mathew meleʒ°in your messe   *speaks*
In sothfol°gospel of God almtʒt   *truthful*
In sample°he can ful grayþely gesse°   *parable / fittingly devise*
500 & lykenʒ hit to heuen lyʒte°   *bright*
My regne he saytʒ is lyk on hyʒt
To a lorde þat hade a uyne° I wate°   *vineyard / know*
Of tyme of ʒere þe terme watʒ tyʒt°   *time was come*
To labor vyne watʒ dere°þe date°   *good / time*

486. fyrst: Go fyrste.
491. Oþer: O Aþer.

489. *damysel*: As Gn points out, this term is here used in a tone of reproof very like the modern use of "miss" or, better still, the southern U.S. "missy."

492. *to dere a date*: Since *date* is needed as the linking word in the next group of stanzas, its meaning and that of *dere* are severely expanded by the poet. A gloss to each of the refrains may be thus helpful. Here the phrase means "it is too high a *goal*."

497. *your messe*: As Go implied, the operative word here is *your*, signifying the detachment of the maiden from earthly worship. The Mass referred to is that of Septuagesima where the parable of the vineyard (Matt. 20:1–16) is read as Gospel.

504. "The *time* to work the vineyard was precious."

43

505 Þat date of ȝere wel knawe þys hyne   (f.46a)
Þe lorde ful erly vp he ros
To hyre werkmen to hys vyne
& fyndeȝ þer summe to hys porpos
Into acorde þay con declyne°   consented
510 For a pene on a day & forth þay gotȝ
Wryþen°& worchen & don gret pyne°   twist / toil
Keruen & caggen°& man°hit clos   cut and bind / make
Aboute vnder þe lorde to marked totȝ°   market goes
& ydel men stande°he fyndeȝ þerate   standing
515 Why stande ȝe ydel he sayde to þos
Ne knawe ȝe of þis day no date°   end

44

Er date of daye hider arn we wonne°   come
So watȝ al samen her answar soȝt
We haf standen her syn ros þe sunne
520 & no mon byddeȝ vus do ryȝt noȝt
Gos°into my vyne dotȝ þat ȝe conne°   go / can
So sayde þe lorde & made hit toȝt°   an agreement

505. þys hyne: Go hys hyne.
510. on: Go omits.

---

505. *þys hyne*: Go and H see these as the "householders," O and Gn, rightly I think, as the "labourers." The word "hind" designating laborers is of such ancient and widespread use, however, that I cannot conceive the poet using it in a way which would certainly confuse his audience.

510. *a pene on a day*: Apparently simply an idiom. Emerson, however, had an ingenious explanation of the presence of *on* here, that "the copyist had corrected his own mistake by writing *a* after *on*, but without erasing the former."

512. *clos*: "neat, trim" (Wright).

516. "Do you know the *time* of day?"

518. *soȝt*: I fully agree with Go and Gn that this is a form of *sech* [OE *sēcan*], "to seek" and should be here rendered "given." O and H derive it from OE *swogan*, "to murmur."

What resonabele hyre be naȝt be runne
I yow pay in dede & þoȝte
525 Þay wente into þe vyne & wroȝte°   *worked*
 & al day þe lorde þus ȝede°his gate°   *went / way*
 & nw men to hys vyne he broȝte
 Welneȝ wyl° day watȝ passed date   *almost until*

45

 At þe date°of day of euensonge   *time*
530 On oure°byfore þe sonne go doun   *one hour*
 He seȝ þer ydel men ful stronge
 & sade to hem wyth sobre soun
 Wy stonde ȝe ydel þise dayeȝ longe
 Þay sayden her hyre watȝ nawhere boun
535 Gotȝ to my vyne ȝemen°ȝonge   *yeomen*
 & wyrkeȝ & dotȝ þat at ȝe moun

523. resonabele: Go resnabele.
524. pay: ms, H pray.
527. nw: Go nwe.
529. date of day: ms, H day of date.
532. sade: O sayde.
532. hem: ms hen.

---

523. "Whatever wage has accumulated by nightfall."

524. pay: Only R. Morris and H accept the ms reading of *pray.* H ends the lord's speech at 521, treats 522–23 parenthetically, then begins the lord's speech at 524 with "I call on [pray] you through bond and intent." As Gn points out, *pay* is "a survival of the old use of the present to express future tense."

524. *in dede & þoȝte:* "in performance and intention" (Gn), or possibly "both by right of contract (522–23)

and by reason of good intentions" (H).

528. "Until the day was almost *past.*"

529. *date of day:* ms *day of date.* Though the ms reading can indeed be justified (note Savage's "At [in] the day at the time of evening"), it seems more likely that the scribe simply inverted the alliterating words.

534. "They said 'their service was nowhere engaged'" (O).

536. *þat at ȝe moun:* "whatever you can."

Sone þe worlde bycom wel broun°   *dark*
Þe sunne watȝ doun & hit wex late
To take her hyre he mad sumoun°   *gave summons*
540 Þe day watȝ al apassed date

X/46

The date of þe daye þe lorde con knaw°   *knew* (f.46b)
Called to þe reue° lede°pay þe meyny° *steward / man / company*
Gyf hem þe hyre þat I hem owe
& fyrre þat non me may reprene°   *reprove*
545 Set hem alle vpon a rawe°   *row*
& gyf vchon inlyche°a peny   *give each one alike*
Bygyn at þe laste þat standeȝ lowe
Tyl to þe fyrste þat þou atteny°   *reach*
& þenne þe fyrst bygonne to pleny°   *complain*
550 & sayden þat þay hade trauayled°sore   *worked*
Þese bot on oure hem con streny
Vus þynk vus oȝe°to take more   *it seems to us we ought*

47

More haf we serued vus þynk so
Þat suffred han þe dayeȝ hete
555 Þenn þyse þat wroȝt°not houreȝ two   *worked*
& þou dotȝ hem vus to counterfete°   *resemble*

538. &: ᴍs, H & &.
542. meyny: Go meny.
543. owe: Go awe.
544. reprene: O, Go, H repreny.
547. lowe: Go lawe.
550. hade: H had.

---

540. "The day was wholly at an end." In spite of my rather free glosses, it is apparent that the basic sense of *date* in this section is "limit," an idea implied in each of its uses noted above and emphasized by the maiden's *þer is no date of hys godnesse* (493).

551. "These only one hour exerted themselves."

Þenne sayde þe lorde to on°of þo°   *one / those*
Frende no waning I wyl þe ȝete
Take þat is þyn owne & go
560 & I hyred þe for a peny agrete
Quy bygynneȝ þou now to þrete°   *quarrel*
Watȝ not a pene°þy couenaunt þore°   *penny / agreement then*
Fyrre þen couenaunde°is noȝt to plete°   *agreement / plead*
Wy schalte þou þenne ask more

48

565 More° weþer louyly° is me my gyfte   *moreover / lawful*
To do wyth myn quatso me lykeȝ
Oþer elleȝ þyn yȝe to lyþer is lyfte
For I am goude & non byswykeȝ°   *cheat no one*
Þus schal I quoþ Kryste hit skyfte°   *ordain*
570 Þe laste schal be þe fyrst þat strykeȝ°   *goes*
& þe fyrst þe laste be he neuer so swyft
For mony ben calle þaȝ fewe be mykeȝ

558. waning: MS, H wanig.
564. ask: Go aske.
565. louyly: O lawely; Go leuyly.
572. calle: O, Go, Gn called.

558. *waning*: D. C. Fowler (MLN 74:581–84) is almost certainly correct in deriving *waning* from OE *wānung*, "lamentation" in spite of the linguistic and scriptural difficulties, rather than from OE *wanung*, "loss, deprivation." The line thus reads, "I will allow you no lamentation."

560. *agrete*: O and Go gloss as "for the particular job," Gn as "all together."

565–67. See Matt. 20:15.

567. *to lyþer is lyfte*: Emerson thought *lyfte* a noun, "weak, worth-

less," and *to lyþer* a strengthening adverb, "too wickedly." The usual construction, however, regards *lyfte* as a participle and *lyþer* as the noun "evil." Thus the line reads "or else your eye is turned to evil."

572. *calle*: There is no need to emend this to *called* since, as Savage points out, *calle* is a legitimate past tense.

572. *mykeȝ*: Used to translate *electi* in *multi sunt enim vocati, pauci autem electi* (Matt. 20:20), this almost certainly derives eventually from Latin

Þus pore men her part ay pykeȝ°   *get*
Þaȝ þay com late & lyttel wore°   *humble were*
575 & þaȝ her sweng wyth lyttel atslykeȝ
Þe merci of God is much þe more

49

More haf I of ioye & blysse hereinne   *(f.47a)*
Of ladyschyp gret & lyueȝ blom°   *bloom of life*
Þen alle þe wyȝeȝ in þe worlde myȝt wynne
580 By þe way of ryȝt to aske dome
Wheþer welnygh now I con bygynne
In euentyde into þe vyne I come°   *came*
Fyrst of my hyre my lorde con mynne°   *remembered*
I watȝ payed anon of al & sum°   *at once in full*
585 ȝet oþer þer werne þat toke more tom°   *time*
Þat swange & swat°for long ȝore° *toiled and sweated | past*
Þat ȝet of hyre noþynk þay nom°   *got*
Paraunter noȝt schal toȝere°more   *this year*

50

Then more I meled°& sayde apert°   *spoke | openly*
590 Me þynk þy tale vnresounable
Goddeȝ ryȝt° is redy & euermore rert°   *justice | exalted*
Oþer holy wyrt is bot a fable
In Sauter°is sayd a verce ouerte°   *the Psalter | plain*
Þat spekeȝ a poynt determynable
595 Þou quyteȝ vchon°as hys desserte   *reward each one*

577. ioye: Go, Gn joye.

---

amicus through OF *amike*, but seems also related to OE *mæcca*, "companion." See H's note for various etymologies.

575. atslykeȝ: Emerson thought this to be derived from OE *slican*,

"strike," and translated "And though their blow strikes with little (effect)."

580. "If they were to ask judgment according to right."

581. *Wheþer*: "Although" (Savage).

Þou hyӡe kyng ay pretermynable
Now he þat stod þe long day stable°   *firm*
& þou to payment com hym byfore
Þenne þe lasse in werke to take more able
600 & euer þe lenger þe lasse þe more

IX/51

Of more & lasse in Godeӡ ryche°   *kingdom*
Þat gentyl sayde lys no joparde°   *lies no doubt*
For þer is vch mon payed inlyche
Wheþer lyttel oþer much be hys rewarde

596. pretermynable: ᴍs pertermynable.

---

596. *pretermynable*: A nonce word, *NED* guesses that it may be an English rendering of a scholastic term *preterminabilis*, "predetermining." Go translates "preordained," O "foreordaining," Gn "who pre-ordains," H "before the terminable," hence "Eternal, Infinite." Kean thinks *per-* or *partermynable*, "who above all others givest just judgment," to be the correct form.

A remarkable explanation has been brought forward by R. E. Kaske (Trad 15:418–28), who declares that the ᴍs form *pertermynable* is correct and that the word, derived from ʟᴍᴇ *ternyne* (from ᴏғ *terminer*) "to declare, affirm" plus the suffix *able* and the prefix *per*, means "endurance in time." Kaske defends this interpretation by reference to the comments of the fathers on Ps. 61:13, referring to the "enduring and immutable speech of God . . . , conventionally explained, in accord with the three following lines of the psalm, as

the enduring expression of His *potentia* and His *misericordia*." The function of the word here is thus to "support . . . the dreamer's mistaken argument for a strict correspondence between earthly works and eternal rewards."

599–600. "Then the less work done the more the ability to earn; and ever the less, the more able to earn."

603–604. *inlyche . . . rewarde*: These lines may contain the theological and perhaps also the thematic center of the poem, since here is argued closely the one issue that seems best to crystallize the widely divergent points of view that separate narrator and child (see Introduction). The maiden, having just recounted the parable of the vineyard and applied its meaning to herself (582–84), sets about to answer the narrator's objection that her account is *vnresounable* since it discounts absolutely the doctrine of reward according to merit in favor of reward by grace. The crux of her

605 For þe gentyl cheuentayn°is no chyche°   *chieftain / niggard*
     Queþersoeuer he dele nesch° oþer harde   *soft*
     He lauez°hys gyftez as water of dyche°   *pours / from a ditch*
     Oþer gotez°of golf°þat neuer
        charde°   *streams / a gulf / would cease*

---

argument lies in these lines and centers in the terms *inlyche* and *rewarde*.

Inlyche, which Emerson called an "historically impossible" form, is difficult because one expects *ilyche*, "alike." Both Emerson and Gn thus understandably regard *inlyche* as an expansion from OE *ilyche*. However, the OE adverb *inlice*, "thoroughly, fully," could very well be the source of the term. The major question here is whether the maiden means that each saved soul is paid "alike," a theory subscribed to by Emerson, Go, O, Gn, and C. Brown (PMLA 19:115–23), or whether she means that each is paid "fully" as suggested by Marie Hamilton (MLN 58:370–72), although Hamilton herself translates *inlyche* in an earlier line (546) as "alike." "Alike" stresses God's impartiality, whereas "fully" stresses His generosity.

This controversy is, I think, more semantic than real and may be resolved, theologically, by means of two doctrines, either or both of which were probably held by the poet. First, as in the quotation from *The Ladder of Perfection* cited in H's note, the medieval church recognized two forms of reward, the first "*Sovereign* and *Principal* . . . called *Essential Reward*" which is given purely by grace—in Protestant terms, Justification—and "*Secondary,* or *Accidental,* which our Lord giveth for special good deeds"— roughly approaching Protestant Sanctification.

A better explanation and solution, however, is contained in the idea that each soul is paid fully and, because fully, alike, though not identically. As J. R. Sledd (MLN 55:379–82) says, "the poet possibly held that all the blessed are rewarded alike, since they are all in the presence of God, but that they are not rewarded equally, since they differ in their spiritual capacity to realize His presence."

The best explanation in lay terms of this apparent paradox is that of Dorothy L. Sayers, made in explanation of the apparent inequalities of Dante's hierarchy in Paradise. Sayers notes that "there is equality in the sense that all the souls alike are as full of bliss as they are capable of being; but between soul and soul there is no formal equality at all. The pint-pot and the quart-pot are *equally full*: but there is no pretense that a pint and a quart are the same thing; neither does the pint-pot ever dream of saying to the quart-pot, 'I'm as good as you are'—still less of saying, 'It isn't fair that you should hold more than I' " (*Introductory Papers on Dante,* 57).

The meaning of *rewarde* in the next line is closely linked to that of *inlyche*. Those who translate *inlyche* "alike"

Hys fraunchyse is large þat euer dard
610 To hym þat matȝ in synne rescoghe

---

prefer that *rewarde* be "regard, consideration," or "what is due as recognition of merit." Those who translate *inlyche* "fully" translate *rewarde* simply "reward." Sledd's article (noted above) reviews the evidence for both opinions.

Whatever the opinion of the reader, he should hold in mind that the purpose of the maiden, and of the poet, is *not* to raise the complex issues of grace vs. merit simply for their own sakes, but to use their inherent paradoxes as a dramatic means of contrasting the full faith and knowledge of the maiden with the limited faith and knowledge of the narrator (see Introduction).

609–10. I can best begin this note by quoting Gn: "A notoriously difficult passage: the reference of the pronouns is uncertain: *fraunchyse* may mean either 'generosity' (of God) or 'privilege, liberation' (of the man *þat ever dard*); and there are two verbs which could give past tense *dard* in Middle English, OE *durran* 'dare' and OE *darian* 'lurk in dread.'" Following are the editors' translations, offered without comment:

Go: Large is his freedom who hath fear'd 'fore Him that rescueth in sin.

Menner: His (God's) liberality, which has ever been unsearchable, abounds to all. To the man who makes amendment for sin (or repents) no blessing shall be denied.

O: That man's privilege is large who (in temptation) ever resorted [*fard* rather than *dard*] to him that giveth succor in sin.

Gn (preferred): That man's privilege is great who ever stood in awe of Him who rescues sinners.

H: Ample is his heritage who always reverence paid / To Him who makes rescue in the case of sin.

Three recent interpretations shed additional light on the passage. F. T. Visser (ES 39:20–23) took *dard/ To hym* as "dared to go to Him" and so translated: "that man's privilege is great who (at a certain moment in his life) had the courage to go or turn to Him [God] who rescues sinners." In a similar vein Savage, following Wright, had derived *dard* from OF *darder*, "gush out."

R. E. Kaske (Trad 15:418–28) referred the lines to John 1:14, 16–18, and to a number of patristical exegeses of these verses. Kaske translated *þat ever dard* as "who was ever hidden *or* unseen" and construed the phrase as modifying *Hys* and as containing an allusion to verse 18. Kaske took the whole of 609 as a reference to God the Father which in turn clarifies 610 as a "characterizing circumlocution for Christ, the 'unigenitus Filius' of John 1:18." Thus Kaske translated: "The 'liberality of intimacy and grace . . . of Him who was ever hidden (God the Father) is abundant to Him who makes rescue in sin (God the Son, incarnate in Christ)." It is difficult to see, however, how Kaske's reconstruction fits the argument of the poem at

No blysse betȝ°fro hem reparde°   *is / withheld*
For þe grace of God is gret inoghe°   *enough*

52

Bot now þou moteȝ° me for to mate°   *argue / confuse* (f.47b)
Þat I my peny haf wrang tan°here   *wrongly taken*
615 Þou sayȝ þat I þat com to late
Am not worþy so gret fere
Where wysteȝ þou euer any bourne abate
Euer so holy in hys prayere
Þat he ne forfeted by sumkyn gate°   *some kind of way*
620 Þe mede°sumtyme of heueneȝ clere   *reward*

615. com: Gn, H come.
616. fere: MS, H lere; O, Go here.

---

this point. Bruce Mitchell (NQ 259: 47), whose note interestingly begins with the assertion that *daren* in the sense of "to stand in awe of" and the referent of *hym* in 610 as God "should now be regarded as settled," takes *fraunchyse* as "spiritual freedom" and so renders the lines: "That man finds a new Paradise (or Eden) who stands in awe of him who rescues sinners."

611. *hem*: Presumably a use, like that of *þay* in 621 and 626 and *her* in 687, of the plural pronoun after an indefinite singular, "the reverent man" referred to in 610, the *bourne* of 617, the *innocent* of 625, and *the ryȝtwys man* of 685.

616. *fere*: Only H keeps the MS reading *lere* which she takes as a variant of *lure*, "recompence," referring to the *peny* promised the laborers. O and Go both amend to *here*, "wages." I much prefer Gn's *fere*, derived ul-

timately from OF *afe(i)re* and meaning here "rank" or "dignity."

617. *abate*: "remain, endure" (Go, O, Gn); "cast down, humbled" (Emerson); "abate, slacken, lose zeal" (H). H's statement that to translate the lines: "Where did you ever know of a man remaining so constant in prayer that he did not somehow forfeit the hope of heaven" is to go counter to Christian teaching hardly seems justified. The maiden here is simply affirming the fallen state of man and the impossibility of human perfectability, doctrines which, in spite of the notion that some men merit sainthood for blameless lives, have always been integral parts of Christian dogma.

618. *holy*: Savage and Wright take this as a variant spelling of "wholly" and regard it as modifying *abate*, "so wholly humbled."

& ay þe ofter° þe alder þay were — *oftener*
Þay laften°ryȝt & wroȝten woghe° — *abandoned / did evil*
Mercy & grace moste hem þen stere° — *guide*
For þe grace of God is gret innoȝe

53

625 Bot innoghe of grace hatȝ innocent° — *the innocent*
As sone as þay arn borne by lyne
In þe water of babtem þay dyssente
Þen arne þay boroȝt into þe vyne
Anon þe day wyth derk endente
630 Þe niyȝt of deth dotȝ to enclyne.
Þat wroȝt neuer wrang er þenne þay wente
Þe gentyle lorde þenne payeȝ hys hyne° — *as his workers*
Þay dyden°hys heste° þay wern
þereine — *followed / commandment*
Why schulde he not her labour alow° — *credit*
635 ȝys° & pay hem at þe fyrst fyne — *indeed*
For þe grace of God is gret innoghe

630. niyȝt: ms *difficult*; O, Go, H myȝt.
635. ȝys & pay: O ȝy . . . & pay.
635. hem: ms, H hym.
635. fyrst: Go fyrste.

---

626. *borne by lyne*: Hamilton agrees with Emerson that this phrase means "born by lineal descent" not "in succession," as O and Go claim. Hamilton translates, " 'The innocent have grace enough, as soon as they are born by lineal descent—as soon as they are regenerate, born to the supernatural order." H translates "in order of birth," but does not explain the basis of her translation.

630. *niyȝt*: ms is very difficult here

and all editors except Gn read *myȝt*, the "might of death," which makes, of course, perfectly good sense. However, *niyȝt* or *nyȝt* (Kölbing and Savage) does complete the image pattern of day and night which the poet began with the day-life, night-death image pattern inherent in the parable of the vineyard. Thus 629–30: "Anon the day, laid over with darkness, sinks to the night of death."

635. *at the fyrst fyne*: Like Gn, I

54

Inoʒe is knawen þat mankyn grete
Fyrste watʒ wrotʒ to blysse parfyt
Oure forme fader°hit con forfete   *first father*
640 Þurʒ an apple þat he vpon con byte
Al wer we dampned for þat mete
To dyʒe in doel out of delyt
& syþen wende to helle hete°   *hell's heat*
Þerinne to won wythoute respyt
645 Bot þeron com a bote astyt°   *remedy at once*
Ryche blod ran on rode°so roghe°   *the cross | cruel*
& wynne°water þen at þat plyt°   *precious | perilous time*
Þe grace of God wex gret innoghe

55

Innoghe þer wax° out of þat welle   *flowed (f.48a)*
650 Blod & water of brode wounde
Þe blod vus boʒt fro bale of helle
& delyuered vus of þe deth secounde

645. þeron com: O þer oncom; Go þer on-com.
649. out: MS out out.

---

much prefer Wright's suggestion that *at the fyrst* "is an adverbial phrase, and *fyne* an adverb, 'Pay them first in full' " to the older editors' "at the first end" and certainly to H's "at the first furrow." Carter Revard (ELN 1:164–66) takes *fyne* to be a noun and translates "according to the original contract."

637–60. Hamilton (PMLA 70:805–24) regards this resume of the Fall and the Redemption as the center of the poem (see Introduction).

642. "To die in sorrow away from joy."

645. *þeron com*: O read *oncom*, "supervene" and Go *on-com*.

647–48. Go and H place a semicolon after *water*, a reading which, as H says, seems to enforce the doctrine that "grace from God increased" at the death of Christ, *at þat plyt*. The phrase *at þat plyt* seems to me, however, clearly to modify *ran* (646) and certainly 648 may stand on its own as a general commentary.

652. *þe deth secounde*: The condemnation of the damned at the Last Judgment.

Þe water is baptem þe soþe to telle

Þat folȝed°þe glayue°so grymly°

    grounde   *followed | spear | cruelly*

655 Þat wascheȝ away þe gylteȝ felle°   *sins deadly*

Þat Adam wyth°inne deth vus drounde   *with which Adam*

Now is þer noȝt in þe worlde rounde

Bytwene vus & blysse bot þat° he

    wythdroȝ°   *except what | removed*

& þat is restored in sely stounde°   *a blessed hour*

660 & þe grace of God is gret innogh

XII/56

Grace innogh þe mon may haue

Þat synneȝ þenne new ȝif him repente

Bot wyth sorȝ & syt° he mot°hit craue   *sorrow and grief | must*

& byde þe payne þerto is bent°   *which is with it bound*

665 Bot resoun of ryȝt þat con noȝt raue°   *cannot stray*

Saueȝ euermore þe innossent

Hit is a dom°þat neuer God gaue   *judgment*

Þat euer þe gyltleȝ schulde be schente°   *discomfited*

Þe gyltyf may°contryssyoun hente°   *guilty can | find*

670 & be þurȝ mercy to grace þryȝt°   *led*

---

653. *Þe water is baptem*: The quotations from St. Anselm and others brought forward by O show this to be a familiar piece of medieval symbolism.

658. *he*: One must agree with H that the antecedent of *he* is Adam (656), who did indeed take away the bliss of intuitive grace.

661ff. I can do no better here than to quote O's excellent summary of the essential doctrine expounded in this passage: "Salvation is granted both to the innocent and the contrite. The innocent ever possess it as their right; the contrite obtain it only through repentance, the pain of remorse, and the grace and mercy of God. It is better, if one can, to win salvation by innocence, than to run the risk of failure and the danger of judgment which the other course involves. But, if one is brought to judgment, let him urge in his defense the words of Solomon and David."

Bot he to gyle þat neuer glente°   *turned*
At inoscente is saf & ryȝte

57

Ryȝt þus I knaw wel in þis cas
Two men to saue is God by skylle
675 Þe ryȝtwys man schal se hys face
 Þe harmleȝ haþel° schal com hym tylle°   *man / to*
 Þe Sauter°hyt satȝ°þus in a pace° *Psalter / says / passage*
 Lorde quo schal klymbe þy hyȝ hylle
 Oþer rest wythinne þy holy place
680 Hymself to onsware he is not dylle°   *slow*
 Hondelyngeȝ°harme þat dyt not ille *with the hands*
 Þat is of hert boþe clene & lyȝt°   *pure*
 Þer schal hys step stable stylle°   *stand firm*
 Þe innosent is ay saf by ryȝt

58

685 The ryȝtwys man also sertayn   (f.43b)
 Aproche he schal þat proper pyle°   *fair castle*

672. At: Gn And.
672. inoscente: Go in-oscence.
672. & ryȝte: Go by ryȝte.
673. þus: MS, H þus þus.
675. face: MS fate.
678. hylle: MS hylleȝ.

---

672. *At inoscente*: Go translated, awkwardly, "in innocence"; O and Emerson suggested *þat inoscente*; Gn emended *at* to *and*, translating "And (he that is) innocent." *At*, however, may perfectly well mean "with" or "along with," as H suggests, and the two lines read "But he that never deviated by guile along with the innocent is (both) saved and sanctified." I agree with Gn that *ryȝte* is here an adjective.

674. *God*: I agree here with H that this is "God" rather than "good." The two men whom God will save are the righteous man (675) and the guiltless man (676). Emerson noted that in *Patience* also (13–28) the first and eighth beatitudes are combined and the same reward promised.

674. *by skylle*: "in a true statement" (Wright), "according to reason" (Bloomfield).

Þat takeȝ not her lyf in vayne
Ne glaquereȝ°her nieȝbor wyth no gyle   *cheats*
Of þys ryȝtwys saȝ Salamon playn
690 How koyntise°onoure con aquyle°   *wisdom / obtained*
By wayeȝ ful streȝt ho con hym strayn°   *guide*
& scheued°hym þe rengne°of God awhyle   *showed / kingdom*
As quo°says lo ȝon louely yle   *one who*
Þou may hit wynne if þou be wyȝte°   *brave*
695 Bot hardyly°wythoute peryle   *surely*
Þe innocent is ay saue by ryȝte

59

Anende° ryȝtwys men ȝet saytȝ a gome°   *about / man*
Dauid in Sauter if euer ȝe seȝ°hit   *saw*
Lorde þy seruaunt draȝ°neuer to dome   *bring*

690. koyntise onoure: ᴍꜱ kyntly onre;
     O kyntly oure King hym; Go kyntly oure
     Koyntyse hym; H kyntly onore.
691. ho: ᴍꜱ, O, Go he.
698. seȝ: Go, Gn syȝ.

---

689. *þys ryȝtwys*: The source of 689–94 is Wisd. of Sol. 10:10 (see also H. Bradley, Acad 38:201). The "just man" here alluded to is probably Jacob, who is described in the source as a man ruled by wisdom. See O's notes for details.

689. *saȝ*: Almost certainly "saw" in the sense of "perceived" rather than "says" as Gn maintains.

690. This is an extremely defective line in the ᴍꜱ requiring extensive reconstruction. Gn and O emended to *How kyntly oure [king hym] con aquyle* though Go later changed to *How kyntly oure [Koyntyse hym] con aquyle*, these emendations being based on the fact that medieval scriptural commentators generally identified wisdom with Christ. I am here following Gn who reconstructs the line to read *How [Koyntise on] oure con aquyle* on the grounds that "some word for Wisdom must come into 690 as the subject, and alliteration indicates the word *Koyntise.*"

690. *onoure*: In accord with H, I read the ᴍꜱ form here as *onre*, rather than as *oure* as did Go, Gn, and O.

691. *ho*: Emended from ᴍꜱ *he* to agree with *Koyntise* in 690.

693–94. Adapted from Gen. 28:10–15, Jacob's dream.

698–700. Adapted from Ps. 142:2.

700 For non lyuyande to þe is justyfyet

Forþy° to corte quen þou schal com   *therefore*

Þer alle oure causeʒ schal be tryed

Alegge þe ryʒt þou may be innome°   *refuted*

By þys ilke spech I haue asspyed°   *observed*

705 Bot he on rode° þat blody dyed   *the cross*

Delfully° þurʒ hondeʒ þryʒt°   *grievously / pierced*

Gyue° þe to passe when þou arte tryed   *may he grant*

By innocens & not by ryʒte

60

Ryʒtwysly° quo con rede   *rightly*

710 He loke on bok & be awayed°   *instructed*

How Jesus hym welke in areþede°   *walked among ancient people*

& burneʒ° her barneʒ° vnto hym

brayde°   *persons / children / brought*

For happe & hele þat fro hym ʒede

To touch her chylder þay fayr hym prayed

715 His dessypeleʒ wyth blame let be hem bede°   *bade them cease*

700. For: MS sor.
701. com: Go come.
702. tryed: Go cryed.
709. quo con: Go quo so con.
711, 717, 721. Jesus: MS ihc̄.
715. hem: MS hym.

---

703. *Alegge*: Go and O both treated this as an imperative: "Renounce your claim" (Go), "Urge your privilege" (O). However, Dorothy Everett and Naomi D. Hurnard in an important article (MÆ 16:9) urged that *alegge* be read as a conditional subjunctive, "If you plead right," rather than as an imperative. This is the reading adopted by both Gn and H. Hamilton, however, thinks Hurnard and Everett to be mistaken, believing that the maiden is here "urging the dreamer to repeat David's plea when he comes to the Last Judgment: 'Claim the right'."

713. "For good fortune and healing that from him issued."

714. *touch*: Having inspected the MS, I agree with H that this is the MS form.

& wyth her resouneʒ ful fele restayed°   *many restrained*
Jesus þenne hem swetely sayde
Do way° let chylder vnto me tyʒt°   *cease | come*
To suche is heuenryche arayed°   *heaven's kingdom prepared*
720 Þe innocent is ay saf by ryʒt

XIII/61

Jesus con calle to hym hys mylde
& sayde hys ryche°no wyʒ myʒt wynne   *kingdom* (f.49a)
Bot he com þyder ryʒt as a chylde
Oþer elleʒ neuermore com þerinne
725 Harmleʒ trwe & vndefylde
Wythouten mote oþer mascle°of
          sulpande°synne   *stain or spot | polluting*
Quen such þer cnoken on þe bylde°   *dwelling*
Tyt°schal hem men þe ʒate vnpynne   *quickly*
Þer is þe blys þat con not blynne°   *end*
730 Þat þe jueler soʒte þurʒ perre pres°   *gems of value*
& solde alle hys goud° boþe wolen & lynne   *goods*
To bye hym a perle watʒ mascelleʒ

62

This makelleʒ°perle þat boʒt is dere   *matchless*
Þe joueler gef fore alle hys god

733. makelleʒ: O, Go maskelleʒ; H makeleʒ.

---

721. *mylde*: Refers to the "tender ones" in the familiar story of Christ's blessing the children (Luke 18:15–17), not as Gn imagines (in his glossary) the disciples.

721. Since no linking word is carried over from 720, this is the sole instance in which the concatenation fails in the poem. Emerson wished to insert *ryʒt* "straightway, at once," before *Jesus*

in 721 to complete the scheme.

733. *makelleʒ*: Probably used by the poet, here and in 757, along with *maskelleʒ* to emphasize by means of word play the peerlessness of the pearl as well as its purity. The two words are brought together, fittingly, in 780, the last line of the "*maskelleʒ* group."

733–44. H is perfectly correct in defending the maiden's exposition of the

735 Is lyke þe reme°of heuenesse clere°   *kingdom / bright*
   So sayde þe fader of folde & flode°   *earth and water*
   For hit is wemleȝ° clene & clere   *spotless*
   & endeleȝ rounde & blyþe of mode°   *spirit*
   & commune to alle þat ryȝtwys were
740 Lo euen inmyddeȝ my breste hit stode
   My lorde þe lombe þat schede hys blode
   He pyȝt hit þere in token of pes
   I rede°þe forsake þe worlde wode°   *advise / insane*
   & porchace þy perle maskelles

63

745 O maskeleȝ perle in perleȝ pure
   Þat bereȝ quod I þe perle of prys°   *excellence*
   Quo formed þe þy fayre fygure
   Þat°wroȝt þy wede° he watȝ ful wys   *he who / garment*
   Þy beaute com neuer of nature

735. heuenesse: Go heuenes.
735. clere: Go spere.
739. ryȝtwys: ᴍꜱ ryȝtywys.

"pearl of great price" against O's charge that it is "confused." The maiden identifies the pearl with the kingdom of heaven (735), the common reward of the saved. Thus the narrator is enjoined by the girl to purchase "his" pearl, i.e. to secure for himself the kingdom of heaven.

740. *stode*: Hamilton denies that this is a form of *stande*, but relates it rather to ᴏᴇ *stōd* and glosses it "shone forth," *hit* referring to the pearl of great price. Cf. 113*n*.

749–52. These lines are usually taken as being reminiscent of that passage in *Roman de la Rose* (16013 ff.

in Langlois's edition) in which it is said that neither the philosopher nor the artist can successfully copy nature. But since, as O says, such comparisons were common enough in the Middle Ages, we cannot be sure of direct borrowing here, even though Aristotle and Pygmalion are particularly mentioned in both works. The point here is somewhat different also. Surely what the poet is emphasizing is not the failure of the philosophers and artists to copy nature, but that the unnatural, unearthly quality of the maiden's beauty is beyond the mere copies of nature. Hamilton imagines the point to be

750 Pymalyon°paynted neuer þy vys°   *Pygmalion* / *face*
    Ne Arystotel nawþer by hys lettrure°   *learning*
    Of carpe°þe kynde°þese propertez   *spoke of* / *nature of*
    Þy colour passez þe flour-de-lys
    Þyn angel-hauyng°so clene
        cortez°   *angelic manner* / *purely gracious*
755 Breue°me bryзt quat kyn offys°   *tell* / *kind of rank*
    Berez þe perle so maskellez

64

    My makelez lambe þat al may bete°   *amend* (f.49b)
    Quoþ scho° my dere destyne   *she*
    Me ches to° hys make° alþaз vnmete°   *chose as* / *spouse* / *unfitting*
760 Sumtyme semed þat assemble°   *union*
    When I wente fro yor worlde wete
    He calde me to hys bonerte°   *goodliness*
    Cum hyder to me my lemman°swete   *beloved one*
    For mote ne spot is non in þe
765 He gef me myзt & als bewte

752. carpe: Go, Gn carped.
752. propertez: O, Gn propertyз.
755. offys: Gn oftriys; Go of triys.
757. makelez: O, Go maskelez.

theological, that Aristotle is named as the "pagan" authority on the soul who could not of course have conceived of a "redeemed soul like Pearl."

753. A possible echo of *Roman de la Rose*, 16239. I feel, however, that the allusion would not have been noted (in the French poem, nature is compared to the fleur-de-lys) were it not in such close proximity to the Pygmalion passage noted immediately above.

755. *offys*: My own inspection agrees with O's and H's that this is the ms form, the second *f* being spaced peculiarly, not *of triys* (Go) or *oftriys* (Gn).

761. *wete*: In spite of most previous editors' "wet," I must agree with H's "woe." Thus *worlde* is an "endingless genitive," a form which does occur in the works of the *Gawain*-poet (see Gn, 109).

THE DREAMER AND THE CHILD

In hys blod he wesch°my wede°on
  dese°   *washed / garment / a dais*
& coronde clene in vergynte
& pyȝt me in perleȝ maskelleȝ

65

Why maskelleȝ byrd°þat bryȝt con flambe°   *bride / shines*
770 Þat reiateȝ hatȝ so ryche & ryf
Quat kyn°þyng may be þat lambe   *kind of*
Þat þe wolde wedde vnto hys vyf
Ouer alle oþer so hyȝ þou clambe
To lede wyth hym so ladyly°lyf   *ladylike a*
775 So mony a comly onvunder cambe
For Kryst han lyued in much stryf
& þou can alle þe dere° outdryf   *those dear ones*
& fro þat maryag al oþer depres°   *drive away*
Al only°þyself so stout & styf°   *exclusively / brave and strong*
780 A makeleȝ may & maskelleȝ

XIV/66

Maskelles quoþ þat myry° quene   *fair*
Vnblemyst I am wythouten blot
& þat may I wyth mensk menteene°   *grace maintain*
Bot makeleȝ quene þenne sade I not
785 Þe lambes vyueȝ in blysse we bene°   *are*

768. &: Go He.
778. maryag: Go maryage.
784. sade: O sayde.
785. lambes: Gn Lambeȝ.

---

770. "That has royal attributes so rich and plentiful."

775. *comly onvunder cambe*: "fair beneath the comb," a conventional courtly compliment.

785–86. *A hondred & forty þowsande*: Possibly the scribe's error for the Bible's 144,000, later given by the

A hondred & forty þowsande flot°   *in all*
As in þe Apocalyppeʒ hit is sene
Sant John hem syʒ al in a knot
On þe hyl of Syon þat semly clot°   *hill*
790 Þe apostel hem segh in gostly drem°   *spiritual vision*
Arayed to þe weddyng in þat hylcoppe°   *hilltop*
Þe nwe cyte o Jerusalem

67

Of Jerusalem I in speche spelle°   *tell* (f.50a)
If þou wyl knaw what kyn he be
795 My lombe my lorde my dere juelle
My ioy my blys my lemman fre°   *fair beloved*
Þe profete Ysaye of hym con melle°   *spoke*
Pitously° of hys debonerte°   *compassionately / meekness*
Þat gloryous gyltleʒ° þat mon con
    quelle°   *innocent / was killed*

786. forty: Go, Gn forty fowre.
788. John: MS john̄.
792. Jerusalem: MS jrlm̄, *and so in following stanzas.*
792. o: MS w.

poet correctly (869–70). Sister Mary Madeleva, in attacking the elegiac position, argued (*Pearl: A Study in Spiritual Dryness*) that no child of two could have a place in the procession of 144,000 virgins following the Lamb in Paradise since the term "virgin" in the Middle Ages "meant a person [of either sex and the 144,000 of Revelations are men] bound by the vow of chastity or living in that state," a state dependent upon choice and renunciation.

E. Hart, however, contended (MLN 42:113–16) that, on the basis of Chaucer's Prioress's Tale and Matt. 2:13–18 (read as the Gospel on Holy Innocents' Day), people in the Middle Ages associated the procession of the virgins with the Holy Innocents, among whom a two-year-old child might well walk.

790. *Þe apostel*: Christian thought has from the earliest Christian times identified the author of Revelations as the "beloved disciple."

799–804. See Isa. 53:7.

800 Wythouten any sake of felonye
    As a schep to þe slaȝt þer lad watȝ he
    & as lombe þat clypper in hande nem°   took
    So closed he hys mouth fro vch query
    Quen Jueȝ hym iugged in Jerusalem

                        68

805 In Jerusalem watȝ my lemman slayn
    & rent on rode wyth boyeȝ bolde
    Al oure baleȝ° to bere ful bayn°   sorrows / willing
    He toke on hymself oure careȝ colde
    Wyth boffeteȝ watȝ hys face flayn
810 Þat watȝ so fayr on to byholde
    For synne he set° hymself in vayn°   valued / at nothing
    Þat neuer hade non° hymself to wolde   any sin
    For vus he lette hym flyȝe & folde°   himself be torn and bent
    & brede° vpon a bostwys bem°   stretched / rough beam
815 As meke as lomp þat no playnt tolde
    For vus he swalt° in Jerusalem   died

        800. felonye: Go felone.
        802. in hande nem: ᴍs in hande men; O, Go, H in lande nem.
        803. query: Go quere.
        804. iugged: Go jugged.
        804. Jerusalem: ᴍs ihr̄m.
        815. lomp: O, Go lomb.

800. *Wythouten any sake of felonye:*
"No criminal charge being proved
against Him" (Gn).

802. *hande:* My own inspection of
the ᴍs agrees with that of Gn rather
than that of H, who read *lande.* Sav-
age, like Go, prefers *honde.*

806. *boyeȝ bolde:* These were the
thieves between whom Jesus was cru-
cified. Morton Bloomfield suggested,
however, that since *wyth* taken with
rent may well mean "by," the *boyeȝ*
might have been the Roman soldiers.

812. *wolde:* Wright thought "con-
trol, power" from ᴏᴇ *geweald,* and
Savage adapted her reading to "in
one's possessions." H thought "sub-
due."

815. *lomp:* "lamb," noted by Gn as
a "western form," a variant of the
usual *lomb.*

69

Jerusalem Jordan & Galalye
Þer as° baptysed þe goude Saynt Jon   *where*
His wordeȝ acorded to°Ysaye   *with*
820 When Jesus con to hym warde°gon   *toward him*
He sayde of hym þys professye
Lo Godeȝ lombe as trwe as ston
Þat dotȝ° away þe synneȝ dryȝe   *does*
Þat alle þys worlde hatȝ wroȝt vpon
825 Hymself ne wroȝt neuer ȝet non
Wheþer° on hymself he con al clem   *yet*
Hys generacyoun°quo recen con°   *ancestry / can tell*
Þat dyȝed for vus in Jerusalem

70

In Jerusalem þus my lemman swatte   (f.50b)
830 Twyeȝ for°lombe watȝ taken þare   *twice as*

817. Jerusalem: Go, Gn In Jerusalem.
818. Jon: H John.
825. wroȝt: Go wroȝte.
829. Jerusalem: Go Ierusalem.
829. swatte: O, Go, Gn swete.
830. þare: O þere.

817. There is no need to supply *in* at the beginning of this line. A pause at the end of the line renders the syntax perfectly clear.

817-18. As Gn remarks, "There is no record of John the Baptist having baptized elsewhere than in Jordan ... ; doubtless the poet's ideas of the geography of Palestine were vague."

823-24. Emerson saw these lines as essentially a paraphrase of the *qui tollet peccatum mundi* of the Vulgate. Although the poet makes "sins" plural in 823, he returns to the singular in 824, "that has wrought upon (affected) all the world."

823. *dryȝe*: Regarded by H as a verb, to "dry, blot."

826. *clem*: Like Menner and H, I would derive this from OE *clǣman*, "smear," "an appropriate word ... as expressing the loathsomeness of sin" (H).

829. *swatte*: O, Go, and Gn emended to *swete*. As Savage notes, the word here means to undergo "severe afflictions."

    By trw recorde of ayþer prophete
    For mode°so meke & al hys fare°   *spirit / demeanor*
    Þe þryde tyme is þerto ful mete°   *fitting*
    In Apokalypeʒ wryten ful ʒare°   *clearly*
835 Inmydeʒ þe trone þere saynteʒ sete
    Þe apostel John hym saytʒ°as bare°   *saw / clearly*
    Lesande° þe boke with leueʒ sware   *opening*
    Þere seuen syngnetteʒ° wern sette in seme° *seals / the border*
    & at þat syʒt vche douth con dare°   *feared*
840 In helle in erþe & Jerusalem

XV/71

    Thys Jerusalem lombe hade neuer pechche°   *a shred*
    Of oþer huee°bot quyt jolyf°   *color / fair*
    Þat mot ne masklle moʒt on streche°   *rest on*
    For wolle quyte so ronk & ryf°   *rich and plentiful*
845 Forþy° vche saule þat hade neuer teche°   *therefore / a stain*
    Is to þat lombe a worthyly° wyf   *worthy*
    & þaʒ vch day a store°he feche°   *multitude / brings*
    Among vus commeʒ non oþer strot° ne stryf   *wrangling*
    Bot vchon enle°we wolde°were fyf   *each one singly / wish*
850 Þe mo°þe myryer so God me blesse   *more*

      836. John: Go, Gn Iohn.
      836. saytʒ: Go, Gn saʒ; O syʒ.
      843. masklle: Go maskelle.
      848. non oþer: Go noþer; Gn nouþer.

---

  831. *ayþer prophete*: Isaiah (Isa. 18:7) and St. John the Baptist (John 1:29).

  837. *leueʒ sware*: While this refers to the scroll of Rev. 5:1–8, the poet has in mind a medieval volume with "square leaves."

  839. *douth*: "So, 'douth,' having dignified associations from its use in old heroic poetry, but having lost the precise significance of the OE *duʒuþ* [a host of noble retainers], is at once impressive and mysterious enough to be used of the hosts of hell, earth, and heaven that gaze upon the Lamb" (Dorothy Everett, *Essays on Middle English Literature*).

  839. *con dare*: H glosses "worshipped."

In compayny gret our luf con þryf
In honour more & neuer þe lesse

72

Lasse of blysse may non vus bryng
Þat beren þys perle vpon oure bereste°   *breast*
855 For þay of mote°couþe neuer mynge°   *dispute / think*
Of spotleʒ perleʒ þat beren þe creste
Alþaʒ oure corses in clotteʒ clynge
& ʒe remen for rauþe° wythouten reste   *cry out in grief*
We þurʒoutly°hauen cnawyng°   *thoroughly / knowledge*
860 Of on dethe ful oure hope is drest
Þe lombe vus gladeʒ° oure care is kest°   *gladdens / driven away*
He myrþeʒ vus alle°at vch a mes°   *makes us all rejoice / mass*
Vchoneʒ°blysse is breme° & beste   *each one's / glorious*
& neuer oneʒ honour ʒet neuer þe les

856. þat: ᴍs, H þa.
860. on: ᴍs *illegible.*
860. dethe: H deth.
861. lombe: ᴍs lonbe; Go loumbe.
862. myrþeʒ: H myrþes.

853ff. See 1n.

856. *creste*: Taken by previous editors to be the crown referred to in 205ff., H translates "top, acme" and takes it to refer to the "best of pearls, . . . symbolizing the Kingdom of Heaven."

860. A difficult line, it is perhaps best taken, as Gn and O suggested, as a statement of man's faith in the atonement of his sins through Christ's death: "In the death of One (Christ) all our hope is placed." H takes the line as an expression of the hope that "the death of their earthly bodies has released their souls into eternal life;

that they will avoid the *mors secunda*." Emerson believes the maiden to be saying that "although our bodies are in the grave and you continue to mourn therefore (the first death), we certainly know that of one death (the second) our hope is fully settled (or established)." Wright interestingly enough read ᴍs *o,* the remainder of the word being illegible, as *our* and translated "from the moment of our death our hope becomes realized."

862. *mes*: O's suggestion that this is ᴏꜰ *mes,* "feast," seems hardly credible.

73

865 Lest les þou leue my tale farande   (f.51a)
In Appocalyppece is wryten in wro°   *a passage*
I seghe says John þe loumbe hym stande
On þe mount of Syon ful þryuen & þro°   *mighty and strong*
& wyth hym maydenneȝ an hundreþe þowsande
870 & fowre & forty þowsande mo
On alle her forhedeȝ wryten I fande
Þe lombeȝ nome hys fadereȝ also
A hue°from heuen I herde þoo°   *cry / then*
Lyk flodeȝ fele laden runnen on resse
875 & as þunder þroweȝ° in torreȝ blo   *rolls*
Þat lote° I leue° watȝ neuer þe les   *sound / believe*

74

Nauþeles þaȝ hit schowted scharpe°   *sounded strongly*
& ledden°loude alþaȝ hit were   *a voice*
A note ful nwe I herde hem warpe°   *utter*
880 To lysten þat watȝ ful lufly dere°   *delightfully pleasant*
As harporeȝ harpen in her harpe

867. þe: H þa.
873. from: O, Go, H fro.
874. laden: Go leden.

---

865. *les*: As Gn points out, *les* is a shortened way of saying "less than desirable" and so translates "lest you should be less inclined to believe my seemly discourse."

869. *maydenneȝ*: The poet so renders *virgines* in Rev. 14:4 in spite of the fact that the 144,000 are there said to be men. However, as *NED* shows, the word *mayden* applied to either sex in the Middle Ages, and the poet prob-ably meant to include both in the procession. See 785*n*.

874. "Like the sound of many rivers running in a rush."

875. *torreȝ blo*: "dark hills," though *NED* suggests that *torr* may mean a "heavy mass of cloud." The common usage in the poet's time, however, would almost certainly have been "hill."

881–84. See *GGK* 118*n*.

Þat nwe songe þay songen ful cler
In sounande° noteȝ a gentyl carpe°   *resounding / noble discourse*
Ful fayre þe modeȝ þay fonge in fere°   *got all together*
885 Ryȝt byfore Godez chayere°   *throne*
   & þe fowre besteȝ þat hym obes°   *revere*
   & þe aldermen°so sadde° of chere°   *elders / serious / countenance*
Her songe þay songen neuer þe les

75

Nowþelese non watȝ neuer so quoynt°   *skillful*
890 For alle þe crafteȝ°þat euer þay knewe   *skills*
Þat of þat songe myȝt synge a poynt°   *note*
Bot°þat meyny°þe lombe þat swe°   *except / company / follow*
For þay arn boȝt° fro þe vrþe aloynte°   *redeemed / far removed*
As newe fryt° to God ful due   *first fruit*
895 & to þe gentyl° lombe hit°arn anioynt°   *noble / they / united*
As lyk to hymself of lote & hwe°   *appearance and color*
For neuer lesyng°ne tale vntrwe   *lie*
Ne towched her tonge for no dysstresse
Þat moteles meyny° may neuer remwe°   *spotless company / part*
900 Fro þat maskeleȝ mayster neuer þe les

76

Neuer þe les let be my þonc°   *my thanks be*
Quoþ I my perle þaȝ I appose°   *question*
I schulde not tempte þy wyt so wlonc°   *noble*
To Krysteȝ chambre þat art ichose

---

892. þat swe: ᴍꜱ þay swe.

---

884. *modeȝ*: C. O. Chapman
(PMLA 46:177) argued that the word
here is used technically in reference
to the modes of ecclesiastical music
and reveals some professional train-
ing of the poet as a musician. How-
ever, as Go points out, the word *modus*
was used during the period to mean
simply "tune, melody," and there is
nothing in the context to suggest any-
thing more complex than this.

903. *tempte*: "to distress" (Wright).

905	I am bot mokke° & mul° among	*filth / dust*
	& þou so ryche° a reken°rose	*splendid / fresh*
	& bydeʒ here by þys blysful bonc	
	Þer lyueʒ lyste° may neuer lose°	*rough*
	Now hynde° þat sympelnesse coneʒ enclose	*life's joy / fade*
910	I wolde þe aske a þynge expresse°	*gracious one*
	& þaʒ I be bustwys°as a blose	*plainly*
	Let my bone vayl°neuer þe lese	*prayer avail*

XVI/77

	Neuer þe lese cler I yow bycalle°	*call on*
	If ʒe con se hyt be to done	
915	As þou art gloryous wythouten galle°	*spot*
	Wythnay° þou neuer my ruful° bone	*deny / piteous*
	Haf ʒe no woneʒ in castel-walle	
	Ne maner þer ʒe may mete & won°	*dwell*

905. among: Go amonc.
911. blose: Go wose.
912. vayl: Go vayle.
918. won: Go wone.

---

905. *among*: Wright and Savage translate *among* adverbially here as "beside you," which is lovely in context and agreed to by the *Middle English Dictionary*. The editors had translated *among* as "meanwhile" (Go and O), "together" (Gn), or "mingled with, mixed" (H). Go emends to *amonc* to fit the rhyme scheme.

909. *sympelnesse*: "simplicity" meaning "lack of guile" (Gn), the "simplicity that is in Christ" (2 Cor. 11:3).

911. *blose*: A nonce word, glossed by Go, Wright, and Emerson as a noun, "churl" or "wild man" from OF adjective *blos, privé de bon sens.*

O tentatively agreed with Morris that it was a noun "flame" derived from ON *blossi*. Gn guessed a "rough uncouth person," an error for ME *bose*, "a leather bottle." In spite of the etymological difficulties of the word, it certainly must be, as H says, "an expression of self-abasement."

917. *castel-walle*: As in the description of the maiden's raiment and the book from which the Lamb reads, the poet here describes the New Jerusalem in terms appropriate to his own age. The Heavenly City has a *castel-walle*; it is also a *manayre* (1029) and has a *bayle* (1083).

Þou tellez me of Jerusalem þe ryche ryalle°   *royal kingdom*
920 Þer Dauid dere watz dyȝt° on trone   *set*
Bot by þyse holtez°hit con not hone°   *woods | be situated*
Bot in Judee hit is þat noble note°   *structure*
As ȝe ar maskelez vnder mone
Your wonez schulde be wythouten mote°   *stain*

78

925 Þys motelez meyny þou conez of mele°   *speak of*
Of þousandez þryȝt° so gret a route°   *crowded | company*
A gret cete°for ȝe arn fele°   *city | many*
Yow byhod°haue wythouten doute   *it behooved you*
So cumly°a pakke of joly°juele   *beautiful | fair*
930 Wer euel° don schulde lyȝ þeroute°   *ill | should they lie outside*
& by þyse bonkez þer I con gele
I se no bygyng nawhere aboute
I trowe alone ȝe lenge & loute
To loke on þe glory of þys gracious gote
935 If þou hatz oþer bygyngez stoute
Now tech me to þat myry mote°   *fair city*

79

That mote þou menez in Judy°londe   *Judea (f.52a)*
Þat specyal spyce°þen to me spakk   *excellent person*
Þat is þe cyte þat þe lombe con fonde

919. þe: H the.
932. I: MS, O, H & I.
934. gracious: MS gracous.
935. bygyngez: MS, O, Go, H lygyngez.

932. I have deleted & at the beginning of the line as superfluous, though O and H both keep it by making 932 a parenthetical aside. Gn translates "And by these slopes where I linger I see no dwelling anywhere about. I be-lieve you make your way (hither) and stay only to look on the beauty of this fair stream."

935. *bygyngez*: Gn's emendation for MS *lygyngez*, a nonce word.

940 To soffer inne sor°for maneȝ sake   *sorrow*
Þe olde Jerusalem to vnderstonde°   *that is to say*
For þere þe olde gulte watȝ don° to slake° *brought / an end*
Bot þe nwe þat lyȝt° of Godeȝ sonde°   *came down / sending*
Þe apostel in Apocalyppce in theme con
    take°   *adopted as a theme*
945 Þe lompe þer wythouten spotteȝ blake
Hatȝ feryed°þyder hys fayre flote°   *led / company*
& as hys flok is wythouten flake
So is hys mote wythouten moote

80

Of motes° two to carpe clene°   *cities / speak exactly*
950 & Jerusalem hyȝt° boþe nawþeles° *are called / nevertheless*
Þat nys to yow no more to mene
Bot cete of God oþer syȝt° of pes°   *vision / peace*
In þat on oure pes watȝ mad°at ene°   *made / once*
Wyth payne to suffer þe lombe hit chese° *chose*
955 In þat oþer is noȝt bot pes to glene
Þat ay schal laste wythouten reles°   *cessation*
Þat is þe borȝ° þat we to pres°   *city / hurry*
Fre þat°oure flesch be layd to rote°   *after / rot*
Þer glory & blysse schal euer encres
960 To þe meyny°þat is wythouten mote° *company / stain*

944. Apocalyppce: H Apocallypce.
945. lompe: O, Go lombe.
958. flesch: MS fresth.

---

944. *theme*: Almost certainly pronounced *teme* and hence alliterates with *take*.

947. *flake*: Probably related to ON *flekkr*, "spot, blemish," as H points out, rather than to ON *flaki* as earlier editors had claimed.

948. *moote*: Not "moat" as Go and O had thought, but "spot, stain," derived from OE *mot*.

950–52. Both meanings of Jerusalem were current in Middle English, though "Vision of Peace" was apparently more common than "City of God" (see Gn's note).

81

Moteleȝ may°so meke & mylde   *spotless maiden*
Þen sayde I to þat lufly flor
Bryng me to þat bygly bylde°   *pleasant dwelling*
& let me se þy blysful bor
965 Þat schene°sayde þat God wyl schylde°   *fair one / prevent*
Þou may not enter wythinne hys tor°   *tower*
Bot of þe lombe I haue þe aquylde°   *obtained permission*
For a syȝt þerof þurȝ gret fauor
Vtwyth°to se þat clene cloystor   *from without*
970 Þou may bot inwyth°not a fote   *from within*
To strech°in þe strete þou hatȝ no vygour°   *walk / power*
Bot°þou wer clene wythouten mote   *unless*

XVII/82

If I þis mote þe schal vnhyde°   *reveal (f.52b)*
Bow°vp towarde þys borneȝ heued°   *go / stream's head*
975 & I anendeȝ° þe on þis syde   *opposite*
Schal sve° tyl þou to a hil be veued°   *follow / brought*
Þen wolde I no lenger byde
Bot lurked°by launceȝ° so
   lufly leued°   *stole / branches / delightfully leaned*
Tyl on a hyl þat I asspyed
980 & blusched° on þe burghe as I forth dreued°   *gazed / rushed*
Byȝonde þe brok fro me warde keued
Þat schyrrer°þen sunne wyth schafteȝ°schon   *brighter / rays*

977. I: *Not in* MS; Go I þer.
981. keued: O breued.

973ff. Kean (208ff.) relates the vision of the New Jerusalem to the visions of Dante in the Earthly Paradise and in *Paradiso* xxxi.

981. ʞeued: "sunken, placed low." Unlike Gn and H, I am inclined to think that this modifies *me* rather than *þat* (presumably the city) in 979. In short, the poet, unlike the Apostle John (and surely 984 need not be taken with absolute literalness), sees from a river valley the

In þe Apokalypce is þe fasoun preued°   *fashion shown*
As deuyseȝ°hit þe apostel Jhon   *pictures*

83

985 As John þe apostel hit syȝ wyth syȝt
    I syȝe þat cyty of gret renoun
    Jerusalem so nwe & ryally dyȝt°   *royally adorned*
    As°hit watȝ lyȝt° fro þe heuen adoun   *as if | had come*
    Þe borȝ watȝ al of brende°golde bryȝt   *refined*
990 As glemande glas burnist broun°   *bright*
    Wyth gentyl gemmeȝ anvnder° pyȝt   *underneath*
    Wyth banteleȝ twelue on basyng boun°   *foundation fixed*
    Þe foundementeȝ°twelue of riche
        tenoun°   *foundations | joining*
    Vch tabelment°watȝ a serlypeȝ°ston   *tier | single*
995 As derely deuyseȝ°þis ilk°toun   *pictures | same*
    In Apocalyppeȝ þe apostel John

84

As John þise stoneȝ in writ con nemme°   *named*
I knew þe name after his tale

984. Jhon: ᴍꜱ Jhōn; O, H John.
985. John: ᴍꜱ Jhn̄.
988. watȝ: Gn was.
986. John: ᴍꜱ Johñ, *and so also in 1008, 1009, 1021, 1032, 1033, 1053.*
997. John: *Not in* ᴍꜱ.
998. name: Go nameȝ.

Heavenly City *on* a hill, not *from* a hill as Gn maintains. He has been told by the maiden to proceed upstream until he *sees* a hill, presumably that of the New Jerusalem. Then we are told that he made his way through woods *Tyl on a hyl þat I asspyed.* In this line, it seems (again contrary to Gn and H) that *on a hyl* refers to *þat* (the city) rather than to *I.*

991. O places a semicolon after *pyȝt.*

992. *banteleȝ:* "bantels," the "tiers or coursings (*tabelment*) which served as foundations (*foundementeȝ*) of the city . . . arranged in the forms of steps" (Gn).

997ff. *As John þise stoneȝ in writ con nemme*: Rev. 21:21. The poet errs only slightly in listing the ruby as the

Jasper hyȝt°þe fyrst gemme   *is called*
1000 Þat I on þe fyrst basse con wale°   *base perceived*
He glente°grene in þe lowest hemme°   *it glinted / course*
Saffer°helde þe secounde stale°   *sapphire / place*
Þe calsydoyne°þenne wythouten wemme°   *chalcedony / flaw*
In þe þryd table con purly pale°   *tier shone pure and pale*
1005 Þe emerade þe furþe so grene of scale°   *surface*
Þe sardonyse°þe fyfþe ston   *sardonyx*
Þe sexte°þe rybe°he con hit wale°   *sixth / ruby / noted it*
In þe Apocalyppce þe apostel John

85

ȝet joyned°John þe crysolyt°   *added / chrysolite* (f.53a)
1010 Þe seuenþe gemme in fundament

999. fyrst: Go fyrste.
1004. þryd: Go þrydde.
1007. rybe: Go sarde.

---

sixth stone. True, John names *sardinus* or *sardius*, a carnelian, but there was a well-founded tradition to the effect that the *sardius* of the Vulgate was actually a ruby (see Gn's note).

In these lines, as with the spices of 43ff., the symbolism of the gems is appropriate to the meaning of the poem. According to M. R. Stern (JEGP 54:684–92), they signify the "lessons the narrator has learned in the conventional debate: Jasper is faith; sapphire is hope; chalcydon is good works; emerald is chastity; sardonyx is repentance; ruby is Jesus; chrysolite is the miracles of Christ, the holy gift, and the Holy Ghost; beryl is the Resurrection; topaz is the nine orders of angels; chrysoprase is travail; jacinth is safety in far places; and amethyst is Christ's robe." The fact that the symbolism of the topaz, jacinth, and amethyst do *not* fit the narrator's situation is an indication to Stern that the "poet did not order the parallel consciously," though he was "fully immersed in the traditions with which he worked."

Robert Blanch (LHR 7:1–12), having surveyed the symbolism of gems and precious metals in *Pearl,* concludes that they are used by the poet to emphasize "the essential difference between the earthly and celestial spheres" and to elucidate "the prerequisites for the dreamer's spiritual peace, including the need for Christ's saving blood."

Þe aȝtþe° þe beryl cler & quyt   *eighth*
Þe topasye twynne-hew° þe nente
        endent°   *topaz twin-hued | ninth set*
Þe crysopase° þe tenþe is tyȝt°   *chrysoprase | fixed*
Þe jacyngh° þe enleuenþe gent   *jacinth*
1015 Þe twelfþe þe gentyleste in vch a plyt°   *state*
Þe amatyst purpre wyth ynde blente°   *indigo mixed*
Þe wal abof þe bantels bent°   *coursings set*
O jasporye° as glas þat glysnande schon   *of jasper*
I knew hit by his deuysement°   *description*
1020 In þe Apocalyppeȝ þe apostel John

86

As John deuysed ȝet saȝ I þare
Þise twelue degres wern° brode & stayre°   *which were | steep*
Þe cyte stod abof ful sware°   *square*
As longe as brode as hyȝe ful fayre°   *exactly*
1025 Þe streteȝ of golde as glasse al bare
Þe wal of jasper þat glent as glayre°   *egg-white glaze*
Þe woneȝ wythinne enurned° ware   *adorned*
Wyth alle kynneȝ perre° þat moȝt
        repayre°   *kinds of gems | come together*
Þenne helde vch sware of þis manayre

1012. twynne-hew: MS, O, Go, H twynne-how.
1014. jacyngh: Go, Gn jacynght.
1015. gentyleste: Go tryeste.
1017. bent: Go brent.
1020. John: MS Jhn̄.

1015. *gentyleste*: Gn quotes various medieval lapidaries to the effect that the amethyst (1) is *comfortable in all sorowes* and (2) that it "is said to have protecting power against a long list of dangers and misfortunes."

1025. *bare*: Gn remarks that *bare* here indicates that the streets shone like glass, not that they were transparent.

1029. *sware*: "square," rather than "side of a square" (O). The poet uses

1030 Twelue forlonge space er euer hit fon° ceased
    Of heȝt° of brede° of lenþe to cayre° height / breadth / extend
    For meten°hit syȝ þe apostel John measured

XVIII/87

    As John hym wryteȝ ȝet more I syȝe
    Vch pane°of þat place had þre ȝateȝ side
1035 So twelue in pourseut I con asspye
    Þe portaleȝ pyked°of rych plateȝ adorned
    & vch ȝate of a margyrye
    A parfyt perle þat neuer fateȝ° fades
    Vchon in scrypture a name con plye° showed forth
1040 Of Israel barneȝ° folewande her dateȝ Israel's children
    Þat is to say as her byrþ-whateȝ

1030. forlonge space: Go þowsande forlonge.
1036. rych: Go ryche.
1041. byrþ-whateȝ: Go byrþe-whateȝ.

---

a solid, rather than a plane, figure for the New Jerusalem; it is *as longe as brode as hyȝe ful fayre* (1024). Of interest is the poet's reduction of the Vulgate's 12,000 furlongs to 12. Go guesses that the omission is a scribal error, Gn that the poet was here using a commentary "in which the verse explained was given in an abbreviated form." It might well be that the poet was attempting to frame here an image that would be credible and imaginable within the framework of the poem. A city encompassing some 1,364 miles on each square side of its cube—*of heȝt, of brede, of lenþe* [1031]—may be quite suited to a vision such as St. John's, but one measuring a little over a mile and a third is much more imaginable, and just as impressive, in terms of the narrator's vantage point and experience.

1035. *pourseut*: Almost certainly not *poursent*, "compass, enclosing wall," as Go and Gn imagine. Translate as "succession."

1041. *as her byrþ-whateȝ*: "according to the fortunes of their birth," in order of birth, the eldest first. Gn points out that this detail does not come from Rev. 21:12, the source of this passage, which describes the gates of the Heavenly City, over which the names of the twelve tribes are inscribed, but from Exod. 228, where it is said that the names of the twelve tribes are to be inscribed on two onyx stones to be set into the high priest's ephod. It may well be that the poet was using a commentary which compared the two scriptural passages.

THE DREAMER AND THE NEW JERUSALEM

Þe aldest ay fyrst þeron watȝ done
Such lyȝt þer lemed°in alle þe strateȝ°　　　　*gleamed | streets*
Hem nedde° nawþer sunne ne mone　　　　　　*they needed*

88

1045 Of sunne ne mone had þay no nede
　　Þe self God°watȝ her lombe-lyȝt　　　　*God himself* (f.53b)
　　Þe lombe her lantyrne wythouten drede°　　　*doubt*
　　Þurȝ hym blysned°þe borȝ al bryȝt　　　　　*shone*
　　Þurȝ woȝe & won°my lokyng
　　　　ȝede°　　　　　*wall and dwelling | gaze pierced*
1050 For sotyle cler noȝt lette no lyȝt
　　Þe hyȝe trone þer moȝt ȝe hede°　　　　　　*behold*
　　Wyth alle þe apparaylmente vmbepyȝte°　　*adornment set around*
　　As John þe appostel in termeȝ tyȝte°　　*exact words set forth*
　　Þe hyȝe Godeȝ self hit set vpone
1055 A reuer of þe trone þer ran outryȝte
　　Watȝ bryȝter þen boþe þe sunne & mone

89

　　Sunne ne mone schon neuer so swete
　　As þat foysoun flode°out of þat flet°　　　*abundant river | flood*
　　Swyþe°hit swange°þurȝ vch a strete　　　　*swiftly | rushed*
1060 Wythouten fylþe oþer galle oþer glet°　　　*scum or slime*
　　Kyrk°þerinne watȝ non ȝete°　　　　　　　*church | yet*
　　Chapel ne temple þat euer watȝ set

1046. self: Go selfe.
1046. lombe-lyȝt: O lompelyȝt; Go lompe-lyȝt.
1050. lyȝt: Go syȝt.
1058. As: ms, H A.

1046. *lombe*: "lamp"; like *lomp* in 815, a Western form.　　and clear, nothing hindered any light" (Gn).
1050. "For (all) being transparent

Þe almyȝty watȝ her mynster mete°   *fitting*

Þe lombe þe sakerfyse þer to refet

1065 Þe ȝateȝ stoken°watȝ neuer ȝet   *gates shut*

Bot euermore vpen°at vche a lone°   *open | lane*

Þer entreȝ non to take reset°   *refuge*

Þat bereȝ any spot anvnder°mone   *under*

90

The mone may þerof acroche no myȝte

1070 To spotty ho is of body to grym

& also þer ne is neuer nyȝt

What° schulde þe mone þer compas° clym *why | circuit*

& to euen°wyth þat worþly°lyȝt   *vie | glorious*

Þat schyneȝ vpon þe brokeȝ brym°   *river's bank*

1075 Þe planeteȝ arn in to pouer a plyȝt°   *state*

& þe self°sunne ful fer to dym   *very*

Aboute þat water arn tres ful schym°   *bright*

Þat twelue fryteȝ of lyf con bere ful sone

Twelue syþeȝ° on ȝer þay beren ful frym° *times | richly*

1080 & renowleȝ° nwe in vche a mone   *renew*

1063. mynster: MS, O, Go mynyster.
1064. refet: MS, O, Go, H reget.
1068. anvnder: MS an vndeȝ.
1076. self: Go selfe.

1063. *mynster*: MS *mynyster*. This renders *templum* in Rev. 21:22, the source for this passage. "Minister" is certainly not intended.

1064. *refet*: This is Wright's emendation, followed by Gn, of MS *reget*; thus "the Lamb, the sacrifice, was there as refreshment." *Reget* is a nonce word, glossed by Go and H from context as a verb "to redeem" and by O as "to reproduce" in heaven the cele-bration of the mass.

1069. *acroche*: The meaning here seems to be that the moon is "too spotty" and "too grim" to have light of her own and so in the normal course of events must steal light from the sun, a privilege denied her in the New Jerusalem. Emerson was the first to suggest that *acroche* might mean "usurp, seize."

91

Anvnder mone so gret merwayle   (f.54a.)
No fleschly hert ne myȝt endeure
As quen I blusched°vpon þat bayle°   *looked / wall (city)*
So ferly° þerof watȝ þe fasure°   *wondrous / fashion*
1085 I stod as stylle as dased quayle
For ferly° of þat frelich fygure°   *wonder / noble form*
Þat felde° I nawþer reste ne trauayle   *felt*
So watȝ I rauyste°wyth glymme°pure   *ravished / radiance*
For I dar say wyth conciens sure
1090 Hade bodyly burne abiden°þat bone°   *man endured / favor*
Þaȝ alle clerkeȝ hym hade in cure°   *care*
His lyf wer loste anvnder mone

XIX/92

Ryȝt° as þe maynful°mone con rys   *just / mighty*
Er þenne°þe day-glem dryue° al doun   *before / goes*
1095 So sodanly on a wonder wyse
I watȝ war of a prosessyoun
Þis noble cite of ryche enpryse°   *splendid renown*
Watȝ sodanly ful wythouten sommoun°   *summons*

1081. gret: Gn great.
1083. bayle: ᴍs baly; O bayly.
1086. frelich: ᴍs, O, Go, H freuch.
1092. wer: Gn were.
1097. enpryse: ᴍs enpresse.

1082. *No fleschly hert*: We are reminded that the narrator's spirit, not his body, is witnessing this vision.

1085. *dased quayle*: O notes *The Clerk's Tale, couche as doth a quayle,* and remarks that such a bird is described as "badly scared" with "its plumage compressed about it as tightly as possible."

1086. *frelich*: In spite of Go, O, H, and Emerson, I cannot make any real sense of ᴍs's *freuch*. *Frelich* (Morris and Gn), however, both fits the context and is palaeographically possible.

1093. The simile of the moon and sun here is used to express the suddenness with which the dreamer becomes aware of the procession.

Of such vergyneʒ in þe same gyse
1100 Þat watʒ my blysful anvnder croun
& coronde wern alle of þe same fasoun
Depaynt° in perleʒ & wedeʒ°qwyte   *arrayed / garments*
In vchoneʒ breste watʒ bounden boun°   *fixed firmly*
Þe blysful perle wyth gret delyt

93

1105 Wyth gret delyt þay glod in fere°   *glided in company*
On golden gateʒ þat glent as glasse
Hundreth þowsandeʒ I wot þer were
& alle in sute°her liureʒ wasse°   *to match / garments were*
Tor°to knaw þe gladdest chere°   *hard / expression*
1110 Þe lombe byfore con proudly passe
Wyth horneʒ seuen of red golde cler°   *bright*
As praysed°perleʒ his wedeʒ wasse   *precious*
Towarde þe throne þay trone a tras°   *made their way*
Þaʒ þay wern fele no pres in plyt°   *no crowding in their order*
1115 Bot mylde as maydeneʒ seme at mas
So droʒ°þay forth wyth gret delyt   *went*

94

Delyt þat hys come encroched°   *coming brought* (f.54b)
To much hit were of for to melle°   *to tell of*
Þise aldermen quen he aproched
1120 Grouelyng to his fete þay felle
Legyounes of aungeleʒ togeder uoched°   *summoned*
Þer kesten°ensens of swete smelle   *cast*
Þen glory & gle watʒ nwe abroched°   *uttered*
Al songe to loue°þat gay°juelle   *praise / fair*

1104. wyth gret: MS wᵗ outen; H wythouten.
1108. liureʒ: Go liure.
1111. golde: MS glode.
1112. wedeʒ: Go wede.
1117. þat: O, Go þat þer.

1125 Þe steuen°moȝt stryke þurȝ þe vrþe to helle   *sound*
    Þat þe Vertues of heuen of°joye endyte°   *for / sing out*
    To loue þe lombe his meyny in melle°   *midst*
    Iwysse I laȝt°a gret delyt   *took*

95

    Delit þe lombe for to deuise°   *look on*
1130 Wyth much meruayle in mynde went
    Best watȝ he blyþest & moste to pryse°   *esteem*
    Þat euer I herde of speche spent°   *speech spent on*
    So worþly°whyt wern wedeȝ hys   *gloriously*
    His lokeȝ symple hymself so gent
1135 Bot a wounde ful wyde & weete con wyse°   *wet showed*
    Anende°hys hert þurȝ hyde torente°   *over / skin all torn*
    Of his quyte syde his blod outsprent°   *gushed forth*
    Alas þoȝt I who did þat spyt°   *evil*
    Ani breste for bale aȝt haf forbrent°   *ought to have burned*
1140 Er he þerto hade had delyt

96

    The lombe delyt non lyste to wene
    Þaȝ he were hurt & wounde hade
    In his sembelaunt°watȝ neuer sene   *demeanor*
    So wern his glenteȝ°gloryous glade   *looks*

1125. þurȝ þe: H þurȝ.

1126. *Vertues of heuen*: One of the nine orders of angels, these being, in ascending order, Angels, Archangels, Principalities, Powers, Virtues, Dominations, Thrones, Cherubim, and Seraphim.

1141. O translates, "(Yet) it would please none to doubt the Lamb's joy." Wright reads it as "The Lamb's delight no one would aspire to conceive," and Go as "To no one was there desire to question the delight of the Lamb." H translates, "The Lamb's delight let no one hope to imagine." *Wene* can mean either "imagine" (as in H and Wright) or "doubt" (as in O and Go).

1145 I loked among his meyny schene
How þay wyth lyf wern laste & lade°   *filled and laden*
Þen saȝ I þer my lyttel quene
Þat I wende°had standen by me in sclade°   *thought / a valley*
Lorde much of mirþe watȝ þat ho made
1150 Among her fereȝ°þat watȝ so quyt   *companions*
Þat syȝt me gart°to þenk to wade   *made*
For luf-longyng in gret delyt

XX/97

Delyt me drof in yȝe & ere   (f.55a.)
My maneȝ mynde to maddyng malte°   *melted*
1155 Quen I seȝ my frely° I wolde be þere   *fair one*
Byȝonde þe water þaȝ ho were walte
I poȝt þat noþyng myȝt me dere
To fech me bur & take me halte
& to start°in þe strem schulde non me stere° *plunge / hinder*
1160 To swymme þe remnaunt° þaȝ I þer
        swalte°   *remainder / might die*
Bot of þat munt°I watȝ bitalt°   *intention / shaken*
When I schulde°start in þe strem astraye   *was about to*
Out of þat caste°I watȝ bycalt°   *purpose / called*
Hit watȝ not at my prynceȝ paye

1152. *luf-longyng*: See 11*n*.

1156. *walte*: H derives this from OE *wælan* and glosses it "vexed."

1158. *To fech me bur & take me halte*: A difficult line. Go thought *to fech me bur* meant "to gather impetus for a leap by taking a short run," a meaning agreed to by H. Gn's "to fetch me a blow" seems sounder etymologically and certainly is closer to the context. If, however, *fech me bur* is thought to be a "gathering of speed,"

then *take me halte* must mean something like "take off" (Go) or "spring high" (H), neither of which expresses the notion of hindrance which the passage (except in H's translation) so clearly demands. It seems better then simply to gloss the phrase, as does Gn, "stop my advance" and render lines 1157–58 as: "I thought that nothing might harm me by fetching me a blow or halting my advance."

98

1165 Hit payed hym not þat I so flonc°   *flung myself*
Ouer meruelous mereʒ° so mad
        arayde°   *waters | madly disturbed*
Of raas°þaʒ I were rasch & ronk°   *rush | overbearing*
ʒet rapely°þerinne I watʒ restayed°   *quickly | restrained*
For ryʒt as I sparred°vnto þe bonc   *rushed*
1170 Þat brathþe°out of my drem me brayde°   *violence | roused*
Þen wakned I in þat erber wlonk°   *garden splendid*
My hede vpon þat hylle watʒ layde
Þer as my perle to grounde strayd
I raxled°& fel in gret affray°   *stretched myself | dismay*
1175 & sykyng° to myself I sayd   *sighing*
Now al be to þat prynceʒ paye

99

Me payed ful ille to be outfleme
So sodenly of þat fayre regioun
Fro alle þo syʒteʒ so quyke & queme°   *lifelike and pleasant*
1180 A longeyng heuy me strok in swone°   *a swoon*
& rewfully þenne I con to reme°   *cried out*
O perle quoþ I of rych renoun
So watʒ hit me dere þat þou con deme
In þys veray avysyoun
1185 If hit be ueray & soth sermoun°   *real and true account*

1170. brathþe: ᴍs bratþe *with* þ *superimposed on* h; *Go, H* brathe.
1179. quyke: ᴍs quykeʒ.
1184. þys: Gn þis.
1185. If: ᴍs if.

1177. *outfleme*: Like Gn, I believe this to be an adjective "driven out, expelled," though the *NED*, O, and Go see it as a noun and Mabel Day (MLR 14:413–15) and H as a past participle without the *-d*.

1183. *dere*: Emerson and Savage think "grievous," as in *GGK* 564.

Þat þou so stykeȝ in garlande gay
So wel is me in þys doel°doungoun   *sorrow*
Þat þou art to þat prynseȝ paye

100

To þat prynceȝ paye hade I ay bente°   *if I had ever bowed* (f.55b)
1190 & ȝerned no more þen watȝ me geuen
    & halden me þer in trwe entent
    As þe perle me prayed þat watȝ so þryuen°   *fair*
    As helde drawen to Goddeȝ present
    To mo of his mysterys I hade ben dryuen°   *brought*
1195 Bot ay wolde man of happe°more hente°   *good fortune | seize*
    Þen moȝten by ryȝt vpon°hem clyuen°   *to | belong*

1186. stykeȝ: O, Go strykeȝ.
1190. geuen: Go, Gn gyuen.
1193. helde: O helder.
1196. moȝten: Go, Gn moȝte.

1186. *stykeȝ*: Go and O emend this to *strykeȝ*, thinking that the *garlande gay* refers to the actual crown described in lines 205–208. However, the *garlande gay* in which the maiden *stykeȝ* is probably the *garlande* of souls which here, as in *Paradiso* X, 91–93, forms a crown. See H's note. Ian Bishop, however, arguing against the H-Gn reading (RES 8:12–21), proposes that the *garlande gay* may be metaphorically the New Jerusalem itself and that *stykeȝ* may be the intransitive "you are set." Iconographically, Bishop claims, the poet may well have in mind chandeliers in the forms of crowns which were hung over altars in the twelfth century and which were set with precious stones and garlanded with flowers.

1193. *As helde*: Go, O, and Gn all felt this to be derived from ON *heldr*, Go translating "belikes," O "rather," and Gn "readily, likely." Emerson and Wright, on the other hand, thought *helde* to be an error for *holde*, and Wright accordingly translated "Thus in steadfast loyalty brought into communion with God." H's suggestion, however, that it is a past participle of *helden*, "disposed," another example of a participle lacking final *d*, certainly seems to be both etymologically possible and to fit the context. H translates 1191–94: "And held me there in true intent/ As the pearl me urged, who was so blessed,/ Thus disposed, drawn to God's Presence,/ To more of His mysteries I would have been led."

Þerfore my ioye watȝ sone toriuen°   *torn apart*
& I kaste of kytheȝ°þat lasteȝ aye   *cast from regions*
Lorde mad hit°arn þat agayn þe stryuen   *they*
1200 Oþer proferen þe oȝt agayn þy paye

101

To pay þe prince oþer sete saȝte°   *set at peace*
Hit is ful eþe° pe god Krystyin   *easy*
For I haf founden hym boþe day & naȝte°   *night*
A god a lorde a frende ful fyin°   *noble*
1205 Ouer þis hyul þis lote°I laȝte°   *fortune / took*
For pyty of my perle enclyin°   *lying prostrate*
& syþen°to God I hit bytaȝte°   *then / committed*
In Krysteȝ dere blessyng & myn
Þat in þe forme of bred & wyn
1210 Þe preste vus scheweȝ vch a daye
He gef°vus to be his homly hyne°   *granted / household servants*
Ande precious perleȝ vnto his pay
Amen   Amen

1198. kytheȝ: H kyþeȝ.
1201. sete: O sete hym.
1205. hyul: O hyiil.

1207. *hit*: the pearl.

1208. Norman Davis (RES 17:403–405) sees the phrase as a formula of greeting characteristic of those used in medieval and Renaissance times "by parents to their children," thus strengthening the elegiac interpreta-tion of the poem.

1209ff. Like H, I do not think *gef* (1211) to be a subjunctive. The poem simply does not end with a prayer, but with the dreamer's affirmation of faith in the sacrament.

· Sir Gawain ·
and the Green Knight

PART I

I

Siþen° þe sege & þe assaut
   wat3 sesed° at Troye   *after | had come to an end* (f.91a)
Þe bor3 brittened & brent°
   to bronde3 & aske3°   *city destroyed and burned | ashes*
Þe tulk° þat þe trammes° of tresoun þer wro3t   *man | plots*

1ff. Similar passages referring to the mythical founding of Britain by the Trojan Brutus are noted by Go at the beginning of *Winner and Waster* and at the conclusion of the alliterative *Morte Arthure*. Ebbs (JEGP 57:522–25) notes in connection with this passage and 2524–25 a recurrent device, present also in *Patience* 1 and 531, *Pearl* 1 and 1212, and, less noticeably, *Purity* 5–6 and 1805–8, of using framing passages as an indication of common authorship of the four poems.

Some mention should be made here of the fact that Laurita A. Hill (Spec 21:67–71) has shown that the capitalization of the MS does not fully support the convenient four-part division of the poem first designated by Madden and reprinted in all subsequent editions. I have, following the practice of the two EETS editions of the poem, here and in the other three poems reproduced the traditional divisions of earlier editions, but I have indicated by 24 point capitals the MS divisions at 619, 763, 1421, 1893, and 2259 as well as the major divisions at 491, 1126, and 1998. In spite of Miss Hill's arguments, the traditional arrangement seems to me to follow best the manuscript division, since the capitals in the MS at 491, 1126, and 1998 are larger and more ornate than the other five, and the natural divisions of the argument.

3. *Þe tulk*: Surely Go and Savage are right in seeing this as a reference to

4 Watȝ tried for his tricherie þe trewest on erthe
  Hit watȝ Ennias° þe athel°
    & his highe kynde°   *Aeneas | noble | kindred*
  Þat siþen depreced°prouinces & patrounes
    bicome   *later conquered*
  Welneȝe° of al þe wele° in þe West Iles   *almost | wealth*
8 Fro riche Romulus to Rome ricchis hym swyþe
  With gret bobbaunce° þat burȝe he
    biges vpon fyrst°   *pride | builds at first*
  & neuenes°hit his aune nome°
    as hit now hat°   *names | own name | is called*
  Ticius°to Tuskan & teldes
    bigynnes°   *Ticius goes | begins to build houses*

11. Ticius: D Tirius.

Antenor, the traditional traitor of Troy, who was in fact *tried for his tricherie* and banished. Earlier editors, confused perhaps by the syntax of *Hit watȝ Ennias* (5), took *þe tulk* to be Aeneas. They were thus forced (see notes in Madden and TG) to bring forward relatively obscure passages from Joseph of Exeter's *De Bello Trojano* which link Aeneas and Antenor as well as the medieval tradition that Aeneas was tried by the Greeks for concealing Polyxena, because of whom Achilles had been killed. Certainly, however, medieval people regarded Antenor as the great Trojan traitor, and the syntax of the poem clearly makes such a reading probable.

4. *tried*: Go glosses as "distinguished, famous." Go's statement, however, that the "first example in *NED* of 'try' used in the legal sense of a person in 1538"is misleading, since the general meaning of "try" in the legal sense of "to examine and determine (a cause or question) judicially" is noted in *Cursor Mundi* (c. 1300) and the transferred meaning could well have been used in the poet's time; certainly it fits the sense of the passage here.

7. *West Illes*: TG note that these are possibly Wight, Man, and the Orkneys. Go says simply "the western world," and D "western lands" generally.

8. Banks translates "then swiftly to Rome rich Romulus journeyed," which in spite of the confused construction (see Go's note) is certainly the sense of the passage. *Riche* here must mean "powerful," eminent.

11. *Ticius*: C. O. Chapman (MLN 63:58–60) thinks the unidentifiable Ticius may well be a scribal error for "Turnus," named in Higden's *Poly-*

12 Langaberde in Lumbardie lyftes vp homes
   & fer ouer þe French flod° Felix Brutus   *sea*
   On mony bonkkes ful° brode Bretayn he setteȝ   *slopes very*
      wyth wynne°   *joy*
16   Where werre & wrake & wonder
     Bi syþeȝ hatȝ wont° þerinne   *at times have dwelled*
     & oft boþe blysse & blunder
     Ful skete° hatȝ skyfted synne°   *swiftly / shifted since*

---

chronicon as *regem Tusciae*. Madden had suggested that the poet might indeed have meant Antenor, and Go, following Madden, suggests that Ticius "may be . . . a confused memory of the Titienses, the ancient Roman tribe said to be called after Titus Tatius, the Sabine king [in *Aeneid* 8:837–38]. . . ." D emends to *Tirius* following Silverstein's argument (MP 62: 189–206) that the father of Tuscus, "the name best suited to the founder of Tuscany," is sometimes referred to as Tirrus or Tirius in early commentaries on Virgil. This is certainly a parallel to *Langaberde* (12), "invented to be the eponymous founder of Tuscany" (TG), and indeed some such form as "Tuscius" may be intended.

12. *Langaberde*: Said by Nennius (*Historia Brittonum*, 17) to be the nephew of Felix Brutus and the legendary ancestor of the Longobardi or Lombards.

13. *Felix Brutus*: The mythical founder of Britain from whose name the name of the island is supposedly derived. First mentioned by Nennius in the ninth century, according to the legend he is either a grandson or great-grandson of Aeneas, and it seems certain that he is an invention of those early Britons who wished to claim for their race a noble Trojan descent like that of the Romans (see J. D. Bruce (1928), Baltimore, *The Evolution of Arthurian Romance*, II:51–53). The name "Felix" is apparently original with the *Gawain*-poet and was possibly coined for the sake of the alliteration, although T. Silverstein (MP 62:189–206) states that the adjective *felix* was traditionally used of founders of cities. D notes that *felix* could well be a corruption of *filius Brutus*, itself a corruption of Nennius' *Silvius Brutus*. B. S. Snell has suggested (NQ 49:75) that *blysse and blunder* (18) may be a pun on the name "Felix Brutus."

16. *wonder*: Clearly "marvels" in contrast to *werre & wrake* just as *blysse* (18) is in contrast to *blunder* (see Bonjour, ES 32:70–72). Wright claimed on the authority of Morris and the *NED* that *wonder* complemented the meaning of *werre & wrake* and should be glossed as "distress" or "disaster." A. MacDonald (MLR 30:343–44) translated *wonder* as "dreadful deeds, destruction" and maintained that it contrasted with *wynne* in 15.

II

20 Ande quen þis Bretayn watȝ bigged°
    bi þis burn rych°   *built / noble man*
  Bolde bredden° þerinne baret
    þat lofden°   *bold men bred / who loved strife*
  In mony turned tyme tene°þat wroȝten   *strife*
  Mo ferlyes° on þis folde han° fallen
    here oft   *more marvels / land have*
24 Þen in any oþer þat I wot° syn þat ilk° tyme   *know of / same*
  Bot of alle þat here bult° of Bretaygne kynges   *dwelt*
  Ay°watȝ Arthur þe hendest° as I haf herde
    telle   *ever / most courteous*
  Forþi° an aunter° in erde I
    attle° to schawe   *therefore / adventure / intend* (f.91b)
28 Þat a selly in siȝt summe men hit holden
  & an outtrage°awenter of Arthureȝ wondereȝ   *extraordinary*
  If ȝe wyl lysten þis laye bot on littel quile
  I schal telle hit as tit° as I in toun herde   *at once*

---

26. *Arthur*: For a convenient short history of the development of the legend of Britain's great mythical king see R. S. Loomis (1963), *The Development of Arthurian Romance*, New York.

28. *a selly in siȝt*: *selly*, normally an adjective, is here used as a noun, and the phrase may be taken to mean "a wondrous sight" as P. G. Thomas suggested (ES, 47:311–13). See also C. T. Onions.

30. *laye*: L. H. Loomis (*Arthurian Literature in the Middle Ages*) suggests that the use of *laye* here, along with a reference to the interlude in 472, suggests that the poet was familiar with current types of literature. Lines 30–31 are noted by Ebbs (JEGP, 57:522–25) as an example, like *Patience* 59–68, *Purity* 1153, and *GGK* 1996–7, of the poet's use of "the popular convention of oral story telling."

31–36. For a discussion of the sources of the poem, see Introduction.

31. *as I in toun herde*: A conventional medieval appeal to authority, this phrase does not imply a direct source for the poem. The verb *herde* may, by the way, very well attest to the existence of a continuing tradition of oral alliterative poetry in the west of England.

32   with tonge
        As hit is stad & stoken
        In stori stif & stronge
        With lel letteres loken
36   In londe so° hatȝ ben longe   *as it*

III

Þis kyng lay at Camylot vpon Krystmasse
With mony luflych°lorde ledeȝ° of þe best   *comely | men*
Rekenly° of þe Rounde Table alle þo rich breþer   *nobly*
40 With rych reuel oryȝt & rechles°merþes   *fitting and carefree*
Þer tournayed tulkes by tymeȝ ful mony

---

33. *stad & stoken*: Emerson suggests "fixed and established," and J. Speirs "as it had been put together or composed" (Scrut 18:195).

35–36. *lel letteres loken*: Probably "in correct letters fastened," a reference to the alliterative measure of the poem and to the "continuity of the alliterative tradition" (TG) *in londe so hatȝ ben longe.* Frankis, however, argues (NQ 85:329–30) that the phrase means "embodied in truthful words."

37. *Camylot*: Probably modern South Cadbury, though a number of sites in England, notably Winchester, have been suggested. See Leslie Alcock (1971), *Arthur's Britain*, New York.

37ff. This is one of several passages, as well as hundreds of words, discussed in terms of their "stylistic" values, both metrical and linguistic, by Marie Borroff in *Sir Gawain and the Green Knight: A Stylistic and Metrical Study*. Most of Borroff's findings, based primarily on the poet's use of words within the traditions of the alliterative line, are illuminating, though some seem highly speculative. Because of Borroff's good sense in providing an "Index of Words Discussed," I have refrained from listing her findings in the notes to this volume.

37ff. The description of Arthur's Christmas feast would seem to reflect very accurately the Christmas celebrations of a great English house in late medieval times. Go notes a number of contemporary accounts, and Elizabeth Salter (MP 64:233–35) draws a number of parallels between the poem and descriptions of Christmas festivities at Tutbury, one of the castles of John of Gaunt. Certainly Christmas Day, along with Easter, Ascension, Whitsunday, and All Saints, are the great feast days of the Arthurian year.

39. *þe Rounde Table*: Several accounts exist of the origins of this fa-

Justed ful jolile þise gentyle kniȝtes

Syþen kayred°to þe court caroles to make   *then rode*

44 For þer þe fest watȝ ilyche°ful fiften dayes   *the same*

With alle þe mete°& þe mirþe

þat men couþe avyse°   *food / could devise*

Such glaum° ande gle glorious to here   *merry sounds*

Dere dyn° vpon day daunsyng on nyȝtes   *pleasant noises*

48 Al watȝ hap°vpon heȝe in halleȝ & chambreȝ   *happiness*

With lordeȝ & ladies as leuest him þoȝt

With all þe wele°of þe worlde þay

woned°þer samen°   *joy / dwelled / together*

Þe most kyd°knyȝteȝ vnder Krystes seluen   *famous*

52 & þe louelokkest°ladies þat euer lif haden   *fairest*

& he þe comlokest°kyng þat þe court haldes°   *comeliest / rules*

46. glaum ande: ᴍꜱ, Go glaumande.

---

mous board. According to Laȝamon, who is elaborating a statement in Wace (there is no mention of it in Geoffrey of Monmouth), the Round Table, at which 1600 could sit, was built by a Cornish carpenter at Arthur's request because of a brawl that had broken out among the knights concerning precedence in seating. Robert de Boron states, however, that the table was made for Uther on the model of the Grail table of Joseph of Arimathea, itself a replica of the table of the Last Supper. Malory reports that Merlin himself made the table "in tokenyng of roundnes of the worlde," but elsewhere in the *Morte Darthur* reports that the Round Table was a part of Guinevere's dowry.

43. *caroles*: Originally simple ring dances accompanied by song, carols evolved into highly complex verse forms. For contemporary accounts, see the notes in Go and TG and *GGK* 1026.

44. *ful*: Go takes *ful* as an adjective modifying *fest* rather than as an adverb modifying *fiften*. Line 45 in turn thus modifies *watȝ ful*.

44. *fiften dayes*: Until Jan. 8. Feasts of great length were apparently not regarded as unusual.

46. *glaum ande gle*: Emerson's suggested reading, followed by TG and D, of ᴍꜱ *glaumande gle*. The scribe, as in 1426, apparently confused the participial ending with the conjunctive, there being no evidence of verbal equivalents of *glaum* and *glauer*.

48. *upon hyȝe*: "aloft" (Wright).

49. *him*: Plural "them."

For al watʒ þis fayre folk in her first age°　　　*their prime*
　　　on sille

56　Þe hapnest° vnder heuen　　　*most fortunate*
　　　Kyng hyʒest mon of wylle°　　　*mind*
　　　Hit were now gret nye°to neuen°　　　*difficulty | name*
　　　So hardy a here°on hille　　　*company of warriors*

IV

60　Wyle Nw ʒer watʒ so ʒep° þat hit watʒ nwe cummen　　　*fresh*
　　　Þat day doubble on þe dece°watʒ þe douth°
　　　　serued　　　*dais | company*
　　　Fro°þe kyng watʒ cummen with knyʒtes into þe halle　　　*when*
　　　Þe chauntre of þe chapel cheued° to an
　　　　ende　　　*came*
64　Loude crye watʒ þer kest of clerkeʒ & oþer
　　　Nowel nayted° onewe neuened
　　　　ful° ofte　　　*celebrated | named very* (f.92a)

58. were: ᴍs werere.
60. Nw ʒer: ᴍs, Go nw ʒer; W New Yer.
60. nwe: Go ʒister-neue; W newe.

---

55. *on sille*: Emerson translates freely "on earth," Banks "seated there," and I might suggest "in the hall."

58–59. See 165–66n.

63. *Þe chauntre of þe chapel*: Savage (JEGP 51:537–44) maintains that the mass celebrated here is that of the *festum subdiaconorum* or "Feast of Fools" appropriate to January 1 and marked by *loude crye* and *nowel nayted onewe*. Savage remarks generally of the poem that one "cannot fail to notice the attention and respect which its [the poem's] hero, and con-sequently its creator, pay to the regular and orderly sequence of the services of the Church." Emerson takes *þe chauntre* to refer to the mass itself and notes that the "order of events [in 63ff.] is hearing of mass in the chapel, the entrance to the hall by the kings and knights, the noisy demanding and receiving of New Year's gifts, the feast itself with the double serving."

63. *cheued*: I read this as a past participle: "When the king came with his knights into the hall—the chapel ceremony having ending—a loud cry. . . ."

& syþen riche° forth runnen to
  reche hondeselle°   *then nobles / give New Year's gifts*
ȝeȝed ȝeres° ȝiftes on
  hiȝ ȝelde hem° bi hond   *cried the year's / give them*
68 Debated busyly aboute þo giftes
Ladies laȝed ful loude þoȝ þay lost haden
& he þat wan°watȝ not wrothe þat may ȝe
  wel trawe°   *won / believe*
Alle þis mirþe þay maden to þe mete tyme
72 When þay had waschen worþyly þay wenten to sete
Þe best burne ay abof as hit best semed
Whene Guenore ful gay grayþed° in þe myddes   *set*
Dressed°on þe dere des dubbed°al aboute   *placed / adorned*

---

67. *ȝeȝed ȝeres-ȝiftes on hiȝ*: The giving of gifts at New Year's dates back at least to the twelfth century (see TG's note), though very little is known about the exact manner in which such gifts were given. Go notes a difference between the *hondeselle* (66) given by the nobles only to their retainers and the gifts (67) given to the guests, a distinction which, even if present, has little effect upon our reading of the poem. The games which accompanied distribution of the gifts have not been reconstructed. The gifts were called out (*ȝeȝed ... on hiȝ*) and possibly were distributed personally *bi hond* by the great lords. There was evidently a great deal of good-humored comparison of the gifts—the guests we learn *debated busyly aboute þo giftes* (68)—and if Emerson and Onions are correct, as I think they are, about that gift which the knights won and the ladies laughed at having lost,

many exchanges of kisses took place. One should perhaps mention in passing that the English are to this day much more casual in kissing on greeting (974) and parting (1300) than are most northern Europeans.

73. *Þe best burne ay abof*: Since no such distinction could be made at Arthur's Round Table, we must envision here a table and a custom of the author's own time. There is a parallel here to the description of the wedding feast in *Purity*. See 107*n*.

74. *Guenore*: For an interesting account of the development of the character of Arthur's queen, see Tom Peete Cross and W. A. Nitze (1930), *Lancelot and Guinevere: A Study in the Origins of Courtly Love,* Chicago.

75. *des dubbed*: Emerson regarded the series of phrases beginning with *dubbed* as modifying *des* and not *Guenore*. *Þe comlokest* in 81 thus refers back to *Guenore*, and the *smal*

76 Smal sendal° bisides a selure° hir ouer   *fine silk | canopy*
    Of tryed Tolouse of Tars tapites innoghe
    Þat were enbrawded & beten°wyth þe best gemmes   *set*
    Þat myȝt be preued of prys wyth penyes to bye
80   in daye°   *ever*
        Þe comlokest to discrye°   *look on*
        Þer glent° with yȝen gray   *glanced*
        A semloker°þat euer he syȝe   *comelier one*
84   Soth moȝt no mon say°   *speak of*

V

    Bot Arthure wolde not ete til al were serued
    He watȝ so joly of his joyfnes° & sumquat child-gered   *youth*

77. Tolouse of Tars: Go Tolouse & Tars.

---

sendal bisides of 76 refers to the curtains at the side of the dais, not at Guinevere's side.

77. *Tolouse*: A red silk fabric, probably originally imported from Toulouse, called generally *tuly* or sometimes (568) *tule*.

77. *Tars*: A rich cloth, probably of gold, its name derived (see *NED*) from the rich kingdom of Tharsia (see 571).

82. *yȝen gray*: A standard attribute of the courtly heroine.

84. *soth*: Emerson emends to *sothly* for the sake of the metrical pattern.

85ff. Hans Schnyder (*Sir Gawain and the Green Knight: An Essay in Interpretation*) uses these lines, along with 492, 280, 682–83, Arthur's willingness to "sacrifice" Gawain, and various references in the literature of the period, to support a theory of Arthur's pride and the corruption of his court. Arthur, according to Schnyder, is "Fortune's fool, he has been spoiled by prosperity, and he consequently fails to meet the test when the Green Knight makes himself known as the herald of adversity to come." Thus Gawain, instead of Arthur, is tempted by various trials of Dame Fortuna, represented in the poem by both Morgan and Bercilak's wife.

86. *child-gered*: Go derives from OF *giere*, a variant of *chiere*, "which should give in ME gere (=jere). Accordingly 'child-gered' may equal 'child-jered,' i.e. child-mannered. . . ." C. A. Luttrell (NQ 86:447–50) derives the term from ME *gere*, "a wild or changeful mood," and translates *child-gered* as "childish excitement." TG's "boyish" seems an accurate rendering, whatever the derivation.

His lif liked hym lyȝt he louied þe lasse
88 Auþer°to longe lye or to longe sitte   *either*
So bisied him his ȝonge blod & his brayn wylde
& also anoþer maner meued° him eke   *habit moved*
Þat he þurȝ nobelay°had nomen he wolde neuer ete   *nobility*
92 Vpon such a dere day er hym deuised were
Of sum auenturus þyng an vncouþe° tale   *strange*
Of sum mayn° meruayle þat he myȝt trawe   *great*
Of alderes° of armes of oþer auenturus   *princes*
96 Oþer sum segg hym bisoȝt of sum siker knyȝt
To joyne wyth hym in iustyng in joparde to lay
Lede lif for lyf leue vchon oþer
As fortune wolde fulsun hom þe fayrer to haue
100 Þis watȝ kynges countenaunce°where he in
    court were   *behavior*
At vch farand fest° among his
    fre meny°   *splendid festival / noble company*
    in halle   (f.92b)
Þerfore of face so fere°   *proud*
104 He stiȝtleȝ stif in stalle
Ful ȝeþ in þat Nw ȝere
Much mirthe he mas° with alle   *makes*

88. longe (1st): MS lenge.
95. Of (1st): MS Of of.
100. watȝ: Go, D watȝ þe.

87. *lyȝt*: As D suggests, this is adjectival: "he liked his life to be gay."

90ff. A common Arthurian custom first noted in the Vulgate *Merlin* (ed. Sommer, II, 320). For parallel instances, see Go's and TG's notes.

96–99. D is certainly correct in taking *lif* (98) as the object of *lay* (97). However, *lede* (98) is perhaps best taken as an attributive use of the noun, here modifying *lif*. The sense of the passage thus reads "Or some man besought him (Arthur) of a worthy opponent to join with him in jousting, to lay in hazard one man's life for another's, each allowing the other the advantage as fate would have it."

104. *in stalle*: TG and D, "standing up"; Go, in a "standing position"; Wright, in a "place of honor."

VI

Thus þer stondes in stale þe stif kyng hisseluen
108 Talkkande bifore þe hyȝe table of trifles ful hende
There gode Gawan watȝ grayþed° Gwenore bisyde   *set*
& Agrauayn a la dure mayn°on þat oþer
    syde sittes   *of the hard hand*
Boþe þe kynges sister sunes & ful siker°kniȝtes   *trusty*
112 Bishop Bawdewyn abof bigineȝ þe table

107ff. TG's diagram of the table arrangements is apparently incorrect. Arthur is correctly seen as sitting in the middle of a "high table" placed at right angles to other tables running down the sides of the hall (*þe sidbordeȝ*, 115), but surely Bishop Baldwin would "begin the board" (112) as guest of honor at Arthur's right and Yvain, his dining partner (128), would in turn be at the bishop's right. The queen would be at the king's left, and Gawain and Agravain, another dining pair, would be seated next to her (see Emerson in JEGP 26:252–54 and SP 22:180–83, and Go's notes). The company would thus be served in pairs (128).

109. *Gawan*: The son of King Loth of Lothian (Malory's King Lot of Lowthean and Orkeney) and son of one of Arthur's half-sisters—Anna in Geoffrey, Morgause in Malory. He is the greatest of the French Arthurian heroes, noted for his courtesy, and probably has his literary descent from a Celtic sun god (see R. S. Loomis, *Celtic Myth and Arthurian Romance*). Loomis, Buchanan (PMLA, 47:315–18), and the great number of "Cel-

ticist" critics of the poem (see Introduction) suggest that Gawain is frequently the counterpart of the Irish hero Cuchulainn. For a comprehensive review of the puzzling changes in his reputation as a hero of chivalry, especially his denigration in the later French romances, see B. J. Whiting MS 9:189–234) and Alan Markman (PMLA 72:574–86). For variant spellings of his name, see TG's note.

110. *Agrauyn a la dure mayn*: One of Gawain's younger brothers, he is in the later French romances and in Malory along with Mordred jealous of Lancelot and a traitor to the king. He is also given *dures mains* in Chrétien's *Perceval* (l. 9510) and *herten hende* in the Middle High German *Parzival* of Claus Wisse and Phillipp Colin.

112. *Bischop Bawdewyn*: Why Bishop Baldwin should have the place of honor is not explained in the poem. He is descended from the Bishop Bedwine of the *Mabinogion* and becomes Arthur's archbishop in the fifteenth-century OF Vulgate Prose Cycle of romances and in Malory. Madden suggests that the name may

& Ywan Vryn son ette wit hymseluen

Þise were diȝt° on þe des & derworþly°   *placed / honorably*
      serued

& siþen mony siker segge at þe sidbordeȝ

116 Þen þe first cors come with crakkyng°of trumpes   *blaring*

Wyth mony baner ful bryȝt þat þerbi henged

Nwe nakryn noyse with þe noble pipes

Wylde werbles & wyȝt wakned lote

120 Þat mony hert ful hiȝe hef at her towches

Dayntes dryuen° þerwyth of ful dere
      metes°   *come / precious foods*

Foysoun° of þe fresche° & on so
      fele disches   *abundance / fresh foods*

Þat pine to fynde þe place þe peple biforne

124 For to sette þe sylueren þat sere sewes° halden   *potages*

---

113. wit: TG, D, W with.
124. sylueren: MS syluener.

---

be taken from "an Archbishop of Canterbury named Baldwin, who held the see from 1184 to 1191."

113. *Ywan, Vryn son*: Like Gawain, one of Arthur's half-nephews, Yvain is the son of King Urien of Gore and one of Arthur's half-sisters, Brimesent (Morgan le Fay in Malory?). TG's note supplies a brief sketch of him.

113. *wit hymselven*: Almost certainly, as D notes, "beside him," that is, Bishop Baldwin. Brett, however, suggests (MLR 22:66) that it may mean "them" and Grattan (RES 1: 486) reads *hymselven* as "the king."

114ff. The description of Arthur's feasting here is very similar to that of Belshazzar's feast in *Purity*.

118ff. These lines (along with *GGK* 1165–66, 1141, 1362–64, 1465–67, 1952–53, 1654–56; with *Pearl* 881–84; and with *Purity* 1080–84, 1210, 1783, and 1413–16) are used by Chapman (PMLA 46:177–81) to demonstrate the poet's knowledge of a variety of forms of court music.

118–120. "The din of new drums along with the noble pipes, the wild and valiant strains, awakened [such a] noise that many a heart swelled at their sound."

118. *nakryn*: Go lists this as a genitive plural, D as an adjective.

119. See 639*n*.

123. *pine*: "it was difficult to" (D).

124. *sylueren*: "silver dishes," first emended from *syluener* by Morris.

on clothe
Iche lede° as he loued° hymselue   *each man / pleased*
Þer laght° withouten loþe   *took*
128   Ay° two had disches twelue   *each*
Good ber & bryȝt wyn boþe

VII

Now wyl I of hor seruise say yow no more
For vch wyȝe may wel wit° no wont þat þer were   *know*
132   An oþer noyse ful newe neȝed biliue
Þat þe lude myȝt haf leue liflode to cach
For vneþe°watȝ þe noyce not a whyle sesed   *hardly*
& þe fyrst cource in þe court kyndely° serued   *properly*
136   Þer hales°in at þe halle dor an aghlich
      mayster°   *comes / ugly knight*
On þe most on þe molde on mesure hyghe
Fro þe swyre°to þe swange°so sware°&
      so þyk   *neck / waist / square*
& his lyndes°& his lymes so longe & so grete   *loins*
Half etayn in erde I hope þat he were   *(f.93a)*
141   Bot mon most°I algate mynn°hym to bene°   *must / think / be*

---

127. *withouten loþe*: "ungrudged" (D); "with pleasure" (Magoun).

132–3. "A different, very new, noise quickly approached, so that the prince might be allowed to take food" (D).

134. *not*: Superfluous in translation: "the sound had scarcely ceased for a moment."

136ff. Wright suggests that in the Green Knight's conduct there is reflected a large degree of play-acting.

137. *On þe moste on þe molde*: "the largest on earth." For this use of "one" as strengthening the superlative, see

NED "one," *numeral*, a. 26. Also cf. *GGK* 2363 and *Purity* 892.

137. L. H. Loomis (*Arthurian Literature in the Middle Ages*) lists the Green Knight's size along with his "fierce eyes, silent as he enters the hall, his great axe. . . , his high praise of the court, his exit carrying his head" as "elements to be found in *GGK*, but not in *Caradoc*."

140–42. "Half a giant on earth I believe he was; but even so I must declare him more like a man."

& þat þe myriest° in his muckel° þat myȝt ride   *fairest / size*
For of bak & of brest al were his bodi sturne
144 Both his wombe°& his wast were worthily°smale *belly / fittingly*
& alle his fetures folȝande°in forme þat he hade *following*
     ful clene° *fair*
For wonder of his hwe men hade
148 Set in his semblaunt sene° *appearance clearly*
He ferde°as freke were fade *acted*
& oueral enker grene

144. Both: ᴍs Bot.

143. *sturne*: Probably both "strong" (G) and "massive" (Savage).

144. *Both*: Emended from *Bot* by Napier and by TG, Go, and D, who compare it with *wit* in 113. In spite of the temptation to see *bot* as enforcing a contrast between this and the preceding line (Emerson; Menner [MLN 41:399]), the concessive *al were* of 143 will not allow for *bot*.

149. *fade*: An interesting word of unknown origin. TG glossed it "bold" and Go "hostile, fierce" from context. Emerson suggested "orderly" as derived from ᴏᴇ *fæd* (*gefæd*). Onions (TLS, Jan. 20 and Feb. 3, 1927) derived it from a dialect "fade" found in Wright's *Dictionary of Obsolete and Provincial English* and designated there as "the decayed part of cheese"; he thus took the term to refer to the Green Knight's color. Kenneth Sisam, replying in the pages of TLS (Jan. 27 and March 17, 1927), disagreed and reiterated the case for "fierce." G. V. Smithers (NQ 74:134–36) suggested that *fade* had reference to a "supernatural being" and derived the term from Lat. *fadius*. Isaac Jackson also found *fade* to have some connection with "fee" though he derived it from Breton *fata*; Jackson's gloss, however, was criticized by Sisam (NQ 74:239) who thought that such a term would have been obscure to the poet's audience. However, "fee" has a meaning somehow related to "fairy" and the supernatural certainly fits the context. It is probably preferable to "fierce" or "bold."

150. *enker grene*: A translation apparently of *vert encré*, "truly" or "very" green (see Go's note).

The Green Knight's color has figured prominently in many interpretations of the poem (see Introduction). The early "myth" critics, e.g. E. K. Chambers (*The Medieval Stage*), W. A. Nitze (MP 33:351–66), A. B. Cook (Folklore, 17:430–41), vigorously maintained that the color green indicated that the Green Knight was essentially some form of the "vegetation spirit," an interpretation even more vigorously denied by G. L. Kittredge (*Sir Gawain and the Green Knight*),

VIII

Ande al grayþed° in grene þis gome & his wedes   *clothed*
152 A strayt° cote ful streȝt þat stek on his sides   *tight*

---

who maintained that neither the *Ga-wain*-poet nor any of his sources "had any notion of associating the challenger with Celtic 'probably arboreal' spirits, Arician groves, spirits of vegetation or the annual death and rebirth of the embodied vital principle. To them he was merely an enchanter, a shape-shifter, or else a human being under spells. . . ."

There have been, as one would expect, a number of attempts to find some reason for the Green Knight's color in the Celtic forbears, known or unknown, of the poem. Loomis (PMLA 48:1000–35; *Celtic Myth and Arthurian Romance*; and *Arthurian Tradition and Chrétien de Troyes*) finds in the Guingambresil episode of Chrétien's *Conte del Graal* a green- or possibly grey-mantled (depending on how one translates OF *glas*) stranger who is both challenger and later host. R. M. Smith (JEGP 45:1–25) in turn claims that Find Ban mac Bresail in the Ossianic cycle may be the prototype of Chrétien's Guingambresil. L. H. Loomis notes (*Arthurian Literature in the Middle Ages*) however, that "the challenger in no version antedating *GGK* appears as a green giant, clad in green and riding a green horse."

Krappe (Spec 13:206–15), Randall (SP 57:479–91), and Zimmer (*The King and the Corpse*) see green as the color of Death and so identify the Green Knight either as the Lord of Hades (Krappe), a testing "fende" from Hell (Randall), or Death himself (Zimmer).

Hulbert (MP 13:433–62 and 689–730) noted that the color green is essentially a "fairy color" and used this fact to support his theory that the Beheading Game and the testing of Gawain existed originally in a single story dealing with the courtship of a Fairy Mistress.

Goldhurst (CE 20:61–65), later supported by J. S. Lewis (CE 21:50–51), thought that green (the "primitive and sometimes brutal forces of nature") and gold (the refinements of civilization) were opposed in the description of the Green Knight and in the poem generally to support the theme that nature makes known its demands "even to those who take shelter behind the civilized comforts of court life."

In a highly influential restatement of the Vegetation Spirit theory, John Speirs (*Medieval English Poetry, the Non-Chaucerian Tradition*) identified the Green Knight as "the Green Man —the Jack-in-the-Green or the Wild Man of the village festivals of England and Europe. He is the descendant of the Vegetation or Nature god of . . . almost universal and immemorial tradition whose death and resurrection mythologizes the annual death and re-birth of nature." He is "wild, uncouth, raw life."

A mere mantile abof mensked° withinne   *adorned*

With pelure pured apert° þe pane

    ful clene°   *fur trimmed clearly / fair*

With blyþe blaunner ful bryȝt & his hod boþe

156 Þat watȝ laȝt° fro his lokkeȝ & layde on his

    schulderes   *caught back*

Heme wel-haled hose of þat same grene

Þat spenet° on his sparlyr° & clene

    spures vnder   *were fastened / calf*

---

157. Heme wel-haled: Go Heme-wel haled.
157. same grene: D same.

There have been a few attempts to use the Green Knight's color to identify him as a known fourteenth-century person. Highfield (MÆ 22: 18–23) sees in the Green Knight an allusion to a Simon Newton referred to as *scutifer viridis*, Braddy (MLN 67:240–42) to one Ralph Holmes, a soldier bearing the nickname "green knight" and decapitated in Spain in 1369, and d'Ardenne (RES 10: 113–26) to the "Green Count," Amadeus VI, Count of Savoy (1334–83), a contemporary of the author of *GGK*.

The most startling theory is that of Hans Schnyder (*Sir Gawain and the Green Knight: An Essay in Interpretation*) who uses the color green to assist in his identification of the Green Knight at the anagogical level with Christ, who is "fertile [hence green] in good works." As Kittredge remarked of the "myth" critics, "thought is free."

153. *mere*: TG and D derive this, wrongly I think, from OE *myrige*, "merry" or "fair." The word also ap-

pears in 878, 924, and 1495 with its usual meaning of "splendid, noble."

154. *pane*: TG, "fur-lining"; Go, "cloth"; Thomas (ES 47:311), "shirt." D's "facing of fur at the edge of the mantle" seems reasonable.

155. *blaunner*: Go, following Kaluza, derives this from a "compound of *blaun* (< OF *blanc*) and OF *neir*, black, hence 'ermine'." TG had derived conjecturally from OF *blanc de mer* and translated it "white fur." Older editors simply gloss it "fur" from the context.

157. *Heme wel-haled*: I am following TG and D here. Go had suggested *Heme-wel*, "fitly." Emerson's suggestion that *heme* is an adverb meaning "closely" seems best to fit the text, although Magoun's "properly" or "neatly" also work well. Onions had suggested that *heme* was actually *hem* and translated the phrase "with the hem." D omits *grene* on the grounds that "the second half-line is too heavy."

Of bryȝt golde vpon silk bordes barred° ful ryche   *striped*
160 & scholes vnder schankes þere þe schalk° rides   *man*
  & alle his vesture uerayly watȝ clene verdure°   *pure green*
  Boþe þe barres of his belt & oþer blyþe stones
  Þat were richely rayled° in his aray clene   *arranged*
164 Aboutte hymself & his sadel vpon silk werkeȝ°   *embroidery*
  Þat were to tor° for to telle of tryfles° þe halue   *hard / details*
  Þat were enbrauded°abof wyth
   bryddes & flyȝes°   *embroidered / birds and butterflies*
  With gay gaudi of grene þe golde ay
   inmyddes°   *ever in the middle*
168 Þe pendauntes of his payttrure° þe proude
   cropure   *horse trappings*
  His molaynes & alle þe metail anamayld was þenne
  Þe steropes þat he stod on stayned of þe same

168. þe (2nd): MS pe.

160. *scholes*: A well-fought term. The majority party would seem to favor the obvious "shoeless" as fitting the primitive, yet unwarlike, appearance of the Green Knight. See Emerson (MLN 36:212–15), C. Clark (RES 6: 174–77 and M. Rigby (RES 7: 173–74). Go, however, takes *scholes* to be supports "covering the sole of the foot, and more especially under the shank . . . on the part between heel and sole." For other theories, see Go's note.

165–66. Noted by Ebbs (JEGP 57: 522–25), along with 58–59 and with *Pearl* 133–36 and *Purity* 1375–76, as examples of the poet's "expressing his inability to describe some feature . . . or to give a satisfactory count of a large group of people."

167. *gaudi*: Probably used in a collective sense, here meaning "ornamentation." Gauds were large beads used in the Rosary "to mark the fifteen mysteries (the first five of which are 'joyful mysteries') to be meditated upon in reciting the fifteen decades of aves" (*NED*). By 1430 the word had come to mean a "showy ornament, a piece of finery" (*NED*) and its use in this passage seems simply a collective extension of this meaning.

169. *molaynes*: H. L. Savage, quoting Kelham's *Dictionary of the Norman Language*, glosses as "bits, bosses for bridles," though the correct gloss, as D notes, is "bosses, bits for bridles."

    & his arsounȝ° al after & his aþel skurtes   *saddlebows*

172 Þat euer glemered & glent° al of grene stones   *glinted*

    Þe fole° þat he ferkkes° on fyn of þat ilke   *horse / rides*

        sertayn

    A grene hors gret & þikke

176 A stede ful stif to strayne°   *hard to restrain*

    In brawden° brydel quik   *embroidered*

    To þe gome he watȝ ful gayne°   *ready* (f.93b)

IX

    Wel gay watȝ þis gome gered in grene

180 & þe here of his hed of his hors swete

    Fayre fannand fax vmbefoldes° his

        schulderes   *waving hair hangs about*

    A much° berd as a busk° ouer his brest henges   *great / bush*

    Þat wyth his hiȝlich° here þat of° his hed reches   *splendid / from*

---

171. skurtes: MS, TG sturtes; D skyrtes; W scurtes.
182. as: MS as as.

---

171. *skurtes*: The MS form *sturtes* is said by TG to be derived from OE *steort*, "tail," and to refer here to some sort of "projection" on the horse's equipment (see *NED* under "start," *n*). Menner (MLR 19:204–8) took the word to refer to the "studded nails" ornamenting the horse's gear. Despite, however, the TLS reviewer (Jan. 25, 1941) who called Go's emendation to *skurtes* unnecessary "if one looks at the manuscript illustration, which shows Gringolet's [not, mind you, the Green Knight's horse's] trappings," I, like D, find Go's emendation illuminating and useful.

173. *fyn of þat ilk*: "was in hue still the same" (Banks); "gay with that same (green)" (TG).

180. *of his horse swete*: Go derives, as in 2518 and 191, from OF *suite*, "the same," the line thus meaning that the Green Knight's hair matched that of his horse, a perfectly reasonable statement following 175 where the horse is said to be "grene." There is no point in attempting, as does Go, to rearrange the syntax. Emerson simplifies the passage by rendering "swete" as "fine, good," a practice followed by Banks: "This hero in green was habited gaily,/ And likewise the hair on the head of his good horse."

184 Watȝ euesed al vmbetorne abof his elbowes

Þat half his armes þervnder were halched° in

    þe wyse   *enclosed*

Of a kyngeȝ capados þat closes his swyre°   *neck*

Þe mane of þat mayn° hors much to hit lyke   *great*

188 Wel cresped & cemmed° wyth knottes

    ful mony   *curled and combed*

Folden in° wyth fildore° aboute þe

    fayre grene   *entwined | gold thread*

Ay a herle° of þe here an oþer of golde   *strand*

Þe tayl of his toppyng twynnen°

    of a sute°   *forelock joined in | match*

192 & bounden boþe wyth a bande of a bryȝt grene

Dubbed wyth ful dere stoneȝ as þe dok

    lasted°   *tail extended*

Syþen þrawen° wyth a þwong° a þwarle knot

    alofte   *twisted | thong*

Þer° mony belleȝ ful bryȝt of brende° golde

    rungen   *where | burnished*

196 Such a fole° vpon folde ne freke þat hym rydes   *horse*

Watȝ neuer sene in þat sale° wyth syȝt er þat tyme   *hall*

---

184. *euesed al vmbetorne*: Onions glosses "clipped all round about" and derives *vmbetorne* from Low German *umtrent*, "roundabout, approximately, very near."

186. *capados*: Clearly a hood or cape, probably from OF **cape à dos*, rather than a "tunic of Cappadocian leather" (TG). Such a hood fit closely at the neck (*closes his swyre* and *closed aloft* [572]). G. L. Hamilton (MP 5:365–76) believes the original of the garment to be like the French *chaperon* worn under the helmet and to have originally been made of Cappadocian leather. Marie Borroff (trans. *GGK*, New York, 1967) suggests a derivation from *cap-à-dos*, "from head to back," by analogy with *cap-à-pie*. For further theories, see Go's note.

194. *þwarle knot*: Onions is probably right in comparing *þwarle knot* to Lancashire dialect *wharl-knot*, "tight knot." There seems no good reason for adopting Go's *þwarte-knot*, "cross knot" or TG's "intricate" from OE *þweorh*.

with yȝe
He loked as layt°so lyȝt°   *lightning | bright*
200 So sayd al þat hym syȝe
Hit semed as no mon myȝt
Vnder his dyntteȝ dryȝe°   *blows survive*

X

Wheþer° hade he no helme
    ne hawbergh nauþer°   *yet | helmet nor coat of mail either*
204 Ne no pysan° ne no plate þat pented°
    to armes   *breastplate | pertained*
Ne no schafte° ne no schelde to schwue° ne
    to smyte   *spear | thrust*
Bot in his on honde he hade a holyn bobbe
Þat is grattest in grene when greueȝ° ar bare   *groves*
208 & an ax in his oþer a hoge &
    vnmete°   *a huge one and monstrous*
A spetos sparþe°to expoun in spelle°
    quoso myȝt   *cruel ax | describe*
Þe lenkþe of an elnȝerde° þe large hede hade   *ell rod*

203. hawbergh: ᴍs hawbrgh.
210. lenkþe . . . hede: ᴍs, TG, Go, W hede . . . lenkþe.

---

206. *holyn bobbe*: Savage notes that
the custom of carrying a holly bob as
a "sign of . . . peaceful intention" per-
sisted in the north of England into the
nineteenth century. Certainly this is
its meaning in the poem. Other uses
of the holly have been suggested:
Krappe points out (Spec 13:206–15)
that it was in Celtic lands "closely asso-
ciated with the powers of death" and
so helps in the poem to identify the
Green Knight with Death; and Ran-
dall notes (SP 57:479–91) that the
holly was often associated with other-
world visitors.

208. *an ax*: Krappe (Spec 206–15)
maintains that the ax identifies the
Green Knight as Death, "the only
deathless executioner known."

210. I am following here D's trans-
position of *hede* and *lenkþe*, a change
which clarifies an otherwise puzzling
line. Apparently the transposition of
similar words within the line was a
habit of the scribe: cf. 785 and 1719.

Þe grayn al of grene stele & of golde hewen
212 Þe bit burnyst bryȝt with a brod egge
As wel schapen to schere°as scharp rasores   *cut*
Þe stele of a stif staf þe sturne hit bigrypte
Þat watȝ wounden wyth yrn to þe wandeȝ° ende   *handle's* (f.94a)
216 & al bigrauen with grene in gracios werkes
A lace°lapped aboute þat louked° at þe hede   *thong / fastened*
& so after þe halme halched° ful ofte   *shaft looped*
Wyth tryed°tasseleȝ þerto tacched
    innoghe°   *fine / fastened many*
220 On botounȝ° of þe bryȝt grene brayden°
    ful ryche   *to bosses / embroidered*
Þis haþel heldeȝ hym in & þe halle entres
Driuande° to þe heȝe dece dut°
    he no woþe°   *coming / feared / danger*
Haylsed°he neuer one bot heȝe he ouer loked   *greeted*
224 Þe fyrst word þat he warp° wher is he sayd   *uttered*
Þe gouernour of þis gyng° gladly I wolde   *assembly*
Se þat segg in syȝt & with hymself speke raysoun
228   To knyȝteȝ he kest his yȝe
    & reled hym vp & doun

---

211. *grayn*: At least four opinions have been offered: the "spiked shaft of the gisarm [the shaft]" (TG); the "forked blade branching off from the pike-head" (Go); "the thick part of the head of the axe, where it, as it were, branches off from the stem of the handle" (Wright); and "the spike at the back of the axe" (Brett in MLR 10:190).

214ff. The syntax here is puzzling because of the otiose *hit*. I would recommend here Go's punctuation (left unexplained by him) which treats *þe stele*, "the shaft" (214), as the object of *lapped aboute* in 217. D suggests treating "the second half of [214] as relative: 'the shaft of a stout staff by which the grim knight gripped it'."

219–20. See 280*n*.

229. *reled hym vp and doun*: Go Emerson, and Wright agree, following Naiper, that *reled hym* refers to *yȝe* in the previous line and that the phrase should be translated "rolled them [his eyes] to and fro." Morton Bloomfield,

He stemmed & con studie°   *stopped and looked closely*
Quo walt° þer most renoun   *had*

XI

232 Ther watȝ lokyng on lenþe þe lude to beholde
     For vch mon had meruayle quat hit mene myȝt
     Þat a haþel & a horse myȝt such a hwe lach°   *hue take*
     As growe grene as þe gres & grener hit semed
236 Þen grene aumayl° on golde glowande bryȝter   *enamel*
     Al studied° þat þer stod & stalked hym nerre   *watched*
     Wyth al þe wonder of þe worlde what he worch schulde
     For fele sellyeȝ had þay sen bot such neuer are°   *before*
240 Forþi for fantoum & fayryȝe þe folk þere hit demed
     Þerfore to answare watȝ arȝe° mony aþel freke   *afraid*
     & al stouned° at his steuen° & stonstil seten   *amazed / voice*
     In a swoghe° sylence þurȝ þe sale riche   *dead*
244 As al were slypped vpon slepe so slaked hor loteȝ
         in hyȝe°   *haste*
     I deme hit not al for doute
     Bot sum for cortaysye
248   Bot let hym þat al schulde loute°   *bow to*
     Cast° vnto þat wyȝe   *speak*

236. glowande: ᴍꜱ lowande.

---

however, has suggested that *hym* may well be reflexive and that the Green Knight "rolled up and down," i.e. back and forth, on his horse.

237. *þat þer stad*: D takes these to be the retainers standing about the hall.

244. *loteȝ*: "uproar" (Savage, in MLN 60:492–93). See 639*n.*

246–47. *al ... sum*: D believes these to be adverbs: "I think it was not entirely owing to fear, but partly out of courtesy."

249. Emerson wished to add *word* or *speche* after *cast* to improve the metrics of the line.

XII

Þenn Arþour bifore þe hiȝ dece þat auenture byholdeȝ
& rekenly°hym reuerenced for rad°was he neuer   *nobly / afraid*
252 & sayde wyȝe welcum iwys to þis place
   Þe hede of þis ostel Arthour I hat°   *am called (f.94b)*
   Liȝt luflych°adoun & lenge° I þe praye   *alight graciously / stay*
   & quatso þy wylle is we schal wyt after
256 Nay as help me quoþ þe haþel he þat on hyȝe syttes
   To wone° any quyle in þis won hit watȝ not myn
        ernde   *stay*
   Bot for þe los° of þe lede° is lyft vp so hyȝe   *renown / sir*
   & þy burȝ & þy burnes best ar holden
260 Stifest vnder stel-gere° on stedes
        to ryde   *most fearless in armor*
   Þe wyȝtest° & þe worþyest of þe worldes kynde   *strongest*
   Preue°for to play wyth in oþer pure
        laykeȝ°   *valiant / noble sports*
   & here is kydde° cortaysye as I haf
        herd carp°   *shown / heard said*
264 & þat hatȝ wayned°me hider iwyis at þis tyme   *brought*
   Ȝe may be seker°bi þis braunch þat I bere here   *sure*
   Þat I passe as in pes & no plyȝt seche°   *danger seek*
   For had I founded° in fere in feȝtyng wyse   *journeyed*
268 I haue a hauberghe°at home & a helme boþe   *coat of mail*
   A schelde & a scharp spere schinande bryȝt
   Ande oþer weppenes to welde I wene wel als
   Bot for I wolde no were° my wedeȝ ar softer   *fighting*
272 Bot if þou be so bold as alle burneȝ tellen
   Þou wyl grant me godly þe gomen° þat I ask   *sport*
        bi ryȝt

---

267. *in fere*: In spite of TG's note to the contrary, Thomas's gloss (ES 47: 312) "array" from OF *effeir* seems correct.

Arthour con onsware
276 & sayd sir cortays knyȝt
If þou craue batayl bare
Here fayleȝ° þou not to fyȝt°   *lack | fighting*

XIII

Nay frayst° I no fyȝt in fayth I þe telle   *seek*
280 Hit arn aboute on þis bench bot berdleȝ chylder
If I were hasped°in armes on a heȝe°stede   *buckled | noble*
Here is no mon me to mach for myȝteȝ so wayke°   *weak*
Forþy I craue in þis court a Crystemas gomen
284 For hit is Ȝol°and Nwe Ȝer & here are
          Ȝep° mony   *Yule | brave men*
If any so hardy in þis hous holdeȝ hymseluen
Be so bolde in his blod brayn°in hys hede   *mad*
Þat dar stifly° strike a strok for an oþer   *fearlessly*
288 I schal gif hym of my gyft þys giserne ryche
Þis ax þat is heue innogh to hondele as hym lykes
& I schal bide þe fyrst bur° as bare°
          as I sitte   *blow | unarmed* (f.95a)
If any freke be so felle to fonde° þat
          I telle   *fierce as to try*

---

282. so: ᴍs fo.
283. gomen: ᴍs goɱe.

---

277. *bare*: Probably, as in 290, "un-armed" rather than "downright, actual" (D).

280. *bot berdleȝ chylder*: This phrase—along with 354, 219–20 (the rod of initiation), the "year and a day" of Gawain's pledge, the pentangle, the chastity test, the blow of initiation, Gawain's costume (1370–75), and the wearing of the baldric—is brought forward by Cargill and Schlauch (PMLA 43:1928) as proof of a connection between the poem and the Order of the Garter. See also the notes to 85 and to *Hony Soyt Qui Mal Pence*.

288. *giserne*: Actually a kind of halberd, the term is used loosely here, and in 2265, as a synonym for ax.

292 Lepe ly3tly me to & lach° þis weppen — *take*

I quitclayme hit for euer kepe hit as his auen

& I schal stonde°hym a strok stif° on þis

  flet° — *endure / fearless / floor*

Elle3 þou wyl di3t° me þe dom to dele hym an oþer — *appoint*

296 barlay

& 3et gif hym respite

A twelmonyth & a day

Now hy3e° & let se tite° — *hurry / me see quickly*

300 Dar any herinne o3t° say — *anything*

XIV

If he hem stowned° vpon fyrst stiller were þanne — *amazed*

Alle þe heredmen° in halle þe hy3 & þe lo3e — *retainers*

Þe renk on his rounce°hym ruched in his sadel — *horse*

304 & runischly his rede y3en he reled aboute

Bende his bresed° bro3e3 blycande°grene — *bristling / shining*

Wayued his berde for to wayte quoso wolde ryse

301. he: MS ee *altered to* he.

---

296. *barlay*: An interjection still used in children's games "as a cry for truce" (Go) and as a shout of "triumph, and also a claim" (M. Haworth, in NQ 1959:104). For derivation and elaboration, see Go's extensive note.

298. See 280*n*. Loomis (JEGP 42: 149–84) finds a parallel to the *twelmonyth and a day* required by the Green Knight in the bargain made by Arawn with Pwyll in the eleventh-century mabinogi of *Pwyll*.

303. *ruched*: Bloomfield suggests a possible comparison with Penn. Dutch *rutch*, "to twist and turn."

304. *runischly*: The most reasonable etymology for this obscure word seems that suggested by Savage (*St. Erkenwald*) who derives it from OE *ryne*, "a mystery." Such a derivation would account not only for the peculiar "oi" (*roynyshe* in *St. Erkenwald* 52), "e" (*renyschly* and *renischche* in *Purity* 1724 and 96), and "u" (*runisch* in *Purity* 1545; *runyschly* in *GGK* 457 and 432) variants in spelling, but also for the variations in meaning from "mysterious" to "rough, fierce, horrible."

306. *wayte*: "await" (Savage).

306. *wayued*: Bloomfield argues for

When non wolde kepe° hym with carp he
    coȝed ful hyȝe   *engage*
308 Ande rimed hym ful richly & ryȝt hym° to speke   *prepared*
    What is þis Arþures hous quoþ þe haþel þenne
    Þat al þe rous rennes of þurȝ ryalmes so mony
    Where is now your sourquydrye°& your conquestes   *pride*
312 Your gryndellayk° & your greme° & your
    grete wordes   *fierceness / anger*
    Now is þe reuel & þe renoun of þe Rounde Table
    Ouerwalt° wyth a worde of on wyȝes speche   *overturned*
    For al dares° for drede withoute dynt schewed   *shrink*
316 Wyth þis he laȝes so loude þat þe lorde greued
    Þe blod schot for scham into his schyre° face   *bright*
    & lere°   *flesh*
    He wex as wroth as wynde
320 So° did alle þat þer were   *as*
    Þe kyng as kene bi kynde°   *one bold in nature*
    Þen stod þat stif mon nere

308. richly: MS *illegible*; TG richley; D richely.
312. gryndellayk: MS gry dellayk.

"waved" rather than "swept from side to side" (TG, D).

307. *coȝed*: D believes this to indicate "a scornful cry, almost a crow."

308. *rimed*: Go saw a parallel here with ON *rymja*, "to cry out," and Dan. *römme*, "to clear one's throat," and so conjectured that the Green Knight "cleared his throat with much parade." The older derivation from OE *ryman* (TG and Wright), however, seems more likely, with some such translation as Wright's "drew himself up" most suitable in context.

310. *rous*: Go thought "praise" from Scand. *hrōs*. Savage's "noise, uproar, boasting" from ON *raus*, however, is more accurate. Bloomfield believes the notion implied here is that of Lat. *fama*.

312. *gryndellayk*: Along with *gryndel*, 2338, and *gryndelly*, 2299 and *Patience*, 524, a "word peculiar to our poet" (Go).

319. *as wroth as wynde*: A West Midland proverb. See *NED* "wroth," a, 3b, and Magoun (ES 19:207). Onions lists a number of examples.

XV

Ande sayde haþel by heuen þyn askyng is nys°   *foolish*

324 & as þou foly hatʒ frayst° fynde

   þe behoues°   *sought / it behooves you to find it*

I know no gome þat is gast° of þy grete wordes *afraid*

Gif me now þy geserne° vpon Godeʒ halue   *ax*

& I schal bayþen° þy bone° þat

   þou boden° habbes   *grant / boon / asked*

328 Lyʒtly lepeʒ he hym to & laʒt at°his honde *took* (f.95b)

Þen feersly þat oþer freke vpon fote lyʒtis

Now hatʒ Arthure his axe & þe halme° grypeʒ *shaft*

& sturnely stureʒ°hit aboute þat stryke wyth

   hit þoʒt   *brandishes*

332 Þe stif mon hym bifore stod vpon hyʒt°   *on high*

Herre° þen ani in þe hous by þe hede & more *taller*

Wyth sturne schere° þer he stod he stroked his berde *expression*

& wyth a countenaunce dryʒe°he droʒ°

   doun his cote   *unchanging / drew*

336 No more mate° ne dismayd for hys mayn dinteʒ *daunted*

Þen any burne vpon bench hade broʒt hym to drynk

   of wyne

  Gawan þat sate bi þe quene

---

328. laʒt at: W laght hit at.
336. hys: MS hȳs.

---

336. *for hys mayn dinteʒ*: This phrase, following its interpretation as "great blows" by Denver E. Baughan (ELH 17:241–45), has come to play a great part in modern theories of the theme of the poem (see Introduction), the issue being whether Arthur struck a number of ineffectual blows at the Green Knight's neck and had to be rescued from an embarrassing position by Gawain as Baughan maintained or whether, as Savage and older critics thought, he was simply taking "practice shots." (Cf. A. B. Friedman, in Spec 35:260–74).

340 To þe kyng he can enclyne°   *bowed*
     I beseche now with saȝeȝ sene°   *words clear*
     Þis melly mot° be myne   *contest may*

XVI

     Wolde ȝe worþilych lorde quoþ Gawan to þe kyng
344 Bid me boȝe° fro þis benche & stonde by yow þere   *go*
     Þat I wythoute vylanye myȝt voyde þis table
     & þat° my legge° lady lyked not ille   *if / liege*
     I wolde com to your counseyl bifore your cort ryche
348 For me þink hit not semly as hit is soþ° knawen   *the truth*
     Þer° such an askyng is heuened° so hyȝe in
           your sale   *where / raised*
     Þaȝ° ȝe ȝourself be talenttyf° to take hit to
           yourseluen   *though / desirous*
     Whil mony so bolde yow aboute vpon bench sytten
352 Þat vnder heuen I hope non haȝerer of wylle
     Ne better bodyes on bent° þer baret°
           is rered°   *field / strife / raised*
     I am þe wakkest I wot and of wyt feblest

---

343. Gawan: TG, Go, D, W Wawan.

342–45. Note Gawain's great courtesy, his most consistently admirable trait, here in his first appearance in the poem.

343. *Gawan*: I am here keeping the MS form although other editors emend to *Wawan*, a legitimate alternate which appears occasionally for the sake of alliteration.

349. *so hyȝe*: "out loud, publicly."

350. The punctuation suggested by C. Brett (MLR 22:451–58) and followed by Go and D makes *to take hit*

dependent on *semly* in 348.

352. *haȝerer*: "goodlier" (Go); "fitter, readier" (TG). The form is unique in ME since the ON nominative ending "r" is retained. Grattan believes "*ar* has dropped out after *haȝerer*, if indeed the right reading is not *haȝer ar*," but the line is defensible as it stands. D translates "many so bold . . . that I think nobody on earth readier in courage."

353. *bodyes*: "people."

354. See 280*n*.

    & lest lur° of my lyf quo laytes° þe soþe   *least loss / seeks*

356 Bot for as much as ȝe ar myn em° I am only to prayse   *uncle*

    No bounte bot your blod I in my bode knowe

    & syþen þis note° is so nys° þat

        noȝt hit yow falles°   *business / foolish / is fitting*

    & I haue frayned° hit at° yow fyrst foldeȝ°

        hit to me   *sought / from / grant*

360 & if I carp° not comlyly let alle þis cort rych°   *speak / decide*

        bout°blame   *without*

    Ryche° togeder con roun°   *nobles / whispered*

    & syþen þay redden°alle same   *advised*

364 To ryd° þe kyng wyth croun   *relieve*

    & gif Gawan þe game

XVII

    Þen comaunded þe kyng þe knyȝt for to ryse   (f.96a)

    & he ful radly°vp ros & ruchched°

        hym fayre   *promptly / prepared*

368 Kneled doun bifore þe kyng & cacheȝ þat weppen

    & he luflyly° hit hym laft° & lyfte vp his

        honde   *graciously / gave*

    & gef hym Goddeȝ blessyng & gladly hym biddes

    Þat his hert & his honde schulde hardi be boþe

372 Kepe þe° cosyn quoþ þe kyng þat þou on kyrf sette   *take care*

    & if þou redeȝ hym ryȝt redly I trowe

---

356. One is struck by the close relationship of uncles and nephews in medieval heroic literature—e.g. Mark-Tristan, Charlemagne-Roland, Hygelac-Beowulf—a motif which probably reflects the custom of younger sons of noble houses sending their sons to be trained at their elder brothers' courts.

372. *on kyrf*: TG's reading of this phrase, "in cutting," seems to strain the sense of the line, as does Grattan's reading of *sette on kyrf* as "deal a straight blow." Instead, it is probable that Arthur is warning Gawain to strike only "one blow," lest he receive more in return.

373. *redeȝ*: Possibly derived from OE *rædan on*, "to attack," the word here has a similar meaning.

Þat þou schal byden þe bur þat he schal bede° after   *offer*

Gawan gotȝ to þe gome with giserne° in honde   *ax*

376 & he baldly hym bydeȝ he bayst° neuer

    þe helder°   *was abashed | more*

Þen carppeȝ to Sir Gawan þe knyȝt in þe grene

Refourme° we oure forwardes° er

    we fyrre° passe   *restate | agreements | farther*

Fyrst I eþe° þe haþel how þat þou hattes   *entreat*

380 Þat þou me telle truly as I tryst° may   *trust*

In god fayth quoþ þe goode knyȝt Gawan I hatte

Þat bede° þe þis buffet quatso bifalleȝ after   *offer*

& at þis tyme twelmonyth take at° þe anoþer   *from*

384 Wyth what weppen so þou wylt & wyth no wyȝ elleȝ

    on lyue

    Þat oþer onswareȝ agayn

    Sir Gawan so mot I þryue

388   As I am ferly fayn°   *marvelously glad*

    Þis dint þat þou schal dryue

XVIII

Bigog quoþ þe grene knyȝt Sir Gawan me lykes°   *it pleases*

Þat I schal fange at° þy fust° þat I

    haf frayst° here   *receive from | fist | sought*

384. so: MS fo.

---

374. *byden*: Bloomfield suggests that this may here, as well as elsewhere, mean "wait for" with the implication that if Gawain does his work well, the blow will never be returned. The usual translation is "endure."

384. *with no wyȝ elleȝ on lyue*: There are a number of interpretations of this curious phrase: Go took it to mean that Gawain "will contract no other engagement for that day." TG and Banks believe Gawain "to mean that he will bring no supporters with him." A. Macdonald (ES 35:15) thinks that Gawain means he will send no substitutes. Napier takes the phrase to mean "at the hands of no one else." All these views can, of course, be defended from context.

392 & þou hatȝ redily rehersed° bi resoun ful trwe   *repeated*
    Clanly° al þe couenaunt þat I þe kynge asked   *wholly*
    Saf þat þou schal siker°me segge bi þi trawþe   *assure*
    Þat þou schal seche me þiself whereso°
        þou hopes°   *wherever / suppose*
396 I may be funde vpon folde & foch° þe such wages   *fetch*
    As þou deles me today bifore þis douþe° ryche   *company*
    Where schulde I wale° þe quoþ Gauan where is
        þy place   *seek*
    I wot neuer where þou wonyes° bi hym þat me wroȝt   *dwell*
400 Ne I know not þe knyȝt þy cort ne þi name
    Bot teche°me truly þerto & telle me howe þou hattes   *direct*
    & I schal ware° alle my wyt to wynne me þeder   *spend*
    & þat I swere þe forsoþe & by my seker traweþ   (f.96b)
404 Þat is innogh in Nwe ȝer hit nedes no more
    Quoþ þe gome in þe grene to Gawan þe hende
    ȝif I þe telle trwly quen I þe tape° haue   *blow*
    & þou me smoþely° hatȝ smyten
        smartly° I þe teche   *duly / promptly*
408 Of my hous & my home & myn owen nome
    Þen may þou frayst my fare & forwardeȝ holde
    & if I spende no speche þenne spedeȝ° þou þe better   *succeed*
    For þou may leng°in þy londe & layt° no fyrre   *stay / seek*
412   bot slokes

---

398. place: ᴍs plate.
401. howe: D how.

---

409. *frayst my fare*: Go says that the sense of this is "call and ask how I am getting on," and Savage reads it as "enquire after my track." D's "try my behaviour" fits the context best, though his evidence seems slim.

412. *bot slokes*: Go renders "but thou remainest idle, inactive" and derives *slokes* from Norw. *slōk*, Icel. *slōkr*, "an ideal lazy fellow," with parallels in other Germanic languages. D derives from ᴏɴ *slokna*, "to go out" (used of fire) and takes *slokes* to be a "general exclamation, 'enough'." This

Ta now þy grymme tole° to þe   *weapon*
& let se how þou cnokeʒ°   *strike*
Gladly sir for soþe
416 Quoþ Gawan his ax he strokes

XIX

The grene knyʒt vpon grounde grayþely
    hym dresses°   *arranges*
A littel lut°with þe hede þe lere° he discouereʒ   *bowed / flesh*
His longe louelych lokkeʒ he layd ouer his croun
420 Let þe naked nec to þe note schewe
Gauan gripped to his ax & gederes°hit on hyʒt   *lifts*
Þe kay°fot on þe folde he before sette   *left*
Let hit doun lyʒtly lyʒt° on þe naked°   *swiftly alight / bare flesh*
424 Þat þe scharp° of þe schalk schyndered°
    þe bones   *sharp blade / shattered*
& schrank° þurʒ þe schyire grece°
    & schade° hit in twynne   *sank / white flesh / severed*
Þat þe bit of þe broun stel bot on þe grounde
Þe fayre hede fro þe halce° hit to þe erþe   *neck*

425. schade: MS, TG scade.

interpretation would explain the plural ending. Go's note reviews other theories.

420. *note*: Go very shrewdly derives this from OE *hnot*, "short-haired," and renders the phrase "where the short hairs were." Banks suggests the "nape of his neck."

425. *schade*: This is Go's emendation, adopted without comment by D. There seems little point in printing the obscure form *scade*.

426. *broun*: D notes that this word is frequently applied to metals in the Middle Ages and apparently in that context means "shining."

427–28. Magoun (ES 19:208–9) notes that this is one of a number of examples in English literature of "football-play with a human head." Go notes a similar passage in *Diu Krone*. Coomeraswamy (Spec 19:104–25) lists a number of parallel instances of the decapitation and restoration of

428 Þat fele° hit foyned° wyth her
     fete þere hit forth roled   *so that many | spurned*
Þe blod brayd° fro þe body þat blykked°
     on þe grene   *spurted | shone*
& nawþer faltered ne fel þe freke neuer þe helder°   *more*
Bot styþly° he start forth vpon styf schonkes   *firmly*
432 & runyschly° he raȝt° out þere as
     renkkeȝ stoden   *fiercely | reached*
Laȝt to his lufly hed & lyft hit vp sone
& syþen boȝeȝ° to his blonk° þe brydel
     he cachcheȝ   *goes | horse*
Steppeȝ into stelbawe° & strydeȝ alofte   *stirrup*
436 & his hede by þe here in his honde haldeȝ
& as sadly° þe segge hym in his sadel sette   *steadily*
As non vnhap had hym ayled þaȝ hedleȝ he were
     in stedde°   *place*
440 He brayde°his bluk aboute   *twisted*
Þat vgly bodi þat bledde   *(f.97a)*
Moni on of hym had doute°   *fear*
Bi þat his resounȝ were redde

432. runyschly: ᴍꜱ ruyschly.
438. he were: ᴍꜱ ho we; W nowe.
440. bluk: D bulk.

---

the Green Knight's head from Indian myth and ritual in order to demonstrate that the "fundamental motive of the challenge derives from a remote antiquity beyond the reach of literary history . . . ."

432. See 304*n*.

438. *he were*: ᴍꜱ *ho we*. Originally Morris's emendation, this reading is followed by TG, Go, and D.

440. *bluk*: Onions suggests that this should be *bulk*, "the trunk of the body," and D so emends. Emerson suggests that the term may be a miswriting of ᴏꜰ *bloc*, a piece of wood, which might well suggest, as TG gloss it, a "headless trunk."

443. "By the time his words were uttered" (D).

THE HEADLESS GREEN KNIGHT

XX

444 For þe hede in his honde he haldeȝ vp euen°   *straight*
    Toward þe derrest on þe dece he dresseȝ þe face
    & hit lyfte vp þe yȝelyddeȝ & loked ful brode
    & meled° þus much with his muthe as ȝe may now here   *spoke*
448 Loke Gawan þou be grayþe° to go as þou
        hetteȝ°   *set / promised*
    & layte° as lelly° til þou me lude° fynde   *seek / faithfully / man*
    As þou hatȝ hette in þis halle herande° þise knyȝtes   *hearing*
    To þe grene chapel þou chose° I charge þe to fotte°   *go / get*
452 Such a dunt as þou hatȝ dalt disserued þou habbeȝ
    To be ȝederly ȝolden° on Nw ȝeres morn   *quickly given*
    Þe knyȝt of þe grene chapel men knowen me mony
    Forþi me for to fynde if þou frausteȝ° fayleȝ þou neuer   *seek*
456 Þerfore com oþer° recreaunt be calde
        þe behoues°   *or / you must be called*
    With a runisch rout þe rayneȝ he torneȝ

449. as: MS *altered from* al.

---

447. *þus much*: "all this" (Savage); "to this purpose" (Bloomfield).

452–531. I would suggest that *disserued þou habbeȝ* is parenthetical. D, however, has suggested that "by this date indirect objects were beginning to be admitted as subjects of passive constructions" and so regards the sentence as beginning with *disserued*. Marie Borroff's translation follows the same reasoning: "You have well deserved/ That your neck should have a knock on New Year's morn." There seems little point in postulating, as does Go, a missing line.

453. *Nw ȝeres*: MS *nwȝeres*. "This should have been written in two words,

since the alliteration falls on the spirant, as in 60, 105, 284, 404, 2244, 2400. When *n* alliterates (1054, 1062, 1669, 1998), or when the alliteration misses the word (1075, 1675, 1968), there is no division. This suggests an unusual feeling for alliteration on the part of the scribe, or a manuscript very close to the original text" (Go). I have, however, in the interest of consistency and with a gesture toward modern typography printed the term as two capitalized words throughout.

456. *þerfore*: "for that purpose" (Bloomfield).

457. *runisch*: See 304n.

457. *rout*: "roar" from ON *rauta*

Halled° out as þe hal dor his hed in his hande   *rushed*

Þat þe fyr of þe flynt flaʒe° fro fole° houes   *flew / the horse's*

460 To quat kyth°he becom°knwe non þere   *region / went*

Neuermore þen þay wyste fram queþen°

    he watʒ wonnen°   *whence / come*

      What þenne

    Þe kyng & Gawen þare

464   At þat grene° þay laʒe & grenne°   *green man / grin*

    ʒet breued° watʒ hit ful bare°   *made known / plainly*

    A meruayl among þo menne

XXI

Þaʒ Arþer þe hende kyng at hert hade wonder

468 He let no semblaunt be sene bot sayde ful hyʒe

To þe comlych quene wyth cortays speche

Dere dame today demay° yow neuer   *be dismayed*

Wel bycommes such craft° vpon Christmasse   *skill*

472 Laykyng° of enterludeʒ to laʒe & to syng   *playing*

Among þise kynde caroles of knyʒteʒ & ladyeʒ

Neuerþelece to my mete I may me wel dres°   *turn*

For I haf sen a selly I may not forsake°   *deny*

476 He glent vpon Sir Gawen & gaynly° he sayde   *graciously*

461. Neuermore: ᴍs Neuer moʒe; TG, D, W Neuermore.
461. fram: ᴍs fram; D from.

(TG); "rush" from ᴏᴇ *hrūtan* (Go); "noise or cry" from Scand. *rut* (C. A. Luttrell, in Neophil 39:207–17); "violent movement, jerk" (D).

464. *laʒe and grenne*: Used by Bowers (MLQ 24:333–34) as an example, along with 510 and 2514, of the "constant laughter that occurs throughout the poem." Thomas Ross has suggested to me, however, that here the laughter seems "very nervous." The two verbs are in the historic present tense.

472. See 30*n*.

473. *kynde caroles*: Go glosses as "carols rightly belonging to knights and ladies, hence noble"; TG as "seemly, courtly"; R. S. Grattan as "natural to."

Now sir heng vp þyn ax þat hatȝ innogh hewen
& hit watȝ don° abof þe dece on doser°
    to henge   *put | a tapestry* (f.97b)
Þer alle men for meruayl myȝt on hit loke
480 & bi trwe tytel þerof to telle þe wonder
Þenne þay boȝed°to a borde° þise burnes togeder   *went | table*
Þe kyng & þe gode knyȝt & kene men hem serued
Of alle dayntyeȝ double as derrest myȝt falle
484 Wyth alle maner of mete & mynstralcie boþe
Wyth wele walt° þay þat day til worþed°
    an ende   *joy enjoyed | came*
      in londe
   Now þenk wel Sir Gawan
488 For woþe°þat þou ne wonde°   *peril | hesitate*
   Þis auenture forto frayn°   *seek*
   Þat þou hatȝ tan on° honde   *taken in*

PART II

I

This hanselle° hatȝ Arthur of auenturus
    on° fyrst   *New Year's gift | at*
492 In ȝonge ȝer for he ȝerned ȝelpyng to here

---

477. *heng vp þyn ax*: This is not necessarily, as TG state, to be taken literally; it is surely a proverbial expression equivalent to "bury the hatchet." Go, D, and Brett (MLR 14: 7) cite examples.

480. *tytel*: Referring to the ax, this should certainly be taken, as D proposes, in the legal sense of "that which justifies . . . a claim," rather than as simply a "description" (TG).

483. *as derrest myȝt falle*: "in the noblest fashion possible" (Go); "as might befit the most noble" (Napier); "in order of rank" (Grattan).

487. *Gawan*: The rhyme would seem to demand the spelling *Gawayn*.

492. *ȝelping*: The usual term for the characteristic boasting of an epic hero. The next line seems then to mean "though such (boasting) words were absent when they (the court) held their court (*to sete wenten*) . . . ."

492. See 85ff*n*.

Thaʒ hym wordeʒ were wane°when þay to
    sete wenten   *wanting*
Now ar þay stoken of° sturne werk
    stafful° her hond   *fully provided with / very full*
Gawan watʒ glad to begynne þose gomneʒ in halle
496 Bot þaʒ þe ende be heuy haf ʒe no wonder
For þaʒ men ben mery in mynde quen þay
    han mayn° drynk   *have strong*
A ʒere ʒernes° ful ʒerne° &
    ʒeldeʒ neuer lyke°   *passes / quickly / the same*
Þe forme° to þe fynisment foldeʒ°
    ful selden°   *beginning / end accords / seldom*
500 Forþi þis ʒol ouerʒede° & þe ʒere after   *Yule passes over*
  & vche sesoun serlepes sued°after oþer   *in turn followed*
After Crystenmasse com þe crabbed Lentoun
Þat fraysteʒ flesch° wyth þe fysche & fode
    more symple   *subdues the flesh*
504 Bot þenne þe weder of þe worlde wyth wynter
    hit þrepeʒ°   *struggles*
Colde clengeʒ° adoun cloudeʒ vplyften   *shrinks*
Schyre schedeʒ° þe rayn in schowreʒ ful warme *falls*
Falleʒ vpon fayre flat° flowreʒ þere schewen *field*
508 Boþe groundeʒ & þe greueʒ° grene ar her wedeʒ *woods*

508. Boþe: Go Boþe þe.

---

493. *hym*: probably "to them," the members of the court, not "to him," i.e. Arthur (Go).

500ff. Opposing the idea that these lines constitute one of the poet's great "original" passages, Derek Pearsall (MLR 50:129–34) states that the poet is here using the medieval rhetorical convention of the *descriptio quatuor temporum anni.* See also Silverstein

(UTQ 33:258–78). Even so, *crabbed Lentoun, colde clengeʒ adoun,* and such phrases surpass conventional description.

504. *þe weder of þe worlde*: "the worldwide storms," "the equinoctial gales" (Grattan).

506. *Schyre*: TG, adj. "bright"; Go, adv. "brightly"; Wright, adv. "mightily."

Bryddeȝ busken° to bylde & bremlych° syngen   *prepare | loudly*

For solace of þe softe somer þat sues þerafter

          bi bonk°   *slope*

512 & blossumeȝ bolne° to blowe°   *swell | bloom*

     Bi raweȝ° rych & ronk°   *hedge rows | luxuriant*

     Þen noteȝ noble innoȝe

     Ar herde in wod so wlonk°   *lovely* (f.98a)

II

516 After þe sesoun of somer wyth þe soft wyndeȝ

     Quen ȝeferus syfleȝ° hymself on sedeȝ & erbeȝ   *blows*

     Welawynne° is þe wort° þat waxes þeroute   *very joyful | plant*

     When þe donkande° dewe dropeȝ of þe leueȝ   *dripping*

520 To bide a blysful blusch° of þe bryȝt sunne   *gleam*

     Bot þen hyȝes° heruest & hardenes

          hym° sone   *hastens | and becomes severe*

     Warneȝ hym for þe wynter to wax ful rype

     He dryues wyth droȝt þe dust for to ryse

524 Fro þe face of þe folde to flyȝe ful hyȝe

     Wroþe° wynde of þe welkyn wrasteleȝ with þe sunne   *fierce*

     Þe leueȝ lancen° fro þe lynde° &

          lyȝten on þe grounde   *fall | linden*

     & al grayes þe gres þat grene watȝ ere

528 Þenne al rypeȝ & roteȝ° þat ros vpon fyrst   *ripens and rots*

     & þus ȝirneȝ° þe ȝere in ȝisterdayeȝ mony   *passes*

526. lancen: Go, W laucen.

---

510. See 464*n*.

521. *hym*: The *wort* of 518.

526. *lancen*: Go, *laucen*. The scribe's *u*'s and *n*'s are well-nigh indistinguishable. Go felt that here, as in 1212 and 2124, the verb is actually *laucen* (ON *lauss*, "loosen"). Since however, the two indisputable instances of *laucen* (1784 and 2376) are transitive, it seems better to read *lancen* here and elsewhere where its meaning is made clear by the context.

& wynter wyndeȝ° aȝayn as þe worlde askeȝ   *returns*

no fage°   *in truth*

532   Til Meȝelmas mone°   *Michaelmas moon*

Watȝ cumen wyth wynter wage°   *challenge*

Þen þenkkeȝ Gawan ful sone

Of his anious uyage°   *wearisome journey*

III

536   Ȝet quyl Al-hal-day° with Arþer he lenges   *until All Saint's Day*

& he made a fare° on þat fest for þe frekeȝ sake   *observance*

With much reuel & ryche of þe Rounde Table

Knyȝteȝ ful cortays & comlych ladies

540   Al for luf of þat lede in longynge° þay were   *grief*

Bot neuerþelece ne þe later° þay

neuened bot° merþe   *nor the less readily / spoke only of*

Mony ioyleȝ° for þat ientyle° iapeȝ

þer maden   *joyless ones / noble one*

For aftter mete with mournyng he meleȝ°

to his eme°   *speaks / uncle*

544   & spekeȝ of his passage & pertly° he sayde   *plainly*

Now lege lorde of my lyf leue I yow ask

Ȝe knowe þe cost° of þis cace kepe I no more   *terms*

---

531. fage: MS sage.

---

531. *as þe worlde askeȝ*: "as nature requires."

531. *No fage*: MS *no sage*. The emendation was originally suggested by C. T. Onions (TLS Aug. 16 and Sept. 20, 1923, and Feb. 5, 1931), and was followed by TG, Go, and D.

532. *Meȝelmas*: Emended to *meȝel-masse* by Emerson for the sake of the metrics.

536. *Al-hal-day*: The Feast of All Saints, Nov. 1, one of the traditional Arthurian feasts. Savage (*The Gawain-Poet*, 27) notes that since on All Saints' Day masses are offered for the dead, "we are to consider [Gawain] a dead man."

538. *reuel & ryche*: An example of hendiadys, as Bloomfield notes.

546–7. I would here suggest the punctuation used by Go, who translated these lines "I desire nothing else.

To telle yow teneȝ þerof neuer bot trifel
548 Bot I am boun to° þe bur barely tomorne   *ready for*
To sech þe gome of þe grene as God wyl me wysse°   *guide*
Þenne þe best of þe burȝ boȝed°togeder   *city went*
Aywan & Errik & oþer ful mony
552 Sir Doddinaual de Sauage þe duk of Clarence   (f.98b)
Launcelot & Lyonel & Lucan þe gode
Sir Boos & Sir Byduer big men boþe
& mony oþer menskful° with Mador de la Port   *dignified ones*
556 Alle þis compayny of court com þe kyng nerre
For to counseyl þe knyȝt with care at her hert

It were but triviality to tell you the trials thereof." D suggests "terms" for *cost.*

551. *Aywan & Errik*: Aywan is almost certainly Ywain (see 113) and Errik the Eric of Chrétien's *Erec et Enide*. TG suggest that the poet may have also identified him with the Arrake fitz Lake of *The Awntyrs of Arthur*. For further information on all Arthurian knights consult R. W. Ackerman (1952), *Index of Arthurian Names*, Stanford.

552. *Sir Doddinaual de Savage*: properly *Dodinel le Sauage*, so named because of his "love of hunting" (Go) not because he is especially fierce (TG).

552. *þe duk of Clarence*: Galachin, cousin (*L'estoire de Merlin*) or brother (*Le Roman de Lancelot*) of Sir Dodinel. Go's note supplies what is known of him. A most interesting passage in the Vulgate *Lancelot* (ed. Sommer, V, 236) names Lancelot (see next line), Gawain, Dodinel, and the Duke of Clarence in the same breath.

553. *Launcelot*: Son of King Ban of Benwick, he is unknown to the chroniclers, is first mentioned in Chrétien's *Erec et Enide*, assumes a leading role in the story as Guinevere's lover in Chrétien's *La Chevalier de la Charrette*, becomes the center of interest in the Vulgate Cycle, and finally is called "the greatest knight of this world" in Malory. *Lyonel* is the son of King Ban's brother, King Bors of Gaul, hence Lancelot's cousin. *Lucan*, frequently called "The Butler" is one of Arthur's final companions after the battle on the Salisbury Plain.

554. *Sir Boos*: Probably Sir Bors of Ganys, son of King Bors of Gaul and Lancelot's cousin. *Sir Byduer* is Sir Bedivere, like Sir Lucan one of Arthur's final companions.

555. *Mador de la Port*: In the Vulgate Cycle he accuses the queen of poisoning the apple that accidentally killed his cousin, Gaheris. Lancelot, after some delay, defends the queen and defeats Mador.

Þere watȝ much derne doel driuen in þe sale°   *hall*
Þat so worthe as Wawan schulde wende on þat ernde
560 To dryȝe° a delful°dynt & dele no more   *suffer | doleful*
    wyth bronde°   *sword*
    Þe knyȝt mad ay god chere
    & sayde quat schuld I wonde°   *fear*
564 Of destines derf & dere
    What may mon do bot fonde°   *try*

IV

He dowelleȝ þer al þat day and dresseȝ on þe morn
Askeȝ erly hys armeȝ & alle were þay broȝt
568 Fyrst a tule tapit° tyȝt° ouer þe
    flet°   *rich red carpet | spread | floor*
& miche watȝ þe gyld gere° þat
    glent° þer alofte   *gilded armor | glinted*
Þe stif° mon steppeȝ þeron & þe stel hondeleȝ   *strong*
Dubbed in a dublet of a dere tars°   *silk from Tharsia*
572 & syþen a crafty capados° closed aloft   *skillfully-made hood*
Þat wyth a bryȝt blaunner° was bounden withinne   *white fur*
Þenne set þay þe sabatounȝ° vpon þe segge foteȝ   *steel shoes*

558. derne: TG, D derue; W derve.

---

558. *derne*: So Go, following Madden. Other editors have *derue*. "Secret," however, seems more appropriate to the grief of a court careful to mask its grief with mirth (540–42) than merely "heavy" or "severe."

564. *dere*: As D remarks, this could be either "pleasant" (ᴏᴇ *dēore*) or "fierce" (ᴏᴇ *dēor*). However, the former seems more appropriate in

context; "In destinies sad or merry,/ True men can but try" (Borroff).

568ff. A passage on the arming of the hero frequently occurs in the medieval romance and would seem to be inherited from the epic. Gawain's armor (see TG's note) is that of the late fourteenth century.

572. *capados closed aloft*: See 186*n*.

His legez lapped° in stel with luflych greuez — *wrapped*
576 With polaynez piched°þerto policed ful clene — *kneepieces fixed*
Aboute his knez knaged° wyth knotez of golde — *riveted*
Queme quyssewes° þen þat
    coyntlych° closed — *good thighpieces / cunningly*
His thik þrawen° þyзez with
    þwonges to tachched° — *brawny / thongs attached*
580 & syþen þe brawden bryne° of bryзt
    stel ryngez — *woven coat of mail*
Vmbeweued° þat wyз vpon wlonk stuffe — *enclosed*
& wel bornyst brace° vpon his
    boþe armes — *burnished armpieces*
With gode cowters° & gay & glouez of plate — *elbowpieces*
584 & alle þe godlych gere þat hym gayn schulde
    þat tyde° — *time*
Wyth ryche cote-armure
His gold sporez spend with pryde° — *fastened splendidly*
588 Gurde° wyth a bront° ful sure — *girt / sword*
With silk sayn vmbe° his syde — *girdle around*

V

When he watz hasped° in armes his harnays
    watz ryche — *buckled (f.99a)*
Þe lest lachet° ouer loupe lemed° of golde — *smallest clasp / shone*
592 So harnayst as he watz he herknez his masse
Offred & honoured at þe heзe auter
Syþen he comez to þe kyng & to his cort-ferez° — *court companions*
Lachez lufly° his leue at° lordez &
    ladyez — *takes graciously / from*
596 & þay hym kyst & conueyed°
    bikende° hym to Kryst — *conducted on his way / commending*

591. ouer: TG, D, W oþer.

Bi þat watȝ Gryngolet grayth° & gurde with a sadel   *set*

Þat glemed ful gayly with mony golde frenges

Ayquere naylet° ful nwe for þat

    note ryched°   *everywhere nailed / occasion enriched*

600 Þe brydel barred° aboute with bryȝt golde bounden   *striped*

Þe apparayl of þe payttrure° & of þe proude skyrteȝ   *neck armor*

Þe cropore° & þe couertor° acorded

    wyth þe arsouneȝ°   *crupper / cloth cover / saddlebows*

& al watȝ rayled° on red ryche golde nayleȝ   *arrayed*

604 Þat al glytered & glent as glem of þe sunne

Þenne hentes° he þe helme & hastily hit kysses   *takes*

Þat watȝ stapled stifly & stoffed wythinne

Hit watȝ hyȝe on his hede hasped bihynde

608 Wyth a lyȝtly vrysoun° ouer þe auentayle°   *light cover / visor*

Enbrawden & bounden wyth þe best gemmeȝ

On brode sylkyn borde° & bryddeȝ on semeȝ   *hem*

As papiayeȝ° paynted peruyng bitwene   *parrots*

612 Tortors° & trulofeȝ entayled° so þyk   *turtledoves / embroidered*

611. peruyng: Go, TG pernyng; W perving.

---

597. *Bi þat*: "by that time" (Bloomfield).

597. *Gryngolet*: The name of Gawain's horse is very similar to and may in fact be derived from Guingelot, the boat of the hero Wade, and was so derived by Go (*Saga Book of the Viking Club*, V, 104). TG's derivation from a Welsh form such as *Gwyngalet, "white-hard," seems more likely.

601–606. TG's notes treat in detail Gringolet's equipment.

611. *peruyng*: D's reading, earlier editors having read *pernyng,* a present participle formed either by metathesis from the verb *prene,* "to preen" (Go, TG) or from dialect *pirn,* "reel" or "bobbin," hence "flitting" (B. James in NQ 85:9). D takes the word to be a variant of *pervink,* "periwinkle," and sees the figure here as that, frequently found in manuscript illumination and embroidery, of birds painted within a border of foliage.

611. *betwene*: TG's reading here and in 791 and 795 as "at intervals (of space)" is surely justified by the context.

612. *trulofeȝ*: D believes the flower "truelove" rather than "true lover's knots."

As mony burde þeraboute had ben seuen wynter
    in toune
    Þe cercle watȝ more o prys
616   Þat vmbeclypped° hys croun   *encircled*
    Of diamaunteȝ a deuys
    Þat boþe were bryȝt & broun°   *shining*

VI

Then þay schewed hym þe schelde þat was
    of schyr gouleȝ°   *bright gules*
620 Wyth þe pentangel depaynt° of pure golde hweȝ   *depicted*

---

620. *þe pentangle*: Enclosed within a circle, the pentangle was the great seal of Solomon and in the Greek world a symbol of perfection and is ascribed as a device neither to Gawain nor, to my knowledge, to any other knight. (For a description of Gawain's arms, see Madden's note to 636). As TG state, "no doubt the poet came upon a description and interpretation of it [the pentangle] in some treatise or commentary of the Alexandrian school, but we have not been able to find his source." However, as D maintains, "the absence of record in England is doubtless accidental, for [the poet] could hardly have expected his audience to follow his description of the figure if they had never seen it."

A number of critics have dealt with the origin of the device, its relation to Gawain, and its general function in the poem. R. S. Loomis (JEGP 42: 149–84), for example, maintains that the pentangle may be traced back to the five golden wheels on Cuchulainn's shield, while John Speirs (*Medieval English Poetry*) identifies the pentangle as an "ancient life symbol" whose "pre-Christian significance" underlies the poem. Savage (*The* Gawain-*Poet,* 158ff.) relates the pentangle with the French Order of the Star as part of his attempt to identify Gawain with Enguerrand de Coucy. Fr. Gervase Mathew (*Studies in Medieval History*) regards the pentangle as symbolizing Gawain's perfection in the greatest knightly virtues, i.e., "prowess and loyalty" to one's word, oneself, and one's code. Since these virtues were augmented by pity, largesse, "franchise," and courtesy, the whole concept of knightly honor could most easily be viewed as a "supplement to conventional Christian morality" and hence could be appropriately symbolized by the pentangle. G. J. Engelhardt in discussing Gawain's morality (MLQ 16:218–25) shows the pentangle to be a "symbol of the complete man, whose integrity admits no imperfection; and it is this integrity in Gawain which the poem will show

He braydeȝ hit by þe bauderyk aboute þe

    hals kestes°   *shield strap*

Þat bisemed° þe segge semlyly° fayre   *befitted | becomingly*

& quy þe pentangel apendeȝ° to þat prynce noble   *belongs*

624 I am intent yow to telle þof tary° hyt

    me schulde   *though delay*

Hit is a syngne þat Salamon set sumquyle°   *once upon a time*

In bytoknyng of trawþe bi tytle° þat hit habbeȝ   *right*

For hit is a figure þat haldeȝ fyue poynteȝ   (f.99b)

628 & vche lyne vmbelappeȝ & loukeȝ° in oþer   *overlaps and locks*

& ayquere° hit is endeleȝ & Englych hit callen   *everywhere*

Oueral as I here þe endeles knot

Forþy hit acordeȝ to þis knyȝt & to his cler armeȝ

632 For ay faythful in fyue & sere fyue syþeȝ

Gawan watȝ for gode knawen & as golde pured°   *refined*

Voyded of vche vylany wyth vertueȝ ennourned°   *adorned*

    in mote°   *castle*

636   Forþy þe pentangel nwe

624. intent: D, W in tent.
629. endeleȝ: MS emdeleȝ.
634. vertueȝ: MS verertueȝ.

---

to be more apparent than real." And R. W. Ackerman (Anglia 76:254–65) shows that the figure of the five wits, five wounds, and five joys was associated with the sacrament of penance and the confessional in the Middle Ages and are used in the poem to characterize Gawain's "deeply religious devotion."

624. *intent*: D and W read as two words, *in tent*, "bent on," mainly on the basis of a space in the manuscript. However, since the meaning is clear either way, it seems to me best not to strain the construction.

630. *þe endless knot*:

632. Banks: "In five ways, and five times each way still faithful."

636. *nwe*: D suggests "newly painted."

He ber in schelde & cote
As tulk of tale° most trwe   *word*
& gentylest knyʒt of lote

VII

640 Fyrst he watʒ funden fautleʒ in his fyue wytteʒ°   *senses*
& efte° fayled neuer þe freke in his fyue fyngres   *then*
& alle his afyaunce° vpon folde watʒ in þe
fyue woundeʒ   *trust*
Þat Cryst kaʒt° on þe croys as þe crede telleʒ   *received*
644 & queresoeuer þys mon in melly° watʒ stad°   *battle / placed*
His þro° þoʒt watʒ in þat þurʒ alle oþer þyngeʒ   *earnest*
Þat alle his forsnes he fong at° þe fyue joyeʒ   *took from*
Þat þe hende heuen quene had of hir chylde
648 At þis cause þe knyʒt comlyche° hade   *fittingly*
In þe inore half of his schelde hir ymage depaynted

646. forsnes: TG fersnes.
646. fong: TG, D feng.
649. inore: TG more; Go inner-more.

---

639. *lote*: Savage (MLN 60:492–3)
argues that here, in 1116, and in *Pearl*
238 and 896 *lote* means "hearing, de-
meanor" rather than simply "speech."
Other meanings noted by Savage are
"noisy sound, din" (in 119, 1623, 1917,
2211, and *Pearl* 876—where it is ap-
plied to thunder); "uproar, babble"
(in 224); "jests" (in 998, 1086, 1116
[?], 1399, and 1954); and "loud noise
(of winds)" (in *Patience* 161).

641. *fyue fyngres*: Sometimes alle-
gorized as five virtues (R. L. Green,
in ELH 29:134).

642. *þe fyve woundeʒ*: In the two
hands, the two feet, and the side. (See

D. Gray, NQ 108:50–51).

646. *þe fyue joyeʒ*: The Annunci-
ation, Nativity, Resurrection, Ascen-
sion, and Assumption.

646. Although TG emends *forsnes*
to *fersnes* and TG and D *fong* to *feng*,
neither emendation seems necessary
since "fortitude" is more appropriate
here than "fierceness," and *fong*,
though an unusual form, is a justifi-
able one and appears in *Pearl* 884.
(See Menner, in MLN 41:339.)

649. *hir ymage depaynted*: An in-
teresting transference of virtues from
Arthur, to whom this habit was first
attributed by Nennius and the later

Þat quen he blusched° þerto his
    belde° neuer payred°   *looked | courage | failed*
Þe fyft fyue þat I finde þat þe frek vsed
652 Watȝ fraunchyse°& felaȝschyp forbe°
    al þyng   *generosity | surpassing*
His clannes° & his cortaysye croked° were
    neuer   *chastity | astray*
& pite þat passeȝ alle poynteȝ þyse pure fyue
Were harder happed° on þat haþel þen on any oþer   *fastened*
656 Now alle þese fyue syþeȝ° forsoþe were
    fetled on° þis knyȝt   *times | joined in*
& vchone halched°in oþer þat non ende hade   *each one fastened*
& fyched°vpon fyue poynteȝ þat fayld neuer   *fixed*
Ne samned°neuer in no syde ne sundred nouþer   *joined*
660 Withouten ende at any noke I oquere° fynde   *anywhere*
Whereeuer þe gomen°bygan or glod°to
    an ende   *device | glided*

659. nouþer: MS nouþ r.
660. I oquere: MS I quere; TG aiquere; Go i-wis no-quere; W I owhere.

---

chroniclers, to the members of his court. For details see TG's note.

649. *inore*: D's reading, founded on what he feels to be "a clear distinction" between the first and other two minims of the first letter, does much to clarify the line. D. Gray (NQ 103: 487–88) had originally suggested "in-nore," and Go, following S. O. Andrew (RES 6:176), had emended to "inner-more." TG glossed the phrase *þe more half* as "the upper and larger portion," the image of the Blessed Virgin thus being described as painted on the upper half of the inner side of the shield where Gawain might see it.

652–54. As D points out, since the virtues here listed do not apply especially to Gawain's conduct in the poem, they were probably "determined more by form than meaning." D's note discusses the precise meanings of the terms used by the poet and, like J. A. Burrow (*A Reading of Gawain and The Green Knight*, 47), prefers "pity" rather than "piety" for *pite* in 654.

660. *I oquere fynde*: D's sensible reading of an almost unintelligible word. G emends the MS's *I quere fynde* to *i-wys no-quere fynde*, an interesting though unnecessary emendation. Madden and Morris had read

Þerfore on his schene schelde schapen watȝ þe knot

Ryally wyth red golde vpon rede gowleȝ°   *gules*

664 Þat is þe pure pentaungel wyth þe peple called   *(f.100a)*

       with lore°   *learning*

    Now grayþed° is Gawan gay   *set*

    & laȝt° his launce ryȝt þore°   *took / there*

668   & gef hem alle goud day

    He wende° for euer more   *thought*

VIII

He sperred þe sted with þe spureȝ & sprong on his way

So stif° þat þe ston-fyr stroke° out

      þerafter   *hard /sparks flew*

672 Al þat seȝ þat semly syked in hert

& sayde soþly al same° segges til° oþer   *together / to*

Carande° for þat comly bi Kryst hit

    is scaþe°   *anxious / a grievous thing*

Þat þou leude schal be lost þat art of lyf noble

676 To fynde hys fere° vpon folde in fayth is

    not eþe°   *equal / easy*

Warloker°to haf wroȝt° had more wyt bene   *more warily / acted*

& haf dyȝt° ȝonder dere a duk to haue worþed°   *made / become*

A lowande° leder of ledeȝ in londe hym wel semeȝ   *shining*

680 & so had better haf ben þen britned° to noȝt   *broken*

Hadet wyth an aluisch°mon for

      angardeȝ° pryde   *other-worldly / arrogance's*

---

ai-quere, and Emerson and Wright had defended this reading by deriving *fynde* from OE *fynde,* the phrase thus translating "anywhere to be found." TG's "aiquere, I fynde" is interesting, though textually indefensible.

670. *sperred:* "spurred, struck."

Onions suggests that this may mean "to spar" or "to dart."

681. *hadet:* Go's derivation, OE *hēaf-dian,* and translation, "beheaded," are clearly right. Go's note reviews older theories.

Who knew euer any kyng such counsel to take

As knyȝteȝ in cauelaciounȝ° on Crystmasse

    gomneȝ   *disputes*

684 Wel°much watȝ þe warme water þat

    waltered of° yȝen   *very / flowed from*

When þat semly syre soȝt° fro þo woneȝ   *went*

    þad° daye   *that*

    He made non abode°   *delay*

688   Bot wyȝtly° went hys way   *quickly*

    Mony wylsum way he rode

    Þe bok as I herde say

IX

Now rideȝ þis renk þurȝ þe ryalme of Logres°   *Britain*

692 Sir Gauan on Godeȝ halue þaȝ hym no gomen poȝt

Oft leudleȝ° alone he lengeȝ on nyȝteȝ   *companionless*

---

683. cauelaciounȝ: MS cavelounȝ.

682–3. See 85*n.*

689. *wylsum*: Usually translated "bewildering" though Wright suggested "dreary, lonely."

691ff. *Logres*: Arthurian Britain south of the Humber. Gawain rides north from Camelot (see 37*n*) into north Wales, what Speirs (1957:231) characteristically calls "the Druid Country, the home of the pre-Christian culture." Presumably he rides eastward through Carnarvonshire, Denbighshire, and Flintshire, always keeping the Anglesey isles on his left. The *fordeȝ*, mentioned in 699, are doubtless those of the small streams of the area, but the Holy Head is puzzling. Go conjectures that "this must have been the place where Gawain crossed the Dee, entering Wirral," a reasonable conclusion, although no such crossing is known except the remains of the one near Holywell Station and at Gayton (see Go's and TG's notes), neither of which is wholly in accord with the poet's description. At any rate, he does seem to be describing a route well known to his audience, a fact that has led G. P. J. (NQ 80:53–54) to connect the poet with the Abbey of Whally near Clitheroe. See 2172*n.* and D's note.

Þer he fonde noȝt hym byfore þe fare þat he lyked
Hade he no fere° bot his fole° bi

    frytheȝ° & douneȝ   *companion / horse / woods*
696 Ne no gome bot God bi gate° wyth to karp°   *road / speak*

    Til þat he neȝed° ful neghe into þe Norþe Waleȝ   *neared*

    Alle þe iles of Anglesay on lyft half°he haldeȝ   *side*

    & fareȝ ouer þe fordeȝ by þe forlondeȝ°   *lowlands*
700 Ouer at þe Holy Hede til he hade

    eft bonk°   *reached the shore again*

    In þe wyldrenesse of Wyrale wonde° þer bot lyte   *there dwelled*

    Þat auþer God oþer gome wyth goud hert louied   *(f.100b)*

    & ay he frayned° as he ferde° at frekeȝ þat he met   *asked / went*
704 If þay hade herde any karp of a knyȝt grene

    In any grounde þeraboute of þe grene chapel

    & al nykked° hym wyth nay þat neuer in her lyue   *denied*

    Þay seȝe neuer no segge þat watȝ of suche hweȝ
708   of grene

    Þe knyȝt tok gates°straunge   *roads*

    In mony a bonk° vnbene°   *slope / unpleasant*

    His cher°ful oft con chaunge   *mood*
712   Þat chapel er he myȝt sene

697. neghe: MS noghe.
705. chapel: MS clapel.

---

694. *fare*: John Conley argues (NQ 81:2) that *fare* has suffered too literal a translation as "food" and should be translated to mean "*going, way,* or something of the sort."

701. *Wyrale*: The Wirral, the great medieval forest north of the Dee. Savage has conclusively demonstrated that its bad name was due to its having become in the mid fourteenth century a notorious resort of criminals, those who loved neither *God oþer gome wyth goud hert.*

709ff. Clearly Gawain's journey continues through the Wirral, and Madden's conjecture that Gawain rides on into Inglewood Forest in Cumberland may well be correct.

X

Mony klyf he ouerclambe in contrayeȝ straunge
Fer floten° fro his frendeȝ fremedly°   *far removed / as a stranger*
      he rydeȝ
At vche warþe oþer water þer þe wyȝe passed
716 He fonde a foo° hym byfore bot ferly° hit were   *foe / marvel*
  & þat so foule & so felle° þat feȝt hym byhode°   *fierce / behooved*
So mony meruayl bi mount° þer þe
      mon fyndeȝ   *in the mountains*
Hit were to tore°for to telle of þe tenþe dole°   *difficult / part*
720 Sumwhyle° wyth wormeȝ° he werreȝ°   *sometimes / dragons / fights*
    & with wolues als
Sumwhyle wyth wodwos° þat woned
      in þe knarreȝ°   *wild men / rocks*
Boþe wyth bulleȝ & bereȝ & boreȝ oþerquyle
& etayneȝ° þat hym anelede° of þe
      heȝe felle°   *giants / pursued / rocks*
724 Nade he° ben duȝty & dryȝe° &
    dryȝtyn had serued   *had he not / brave and enduring*
Douteles he hade ben ded & dreped°ful ofte   *killed*
For werre wrathed° hym not so much þat
    wynter was wors   *troubled*
When þe colde cler water fro þe cloudeȝ schadde
728 & fres er°hit falle myȝt to þe fale°erþe   *froze before / pale*
Ner slayn wyth þe slete he sleped in his yrnes
Mo nyȝteȝ þen innoghe in naked rokkeȝ

718. so: ms fo.
726. was: D, W nas.
727. schadde: ms schadden.

---

715. *warþe*: Usually glossed "shore,"   NQ 91:171–72).
this may mean "ford" (P. Haworth, in   726. *þat*: "but that" (Go).

Þer as claterande fro þe crest þe colde borne°

    renneʒ   *stream*

732 & henged heʒe ouer his hede in hard ysse-ikkles

    Þus in peryl & payne & plytes°ful harde   *straits*

    Bi contray caryeʒ° þis knyʒt tyl   *over the land rides*

        Krystmasse euen

          al one

736   Þe knyʒt wel þat tyde°   *time*

    To Mary made his mone°   *complaint*

    Þat ho hym red° to ryde   *might advise where*

    & wysse° hym to sum wone°   *guide | dwelling* (f.101a)

XI

740 Bi a mounte on þe morne meryly he rydes

    Into a forest ful dep þat ferly°watʒ wylde   *marvelously*

    Hiʒe hilleʒ on vche a halue & holt-wodeʒ° vnder   *woods*

    Of hore okeʒ ful hoge a hundreth togeder

744 Þe hasel & þe haʒþorne were harled al samen°   *twisted together*

    With roʒe raged mosse rayled° aywhere   *arrayed*

    With mony bryddeʒ vnblyþe vpon bare twyges

---

732. ysse-ikkles: MS *originally* iisse-ikkles *altered to* ysse-ikkles; TG,
D, W iise-ikkles.

734. caryeʒ: TG, Go cayreʒ.

730ff. This is the sort of wry, brusque soldier's humor typical of the poet, though impossible to analyze.

734. *caryeʒ*: Even though *cayreʒ* would be the expected form, there is evidence (C. A. Luttrell, in Neophil 39:207–17) that *caryeʒ*, through a confusion of *cayren* and *carien*, may be intended.

736. Emerson inserts *ryʒt* before *wel* to preserve the meter.

745. *raged*: Go, following Wright, compares this with *EDD rag*, "hoarfrost," and suggests "hoar-frosted." C. A. Luttrell, however (Neophil 39: 207–17), derives *raged* from the "rag" of various plants and renders it "shaggy, tufted," which fits better in context.

Þat pitosly þer piped for pyne of þe colde
748 Þe gome vpon Gryngolet glydeʒ hem vnder
Þurʒ mony misy°& myre mon al hym
    one°   *many a quagmire / alone*
Carande° for his costes lest he ne keuer°
    schulde   *worrying / arrive*
To se þe seruyse of þat syre þat on þat self°nyʒt   *same*
752 Of a burde°watʒ borne oure baret° to quelle   *maiden / grief*
& þerfore sykyng°he sayde I beseche þe lorde   *sighing*
& Mary þat is myldest moder so dere
Of sum herber þer heʒly° I myʒt
    here masse   *lodging where devoutly*
756 Ande þy matyneʒ tomorne mekely I ask
& þerto prestly°I pray my Pater & Aue   *promptly*
    & Crede
    He rode in his prayere
760   & cryed for his mysdede
    He sayned hym in syþes sere°   *crossed himself several times*
    & sayde cros Kryst me spede

XII

Nade° he sayned hymself segge bot þrye°   *had not / thrice*
764 Er he watʒ war in þe wod of a won in a mote
Abof a launde° on a lawe° loken vnder boʒeʒ   *plain / hill*
Of mony borelych bole° aboute bi þe diches   *burly tree*

---

751. seruyse: MS seruy.

---

749. *al hym one*: "alone" (Bloomfield).

750. *costes*: Wright thought "labors."

762. *cros Kryst me spede*: Surely Gawain here makes the sign of the Cross, though the regular form would seem to have been *Kryst cros me spede*. This formula of prayer was used in schools before reciting the alphabet which was printed in horn books in the form of a cross, hence a Christ-cross, later criss-cross.

A castel þe comlokest° þat euer knyȝt aȝte°   *comeliest | owned*
768 Pyched° on a prayere°a park al aboute   *set | meadow*
With a pyked palays° pyned° ful þik *spiked palisade | fastened*
Þat vmbeteȝe°mony tre mo þen two myle   *enclosed*
Þat holde°on þat on syde þe haþel auysed° *castle | observed*
772 As hit schemered & schon þurȝ þe schyre okeȝ
Þenne hatȝ he hendly of° his helme &
  heȝly he þonkeȝ   *he courteously takes off*
Jesus & Saynt Gilyan þat gentyle ar boþe
Þat cortaysly hade hym kydde° & his cry
  herkened   *shown* (f.101b)
776 Now bone hostel° coþe þe burne I
  beseche yow ȝette° *good lodging | to grant*
Þenne gedereȝ° he to Gryngolet with þe gilt heleȝ *spurs*
& he ful chauncely° hatȝ chosen°
  to þe chef gate° *by chance | gone | main road*
Þat broȝt bremly° þe burne to þe bryge ende *clearly*
780   in haste
  Þe bryge watȝ breme vpbrayde° *stoutly pulled up*
  Þe ȝateȝ°wer stoken° faste *gates | shut*
  Þe walleȝ were wel arayed° *constructed*
784 Hit dut° no wyndeȝ blaste *feared*

769. pyned: Go pynned.
774. Saynt: MS say; TG, Go, D, W sayn.
775. hade: TG, D, W had.
777. gedereȝ: TG, D gerdeȝ.

768ff. Speirs (1957:231) sees the castle as a "version of the Grail Castle," close to "the hidden source of life."

772. *schyre*: "clearly defined" (Wright).

774. *Saynt Gilyan*: MS *say*; TG and Go *sayn*. It seems unduly pedantic as long as an emendation is called for

not to emend to a recognizable form. St. Julian is the patron saint of hospitality; cf. the General Prologue to *The Canterbury Tales, House of Fame,* and *Ancrene Rwle.*

777. *gedereȝ*: TG and D, following Napier, read *gerdeȝ.*

XIII

Þe burne bode on blonk þat on bonk houed

Of þe depe double dich þat drof to°þe place   *enclosed*

Þe walle wod°in þe water wonderly depe   *stood*

788 Ande eft°a ful huge heȝt°hit haled

    vpon lofte°   *again / height / rose aloft*

Of harde hewen ston vp to þe tableȝ°   *cornices*

Enbaned vnder þe abataylment in þe best lawe°   *style*

& syþen garyteȝ° ful gaye gered

    bitwene°   *towers / built at intervals*

792 Wyth mony luflych loupe°þat louked°

    ful clene°   *loophole / shut / neatly*

A better barbican þat burne blusched° vpon neuer   *looked*

& innermore he behelde þat halle ful hyȝe

Towres telded°bytwene trochet ful þik   *erected*

796 Fayre fylyoleȝ°þat fyȝed° & ferlyly long   *pinnacles / fitted*

---

785. blonk ... bonk: MS, TG, Go, W bonk ... blonk.
795. Towres: MS towre.

---

785. I am adopting here, as in 210, a transposition suggested by D, here of *blonk* and *bonk*. The line thus reads "the knight stayed on his horse, which halted on the bank . . . ."

790. *Enbaned*: In *Purity* 1458–59 the cups brought forth at Belshazzar's feast are *as casteles arayed/ Enbaned under batelment with bantelles quoynt*. The term is derived from Provencal *embanamen*, "horn-work," and thus would seem to suggest fortifying with some form of barbican (see Brett, in MLR 22:456), perhaps, as TG suggest, "horizontal courses of masonry set near the top of the wall to render assault by means of scaling ladders more difficult" or simply "outworks" (Banks). Emerson says that *Enbaned* modifies the preceding *tableȝ* and means "copings."

794ff. The architecture here described is that of the late fourteenth century.

795. *trochet*: Go connects this term with *troches*, the cluster of short tips near the tip of a stag's antlers, and so glosses it "adorned with small pointed pinnacles." Wright (ES 47:312) connects it with OF *troche, trochet*, "cluster." Thomas (ES 47:913) renders it "crowded."

With coruon coprounes craftyly
    sleȝe°   *carved tops skillfully ingenious*

Chalk-whyt chymnees þer ches°he innoȝe   *saw*

Vpon bastel roueȝ° þat blenked° ful quyte   *tower roofs | shone*

800 So mony pynakle payntet watȝ poudred
    ayquere°   *scattered everywhere*

Among þe castel carneleȝ clambered°so þik° *embrasures | clustered*

Þat pared° out of papure purely hit semed   *cut*

Þe fre° freke on þe fole hit fayr innoghe þoȝt   *noble*

804 If he myȝt keuer° to com þe cloyster wythinne   *succeed*

To herber in þat hostel whyl halyday lested
    aunant

He calde & sone þer com

808 A porter pure plesaunt

On þe wal his ernd he nome°   *took*

& haylsed° þe knyȝt erraunt   *greeted*

---

803. innoghe: MS ĩnghe.
806. aunant: MS *illegible*; TG, D, W auinant.

---

802. *pared out of papure*: The same phrase is found in *Purity* 1408 to describe ornaments used to decorate the food at Belshazzar's feast. R. Ackerman (JEGP 56:410–17) states that these ornaments were not the sugar "subtleties" mentioned by Menner (*Purity*, 1408n) but the paper cutouts used to decorate food, as described in Chaucer's Parson's Tale. On the basis of this line and the plural of "þe chapeles" of 930, Go suggests that the poet may have in mind Caernarvon Castle in Wales. However, the main purpose of the image is surely to suggest a magnificent imagined artifice, a child's dream of a castle.

806. *aunant*: TG, D and the older editors read *auinant*, except for Madden, *amnant*. King (RES 5:540) suggested the adverb, "pleasantly."

808. Thomas Ross reminds me that most porters, as for example Glewlwyd in *Culhwch and Olwen*, are rude. The obliging charm of this fellow may indicate the otherworldly atmosphere of Bercilak's court.

XIV

Gode sir quoþ Gawan woldeȝ þou go myn ernde
812 To þe heȝ lorde of þis hous herber to craue
Ȝe Peter quoþ þe porter & purely I trowee°   *believe* (f.102a)
Þat ȝe be wyȝe welcum to won quyle yow lykeȝ
Þen ȝede° þe wyȝe aȝayn swyþe°   *went / quickly*
816 & folke frely°hym wyth to fonge°þe knyȝt   *readily / receive*
Þay let doun þe grete draȝt & derely°
    out ȝeden   *drawbridge and courteously*
& kneled doun on her knes vpon þe colde erþe
To welcum þis ilk wyȝ as worþy hom°þoȝt   *to them*
820 Þay ȝolden° hym þe brode ȝate ȝarked vp wyde   *yielded*
& he hem raysed rekenly & rod ouer þe brygge
Sere° seggeȝ hym sesed° by sadel quel
    he lyȝt°   *several / took / alighted*
& syþen stabeled his stede stif men innoȝe
824 Knyȝteȝ & swyereȝ° comen doun þenne   *squires*
For to bryng þis buurne wyth blys into halle
Quen he hef° vp his helme þer hiȝed° innoghe   *raised / hastened*
For to hent°hit at his honde þe hende to seruen   *take*
828 His bronde°& his blasoun boþe° þay token   *sword / shield too*
Þen haylsed°he ful hendly þo haþeleȝ vchone   *greeted*
& mony proud mon þer presed þat prynce to honour
Alle hasped°in his heȝ wede° to
    halle þay hym wonnen°   *buckled / noble armor / brought*
832 Þer fayre fyre vpon flet° fersly brenned°   *the hearth / burned*

---

813. trowee: ᴍꜱ *trowoe*.
814. yow: W you.
815. wyȝe aȝayn: Go wyȝe ȝare & com aȝayn; D wyȝe ȝerne and com aȝayn; W wye yerne and com ayayn.

---

815. This line, despite the attempts of editors to fill it out, makes per- fectly good sense as it stands. 820. *ȝarked vp*: Go glossed as

Þenne þe lorde of þe lede louteȝ° fro his chambre   *turns*
For to mete wyth menske° þe mon on þe flor   *courtesy*
He sayde ȝe are welcum to welde° as yow lykeȝ   *take*
836 Þat here is al is yowre awen° to haue at yowre wylle   *own*
    & welde°   *control*
    Graunt mercy quoþ Gawayn
    Þer Kryst hit yow forȝelde
840   As frekeȝ þat semed fayn°   *glad*
    Ayþer oþer in armeȝ con felde°   *embraced*

XV

Gawayn glyȝt° on þe gome þat godly hym gret°   *looked / greeted*
& þuȝt hit a bolde burne þat þe burȝ aȝte°   *city owned*
844 A hoge haþel for þe noneȝ & of hyghe eldee°   *and in prime of life*
Brode bryȝt watȝ his berde & al beuer-hwed
Sturne stif on þe stryþþe° on stalworth
    schonkeȝ°   *firm standing / legs*
Felle face as þe fyre & fre of hys speche
848 & wel hym semed forsoþe as þe segge þuȝt

835. welde: Go wone.

"opened," but Emerson's "thrown up" seems better. See also Savage (MLN 49:342–50).

835–36. D's punctuation here, which makes *þat here is* the object of *welde*, seems more natural than that of Go and TG, both of whom place a semicolon at the end of 835.

835. *welde*: Go emends to *wone*, "dwell," on the grounds that the scribe picked up *welde* from the bob, which is here written on the same line. There is, however, little reason to emend the text since *welde* may be intransitive.

839. *þer*: Used in ME to introduce a wish. Borroff renders "May Christ your pains repay!"

847. *Felle face as þe fyre*: Cf. the sun god in the *Wars of Alexander*, 4922: *fell face as þe fire*. As M. Day points out, this and other sun god parallels in *GGK* all refer to the green knight, though interestingly to both of "his two roles" (see Go 847n and xviii).

To lede a lortschyp in lee of leudeȝ ful gode
Þe lorde hym charred° to a chambre
    & chefly° cumaundeȝ   *turned / particularly* (f.102b)
To delyuer hym a leude hym loȝly° to serue   *humbly*
852 & þere were boun°at his bode° burneȝ innoȝe   *ready / command*
Þat broȝt hym to a bryȝt boure° þer beddyng
    watȝ noble   *bedroom*
Of cortynes of clene sylk wyth cler golde hemmeȝ
& couertoreȝ° ful curious with comlych paneȝ° *coverlets / panels*
856 Of bryȝt blaunner° aboue
    enbrawded bisydeȝ°   *white fur / embroidered at the sides*
Rudeleȝ rennande° on ropeȝ red golde
    ryngeȝ   *curtains running*
Tapyteȝ tyȝt to þe woȝe of Tuly° & Tars° *Toulouse and Tharsia*
& vnder fete on þe flet° of folȝande sute° *floor / matching sort*
860 Þer he watȝ dispoyled° wyth specheȝ of myerþe *disrobed*
Þe burn of his bruny° & of his bryȝt wedeȝ° *coat of mail / armor*
Ryche robes ful rad° renkkeȝ hym broȝten   *quickly*
For to charge & to chaunge & chose of þe best
864 Sone as he on hent & happed°
    þerinne   *took one and enclosed himself*
Þat sete on hym semly wyth saylande° skyrteȝ   *flowing*

---

850. chefly: ᴍꜱ clesly.
856. blaunner: ᴍꜱ *illegible*; TG, W blaunmer.
862. hym: ᴍꜱ hem.
864. & happed: Go & watȝ happed.
865. hym: ᴍꜱ hyn.

---

849. *in lee*: Obscure. TG and D prefer "in hall," an alliterative variant of *on flet and in mote*, to either "in peace" (*NED*) or "as protector."

850. *chefly*: Originally Madden's reading from ᴍꜱ *clesly*.

856. *blaunner*: I am following Go's reading of this obscure word. Madden had *blaunner*, Morris *blaunnier* and TG *blaunmer*. See 155*n*.

863. *charge*: "put on" (Wright).

Þe ver by his uisage verayly hit semed
Wel neȝ to vche haþel alle on hwes
868 Lowande & lufly alle his lymmeȝ vnder
Þat a comloker knyȝt neuer Kryst made
    hem þoȝt°   *it seemed to them*
Wheþen° in worlde he were   *from wherever*
872 Hit semed as he moȝt
Be prynce withouten pere
In felde þer felle° men foȝt   *fierce*

XVI

A cheyer byfore þe chemne þer charcole brenned
876 Watȝ grayþed for Sir Gawan grayþely with cloþeȝ
Whyssynes° vpon queldepoyntes° þat
    koynt wer boþe   *cushions | quilted coverings*
& þenne a mere° mantyle watȝ on þat mon cast   *fair*

---

867. on: Go ouer.
872. moȝt: MS myȝt.
874. foȝt: MS fyȝt.
877. þat: MS þa.

866–68. The difficulty of these lines is greatly augmented by the various ways in which *ver* in 866 may be translated. The usual and best definition is simply "spring" from OF *ver*. This meaning is upheld by Emerson, TG, Go, and D. Morris, however, glosses it as "man" after ON *ver*. Menner (MLR 19:205–06) derived it from OF *vair*, "fur," translating the half-line as the "fur-trimming by his face." This is the reading followed in Banks' translation. Savage, however, maintained that *ver* referred to the heraldic pattern in fur on Gawain's robe, but this is a difficult meaning to fit into the context. All, moreover, offer translations in support of their readings. See Savage's full discussion in *The* Gawain-*Poet,* pp. 176–90. Go changes MS *on* to *over* in l. 867 for the sake of the meter.

875. Apparently chairs were considered luxuries. See Savage, in Expl 3:6.

877. *Whyssynes*: Go reads *Quyssynes* which, of course, simply alters the poet's spelling.

Of a broun bleeaunt° enbrauded ful ryche   *silk*
880 & fayre furred wythinne with felleȝ° of þe best   *skins*
Alle of ermyn in erde° his hode of þe same   *actually*
& he sete in þat settel semlych° ryche   *excellently*
& achaufed hym chefly° & þenne his
    cher° mended   *warmed himself quickly | mood*
884 Sone watȝ telded°vp a tabil on tresteȝ° ful fayre   *set | trestles*
Clad wyth a clene cloþe þat cler quyt schewed
Sanap & salure°& syluerin sponeȝ   *napkin and saltcellar*
Þe wyȝe wesche° at his wylle & went to
    his mete   *washed (f.103a)*
888 Seggeȝ hym serued semly° innoȝe   *properly*
Wyth sere sewes & sete° sesounde of
    þe best   *various broths and fitting*
Double-felde as hit falleȝ & fele kyn
    fischeȝ°   *and many kinds of fish*
Summe baken in bred summe brad° on þe
    gledeȝ°   *grilled | coals*
892 Summe soþen° summe in sewe sauered with spyces   *boiled*
& ay sawses so sleȝe° þat þe segge lyked   *cunningly made*
Þe freke calde hit a fest ful frely & ofte
Ful hendely quen alle þe haþeles rehayted°
    hym at oneȝ°   *exhorted | together*
896   as hende

881. in erde: TG inurnde.
883. chefly: MS cefly.
884. tabil: MS tapit.
893. sawses: MS, TG, D sawes.
893. sleȝe: MS sleȝeȝ.

881. *in erde*: TG had read *inurnde,* "adorned," and Go in his 1925 reprint of Morris had suggested *enurnde.*

884. *telded vp a tabil*: The tables, actually planks on trestles, were obvi-ously stored away after meals; thus Chaucer emphasizes the Franklin's Epicurianism by noting that his table *stood redy covered al the longe day.*

896. *as hende*: D includes this

Þis penaunce now ȝe take
& eft° hit schal amende   *later*
Þat mon much merþe con make°   *made*
900 For wyn in° his hed þat wende°   *to / went*

XVII

Þenne watȝ spyed & spured vpon
    spare wyse°   *inquired and asked in a tactful manner*
Bi preue° poynteȝ of þat prynce put to hymseluen   *discreet*
Þat° he beknew° cortaysly of þe court þat
    he were   *so that / acknowledged*
904 Þat aþel Arthure þe hende haldeȝ hym one°   *rules alone*
Þat is þe ryche ryal kyng of þe Rounde Table
& hit watȝ Wawen hymself þat in þat won synteȝ
Comen to þat Krystmasse as case° hym þen
    lymped°   *chance / befell*
908 When þe lorde hade lerned þat he þe leude hade
Loude laȝed he þerat so lef° hit
    hym þoȝt°   *pleasant / seemed to him*
& alle þe men in þat mote° maden much joye   *castle*
To apere in his presense prestly þat tyme
912 Þat° alle prys & prowes & pured þewes   *since*
Apendes to hys persoun & praysed is euer
Byfore alle men vpon molde his mensk is þe most
Vch segge ful softly sayde to his fere°   *companion*
916 Now schal we semlych° se sleȝteȝ°
    of þeweȝ°   *pleasantly / skillful acts / manners*
& þe teccheles° termes of talkyng noble   *spotless*

---

phrase in the speech of the *haþeles*. However, if it is translated "with equal courtesy" (Wright) it can well be taken to modify *rehayted* and thus not repeat the function of *hendely*

which modifies *calde*.

897. *Þis penaunce*: Go explains that "as it is Christmas Eve, no meat is served, hence the meal is referred to as a penance."

Wich spede is in speche vnspurd may we lerne
Syn we haf fonged° þat fyne fader of
    nurture°   *received | good breeding*
920 God hatȝ geuen vs his grace godly forsoþe
    Þat such a gest as Gawan graunteȝ vs to haue
    When burneȝ blyþe of his burþe schal sitte
        & synge
924 In menyng° of manereȝ mere   *understanding*
    Þis burne now schal vs bryng   (f.103b)
    I hope þat° may hym here   *suppose that one who*
    Schal lerne of luf-talkyng

XVIII

928 Bi þat° þe diner watȝ done & þe dere°vp   *when | noble ones*
    Hit watȝ neȝ° at þe nyȝt neȝed° þe tyme   *almost | drawn near*
    Chaplayneȝ to þe chapeles chosen þe gate°   *took the way*
    Rungen° ful rychely ryȝt as þay schulden   *rang the bells*
932 To þe hersum euensong of þe hyȝe tyde°   *festival*
    Þe lorde loutes° þerto & þe lady als   *goes*
    Into a cumly closet coyntly ho° entreȝ   *pew graciously she*
    Gawan glydeȝ° ful gay & gos þeder sone   *hastens*
936 Þe lorde laches° hym by þe lappe° &
    ledeȝ hym to sytte   *takes | fold of his garment*

929. nyȝt: ᴍѕ myȝt; TG, D, W niyȝt.
930. chaplayneȝ: ᴍѕ claplayneȝ.

918. *spede*: "excellence, perfection" (Wright); "success" (King, in RES 5:449–52). King translates: "What is (i.e. what-sort-of-thing makes) success in conversation we may learn without asking," using *Wich* as a pronoun.
920. For a discussion of the form *vus* for *us* see Magoun.
930. *þe chapeles*: See 802n.
932. *hersum*: Emerson's and Go's rendering of "festal" from ᴏᴇ *hēr*, *hersum, "noble, exalted," is doubtless more accurate than the "devout" (ᴏᴇ *hiērsum*) of D and the older editors.

   & couþly° hym knoweȝ & calleȝ hym his nome   *familiarly*

   & sayde he watȝ þe welcomest wyȝe of þe worlde

   & he hym þonkked þroly° & ayþer halched oþer   *earnestly*

940 & seten soberly samen þe seruisequyle

   Þenne lyst° þe lady to loke on þe knyȝt   *it pleased*

   Þenne com ho of hir closet with mony cler burdeȝ

   Ho watȝ þe fayrest in felle° of flesche & of lyre°   *skin / face*

944 & of compas° & colour & costes° of alle oþer *proportion / manners*

   & wener þen Wenore as þe wyȝe þoȝt

   He ches° þurȝ þe chaunsel to cheryche° þat hende   *went / greet*

   An oþer lady hir lad bi þe lyft honde

948 Þat watȝ alder þen ho an auncian° hit semed   *aged one*

   & heȝly honowred with haþeleȝ aboute

946. He: D, W Ho.

---

939. S. O. Andrew (RES 6:175–82) recommends emending *þroly* to *hiȝly* for the sake of the alliteration.

939. *halched*: Despite Go's argument that *halched* may well designate a spoken greeting, the fact that the two men have already greeted (36ff.), as well as the common use of the term, leads me to conclude that an embrace, a common practice among men in the Middle Ages, is here designated.

941. *Þenne*: Surely here with the sense of "when."

943. *in felle of flesche*: The phrase "flesh and fell" generally meant "bodily" in the Middle Ages. See Go's note.

944. *of alle oþer*: This construction, called "illogical" by TG, was apparently common enough historically (See R. W. King, in RES 5:449–52). It is to be

taken with *fayrest*: "She was the fairest of all."

945. *wener þen Wenore*: A conventional comparison, although in a poem actually involving Guinevere it may have a special force (See C. Moorman, in MS 18:158–72).

946. D, following Wright and others, emends *He* to *Ho* in order to allow the pronoun to refer to the lady, since "Gawain does not leave his seat until the lord gives him permission to do so at 971." However, it would seem natural that Gawain, somewhat overpowered by the lady's beauty, should spring forward to greet her, but that he should on second thought restrain his impetuosity until properly introduced by her husband (971).

Bot vnlyke on to loke þo ladyes were

For if þe 3onge wat3 3ep 3ol3e° wat3 þat oþer — *yellow*

952 Riche red on þat on rayled° ayquere — *arrayed*

Rugh ronkled cheke3 þat oþer on rolled° — *hung*

Kerchofes of þat on wyth mony cler perle3

Hir brest & hir bry3t þrote bare displayed

956 Schon schyrer þen snawe þat schede3 on hille3

Þat oþer wyth a gorger° wat3 gered°

ouer þe swyre — *neckerchief / clothed*

Chymbled° ouer hir blake chyn with mylk-quyte

vayles — *wrapped*

Hir frount° folden in sylk enfoubled°

ayquere — *forehead / muffled*

960 Toret & treleted with tryfle3 aboute

Þat° no3t wat3 bare of þat burde bot þe

blake bro3es — *so that* (f.104a)

Þe tweyne y3en & þe nase þe naked lyppe3

& þose were soure to se & sellyly blered

964 A mensk° lady on molde mon may hir calle — *dignified*

for° Gode — *before*

956. schede3: MS scheder.
958 mylk-quyte: TG, Go, D chalk-quyte; W chalk-whyte.
960. Toret: D Toreted.

950ff. D. A. Pearsall (MLR 50: 129–34) notes that in this passage the poet is using "description by contrast," a standard medieval rhetorical device, here eschewing the use of the more conventional *descriptio feminae*.

955–56. *Schon schyrer* certainly describes the lady's *brest* and *throte* rather than her *kerchofes*. I would therefore take *displayed* to be the predicate of *kerchofes* and *schon* of *brest*

and *throte*. The lady was, I think, almost topless.

958. *mylk quyte*: Following Onions TG, Go and D read *chalk-quyte*, for the sake of the alliteration. Brett, however (MLR 22:221), objects to the emendation.

960. *Toret and treleted*: "turreted and trellised." Madden reads *trejeted* and TG *treieted*, "adorned."

Hir body watȝ schort & þik
Hir buttokeȝ bay & brode
968 More lykkerwys on to lyk
Watȝ þat scho hade on lode°   *in tow*

XIX

When Gawayn glyȝt° on þat gay þat graciously loked   *looked*
Wyth leue laȝt° of þe lorde he went hem aȝaynes   *permission*
972 Þe alder he haylses heldande° ful lowe   *greets bowing*
Þe loueloker° he lappeȝ° a lyttel in
    armeȝ   *lovelier one | embraces*
He kysses hir comlyly & knyȝtly he meleȝ°   *speaks*
Þay kallen hym of aquoyntaunce & he hit quyk askeȝ
976 To be her seruaunt sothly if hemself lyked
Þay tan hym bytwene hem wyth talkyng hym leden

967. bay: TG, D balȝ; W balw.
971. went: Go, D, W lent.

---

967. *bay*: TG and D read *balȝ*, a
"swelling with round smooth surface"
on the supposition that *bay* could only
mean "bay-coloured," which I agree
is hardly appropriate. Brett, however,
defending the almost unintelligible
MS reading (MLR 8:162–63), sug-
gests that this is the "bay" of "bay-
windowed," a most interesting ex-
ample of physical metathesis, but a
reading to which D objects on the
grounds that bay "denoted the interior
opening, not the exterior bulge." How-
ever, the term is now used to denote a
paunch and may have had a similar
meaning in the poet's day.
968. *lykkerwys on to lyk*: TG gloss
lyk here, wrongly I think, in the
sense of "taste" (cf. *Purity* 1521) and
translate the two lines "Sweeter to
taste was she whom she was leading."
Go takes *lyk* as a variant of *lyke* and
reads "more pleasing to take pleasure
in."

971. *went*: Go and D following An-
drew (RES 6:175) emend to *lent* for
the sake of the alliteration.

975. *Þay kallen hym of aqoynt-
aunce*: "They ask to make his ac-
quaintance."

977. *tan hym bytwene hem*: Luttrell
(NQ 9:447–50) translates "to take
aside."

To chambre to chemne & chefly þay asken

Spyceʒ þat vnsparely° men speded hom to bryng   *eagerly*

980 & þe wynnelych°wyne þerwith vche tyme   *joyous*

Þe lorde luflych aloft lepeʒ ful ofte

Mynned°merthe to be made vpon mony syþeʒ   *devised*

Hent heʒly of° his hode & on a spere henged   *took gaily off*

984 & wayned hom to wynne þe worchip þerof

Þat most myrþe myʒt meue° þat Crystenmas whyle   *make*

& I schal fonde° bi my fayth to fylter°

wyth þe best   *try / contend*

Er me wont° þe wede° with help of my

frendeʒ   *before I lack / garment*

988 Þus wyth laʒande loteʒ° þe lorde hit tayt

makeʒ   *laughing words*

For to glade Sir Gawayn with gomneʒ in halle

þat nyʒt

Til þat hit watʒ tyme

992 Þe kyng comaundet lyʒt°   *lights*

Sir Gawen his leue con nyme°   *took*

& to his bed hym diʒt°   *went*

---

984. wayned: TG wayued.

987. wede: ᴍꜱ wedeʒ.

992. kyng: TG, Go, D, W lord.

---

979. *spyceʒ*: Probably "spiced cakes" (Ker, according to Wright).

984. *wayned*: TG had read *wayued*, "waved," but see Wright (JEGP 34: 157–79) who translated the line "And called up [lit. sent] them to win the honor [conferred by possession] thereof." D notes that the etymological sense of the verb *wayne*, "to move," "could develop to a figurative 'urge, challenge'."

988. *hit tayt makeʒ*: "makes things merry" (Go).

991. *kyng*: TG, Go and D read *lord*, Hulbert (MP 23:246–49) *knyʒt*, on the basis that Bercilak is not a king. Emerson's argument (JEGP, 21:378), however, that the host is here assuming the traditional role and title of "King of Christmas" more than justifies retaining the ᴍꜱ reading.

XX

On þe morne as vch mon myneʒ° þat tyme   *recalls*
996 Þat dryʒtyn for oure destyne to deʒe watʒ borne
Wele waxeʒ° in vche a won in worlde for his sake   *joy grows*
So did hit þere on þat day þurʒ dayntes° mony   *courtesies*
Boþe at mes & at mele messes ful
      quaynt°   *cunningly made* (f.104b)
1000 Derf°men vpon dece drest° of þe best   *strong / arranged*
Þe olde auncian wyf heʒest ho sytteʒ
Þe lorde lufly her by lent° as I trowe   *stayed*
Gawan & þe gay burde togeder þay seten
1004 Euen inmyddeʒ as þe messe metely come
& syþen þurʒ al þe sale as hem best semed
Bi vche grome at his degre grayþely° watʒ serued   *speedily*
Þer watʒ mete þer watʒ myrþe þer watʒ much ioye
1008 Þat for to telle þerof hit me tene° were   *trouble*
& to poynte hit ʒet I pyned° me parauenture°   *troubled / perhaps*
Bot ʒet I wot þat Wawen & þe wale burde
Such comfort of her compaynye caʒten°togeder   *got*
1012 Þurʒ her dere dalyaunce of her derne° wordeʒ   *private*
Wyth clene cortays carp closed° fro fylþe   *talk free*
Þat hor play watʒ passande°vche
      prynce gomen°   *surpassing / princely sport*

1014. Þat: MS &.

---

998. See 639*n*.

999. *at mes & at mele*: "at light meals and at feasts." The older reading of *mes* as "Mass" simply does not fit the context here.

1004. *in myddeʒ*: D thinks "in the middle (of the high table)," Wright the space between the tables.

1006. *grome*: Clearly here "man," rather than "servant," possibly through a confusion with *gome*. See TG's note.

1009. *& . . . ʒet*: "even though." See TG's note.

1009. *to poynte*: Grattan believes this may refer to "rhyming by letter, to making alliterative verse."

1014. *Þat*: TG's emendation, as is the same change in 1032 and 1386.

in vayres°   *truth*

1016 Trumpeʒ & nakerys°   *kettledrums*

Much pypyng þer repayres°   *is present*

Vche mon tented hys°   *attended to his business*

& þay two tented þayres

XXI

1020 Much dut° watʒ þer dryuen° þat day & þat

oþer   *mirth | made*

& þe þryd as þro þronge° in þerafter   *equally delightful*

Þe ioye of Sayn Joneʒ day watʒ gentyle to here

& watʒ þe last of þe layk° leudeʒ þer

þoʒten   *entertainment*

1024 Þer wer gestes to go vpon þe gray morne

Forþy°wonderly þay woke & þe wyn dronken   *so*

Daunsed ful dreʒly° wyth dere caroleʒ   *unceasingly*

At þe last when hit watʒ late þay lachen° her leue   *took*

1028 Vchon to wende on his way þat watʒ wyʒe stronge

1024. wer: W were.
1028. stronge: Go strange.

1016. Emerson inserts *þe* before *trumpeʒ* for the sake of the metrics.

1020ff. These lines have given rise to some conjecture concerning the chronology of the poem. Go states that although it appears that the poet has erroneously written St. John's Day, the last of the four days following Christmas, line 1022 actually refers to the *þyrd* day of 1021 and a line following the present line 1022 has been omitted. M. R. Watson (MLN 64:85–86) suggests that the poet has solved the problem of what would have been an extra day in his narrative scheme by

telescoping the third and fourth days of Christmas into a single day.

1025. *Forþy wonderly þay woke*: The guests stayed awake all night to dance caroles.

1028. *stronge*: Go prints *strange* explaining that the "sense of the line is that the guests, each of whom had come from afar, were to wend homeward," and though printing *stronge* D agrees that the meaning is "not belonging to the household." Savage, however, defends *stronge* and argues that only the sober guests could make their way unaided to bed.

Gawan gef hym god day þe god mon hym lachcheʒ
Ledes hym to his awen chambre þe chymne bysyde
& þere he draʒeʒ hym on dryʒe & derely hym þonkkeʒ
1032 Of þe wynne worschip þat he hym wayned°hade   *brought*
    As to honour his hous on þat hyʒe tyde°   *festival*
    & enbelyse his burʒ with his bele chere
    Iwysse sir quyl I leue me worþeʒ þe better
1036 Þat Gawayn hatʒ ben my gest at Goddeʒ awen fest   (f.105a)
    Grant merci sir quoþ Gawayn in god fayth hit is
        yowreʒ
    Al þe honour is your awen þe heʒe kyng yow
        ʒelde°   *reward*
    & I am wyʒe at your wylle to worch youre hest
1040 As I am halden þerto in hyʒe & in loʒe
        bi riʒt
    Þe lorde fast can hym payne
    To holde lenger þe knyʒt
1044   To hym answreʒ Gawayn
    Bi non way þat he myʒt

XXII

Then frayned° þe freke ful fayre at himseluen   *asked*
Quat derue° dede had hym dryuen at þat dere tyme   *brave*

1030. þe chymne: ᴍs þehȳne.
1032. þat: ᴍs &.
1032. wayned: TG, D wayued.
1037. merci: ᴍs nerci.
1044. answreʒ: TG, D answareʒ.

1031. *draʒeʒ hym on dryʒe*: "de-lays him" or possibly "draws him aside."

1032. *wayned*: TG and D read *wayued* "offered." See 984*n*.

1045. *Bi non way*: "by no means."

1047. *derue*: So TG, Go and D. Madden and Morris read *derne*, "se-cret." R. A. Waldron (NQ 207:366) suggests that the Green Knight is ironic in suggesting that Gawain has done some "grievous" deed since he

1048 So kenly° fro þe kyngeȝ kourt to kayre°
      al his one°   *boldly / ride / alone*
    Er þe halidayeȝ holly°were halet° out of toun   *wholly / gone*
    For soþe sir quoþ þe segge ȝe sayn bot þe trawþe
    A heȝe ernde & a hasty°me hade fro þo woneȝ   *urgent one*
1052 For I am sumned myselfe to sech to a place
    I ne wot in worlde whederwarde to wende hit to fynde
    I nolde bot if° I hit negh° myȝt on
           Nw ȝeres morne   *would not unless / reach*
    For alle þe londe inwyth Logres so me oure lorde help
1056 Forþy sir þis enquest I require yow here
    Þat ȝe me telle with trawþe in euer ȝe tale herde
    Of þe grene chapel quere hit on grounde stondeȝ
    & of þe knyȝt þat hit kepes of colour of grene
1060 Þer watȝ stabled bi statut° a
           steuen° vs bytwene   *established by agreement / tryst*
    To mete þat mon at þat mere° ȝif I myȝt last   *appointed place*
    & of þat ilk Nw ȝere bot neked° now
           wonteȝ°   *only a little / it wants*
    & I wolde loke on þat lede if God me let wolde
1064 Gladloker bi Goddeȝ sun þen any god welde
    Forþi iwysse bi ȝowre wylle wende
           me bihoues°   *it behooves me to go*
    Naf° I now to busy° bot bare°
           þre dayeȝ   *have not / be active / except barely*
    & me als fayn to falle feye° as fayly°
           of myyn ernde   *as fain doomed to death / fail*

1053. ne wot: MS wot; W not.

of course knows why Gawain is search-
ing for the Green Chapel.

   1053. *I ne wot*: The *ne* was first

inserted by TG to complete the obvi-
ous sense of the passage.

1068 Þenne laȝande quoþ þe lorde now leng þe byhoues

For I schal teche yow to þat terme° bi þe

  tymeȝ ende   *appointed place*

Þe grene chapayle vpon grounde greue yow no more

Bot ȝe schal be in yowre bed burne at þyn ese

1072 Quyle forth dayeȝ° & ferk° on þe

  fyrst of þe ȝere   *till late in the day / and go*

& cum to þat merk° at mydmorn to

  make quat yow likeȝ   *appointed place (f.105b)*

    in spenne

  Dowelleȝ whyle New ȝeres daye

1076 & rys & raykeȝ° þenne   *leave*

  Mon schal yow sette in waye

  Hit is not two myle henne°   *hence*

XXIII

Þenne watȝ Gawan ful glad & gomenly° he laȝed   *happily*

1080 Now I þonk yow þryuandely þurȝ° alle

  oþer þynge   *heartily beyond*

Now acheued is my chaunce I schal at your wylle

1069. þat. MS þa.

1070. The sense is "Do not worry about the location of the Green Chapel."

1071. Note that Bercilak here, as elsewhere, uses the singular form of address in speaking to Gawain, presumably in friendliness. Go's note on this line contains a detailed analysis of the uses of the second-person forms of address found in the poem.

1074. *in spenne*: Both TG and Go gloss as "field" or "ground" on the basis of *Wars of Alexander*, 4162, *all at was sperpolid on þe spene*, a reference to Alexander's tents falling in a gale. Emerson, however, suggests "space, interval" from Scand. *sponn*. Bloomfield thought that it may have been a cliche for "there."

Dowelle & elleȝ do quat ȝe demen
Þenne sesed hym þe syre & set hym bysyde
1084 Let þe ladieȝ be fette° to lyke hem þe better   *brought*
Þer watȝ seme solace° by hemself
    stille°   *seemly pleasure / privately*
Þe lorde let for luf loteȝ so myry
As wyȝ þat wolde of his wyte ne wyst quat he myȝt
1088 Þenne he carped to þe knyȝt criande loude
ȝe han demed to do þe dede þat I bidde
Wyl ȝe halde þis hes° here at þys oneȝ°   *promise / time*
ȝe sir forsoþe sayd þe segge trwe
1092 Whyl I byde in yowre borȝe be bayn° to
    ȝowre hest°   *obedient / behest*
For° ȝe haf trauayled quoþ þe tulk towen°
    fro ferre   *since / come*
& syþen waked me wyth ȝe arn not wel waryst°   *recovered*
Nauþer of sostnaunce ne of slepe soþly I knowe
1096 ȝe schal lenge in your lofte & lyȝe°
    in your ese   *room and lie*
Tomorn quyle þe messe-quyle & to mete wende°   *go*
When ȝe wyl wyth my wyf þat wyth yow schal sitte
& comfort yow with compayny til I to cort torne
1100   ȝe lende°   *stay*
    & I schal erly ryse
    On huntyng wyl I wende
    Gauayn granteȝ alle þyse
1104 Hym heldande° as þe hende° *bowing to him / courteous one does*

1092. ȝowre: MS ȝowe.

1086. See 639*n*.

1102. Loomis (JEGP 42:149–84) finds a parallel to Bercilak's love of hunting in the eleventh-century mabinogi of *Pwyll* in the figure of Arawn, the winter god who is Pwyll's host. Loomis (*Arthurian Tradition and Chretien de Troyes*) also sees much of Curoi, Cuchulainn's host, in Bercilak (see 2445*n*).

XXIV

ȝet firre quoþ þe freke a forwarde we make
Quatsoeuer I wynne in þe wod hit worþeȝ to°youreȝ   *becomes*
& quat chek so ȝe acheue chaunge me°
   þerforne   *exchange with me*
1108 Swete swap we so sware with trawþe
Queþer leude so lymp lere oþer better
Bi God quoþ Gawayn þe gode I grant þertylle
& þat yow lyst for to layke lef hit me þynkes   (f.106a)
1112 Who bryngeȝ vs þis beuerage þis bargayn is maked
So sayde þe lorde of þat lede þay laȝed vchone
Þay dronken & daylyeden & dalten vntyȝtel
Þise lordeȝ & ladyeȝ quyle þat hem lyked
1116 & syþen with frenkysch fare & fele fayre loteȝ
Þay stoden & stemed & stylly° speken   *arose and stopped and softly*
Kysten ful comlyly & kaȝten° her leue   *took*
With mony leude ful lyȝt & lemande°
   torches   *gleaming*
1120 Vche burne to his bed watȝ broȝt at þe laste
   ful softe
To bed ȝet er þay ȝede°   *went*

1112. þis (1st): Go þe.

1107. *chek*: "booty, gain," rather than "mere fortune" (Menner, in MLN 41:400); "swap, bargain" (Wright).

1108–09. "Good sir, let us exchange—swear honestly now!—whatever falls to our lot, sir, whether worthless or worthwhile."

1112. *who*: Go is surely correct in thinking *who* to be used indefinitely here: "if someone will bring us the drink." King (RES 5:449–52) thinks this neither interrogative (TG) or indefinite (D), but an "alternative spelling of the interjection 'Hoo'." *Bryngeȝ* is thus to King an imperative.

1114. *dalten vntyȝtel*: "talked nonsense" (Wright).

1116. See 639*n*.

1116. *frenkysch fare*: Used satirically in the Chester *Noah's Flood*, 100. Here, however, it would seem to be used in a "good sense" as "French manners, politeness" (see Emerson).

Recorded° couenauntez ofte   *they repeated*
1124 Þe olde lorde of þat leude
Cowþe wel halde layk alofte°   *carry on a game*

PART III

I

Ful erly bifore þe day þe folk vprysen
Gestes þat go wolde hor gromez° þay calden   *their servants*
1128 & þay busken vp bilyue blonkkez° to sadel   *hurry up quickly horses*
Tyffen° her takles trussen° her males°   *prepare / pack / bags*
Richen hem° þe rychest to ryde alle arayde   *dress*
Lepen vp lyȝtly lachen her brydeles
1132 Vche wyȝe on his way þer hym wel lyked
Þe leue lorde of þe londe watz not þe last
Arayed for þe rydyng with renkkez ful mony
Ete a sop hastyly when he hade herde masse
1136 With bugle to bent-felde° he
     buskez bylyue°   *open field / hurries quickly*
By° þat any daylyȝt lemed vpon erþe   *by the time*
He with his haþeles on hyȝe horsses weren
Þenne þise cacheres° þat couþe°
     cowpled hor houndez   *hunters / knew how*

1129. her (1st): MS he.
1137. þat: MS þat þat.

1124. *olde*: Wright and Savage gloss this "eminent."

1133. The description of the three hunts, almost certainly the work of the *Gawain*-poet, has been analyzed from a number of points of view. Perhaps the most famous theory regarding them is that of H. L. Savage, who sees in the three hunts parallels to the three temptations of Gawain in the lady's bower (see Introduction for details). Speirs, looking at the poem from the viewpoint of myth, sees in the hunts the "doing-to-death of the qualities of the natural man which Courtesy has to vanquish . . ." (*Medieval English Poetry*). The technicalities of the hunt have also been thoroughly explored and are commented on in the notes that follow.

1140 Vnclosed þe kenel dore & calde hem þeroute

Blwe bygly in bugleȝ þre bare mote°   *single notes*

Braches bayed þerfore & breme noyse maked

& þay chastysed & charred on chasyng þat went

1144 A hundreth of hunteres as I haf herde telle

of þe best

To trystors vewters ȝod° *stations deerhound-keepers went*

Couples huntes of kest° *leashes huntsmen cast off*

1148 Þer ros for blasteȝ gode   (f.106b)

Gret rurd°in þat forest   *noise*

II

At þe fyrst quethe° of þe quest quaked þe wylde *sound*

Der drof° in þe dale doted° for drede *rushed / grew mad*

1152 Hiȝed° to þe hyȝe° bot heterly° þay

were   *sped / high ground / quickly*

1141. þre: W three.
1141. mote: Go moteȝ.
1145. of þe: Go þe.

1141. See 118n. Since the word *mote* is in essence both singular and plural, the fourteenth-century horn having but one note or tone, there is no need to emend the form of the word, as does Go to *moteȝ*.

1142. *branches*: Much like the modern beagle, these scenting hounds were most often used as *taysours*, "teasers," their duty being "to hunt up [rouse] the game . . . when the deer was to be shot with the bow" (*The Master of Game*).

1143. *chastysed*: Probably "disciplined" (Wright) rather than "rebuked" (Go).

1144. *hundreth of hunteres*: The men, not the dogs. *Hundreth* is probably hyperbolical.

1146. *ȝod*: Emerson emends to *ȝode* for the sake of the metrics.

1147. TG believe that the dogs here released are the greyhounds which did the actual hunting. Savage, however, believes that the *braches* are here meant.

1150. *quest*: While this term may refer to the hunt itself (see 1421 and TG's note), it more than likely in this passage has specific reference to the cry of the hounds.

1150ff. As TG note, this whole passage may be glossed from the *Master of Game* where the same procedure

Restayed with° þe stablye° þat
    stoutly ascryed°   *turned by | beaters | shouted*
Þay let þe hertteʒ haf þe gate° with þe hyʒe hedes   *go free*
Þe breme bukkeʒ also with hor brode paumeʒ°   *antlers*
1156 For þe fre° lorde hade defende° in fermysoun
    tyme   *forbidden*
Þat þer schulde no mon meue to° þe male
    dere   *hunt*
Þe hindeʒ were halden in with hay & war
Þe does dryuen with gret dyn to þe depe sladeʒ°   *valleys*
1160 Þer myʒt mon se as þay slypte slentyng° of arwes   *a rush*
At vche wende vnder wande wapped° a
    flone°   *rushed | arrow*
Þat bigly bote° on þe broun° with
    ful brode hedeʒ   *bit | brown hides*
What þay brayen & bleden bi bonkkeʒ þay deʒen
1164 & ay rachches° in a res radly hem folʒes   *hounds*

---

of deer hunting is described. "Men and hounds were stationed at various points around the district in which the game was to be hunted. Light greyhounds and other *taysours* (hounds for putting up and driving game) were slipped, and as they drove the deer the *stablye* or beaters belonging to the ring of stations directed their course to where the lord and his party stood ready to shoot them. The man of the *stablye* also tried to strike down the deer if they came near enough, and at any of the stations might be some of the larger greyhounds ('receivers') to pull the deer down. The stations where special preparations were made to kill the deer constituted the *resayt* (1168)."

1154. *hertteʒ*: Savage believes that *hertteʒ* here and *hindeʒ* in 1158 denote males and females of the red deer (*cervus elaphus*), and *bukkeʒ* (1155) and *does* (1159) males and females of the fallow deer (*cervus dama*). See also W. J. Ong (MLN 65:537–39) for corroborative evidence.

1156. *fermysoun tyme*: The "closed season" on harts and bucks was, according to the *Master of Game*, from September 14 until May 3. Hinds and does might be hunted from September 14 until February 2.

1161. *wende*: Grattan takes this to be a preterite singular verb, the nominative relative of which has been omitted: "each that passed from the wood."

Hunterez wyth hyȝe horne hasted hem after
Wyth such a crakkande kry as klyffes haden brusten
What wylde so atwaped wyȝes° þat
      schotten   *whatever animal escaped the men*
1168 Watȝ al toraced° & rent at þe resayt°   *seized / receiving station*
    Bi° þay were tened° at þe hyȝe &
       taysed° to þe wattreȝ   *after / worried / driven*
    Þe ledeȝ were so lerned at þe loȝe trysteres°   *low stations*
    & þe grehoundeȝ so grete þat geten hem bylyue
1172 & hem tofylched as fast as frekeȝ myȝt loke
        þer ryȝt
    Þe lorde for blys abloy
    Ful oft con launce & lyȝt°   *did gallop and alight*
1176 & drof° þat day wyth joy   *spent*
    Thus to þe derk nyȝt

III

Þus laykeȝ° þis lorde by lynde-wodeȝ eueȝ°   *plays / edge*
& Gawayn þe god mon in gay bed lygeȝ

1179. Gawayn: MS G.

1165. See 118*n*.

1168–69. I would recommend here the punctuation of TG and Go, who think of 1170–71 as explaining the actions of the men at the *resayt* in 1167–69. See TG's note for a translation based on this punctuation.

1169. *taysed*: See 1142*n*.

1169. *þe wattreȝ*: According to *The Boke of St. Albans* the hunted deer seeks a stream "the howndes . . . to begyle" by causing them to lose his track in water.

1172. *tofylched*: A unique word. Go

glosses as "seized fiercely" from context and suggests a possible derivation from "flick," "meaning, of a dog, to seize by the fur."

1174. *abloy*: Wright (MLR 18:86), supported by C. T. Onions, derived this from OF *esbloir*, "dazzled, transported, reckless." Grattan, however (RES 1:487), took the word to be an interjection: "the lord for joy oft shouted 'tally-ho'."

1177. *derk*: Emerson would amend to *derke* for the sake of the meter.

1178ff. L. H. Loomis (*Arthurian*

1180 Lurkkeȝ quyl þe daylyȝt lemed° on þe wowes°   *shone | walls*
     Vnder couertour ful clere cortyned aboute
     & as in slomeryng he slode° sleȝly° he
          herde   *slept softly | stealthily*
     A littel dyn at his dor & derfly vpon°   *open*
1184 & he heueȝ vp his hed out of þe cloþes
     A corner of þe cortyn he caȝt vp a lyttel   (f.107a)
     & wayteȝ° warly þiderwarde quat hit be myȝt   *looks*
     Hit watȝ þe ladi loflyest to beholde
1188 Þat droȝ þe dor after hir ful dernly° & stylle   *secretly*
     & boȝed° towarde þe bed & þe burne schamed   *turned*
     & layde hym doun lystyly° & let as he slepte   *craftily*
     & ho stepped stilly & stel to his bedde
1192 Kest vp þe cortyn & creped withinne
     & set hir ful softly on þe bedsyde
     & lenged þere selly° longe to loke quen he wakened   *very*
     Þe lede lay lurked a ful longe quyle
1196 Compast° in his conscience° to quat
          þat cace° myȝt   *pondered | mind | happening*

1183. derfly: D dernly.

Literature in the Middle Ages) traces much of the temptation scenes that follow to the twelfth-century German *Lanzelet*, which, although it does not identify the temptress as the wife of the host, does include a great number of parallels to *GGK*. The thirteenth-century French romance *Yder*, on the other hand, does identify the temptress as the lady of the castle. The earliest instance of the temptation motif, however, is generally conceded to be found in the eleventh-century mabinogi of *Pwyll*, although Friedman (Spec 35: 260–74), sees "no temptation in the

Pwyll episode." For a full review of the place of the temptation scenes in *GGK*, see the Introduction.

1183. *derfly*: Both TG and Go suggest that the scribe may have copied *deruely* (*derfly*), "promptly," for the poet's *dernely*, "stealthily," and D prints *dernly*. However, *derfly* is perfectly legible in the MS and may well here mean "quickly" rather than "boldly."

1187. Loomis (JEGP 42:149–84) finds a parallel to Gawain's spurning the advances of his hostess's wife in *Pwyll* (see 1178n and Introduction).

Meue oþer amount to meruayle hym þoȝt
Bot ȝet he sayde in hymself more semly hit were
To aspye° wyth my spelle in space°   *discover / words soon*
        quat ho wolde
1200 Þen he wakenede & wroth° & tohirwarde torned   *stretched*
   & vnlouked his yȝelyddeȝ & let as hym
        wondered°   *pretended to be surprised*
   & sayned hym as bi his saȝe þe sauer° to
        worthe°   *safer / become*
        with hande
1204   Wyth chynne & cheke ful swete
    Boþe quit & red in blande°   *together*
    Ful lufly con ho lete°   *graciously she behaved*
    Wyth lyppeȝ smal laȝande°   *laughing*

IV

1208 God moroun Sir Gawayn sayde þat fayr lady
   Ȝe are a sleper vnslyȝe° þat mon° may
        slyde° hider   *unwary / one / steal*
   Now ar ȝe tan astyt° bot true° vs may
        schape   *in a moment / truce*
   I schal bynde yow in your bedde þat be ȝe trayst°   *sure*
1212 Al laȝande þe lady lanced þo bourdeȝ°   *uttered those jests*

1199. in: MS *illegible.*
1208. fayr: TG, Go, D, W gay.
1209. are: MS, TG, D, W ar.
1212. lanced: Go, W lauced.

1202. *saȝe*: Go's conjecture that *saȝe* here means "pious ejaculation" and that Gawain said something like "Cros Kryst me spede" (762) upon crossing himself is certainly to be preferred to Wright's theory that *saȝe* refers back to Gawain's words to himself in 1198–99.

1208. *fayr*: Both TG and Go emend to *gay* for the sake of the alliteration.

1208. See 280*n.*

Goud moroun gay quoþ Gawayn þe blyþe
Me schal worþe at your wille & þat me wel lykez
For I зelde me зederly & зeзe° after

    grace°   *promptly and cry / mercy*

1216 & þat is þe best be my dome for me byhouez nede
  & þus he bourded aзayn with mony a blyþe laзter
  Bot wolde зe° lady louely þen leue me grante   *if you would*
  & deprece° your prysoun° & pray hym to ryse   *release / prisoner*
1220 I wolde boзe of° þis bed & busk° me better   *leave / dress*
  I schulde keuer° þe more comfort to karp yow wyth   *get*
  Nay for soþe beau sir sayd þat swete   (f.107b)
  зe schal not rise of your bedde I rych° yow better   *intend*
1224 I schal happe° yow here þat oþer

    half als°   *wrap / on the other side also*

  & syþen karp wyth my knyзt þat I kaзt haue
  For I wene wel iwysse Sir Wowen зe are
  Þat alle þe worlde worchipez quere so зe ride
1228 Your honour your hendelayk° is hendely praysed   *courtesy*
  With lordez wyth ladyes with alle þat lyf bere
  & now зe are here iwysse & we bot oure one°   *alone*
  My lorde & his ledez ar on lenþe faren°   *have gone afar*
1232 Oþer burnez in her bedde & my burdez als
  Þe dor drawen & dit° with a derf° haspe   *locked / strong*
  & syþen I haue in þis hous hym þat al lykez
  I schal ware° my whyle wel quyl hit lastez   *spend*
1236   with tale°   *speech*
  зe ar welcum to my cors°   *body*

1213. gay: MS *illegible*.

1220–21. Gawain is probably naked.
1237. It is difficult to see the logic
of Go's remark that the "lady's blunt-
ness in coming to the point testifies to
her inexperience in such a role." Surely

the lady, *lykkerwys on to lyk* (968)
and directed by Morgan—if she herself
be not Morgan (see Introduction)—is
more interested in testing Gawain in
the most direct way rather than in

GAWAIN AND THE LADY

Yowre awen won to wale°   *take*
Me behoueʒ of fyne force°   *necessity*
1240 Your seruaunt be & schale

V

In god fayth quoþ Gawayn gayn hit me þynkkeʒ
Þaʒ I be not now he þat ʒe of speken
To reche to such reuerence as ʒe reherce here
1244 I am wyʒe vnworþy I wot wel myseluen
Bi God I were glad & yow god þoʒt
At saʒe° oþer at seruyce° þat I sette°
      myʒt   *by word | deed | set myself*
To þe plesaunce° of your prys hit were a pure ioye *pleasure*
1248 In god fayth Sir Gawayn quoþ þe gay lady
Þe prys & þe prowes þat pleseʒ al oþer
If I hit lakked° oþer set at lyʒt hit were littel
      daynte   *belittled*
Bot hit ar ladyes innoʒe þat leuer wer nowþe
1252 Haf þe hende in hor holde as I þe habbe here
To daly with derely your daynte wordeʒ
Keuer hem comfort & colen° her careʒ   *relieve*
Þen much of þe garysoun° oþer golde þat
      þay hauen   *treasure*
1256 Bot I louue° þat ilk lorde þat þe lyfte°
      haldeʒ   *praise | sky*

1255. þat: MS þat þat.

---

demonstrating her knowledge of the niceties of the courtly game. D, on the other hand, feels that *my cors* here means no more than "me" and that the line should be translated "You are welcome to me," that is, "I am glad to have you here." Both meanings, of course, may be intended simultaneously.

1238. *won*: P. G. Thomas (ES 47: 311) derives this from OE *wun*, "pleasure."

1256. See 2441–42n.

I haf hit holly in my honde þat al desyres
      þurȝe grace
  Scho made hym so gret chere
1260 Þat watȝ so fayr of face   (f.108a)
  Þe knyȝt with speches skere°   *pure*
  Answared to vche a cace°   *speech*

VI

Madame quoþ þe myry mon Mary yow ȝelde
1264 For I haf founden in god fayth yowre fraunchis nobele
  & oþer ful much of oþer folk fongen hor dedeȝ
  Bot þe daynte þat þay delen for my disert nysen
  Hit is þe worchyp of yourself þat noȝt bot wel conneȝ
1268 Bi Mary quoþ þe menskful° me þynk hit
      anoþer°   *honorable lady / otherwise*
  For were I worth al þe wone° of wymmen alyue   *multitude*
  & al þe wele of þe worlde were in my honde

1262. Answared: MS Aswared.
1265. fongen: D fongen bi; W fongen for.
1266. delen for: W delen.
1266. nysen: D, W nys euen.

1263–67. A notoriously difficult passage. Both TG and Go offer strained translations, but Banks seems best to capture the sense of the lines:

"Quoth the merry man, "Madam,
    Mary reward you,
For noble, in faith,
    I've found you, and generous.
People by others
    pattern their actions,
But more than I merit
    to me they give praise;
'Tis your courteous self who
    can show naught but kindness."

The awkwardness of this passage is due to the difficulty in glossing *nysen* (1266) and to the fact that Gawain in his embarrassment may well be speaking in some sort of formula of polite expression. Go glosses *nysen* as "nothing," which suits the context; TG, following Morris, reads the word as a verb meaning "to make foolish by over-refinement." Menner (MLR 19: 206–08) reads it as the verb *uysen*, "to devise or make." And, D emends *rysen* to *nys even*, "is not equal to it [honor]."

&°I schulde chepen° & chose to cheue me a lorde   *if* / *bargain*

1272 For þe costes° þat I haf knowen vpon þe knyʒt here   *manners*

Of bewte & debonerte° & blyþe semblaunt   *courtesy*

& þat I haf er herkkened° & halde hit here° trwee   *heard of* / *now*

Þer schulde no freke vpon folde bifore yow be chosen

1276 Iwysse worþy quoþ þe wyʒe ʒe haf waled° wel better   *taken*

Bot I am proude of þe prys þat ʒe put on me

& soberly your seruaunt my souerayn I holde yow

& yowre knyʒt I becom & Kryst yow forʒelde°   *reward*

1280 Þus þay meled° of muchquat° til myd-morn

   paste   *spoke* / *many things*

& ay þe lady let lyk a hym loued mych

Þe freke ferde° with defence & feted°

   ful fayre   *acted* / *caution and behaved*

Þaʒ I were burde bryʒtest þe burde in mynde hade

1281. a: TG, D as.

1283. I: Go, W ho.

1283. burde (2nd): Go, W burne.

1278. Surely the sovereign-servant relationship suggested here by Gawain is conventional and formulaic, the sort of phrase expected of this knight *þat alle þe worlde worchipeʒ*.

1281. *a*: Both Madden and Morris emended to "and," TG and D to "as." But as G points out, *a* here can well be the feminine personal pronoun.

1283–87. I would recommend the punctuation suggested by Emerson which makes the whole passage an interior monologue by the lady. D, however, objects to treating these lines as an interior monologue on the grounds that "it would imply that [the lady] knew that Gawain was obliged to face the blow from the Green Knight," this constituting to D a "serious flaw in the handling of the plot." However, Bercilak's explanation (2444–66) clearly implies that his lady was a part of the conspiracy, and her statement here would add to the suspense by alerting the audience, though not Gawain, to the connection between his conduct in the bower and the outcome of the beheading game. Morris and G somewhat pointlessly emend *I* to *ho* and *burde* to *burne* in 1283.

1284 Þe lasse luf in his lode° for lur°
   þat he soȝt   *with him | because of the penalty*
     boute hone°   *without delay*
   Þe dunte° þat schulde hym deue°   *blow | stun*
   & nedeȝ hit most be done
1288 Þe lady þenn spek of leue
   He granted hir ful sone

VII

   Þenne ho gef hym god day & wyth a glent° laȝed   *glance*
   & as ho stod ho stonyed° hym wyth ful stor wordeȝ   *astonished*
1292 Now he þat spedeȝ° vche spech þis
     disport ȝelde° yow   *blesses | entertainment reward*
   Bot þat ȝe be Gawan hit gotȝ in mynde
   Querfore quoþ þe freke & freschly° he askeȝ   *eagerly*
   Ferde° lest he hade fayled in fourme of his castes   *afraid*
1296 Bot þe burde hym blessed & bi þis skyl sayde
   So god as Gawayn gaynly° is halden   *fittingly* (f.108b)

1286. schulde: ᴍꜱ sclulde.
1289. granted: W graunted.
1293. gotȝ: Go gotȝ not; W gos.
1295. castes: Go costes.

1292. See 2441–42.

1293. *hit gotȝ in mynde*: Go assumed that "not" had been omitted after *gotȝ*, but the line is already negative (see Emerson and TLS, January 25, 1941). TG render the phrase "it is debated in my mind."

1295. *castes*: Go emends to *costes*, "manners, behavior," by analogy with 1272. However *castes*, "speech," makes equally good sense here.

1296. *Bi þis skyle*: D treats the phrase, glossed "for this reason," as a part of the lady's speech.

1296. *blessed*: Go, following P. G. Thomas (ES 47:311), notes that *blessed* here may be derived from ᴏᴇ *blissian*, "to rejoice." The lady probably reassures Gawain simply by a smile or glance.

& cortaysye is closed so clene° in hymseluen   *fully*
Couth not lyȝtly haf lenged so long wyth a lady
1300 Bot he had craued a cosse bi his courtaysye
Bi sum towch° of summe tryfle at sum
       taleȝ° ende   *hint / speech's*
Þen quoþ Wowen iwysse worþe° as yow lykeȝ   *let it be*
I schal kysse at your comaundement as a
       knyȝt falleȝ°   *is fitting for*
1304 Þat feres° lest he displese yow so plede hit no more   *further*
Ho comes nerre with þat & cacheȝ hym in armeȝ
Louteȝ° luflych adoun & þe leude kysseȝ   *bends*
Þay comly bykennen° to Kryst ayþer° oþer   *commend / each*
1308 Ho dos hir° forth at þe dore withouten dyn more   *goes*
& he ryches° hym to ryse & rapes° hym sone   *readies / hastens*
Clepes°to his chamberlayn choses his wede   *calls*
Boȝeȝ forth quen he watȝ boun° blyþely to masse   *ready*
1312 & þenne he meued to his mete þat menskly°
       hym keped°   *duly / occupied*
& made myry al day til þe mone rysed
      with game
Watȝ neuer freke fayrer fonge°   *received*
1316   Bitwene two so dyngne dame

           1304. Þat feres: MS & fire.
           1304. so: MS fo.
           1315. Watȝ: MS With.

1298. *cortaysye*: Here and elsewhere the lady uses the words "courtesy" and "courteous" in what we assume to be their traditional courtly-love senses (see J. F. Kitely, in *Anglia* 79:7–16), though in *GGK* the lady in her role as temptress (see 1237*n*) assumes the active role of the lover and Gawain that of the reluctant lady.

1304. *Þat feres . . . so*: MS *& fire . . . fo*. I am adopting here Go's reading of the line. D suggests *firre*, "further," and translates "I shall kiss at your command, and more, as is the duty of a knight. . . ."

1316. *dame*: Plural in function, perhaps because of the rhyme, though not in form.

Þe alder & þe ȝonge
Much solace° set þay same   *joy*

VIII

And ay þe lorde of þe londe is lent° on his gamneȝ   *gone*
1320 To hunt in holteȝ & heþe at hyndeȝ barayne
Such a sowme° he þer slowe bi þat þe sunne heldet°   *number / set*
Of dos & of oþer dere to deme were wonder
Þenne fersly° þay flokked in folk at þe laste   *quickly*
1324 & quykly of þe quelled dere a querre þay maked
Þe best boȝed þerto with burneȝ innoghe
Gedered þe grattest of gres° þat þer were   *fattest*
& didden hem derely°vndo as þe dede
        askeȝ°   *neatly / task demands*
1328 Serched hem at þe asay summe þat þer were
Two fyngeres þay fonde of þe fowlest of alle

1320. *hyndeȝ barayne*: Of the hinds "þat bene bareyn here sesoun begynneþ whan þe sesoun of þe hert failleþ [September 14], and lasteþ to lenton" (*The Master of Game*).

1322. *oþer dere*: Ong (MLN 65: 539) thinks that this may refer to the roe.

1323–64. For an excellent general summary review of the technical studies of this passage on the "breaking" or dressing of the deer, see J. D. Bruce (ES 32:23–26). H. L. Savage has examined the technicalities of fourteenth-century hunting with great thoroughness and his articles dealing with specific problems (e.g., PMLA 46:169–76) should always be consulted. *The Boke of St. Albans* is the most useful of the old handbooks, and the hunting scenes of *The Parlement of the Thre Ages* present interesting parallels to those of *GGK*.

1324. *querre*: Not simply quarry, but the collection of slain animals. TG note that the word derives from OF *cuirée*, the offal given to the dogs after the kill, a word in turn derived from the *cuir* or "hide" from which it was served.

1325. *þe best boȝed thereto*: Evidently then, as now, it was considered proper for all degrees of hunters to be skilled in dressing the slain animal.

1328. *þe asay*: The initial cut made from brisket to belly "to see the goodnesse of the flesh, and howe thicke it is" (Turberville), usually by the man of greatest rank present.

1329. The hunters found two fingers

Syþen þay slyt þe slot sesed þe erber
Schaued wyth a scharp knyf & þe schyre knitten
1332 Syþen rytte° þay þe foure lymmes & rent of þe hyde   *cut*
Þen brek þay þe bale þe bauleȝ° out token   *bowels*
Lystily forlancyng° & lere of þe knot   *throughout* (f.109a)
Þay gryped° to þe gargulun° &
    grayþely departed°   *seized / throat / promptly separated*
1336 Þe wesaunt° fro þe wynt-hole &
    walt° out þe gutteȝ   *gullet / windpipe and flung*
Þen scher° þay out þe schuldereȝ with
    her scharp knyueȝ   *cut*
Haled°hem by a lyttel hole to haue hole sydes   *drew*
Siþen britned° þay þe brest & brayden°
    hit in twynne   *cut open / pulled*

1331. knitten: Go kitten.
1333. bauleȝ: ᴍs baleȝ; Go boueleȝ; D, W boweleȝ.
1334. &: Go, D, W þe.
1334. lere: ᴍs bere.
1334. forlancying: Go, D, W for laucying.

---

depth of fat even on the leanest deer. Falstaff, remember, is "three fingers on the ribs" (*I Henry IV*, IV, ii).

1330. *þe slot*: The hollow at the base of the throat. Through this opening the *erber* or upper stomach can be easily grasped (*sesed*), the flesh around it scraped loose (*schaued*), filled with blood and grease, and the flesh of the stomach (*schyre*) sewn up again (*knitten*). *The Boke of St. Albans* reminds the hunter to carry thread and needle for this purpose. Go refused to take *schyre* as referring to the flesh of the stomach, glossed it as "intestines generally," and so emended *knitten* to

kitten, "cut," thus describing an operation unknown to hunters, then or now.

1333. *bauleȝ*: ᴍs *baleȝ*. TG's emendation: "bowels."

1334. *lere*: ᴍs *bere* (?). The ᴍs letters are here quite cramped and of the two readings *lere*, "flesh," is preferable. Thus the hunters broke out the skin wall of the belly and took out the bowels, which they quickly (*lystily*) threw away with the knot, which is not, as Go and D insist, the knot of the *erber* described in 1331, but, as TG say, one of the two knots or *nuttes* (ᴏꜰ *neuz*) of flesh found between the neck and the shoulders.

1340 & eft at þe gargulun bigyneʒ on
    þenne
  Ryueʒ° hit vp radly° ryʒt to þe
    byʒt°   *rips / quickly / fork of the legs*
  Voydeʒ out þe avanters° & verayly þerafter   *intestines*
  Alle þe rymeʒ by þe rybbeʒ radly þay lance
1344 So ryde þay of by resoun° bi þe
    rygge° boneʒ   *they cleared off rightly / back*
  Euenden to þe haunche þat henged alle samen
  & heuen hit vp al hole & hwen hit of þere
  & þat þay neme for°þe noumbles°bi nome
    as I trowe   *name as / entrails*
1348   bi kynde
  Bi þe byʒt° al of þe þyʒes   *fork*
  Þe lappeʒ° þay lance bihynde   *folds*
  To hewe hit in two þay hyʒes°   *hasten*
1352 Bi° þe bakbon to vnbynde°   *along / cut open*

IX

  Boþe þe hede & þe hals° þay hwen of þenne   *neck*
  & syþen sunder þay þe sydeʒ swyft fro þe chyne° *backbone*
  & þe corbeles fee þay kest in a greue°   *thicket*

1343. lance: Go, W lauce.
1344. So: ᴍꜱ fo.
1345. Euenden: Go Euendoun.
1350. lance: Go, W lauce.

1343. *rimeʒ*: Despite the plural form, Savage (MLN 66:216) sees this as connected with dialect *rim*, "the peritoneum enclosing the intestines."

1345. *Euenden*: Emerson suggests that this is the correct past tense of *euenden*, "to make even." Madden had suggested an adverbial use, "evenly."

Go emends to *euendoun*, the adverb "even down."

1347. *þat*: As TG suggests, *þat* here refers to the parts cut away from the deer.

1355. *þe corbeles fee*: Turberville explains: "There is a little gristle which is vpon the spoone of the brysket [i.e.,

1356 Þenn þurled° þay ayþer þik side þurȝ bi þe rybbe   *pierced*

& henged þenne ayþer bi hoȝes° of þe

fourcheȝ°   *hocks / haunches*

Vche freke for his fee as falleȝ° forto haue   *is fitting*

Vpon a felle° of þe fayre best fede þay þayr houndes   *skin*

1360 Wyth þe lyuer & þe lyȝteȝ° þe leþer° of þe

pauncheȝ   *lungs / skin*

& bred baþed in blod blende°þeramongeȝ   *mixed*

Baldely þay blw prys bayed þayr rachcheȝ

Syþen fonge þay her flesche folden° to home   *packed*

1364 Strakande° ful stoutly mony stif moteȝ°   *sounding / loud notes*

Bi þat þe daylyȝt watȝ done þe douthe° watȝ

al wonen°   *company / come*

Into þe comly castel þer þe knyȝt bideȝ

ful stille

1368   Wyth blys & bryȝt fyr bette°   *fire kindled*

Þe lorde is comen þertylle

When Gawayn wyth hym mette

Þer watȝ bot wele at wylle

1357. ayþer: ᴍs aþer.

---

at the end of the breast bone] which we cal the Rauens bone, bycause it is cast vp to the Crowes and Rauens which attende hunters."

1358. *Vche freke for his fee*: *The Boke of St. Albans* explains in detail the prescribed allotment of the various parts of the deer to the hunters, the hide to the killer, the right shoulder to the forester, etc. See TG's note.

1362–64. See 118*n*.

1362. *prys*: The call, consisting of four notes, blown to signal the taking of the deer.

1368. *wyth blys*: " 'Wyth' is here used idiomatically in connection with 'comen' in the sense of 'against, towards,' *i.e.* the lord has come to bliss and bright blazing fire . . ." (Go). Grattan thinks *bette* a scribal error for *bet*.

1370–75. See 280*n*.

X

1372 Thenne comaunded þe lorde in þat sale to samen°
    alle þe meny   *gather* (f.109b)
  Boþe þe ladyes on loghe° to lyȝt° with her
    burdes   *down* / *come*
  Bifore alle þe folk on þe flette° frekeȝ he beddeȝ   *floor*
  Verayly his venysoun to fech hym byforne
1376 & al godly in gomen Gawayn he called
  Techeȝ hym to° þe tayles° of ful
    tayt° bestes   *shows to him* / *tally* / *lively*
  Scheweȝ hym þe schyree grece schorne vpon rybbes
  How payeȝ° yow þis play haf I prys wonnen   *pleases*
1380 Haue I þryuandely° þonk þurȝ my craft
    serued°   *heartily* / *skill deserved*
  Ȝe iwysse quoþ þat oþer wyȝe here in wayth°
    fayrest   *hunting spoils*
  Þat I seȝ þis seuen ȝere in sesoun of wynter
  & al I gif yow Gawayn quoþ þe gome þenne
1384 For by acorde of couenaunt ȝe craue° hit as
    your awen   *may ask for*
  Þis is soth quoþ þe segge I say yow þat ilke
  Þat I haf worthyly wonnen þis woneȝ wythinne
  Iwysse with as god wylle hit worþeȝ to° ȝoureȝ   *becomes*
1388 He hasppeȝ° his fayre hals his armeȝ wythinne   *grasps*
  & kysses hym as comlyly as he couþe awyse°   *devise*

           1372. lorde: Go syre.
           1376. Gawayn: ᴍs Gaway.
           1386. Þat: ᴍs &.
           1386. wonnen: *Not in* ᴍs.
           1389. he: ᴍs ho.

1380. Savage thinks that in this line
Bercilak is alluding to his skill in
breaking the deer.

1386. *wonnen*: Like TG, Go, and D,
I have supplied this word to complete
the obvious sense of the line.

Tas° yow þere my cheuicaunce° I cheued°

    no more   *take | winnings | won*

I wowche hit saf fynly° þaʒ feler°

    hit were   *would grant it completely | more*

1392 Hit is god quoþ þe god mon grant mercy þerfore

Hit may be such hit is þe better &° ʒe me breue°

    wolde   *if | tell*

Where ʒe wan þis ilk wele bi wytte of ʒorseluen

Þat watʒ not forward° quoþ he frayst me no

    more   *an agreement*

1396 For ʒe haf tan þat yow tydeʒ trawe ʒe° non oþer   *be sure*

    ʒe mowe°   *can get*

Þay laʒed & made hem blyþe

Wyth loteʒ þat were to lowe°   *praise*

1400 To soper þay ʒede asswyþe°   *straightaway*

Wyth dayntes nwe innowe

XI

And syþen by þe chymne in chamber þay seten

Wyʒeʒ þe walle° wyn weʒed° to hem oft   *choice | carried*

1404 & efte in her bourdyng° þay bayþen° in þe

    morn   *jesting | agree*

To fylle þe same forwardeʒ þat þay byfore maden

Þat chaunce so bytydeʒ hor cheuysaunce to chaunge

What nweʒ so þay nome at naʒt quen þay metten

1408 Þay acorded of þe couenaunteʒ byfore þe court alle

1394. ʒorseluen: ᴍs hor seluen; TG, D, W yorseluen.
1396. For ʒe: Go Forʒe.
1406. Þat: TG, D, W Wat.

1393–94. TG take these two lines as demonstrating that Bercilak knows exactly where Gawain procured the kiss he has just given him.

1399. See 639*n*.
1406. *Þat*: TG and D *wat*. I believe the two halves of the line to be reversed.

Þe beuerage watʒ broʒt forth in bourde at þat tyme   (f.110a)
Þenne þay louelych leʒten° leue at þe last   *took*
Vche burne to his bedde busked bylyue°   *hurried quickly*
1412 Bi þat þe coke hade crowen & cakled bot þryse
Þe lorde watʒ lopen of his bedde þe leudeʒ vch one
So þat þe mete & þe masse watʒ metely° delyuered   *duly*
Þe douthe dressed° to þe wod er any day
       sprenged°   *company repaired | broke*
1416   to chace
      Heʒ° with hunte° & horneʒ   *loudly | huntsman*
      Þurʒ playneʒ þay passe in space°   *a short while*
      Vncoupled among þo þorneʒ
1420   Racheʒ þat ran on race

XII

Sone þay calle of° a quest in a ker° syde   *for | marsh*
Þe hunt rehayted þe houndeʒ þat hit fyrst mynged°   *noted*
Wylde wordeʒ° hym warp° wyth a wrast noyce   *cries | uttered*
1424 Þe howndeʒ þat hit herde hastid þider swyþe
& fellen as fast to þe fuyt° fourty at ones   *trail*
Þenne such a glauer ande glam° of gedered
       rachcheʒ   *clamor and noise*
Ros þat þe rochereʒ rungen aboute

1412. *crowen:* MS croweʒ.

1409. *in bourde:* "by way of enter-
tainment" (Wright).

1412ff. Both Turberville and *The
Master of Game* have sections on the
hunting of boar.

1419. *þo þorneʒ:* A usual resort of
the boar.

1422. *rehayted þe houndeʒ:* The
chief huntsman cheered on the hounds
by calling the names of the leaders
(see TG's note).

1423. *wrast:* "furious, angry." Go's
gloss of "noble, goodly" is surely mis-
taken. See Savage, who quotes the rele-
vant passage from Turberville.

1426. See 46n.

1427. *rochereʒ:* a "steep rocky
bank" (Emerson and Wright).

1428 Hunterez hem hardened°with horne & wyth muthe   *urged*
   Þen al in a semble sweyed°togeder   *pack rushed*
   Bitwene a flosche° in þat fryth° & a
      foo°cragge   *pool / wood / forbidding*
   In a knot bi a clyffe at þe kerre syde
1432 Þer as° þe rogh rocher vnrydely° watz fallen   *where / ruggedly*
   Þay ferden° to þe fyndyng & frekez hem after   *went*
   Þay vmbekesten° þe knarre° & þe knot boþe   *cast about / crag*
   Wyʒez whyl° þay wysten wel wythinne hem hit were   *until*
1436 Þe best þat þer breued° watz wyth°þe
      blodhoundez   *announced / by*
   Þenne þay beten on þe buskez & bede° hym
      vp ryse   *bushes and bade*
   & he vnsoundyly out soʒt seggez ouerþwert°   *through*
   On° þe sellokest° swyn swenged°
      out þere   *one of / most wonderful / rushed*
1440 Long sythen fro þe sounder° þat wiʒt for olde   *herd*
   For he watz breme bor alþer-grattest°   *greatest of all*

    1434. knot: Go kerre.
    1435. wythinne: MS wytinne.
    1440. fro: MS for.
    1440. wiʒt: Go synglere; D siʒed; W soght.
    1441. breme bor: MS lines 1441–45 *illegible*; Go bronde bor; W borelych
      and brode, bor.

1431, 1434. *knot*: Go is surely right in glossing *knot* in 1431 as "cluster," rather than as "hill," though this is not its meaning in 1434 where it clearly refers to a rocky, wooded hill.

1436. *þe blodhoundez*: These are larger dogs than the *braches* of the deer hunt, hence more suitable for hunting the strong, fierce, and aggressive boar. See TG's note.

1440. *wiʒt*: Go, following suggestions made by Brett (MLR 8:163) and TG, emended to *synglere*, for which

wiʒt might indeed be a scribal misreading. *Synglere* is the technical term for a lone, fully-grown wild boar. D emends *wiʒt* to *siʒed*, "gone," on the grounds that the second half of the line lacks alliteration and that the construction calls for a verb following *þat*. The line thus means "which had long since gone from the herd because of his age." The general *wiʒt*, "one," however, seems appropriate.

1441. *breme*: Only the "b" of the MS being intelligible, Morris reads

Ful grymme quen he gronyed þenne greued mony
For þre at þe fyrst þrast° he þryȝt° to þe erþe   *thrust / threw*
1444 & sparred° hym forth good sped
    boute spyt° more   *sprang / quickly without injury*
Þise oþer halowed hyghe ful hyȝe° & hay hay cryed   *loudly*
Haden horneȝ to mouþe heterly
    rechated°   *quickly sounded the recall* (f.110b)
Mony watȝ þe myry mouthe° of men & of houndeȝ   *voice*
1448 Þat buskkeȝ° after þis bor with bost° & wyth
    noyse   *hurry / outcry*
    To quelle
  Ful oft he bydeȝ° þe baye   *stands at*
  & maymeȝ þe mute inn melle°   *packs on all sides*
1452 He hurteȝ of þe houndeȝ & þay
  Ful ȝomerly° ȝaule & ȝelle   *piteously*

XIII

Schalkeȝ to schote at hym schowen to° þenne   *pushed forward*
Haled° to hym of her areweȝ hitten hym oft   *loosed*

1444. sparred: MS *illegible*; Go spede hym.
1447. myry: MS *illegible*; TG miyry.

---

beste and Go *bronde,* "brawny." Menner, however, follows Knott in reading *hor* for *bor* and "in seeing traces [which I cannot] of what looks like *hoge* beneath the blot" (MLN 41: 399). I am following TG and D since here the fierceness rather than the strength of the boar seems to be stressed and since *breme* is frequently used by the author.

1442. *grymme:* Like *ful, groyned, sparred,* and other words of this almost unintelligible passage, *grymme* has been reconstructed from the offset impression made by the writing on the blank page opposite.

1444. *sparred:* So Menner (MLN 41:398) and TG (1930 rev.) Go reads *spede.*

1445. *hyghe . . . hay:* Surely these are exclamations as TG suggest. See also 1158.

1451. *þe mute:* The pack of hounds.

1452. *of þe houndeȝ:* Partitive genitive: "some of the dogs."

1456 Bot þe poyntez payred° at þe pyth° þat
        pyȝt° in his scheldez°   *failed | toughness | struck | flanks*
  & þe barbez of his browe bite non wolde
  Þaȝ þe schauen schaft schyndered° in pecez   *splintered*
  Þe hede hypped° aȝayn weresoeuer hit hitte   *bounded*
1460 Bot quen þe dyntez hym dered of her dryȝe° strokez   *heavy*
  Þen braynwod° for bate° on burnez
        he rasez°   *frenzied | strife | rushes*
  Hurtez hem ful heterly° þer he forth hyȝez°   *fiercely | hastens*
  & mony arȝed° þerat & on lyte droȝen   *grew afraid*
1464 Bot þe lorde on a lyȝt° horce launces° hym after   *swift | gallops*
  As burne bolde vpon bent° his bugle he blowez   *battlefield*
  He rechated° & rode þurȝ ronez ful þyk   *sounded the recall*

1457. brawe: TG browen.
1466. rode: MS r de.

1457. *browe*: "The barbs would not penetrate his brow." TG emend to *browen*, "boar's flesh," but as Savage (MLN 52:36–38) points out, the midwinter coat of the boar is especially thick around the head.

1460. *dered*: Savage's "frightened" seems more appropriate to the action here than Go's "injured."

1463. *on lyte droȝen*: Emerson thought *lyte* a pronoun and *on* an adjective; thus, "few drew on." D, however, takes *lyte* to be a noun and *on* a preposition and glosses the phrase "back (in fear)," a reading which does not strain the syntax.

1465–67. See 118n.

1466. *ronez ful þyk*: Wright thought this was related to the dialect term "rone, roan" mentioned in *EDD*

as a "tangle of brushwood," though *NED* derives it from ON *runnr*, "thicket." Savage (MLN 64:1949) thought the term to refer here to the "whin" or common gorse of England.

1467. *schafted*: A puzzling term since the most obvious meaning, "set," manifestly does not fit the narrative: the hunt continues after this point. TG, following Emerson, suggest that since *schafted* derives from the noun *schaft*, "a beam of the sun," its meaning might well be "shone forth" and the verb here might refer not to the coming of daylight, but to the first clear sunlight of the day.

D, on the other hand, takes "set" as the proper meaning and thinks 1467 to be a summary statement, the details of which are supplied in subsequent

Suande° þis wylde swyn til þe sunne schafted   *pursuing*

1468 Þis day wyth þis ilk dede° þay dryuen

on° þis wyse°   *task / spend in / manner*

Whyle oure luflych lede lys in his bedde

Gawayn grayþely° at home in gereȝ ful ryche   *properly*

of hewe

1472   Þe lady noȝt forȝate

Com to hym to salue

Ful erly ho watȝ hym ate

His mode° forto remwe°   *mood / alter*

XIV

1476 Ho commes to þe cortyn & at þe knyȝt totes°   *peeps*

Sir Wawen her welcumed worþy on fyrst

& ho hym ȝeldeȝ aȝayn° ful ȝerne° of hir

wordeȝ   *replies / eagerly*

Setteȝ hir sofly by his syde & swyþely° ho laȝeȝ   *much*

1480 & wyth a luflych loke ho layde° hym þyse wordeȝ   *set forth to*

Sir ȝif ȝe be Wawen wonder me þynkkeȝ

Wyȝe þat is so wel wrast° alway to god   *disposed*

& conneȝ° not of compaynye° þe

costeȝ vndertake°   *can / society / manners understand*

1484 & if mon kennes° yow hom to knowe ȝe

kest° hom of your mynde   *teaches / put* (f.111a)

Þou hatȝ forȝeten ȝederly þat° ȝisterday

I taȝtte   *forgotten quickly what*

1473. Come to: W To com.
1479. sofly: D softly.
1485. taȝtte: W taght te.

---

lines, a technique employed by the poet
in 1176–77, where the coming of *derk*
nyȝt is described only to be followed

by the breaking of the deer in 1319ff.
Go's note, by the way, confuses the
statements of earlier critics.

Bi alder-truest° token of talk þat I cowþe   *truest of all*
What is þat quoþ þe wyghe iwysse I wot neuer
1488 If hit be sothe þat ȝe breue° þe blame is myn awen   *declare*
ȝet I kende° yow of kyssyng quoþ þe clere þenne   *taught*
Quereso countenaunce is couþe° quikly to clayme   *evident*
Þat bicumes vche a knyȝt þat cortaysy vses
1492 Do way° quoþ þat derf mon my dere þat speche   *cease from*
For þat durst I not do lest I denayed° were   *refused*
If I were werned° I were wrang iwysse ȝif I profered   *refused*
Ma fay quoþ þe mere wyf ȝe may not be werned
1496 ȝe are stif innoghe to constrayne wyth strenkþe
        ȝif yow lykeȝ
ȝif any were so vilanous þat yow devaye° wolde   *deny*
ȝe be God quoþ Gawayn good is your speche
Bot þrete is vnþryuande° in þede
        þer I lende°   *unlucky / live*
1500 & vche gift þat is geuen not with goud wylle
I am at your comaundement to kysse quen yow lykeȝ
ȝe may lach° quen yow lyst & leue° quen yow
        þynkkeȝ   *take / leave*
        in space°   *a short time*
1504 Þe lady louteȝ adoun
    & comlyly kysses his face
    Much speche þay þer expoun
    Of druryes greme & grace°   *love's grief and joy*

1493. denayed: Go, D, W deuayed.
1493. were (2nd): W wer.

1493. *denayed*: Go, D, and W by analogy with 1497 read *devayed*, "refused." *Deuaye* in 1497, however, is the proper reading.

1495. *mere wyf*: The context would point to a variant spelling of *mery*, as TG and D suggest, rather than to a derivative of OE *mære*, "beautiful" with connotations of nobility. Go's note speculates interestingly on the possibilities for *mere-wyf* from OE *mere-wif*, "mermaid."

XV

1508 I woled wyt at° yow wyȝe þat worþy þer
   sayde   *would learn from*
  &°yow wrathed°not þerwyth what were
   þe skylle°   *if | be angry | reason*
  Þat so ȝong & so ȝepe° as ȝe at þis tyme   *brisk*
  So cortayse so knyȝtyly as ȝe ar knowen oute°   *widely*
1512 & of alle cheualry to chose þe chef þyng alosed°   *praised*
  Is þe lel layk° of luf þe lettrure of armes   *faithful game*
  For to telle of þis teuelyng of þis trwe knyȝteȝ

1514. For: MS *illegible.*

1508ff. This long sentence is easiest read (as TG suggest) as a single period interrupted (1512–19) by a lengthy aside dealing with the general duties of knights in the service of love. Banks translates the enveloping period (1508–11, 1520ff.) (though his numbering is different) as:

 "I should like," said the lady,
  "from you, sir, to learn,
 If I roused not your anger
  by asking, the reason
 Why you, who are now
  so young and valiant,
 So known far and wide
  as knightly and courteous
 . . . ,
 Why you, thought the noblest
  knight of your time,
 Whose renown and honor
  are everwhere noted,
 Have so let me sit . . . ."

This manner of dealing with the structure of the passage seems more satisfying than either that of Go, who feels that a line has been omitted, or Savage, who thinks that the lady simply changes thought and syntax in mid-sentence.

1509ff. Dorothy Everett (*Essays on Middle English Literature*) remarks on this passage that "the lady of the castle thinks (or pretends to think) that Gawain's reluctance to make love to her is unexpected and even unnatural and, in spite of his disclaimers, he does know how to speak the language of love and is not, therefore, quite as ignorant of the art as he tries to make out."

1513. *lettrure*: "doctrine" (Go); "lore or science" (TG); "literature (about)" (Wright).

1514. *teuelyng*: Derived from ON *tefla*, "to play at draughts," the noun here means "struggle, contention." Emerson glosses "sport," TG "labour."

Hit is þe tytelet token & tyxt of her werkkeȝ

1516 How ledes for her lele° luf hor lyueȝ   *their true | have ventured*

   han auntered°

Endured for her drury dulful stoundeȝ°   *love doleful times*

& after wenged° with her walour &

   voyded her care°   *avenged themselves | sorrow*

& broȝt blysse into boure with bountees° hor awen   *virtues*

1520 & ȝe ar knyȝt comlokest kyd° of your

   elde°   *comeliest known | age*

Your worde & your worchip° walkeȝ ayquere   *honor* (f.111b)

& I haf seten by yourself here sere twyes°   *two separate times*

Ȝet herde I neuer of your hed° helde no wordeȝ   *from you*

1524 Þat euer longed to luf lasse ne more

& ȝe þat ar so cortays & coynt° of your hetes°   *polite | vows*

Oghe to a ȝonke þynk ȝern° to schewe   *young girl eagerly*

& teche sum tokeneȝ of trweluf craftes

1528 Why ar ȝe lewed° þat alle þe los weldeȝ°   *ignorant | renown have*

Oþer elles ȝe demen me to dille° your dalyaunce

   to herken   *silly*

    For schame

   I com hider sengel & sitte

1532   To lerne at° yow sum game   *from*

   Dos techeȝ° me of your wytte   *do teach*

   Whil my lorde is fro hame

1516. ledes: ᴍꜱ illegible.

1515. A very apt comparison of the service of knighthood to a book of romance, the "title inscribed and the text of their deeds" (Banks). One is forcibly reminded of Lady Capulet's extravagant comparison of Paris to a book (*Romeo and Juliet*: I, iii, 82ff.).

1515. *tytelet token*: As Go says, "almost 'table of contents', main theme. . . . The poet is thinking of the romances of chivalry, where the summary of the sections often starts with the word 'how'."

XVI

In goud fayþe quoþ Gawayn God yow forȝelde°   *reward*
1536 Gret is þe gode gle & gomen to me huge
    Þat so worþy as ȝe wolde wynne° hidere   *come*
    & pyne° yow with so pouer a mon as play
        wyth your knyȝt   *trouble*
    With anyskynneȝ countenaunce° hit
        keuereȝ° me ese   *any kind of favor | brings*
1540 Bot to take þe toruayle° to myself to trwluf expoun   *travail*
    & towche þe temeȝ° of tyxt° & taleȝ of armeȝ   *themes | that text*
    To yow þat I wot wel weldeȝ° more slyȝt°   *has | skill*
    Of þat art bi þe half or° a hundreth of seche°   *than | such*
1544 As I am oþer euer schal in erde þer I leue°   *while I live*
    Hit were a fole felefolde° my fre°
        by my trawþe   *foolishness manifold | noble one*
    I wolde yowre wylnyng worche° at my myȝt°   *will do | power*
    As I am hyȝly bihalden & euermore wylle
1548 Be seruaunt to yourseluen so saue me dryȝtyn
    Þus hym frayned° þat fre & fondet° hym ofte   *asked | tempted*
    For to haf wonnen hym to woȝe whatso scho°
        þoȝt elleȝ   *whatsoever she*
    Bot he defended hym so fayr° þat no
        faut semed°   *graciously | fault appeared*
1552 Ne non euel on nawþer halue° nawþer þay wysten   *side*
        bot blysse

1549–51. Dorothy Everett (*Essays on Middle English Literature*) states that Gawain here and in 1774–75 "regards the love which the lady offers and demands as a sin, a temptation to be guarded against. At no point in the poem is there any trace of the idea, stressed, for example, in Chaucer's *Troilus and Criseyde* and common among apologists for courtly love, that love is an ennobling force, the source of knightly virtues."

1550. *woȝe*: D derives from OE *wōgian*, "to woo."

1550. *whatso scho þoȝt elleȝ*: Go thought that this line pointed to "some hidden motive" in the lady's behavior.

Þay laȝed & layked° longe   *played*
At þe last scho con hym kysse
1556 Hir leue fayre con scho fonge
& went hir waye iwysse

XVII

Then ruþes hym þe renk & ryses to þe masse
& siþen° hor diner watȝ dyȝt
& derely° serued   *later / prepared and nobly* (f.112a)
1560 Þe lede with þe ladyeȝ layked° alle day   *played*
Bot þe lorde ouer þe londeȝ launced° ful ofte   *spurred*
Sweȝ° his vncely° swyn þat swyngeȝ°
bi þe bonkkeȝ   *follows / ill-fated / rushes*
& bote þe best of his bracheȝ þe bakkeȝ in sunder
1564 Þer he bode in his bay° tel bawemen
hit breken°   *stood at bay / overcame*
& madee hym mawgref his hed° for
to mwe vtter°   *despite himself / move out*
So felle floneȝ° þer flete° when þe folk
gedered   *many arrows / sped*
Bot ȝet þe styffest to start bi stoundeȝ°
he made   *flinch at times*
1568 Til at þe last he watȝ so mat° he myȝt no more
renne   *exhausted*
Bot in þe hast þat he myȝt he to a hole wynneȝ°   *goes*
Of a rasse bi a rokk þer renneȝ þe boerne°   *stream*
He gete þe bonk at his bak bigyneȝ to scrape

1558. *ruþes*: There is no clear deri-
vation for this word, though TG sug-
gest ON *hryðja*, "shake," and Go a
dialect variant of "rouse."
   1570. *rasse*: "terrace" (Brett, MLR
24:457). D's "ledge" seems more suit-

able, however.
   1571. *bigyneȝ to scrape*: Go, "to paw
the ground," though Savage's case
(*TLS*, Sept. 26, 1936; and MLN 49:
342–50) that the phrase means "sharp-
ens his nether tusks" seems firmly

1572 Þe froþe femed° at his mouth vnfayre°   *foamed / horribly*
    bi þe wykeȝ
   Whetteȝ his whyte tuscheȝ with hym þen irked°   *were weary*
   Alle þe burneȝ so bolde þat hym by stoden
   To nye° hym onferum° bot neȝe°
     hym non durst   *of annoying / from afar / to approach*
1576   for woþe°   *danger*
    He hade hurt so mony byforne
    Þat al þuȝt þenne ful loþe°   *dangerous*
    Be more° wyth his tuscheȝ torne   *to be any more*
1580   Þat breme watȝ & braynwod° bothe   *frenzied*

XVIII

   Til þe knyȝt com hymself kachande° his blonk   *spurring*
   Syȝ hym byde at þe bay his burneȝ bysyde
   He lyȝtes luflych adoun leueȝ his corsour
1584 Braydeȝ° out a bryȝt bront° & bigly forth
    strydeȝ   *draws / sword*
   Foundeȝ° fast þurȝ þe forth° þer
    þe felle° bydeȝ   *comes / stream / fierce one*
   Þe wylde watȝ war of þe wyȝe with weppen in honde
   Hef° hyȝly þe here° so hetterly°
    he fnast°   *rose / bristles / fiercely / snorted*
1588 Þat fele ferde° for þe freke lest felle°
    hym þe worre°   *many feared / befall / worse*

1580. &: *Not in* MS.
1583. luflych: MS luslych.
1588. freke: MS frekeȝ.

---

documented from *The Master of Game.* *Whetteȝ his whyte tuscheȝ* in 1573 is an amplification of this action.

1582. *syȝ*: Morton Bloomfield has suggested that this may well be the imperative "see." The line would thus mean "See him waiting at the bay beside his men." This interpretation avoids the mixing of pronoun references in 1581–85.

Þe swyn setteʒ hym out on° þe segge
    euen°   *rushes out at / straight*
Þat þe burne & þe bor were boþe vpon hepeʒ°   *in heaps*
In þe wyʒt-est° of þe water þe worre° hade
    þat oþer   *strongest / worst of it*
1592 For þe mon merkkeʒ° hym wel as þay mette fyrst   *aims at*
Set sadly° þe scharp° in þe slot°
    euen   *firmly / sharp blade / hollow of the breast*
Hit hym vp to þe hult þat þe hert schyndered
& he ʒarrande° hym ʒelde° & ʒedoun þe water *snarling / yielded*
1596   ful tyt°   *quickly*
    A hundreth houndeʒ hym hent°   *caught* (f.112b)
    Þat bremely con hym bite
    Burneʒ him broʒt to bent°   *the bank*
1600   & doggeʒ to dethe endite°   *put to death*

XIX

    There watʒ blawyng of prys in mony breme horne
    Heʒe halowing on hiʒe with haþeleʒ þat myʒt
    Brachetes bayed þat best as bidden þe maystereʒ

1591. wyʒt-est: *Hyphen in* MS.
1595. ʒedoun: TG ʒed over.

1593. The usual manner of killing a boar was with a spear. Bercilak's action in using a sword is proof of unusual bravery, a "fairer thing and more noble" than employing a spear (*The Master of Game*).

1595. *ʒedoun:* A contraction, as Morris suggests, of *ʒede doun*, "went down." TG, following Napier, emend to *ʒed over*. But as D says "this gives the wrong sense because 1599 shows that the boar remained in the water."

1603. Savage notes that *The Master of Game* claims that three "bays" were blown "to accustom the hounds to respond to the voice of the huntsman and the notes of the horn . . . ." These three bays are reflected in 1450, 1603, and 1362.

1572 Þe froþe femed° at his mouth vnfayre°
        bi þe wykeʒ   *foamed / horribly*
Whetteʒ his whyte tuscheʒ with hym þen irked°   *were weary*
Alle þe burneʒ so bolde þat hym by stoden
To nye° hym onferum° bot neʒe°
        hym non durst   *of annoying / from afar / to approach*
1576   for woþe°   *danger*
      He hade hurt so mony byforne
      Þat al þuʒt þenne ful loþe°   *dangerous*
      Be more°wyth his tuscheʒ torne   *to be any more*
1580   Þat breme watʒ & braynwod° bothe   *frenzied*

XVIII

Til þe knyʒt com hymself kachande° his blonk   *spurring*
Syʒ hym byde at þe bay his burneʒ bysyde
He lyʒtes luflych adoun leueʒ his corsour
1584 Braydeʒ° out a bryʒt bront° & bigly forth
        strydeʒ   *draws / sword*
Foundeʒ° fast þurʒ þe forth° þer
        þe felle° bydeʒ   *comes / stream /fierce one*
Þe wylde watʒ war of þe wyʒe with weppen in honde
Hef° hyʒly þe here° so hetterly°
        he fnast°   *rose / bristles / fiercely / snorted*
1588 Þat fele ferde° for þe freke lest felle°
        hym þe worre°   *many feared / befall / worse*

1580. &: *Not in* MS.
1583. luflych: MS luslych.
1588. freke: MS frekeʒ.

---

documented from *The Master of Game.*
Whetteʒ his whyte tuscheʒ in 1573
is an amplification of this action.

    1582. *syʒ*: Morton Bloomfield has
suggested that this may well be the imperative "see." The line would thus
mean "See him waiting at the bay beside his men." This interpretation
avoids the mixing of pronoun references in 1581–85.

Þe swyn setteʒ hym out on° þe segge
  euen°   *rushes out at / straight*
Þat þe burne & þe bor were boþe vpon hepeʒ°   *in heaps*
In þe wyʒt-est° of þe water þe worre° hade
  þat oþer   *strongest / worst of it*
1592 For þe mon merkkeʒ° hym wel as þay mette fyrst *aims at*
Set sadly° þe scharp° in þe slot°
  euen   *firmly / sharp blade / hollow of the breast*
Hit hym vp to þe hult þat þe hert schyndered
& he ʒarrande° hym ʒelde° & ʒedoun þe water *snarling / yielded*
1596   ful tyt°   *quickly*
A hundreth houndeʒ hym hent°   *caught* (f.112b)
Þat bremely con hym bite
Burneʒ him broʒt to bent°   *the bank*
1600 & doggeʒ to dethe endite°   *put to death*

XIX

There watʒ blawyng of prys in mony breme horne
Heʒe halowing on hiʒe with haþeleʒ þat myʒt
Brachetes bayed þat best as bidden þe maystereʒ

1591. wyʒt-est: *Hyphen in* MS.
1595. ʒedoun: TG ʒed *over.*

1593. The usual manner of killing a boar was with a spear. Bercilak's action in using a sword is proof of unusual bravery, a "fairer thing and more noble" than employing a spear (*The Master of Game*).

1595. ʒedoun: A contraction, as Morris suggests, of ʒede doun, "went down." TG, following Napier, emend to ʒed over. But as D says "this gives the wrong sense because 1599 shows that the boar remained in the water."

1603. Savage notes that *The Master of Game* claims that three "bays" were blown "to accustom the hounds to respond to the voice of the huntsman and the notes of the horn . . . ." These three bays are reflected in 1450, 1603, and 1362.

1604 Of þat chargeaunt° chace þat were chef huntes   *difficult*
    Þenne a wyȝe þat watȝ wys vpon° wodcrafteȝ   *in*
    To vnlace° þis bor lufly bigynneȝ   *cut up*
    Fyrst he hewes of his hed & on hiȝe setteȝ
1608 & syþen rendeȝ him al roghe bi þe rygge° after   *backbone*
    Braydeȝ° out þe boweles brenneȝ° hom
        on glede°   *Pulls / broils / coals*
    With bred blent° þerwith his braches rewardeȝ   *bread mixed*
    Syþen he britneȝ° out þe brawen° in bryȝt
        brode cheldeȝ°   *cuts / flesh / slabs*
1612 & hatȝ out þe hastletteȝ as hiȝtly° bisemeȝ   *fitly*
    & ȝet hem halcheȝ° al hole þe halueȝ togeder   *fastens*
    & syþen on a stif stange° stoutly hem henges   *pole*
    Now with þis ilk swyn þay swengen° to home   *hurry*
1616 Þe bores hed watȝ borne bifore þe burnes seluen
    Þat him forferde° in þe forþe° þurȝ forse of his
        honde   *slew / stream*
        so stronge
      Til he seȝ Sir Gawayne
1620   In halle hym þoȝt ful longe
      He calde & he com gayn°   *came promptly*
      His feeȝ þer for to fonge

1611. cheldeȝ: Go scheldeȝ.

1604. *chef huntes*: The lord and the master of game (Savage, PMLA 56: 169–76).

1610. *rewardeȝ*: The technical term for the bowels boiled or broiled with bread and given to the dogs on a "quyrrye" (see 1324*n*).

1612. *hastletteȝ*: The specialized meaning in hunting is the "edible entrails of the pig," not, as the etymology (OF *hastelet*) might suggest, "roast meat."

1613. *hem*: Although Go thinks this may be a scribal error for "he," it in all probability refers to *cheldeȝ* in 1611.

XX

Þe lorde ful lowde with lote° laȝed myry   *word*
1624 When he seȝe Sir Gawayn with solace° he spekeȝ   *delight*
Þe goude ladyeȝ were geten° & gedered þe meyny   *brought*
He scheweȝ hem þe scheldeȝ &
     schapes° hem þe tale°   *slabs of flesh and gives / tally*
Of þe largesse° & þe lenþe þe liþerneȝ alse°   *size / ferocity also*
1628 Of þe were° of þe wylde swyn in wod þer he fled   *fight*
Þat oþer knyȝt ful comly comended his dedeȝ
& praysed hit as gret prys þat he proued hade
For suche a brawne° of a best þe bolde burne sayde   *flesh*
1632 Ne such sydes of a swyn segh he neuer are°   *before*
Þenne hondeled þay þe hoge hed þe hende mon hit praysed
& let lodly þerat þe lorde for to here°   *praise* (f.113a)
Now Gawayn quoþ þe god mon þis gomen is your awen
1636 Bi fyn forwarde & faste faythely°
     ȝe knowe   *final agreement and firm truly*
Hit is sothe quoþ þe segge & as siker° trwe   *surely*
Alle my get° I schal yow gif agayn bi my trawþe   *booty*

1623. laȝed: ms TG & laȝed; D, W and laȝter.
1624. Gawayn: ms G.

1623. See 639*n*.
1623. *lote laȝed*: ms *lote & laȝed*. As most editors have suggested, a verb is needed after "lorde" if the ms reading is to stand, though any insertion would harm the meter. Morris suggests *lalede*, Emerson *watȝ*, and D converts *laȝed* to the noun *laȝter*. The form adopted here (the omission of *&*) is that suggested by Go.
1634. *let lodly þerat*: "expressed horror thereat" (TG), a comment which demonstrates Gawain's amazement at the size of the boar and hence at Bercilak's skill and bravery. He is not making a "show of abhorrence" (Go).
1637. *trwe*: Here an adverb although Wright suggests that it might be taken as a noun, which along with *siker*, taken as an adjective, would form a phrase meaning "according to sure agreement."

He hent° þe haþel aboute þe halse° & hendely
　　hym kysses　　　　　　　　　　　　　　　　　*took / neck*

1640 & eftersones° of þe same he serued hym þere　　*again*

　　Now ar we euen quoþ þe haþel in þis euentide

　　Of alle þe couenauntes þat we knyt syþen I com hider
　　　　bi lawe

1644　　Þe lorde sayde bi Saynt Gile

　　　　ʒe ar þe best þat I knowe

　　　　ʒe ben°ryche in a whyle　　　　　　　　　　*will be*

　　　　Such chaffer &° ʒe drowe　　　　　　　　　　*trade if*

XXI

1648 Þenne þay teldet° tableʒ trestes alofte　　　　*erected*

　　Kesten° cloþeʒ vpon clere lyʒt þenne　　　　　　*put*

　　Wakned bi woʒeʒ waxen torches

1639. hent: *Not in* MS.
1645. knowe: Go, W knawe.
1647. drowe: Go, W drawe.

1639. *hent*: not in MS but suggested by Madden and followed by TG, Go, and D.

1644. *Saynt Gile*: St. Giles, a seventh-century hermit, lived in secrecy near Nîmes with a lone hind. The hind once led the king to Saint Giles' retreat, whereupon the king persuaded the hermit to build a Benedictine monastery. Saint Giles is nearly always represented by a hind and he is, as Go says, an eminently suitable patron for Bercilak.

1645. *knowe*: Go emends this to *knawe* and *drowe* in 1647 to *drawe*. D suggests that the scribe altered *drawe* to *drowe* (best taken as present) in order to rhyme with *knowe*, which is an alternate form of *knawe*.

1647. *drowe*: Magoun derives this directly from *drive* and here translates "to drive a bargain."

1648. *trestes alofte*: Madden and Morris insert *on* before *trestes*. Emerson, TG, and D, however, take *aloft* as a preposition and read the phrase either "above" (Emerson) or "upon" (TG and D) the trestles. Go, however, takes the words to mean "trestles being erected," *alofte* here functioning adverbially.

1650. *waxen*: Bloomfield suggests that this could be a verb with *torches* as subject and *lyʒt* (1649) as object.

Seggeȝ sette & serued in sale al aboute
1652 Much glam & gle glent° vp þerinne   *sprang*
Aboute þe fyre vpon flet° & on fele wyse°   *in the hall / ways*
At þe soper & after mony aþel° songeȝ   *splendid*
As coundutes of Krystmasse & caroleȝ newe
1656 With alle þe manerly merþe þat mon may of telle
& euer oure luflych knyȝt þe lady bisyde
Such semblaunt° to þat segge semly ho made   *manner*
Wyth stille stollen° countenaunce þat stalworth
    to plese   *secret stealthy*
1660 Þat al forwondered° watȝ þe wyȝe & wroth
    with hymseluen   *astonished*
Bot he nolde° not for his nurture nurne hir aȝayneȝ   *would*
Bot dalt with hir al in daynte° howseeuer þe dede
    turned   *courtesy*
        towrast
1664 Quen þay hade played in halle
As longe as hor wylle hom last
To chambre he con hym calle
& to þe chemne þay past

Wakned could be either a finite verb or a participle. Thus, either "the waxen torches then kindled bright lights (reflections) along the walls" or "the waxen torches, kindled along the walls, shed bright lights." I generally prefer the latter since the candle holders were probably mounted in the walls.

1654–46. See note to 118.

1655. *coundutes of Krystmasse*: The motet-like *conduit* originally consisted of "a tenor part with two added descants" (Go) and was sung as the priest approached the altar during the Christmas liturgy. Later the *coundutes* became simply Christmas songs and are

perhaps the ancestors of the modern Christmas carol.

1661. *nurne*: This word appears five times in *GGK*, three times in *Purity*, three times, interestingly enough, in *St. Erkenwald*, and nowhere else in ME. Though of uncertain meaning it probably here means "repel" (D) rather than "proffer" (Go).

1663. *towrast*: Go's gloss as "virtue" hardly seems to fit the sense. TG, following Thomas (ES 47:311), see it as an adjective, "twisted aside" or "amiss," and D calls it a past participle. Both Wright and Savage gloss it as "against the grain."

XXII

1668 Ande þer þay dronken & dalten & demed eft nwe°   *once again*
   To norne° on þe same note° on Nwe ȝereȝ
      euen   *propose / fashion*
   Bot þe knyȝt craued leue to kayre° on þe morn   *go*
   For hit watȝ neȝ at° þe terme þat he to schulde   *near*
1672 Þe lorde hym letted° of þat to lenge hym
      resteyed   *deterred* (f.113b)
   & sayde as I am trwe segge I siker my trawþe
   Þou schal cheue° to þe grene chapel þy charres°
      to make   *come / affairs*
   Leude on Nw ȝereȝ lyȝt° longe bifore pryme   *dawn*
1676 Forþy þow lye in þy loft° & lach þyn ese   *room*
   & I schal hunt in þis holt & halde° þe
      towcheȝ°   *wood and keep / terms*
   Chaunge wyth þe cheuisaunce bi þat I charre°hider   *return*
   For I haf fraysted° þe twys & faythful I fynde þe   *tried*
1680 Now þrid tyme þrowe best þenk on þe morne
   Make we mery quyl we may & mynne° vpon joye   *think*
   For þe lur° may mon lach whenso° mon
      lykeȝ   *sorrow / get whenever*
   Þis watȝ grayþely graunted & Gawayn is lenged
1684 Bliþe broȝt watȝ hym drynk & þay to bedde ȝeden
      with liȝt

1668. *dalten*: Go, "exchanged" words; TG, "contended (in sport)." Go sees some affinity here with OF *dalier*, "to chat."

1671. *to schulde*: *to* is almost certainly here a form of the verb *take*, "to go," as in *tone*, 2159, and *toȝ*, *Pearl* 513.

1672. *resteyed*: Generally used to mean "paused" or "checked" (1153 and *Pearl* 437, 716, 1168), the context

here suggests "restrained."

1673. *I siker my trawþe*: "I give you my word."

1680. *þrid time þrowe best*: "may the third time turn out best." Thomas (ES 47:313) points out a parallel in *Seven Sages*, "Men sais þe thrid time thrawes best." Go thinks the form of *þrowe* to be imperative, but D regards it as a subjunctive, and I have so translated it. It is, of course, a proverb.

Sir Gawayn lis & slepes
Ful stille & softe al niȝt
1688 Þe lorde þat his crafteȝ kepes
Ful erly he watȝ diȝt°   *ready*

XXIII

After messe a morsel he & his men token
Miry watȝ þe mornyng his mounture he askes
1692 Alle þe haþeles þat on horse schulde helden° hym after   *go*
Were boun busked° on hor blonkkeȝ
bifore þe halle ȝateȝ   *already dressed*
Ferly fayre watȝ þe folde for þe forst clenged
In rede rudede° vpon rak° rises þe
sunne   *redness fiery / cloud drift*
1696 & ful clere costeȝ° þe clowdes of þe
welkyn   *brightly passes above*
Hunteres vnhardeled°bi a holt syde   *unleashed hounds*
Rocheres roungen bi rys° for rurde°
of her hornes   *rocks rang in woods / noise*
Summe fel in° þe fute° þer þe fox bade°   *hit on / track / waited*
1700 Trayleȝ ofte a trayteres bi traunt° of her wyles   *cunning practice*

1686. Gawayn: MS G.
1690. morsel: MS. nnorsel.
1693. bifore: MS. bi forere.
1696. costeȝ: Go, W casteȝ.
1700. trayteres: TG, Go, D, W traueres.

1700. *trayteres*: This, the MS reading, was emended to *trayveres* by Morris and to *traueres*, "cross-wise" by TG, Go, and D, though TG suggest that *trayteres* may derive from OF *al tretour*, "in a detour." The meaning of the line is quite clear, however, if *trayteres* is allowed to remain as "trai-toress (that is a vixen or some other game)" (Emerson): "Some dogs . . . trail oft a traitoress using her tricks" (Banks).

1700. *Trayleȝ*: Savage (MÆ 4:199–202) suggests "draw, to search a trail" from OF *traillier*.

A kenet° kryes þerof þe hunt° on hym
      calles   *small hound / huntsman*
His felaʒes fallen hym to þat fnasted° ful þike   *panted*
Runnen forth in a rabel in his ryʒt fare°   *track*
1704 & he fyskeʒ hem byfore þay founden hym sone
    & quen þay seghe hym with syʒt þay sued hym fast
    Wreʒande° hym ful weterly° with a wroth
      noyse   *reviling / clearly*
    & he trantes & tornayeeʒ° þurʒ mony tene
      greue   *dodges and doubles*
1708 Hauilouneʒ & herkeneʒ° bi heggeʒ
      ful ofte   *doubles back and listens*
    At þe last bi a littel dich he lepeʒ ouer a spenne° *hedge (f.114a)*
    Steleʒ out ful stilly bi a strothe rande
    Went haf wylt° of þe wode with wyleʒ fro
      þe houndes   *thought to have escaped*
1712 Þenne watʒ he went° er he wyst to a
      wale tryster°   *gone / choice hunting station*
    Þer þre þro° at a þrich
      þrat° hym at ones   *fierce ones / rush attached*

1706. hym: MS. *illegible.*
1706. weterly: MS *illegible.*
1712. to: MS to to.

1704. *he fyskeʒ hem byfore*: "he [the kenet] scampering before them [the pack]" (Banks). See Savage (MLN 44:249) for a review of the various theories of the referents of *he* and *hem*. *He* may be either the fox or the kenet mentioned in 1701, though the kenet seems the more logical candidate. There is no reason in either case, however, not to derive *fyskeʒ* from OE *fȳsan*, "to drive." Certainly *hym* in the second part of the line refers to the fox.

1710. *bi a strothe rande*: Clearly the context supports TG's "patch of tall herbage or low brushwood," rather than Go's "valley." Banks' "skirting a thicket" is an excellent translation.

al graye
He blenched° aʒayn bilyue   *drew back*
1716 & stifly start onstray°   *aside*
With alle þe wo on lyue°   *earth*
To þe wod he went away

XXIV

Thenne watʒ hit list° vpon lif to lyþen° þe houndeʒ   *joy / hear*
1720 When alle þe mute° hade hym met menged togeder   *pack*
Suche a sorʒe at þat syʒt þay sette on his hede
As alle þe clamberande clyffes hade clatered on hepes
Here he watʒ halawed when haþeleʒ hym metten
1724 Loude he watʒ ʒayned° with ʒarande° speche   *met / snarling*
Þer he watʒ þreted°& ofte þef called   *threatened*
& ay þe titleres at his tayl þat tary he ne myʒt
Ofte he watʒ runnen at when he out rayked°   *went for the open*
1728 & ofte reled° in aʒayn so Reniarde watʒ wyle   *turned*
& ʒe° he lad hem bi lagmon þe lorde & his meyny   *indeed*
On þis maner bi þe mountes quyle myd-ouer-vnder

1719. list vpon lif: ᴍꜱ, TG lif vpon list.
1724. Loude: Go ʒonde.

1719. *list vpon lif*: Go and D, fol-
lowing Morris, emended the ᴍꜱ's *lif
vpon list* on the grounds that the allit-
erating words had simply become re-
versed. Certainly the sense of the
phrase demands some such change.
See Go's note.

1726. *titlers*: Neither "ticklers"
(*NED*) nor "entitlers" (Grattan),
these are the hounds stationed stra-
tegically at relays which are released
as the fox passes. See D's note.

1728. *reled*: Savage sees this as the
past participle of *NED*'s *reel*, v¹ or v².

1729. *lad hem bi lagmon*: Obscure.
Menner (PQ 10:166–68) suggests "led
them astray" and quotes a line from
Audelay: *hit ledys ʒoue be lagmon be
lyus*, "fleshly lust deceives you." Go
suggests that the *English Dialect Dic-
tionary's* definition of a "lagman" as
the "last of a gang of reapers in Shrop-
shire" may lead to some such transla-
tion as "leads you so that you come out
last."

1730. *myd-over-vnder*: "the middle
of the afternoon" (D).

Whyle þe hende knyȝt at home holsumly slepeȝ
1732 Withinne þe comly cortynes on þe colde morne
Bot þe lady for luf let° not to slepe　　　　　*allowed him*
Ne þe purpose to payre°þat pyȝt° in hir hert　　*fail / was set*
Bot ros hir vp radly rayked hir þeder
1736 In a mery mantyle mete° to þe erþe　　　　　*extending*
Þat watȝ furred ful fyne with felleȝ° wel pured°　*pelts / trimmed*
No hwe goud on hir hede bot þe haȝer stones
Trased aboute hir tressour be twenty in clusteres
1740 Hir þryuen°face & hir þrote þrowen° al naked　　*fair / exposed*
Hir brest bare bifore & bihinde eke
Ho comeȝ withinne þe chambre dore & closes hit hir after
Wayueȝ° vp a wyndow & on þe wyȝe calleȝ　　　*throws*
1744 & radly þus rehayted° hym with hir riche wordeȝ　*rallied*

1735. Bot: W But.
1738. hwe: MS, TG, D hweȝ; W howes.

1733. *for luf*: Go suggests that the use of *luf* here, as in 1802, does not signify that the lady is in the least in love with Gawain, but that she is simply looking forward to "pleasure in his company." Certainly there is no suggestion made anywhere in the poem that the lady is "in love" with Gawain. The only motive even hinted at in the poem for her actions is that she is testing Gawain by order of Morgan le Fay (see 2456ff.).

1738. *hwe*: The MS *hweȝ* was emended by Go to *hwe*, the "howe" or head covering of a married woman (OE *hūfe*), a reading which certainly improves the line. The two lines would thus read "no proper cap she wore, but pearls in myriad clusters ornamented her hairband," a hair style certainly chosen to complement her extremely provocative attire (see 1740–41).

1738–39. *þe haȝer stones/ Trased aboute hir tressour*: The *tressour* or "hairfret" was a "remarkable feature of the female coiffure" (Madden) in the poet's time and can be clearly seen in the MS illustration of the lady's visit to Gawain. Here it is ornamented (*trased*) with *haȝer stones*, "precious stones," possibly pearls (see Go's note and 954) in clusters of twenty, a number signifying plenteousness in the Shetland dialect.

1743. *wyndow*: Doubtless that formed by the curtains of Gawain's bed (see Savage and Wright).

with chere
A mon how may þou slepe
Þis morning is so clere (f.114b)
1748 He watȝ in drowping depe
Bot þenne he con hir here

XXV

In dreȝ° droupyng of dreme draueled° þat
noble   *heavy / muttered*
As mon þat watȝ in mornyng of mony þro þoȝtes
1752 How þat destine schulde þat day dele hym his wyrde
At þe grene chapel when he þe gome metes
& bihoues his buffet abide withoute debate more
Bot quen þat comly com he keuered° his wyttes   *recovered*
1756 Swenges° out of þe sweuenes & swareȝ°
with hast   *hastens / dreams and answers*
Þe lady luflych com laȝande swete
Felle°ouer his fayre face & fetly°hym kyssed   *bent / gracefully*
He welcumeȝ hir worþily with a wale chere
1760 He seȝ hir so glorious & gayly atyred
So fautles of hir fetures & of so fyne hewes
Wiȝt wallande joye warmed his hert
With smoþe smylyng & smolt° þay smeten°
into merþe   *gentle / fell*

1752. dele hym: *Not in* MS.
1752. his: W hys.
1755. comly com: MS, Go comly.

1746. Though it seems gratuitous to mention it, the contrast between the witty, topless lady and the embarrassed, defenceless Gawain is one of the poet's great accomplishments.

1748. *drowping*: Wright, "torpor."
1752. *dele hym*: TG added this by analogy with 2418 and was followed by Go. *Þat* day is the antecedent of *when* in 1753.

1764 Þat al watȝ blis & bonchef° þat breke him bitwene   *happiness*
    & wynne°   *joy*
    Þay lanced wordes gode
    Much wele þen watȝ þerinne
1768 Gret perile bitwene hem stod
    Nif Mare of hir knyȝt mynne

XXVI

    For þat prynces of pris depresed°
        hym so þikke°   *importuned / hard*
    Nurned° hym so neȝe þe þred° þat nede hym
        bihoued   *urged / limit*
1772 Oþer lach þer hir luf oþer lodly° refuse   *or offensively*
    He cared° for his cortaysye lest craþayn° he
        were   *feared / villain*
    & more for his meschef ȝif he schulde make synne
    & be traytor to þat tolke þat þat telde aȝt°   *house owned*
1776 God schylde° quoþ þe schalk þat schal not befalle   *forbid*
    With luf-laȝyng° a lyt he layd hym bysyde   *loving laugh*
    Alle þe specheȝ of specialte° þat sprange of her
        mouthe   *partiality*
    Quoþ þat burde to þe burne blame ȝe disserue
1780 Ȝif ȝe luf not þat lyf° þat ȝe lye nexte   *person*
    Bifore alle þe wyȝeȝ in þe worlde wounded in hert

1766. lanced: Go, W lauced.
1769. Mare: Go Marye.
1769. knyȝt: Go knyȝt con.
1770. prynces: MS prynce; TG pryncece.

1768. *stod*: D suggests taking *stod* as indicative and *mynne* as subjunctive: "There *was* in fact great danger, if Mary should not take care of her knight."

1770. *prynces*: Originally suggested by Emerson and followed by Go, TG, and D (*pryncece*), this emendation is "demanded by the sense of the lines" (Go).

Bot if ȝe haf a lemman° a leuer° þat yow
      lykeȝ better   *sweetheart | dearer one*
& folden fayth to þat fre festned so harde
1784 Þat yow lausen° ne lyst° & þat I leue°
      nouþe   *to break | wish | believe* (f.115a)
And þat ȝe telle me þat now trwly I pray yow
For alle þe lufeȝ vpon lyue layne° not þe soþe   *hide*
      for gile°   *guile*
1788   Þe knyȝt sayde be Sayn Jon
     & smeþely° con he smyle   *gently*
     In fayth I welde riȝt non°   *have none at all*
     Ne non wil welde þe quile°   *at present*

XXVII

1792 Þat is a worde quoþ þat wyȝt þat worst is of alle
     Bot I am swared forsoþe° þat sore°
       me þinkkeȝ   *answered truly | painful*
     Kysse me now comly & I schal cach heþen°   *go hence*
     I may bot mourne vpon molde as may þat much louyes
1796 Skyande° ho sweȝe° doun & semly hym
       kyssed   *sighing | stooped*
     & siþen ho seueres° hym fro & says as ho stondes   *parts*
     Now dere at þis departyng do me þis ese
     Gif me sumquat of þy gifte þi gloue if hit were
1800 Þat I may mynne° on þe mon my mournyng to lassen   *think*

1799. if: MS of.

1786. *For alle þe lufeȝ vpon lyue*:
TG note that the lady is here referring
to "the practise of swearing by God's
love, Christ's love, etc., and includes all
these oaths in one . . . ."

1795. *may*: Savage (MLN 55:604)
suggests that this is probably "woman"
from OE *mæg*, "kinswoman" rather
than "maiden" from ON *mær*.

Now iwysse quoþ þat wyӡe I wolde I hade here
Þe leuest° þing for þy luf þat I in londe welde · · · · · · *dearest*
For ӡe haf deserued forsoþe sellyly° ofte · · · · · · · · *very*
1804 More rewarde bi resoun° þen I reche° myӡt · · · · · *rights / offer*
Bot to dele°yow for drurye° þat dawed°
bot neked° · · · · · *give / a token for love / would avail / little*
Hit is not your honour to haf at þis tyme
A gloue for a garysoun° of Gawayneӡ gifteӡ · · · · · · · *warrant*
1808 & I am here on erande in erdeӡ vncouþe
& haue no men wyth no maleӡ° with
menskful þingeӡ · · · · · · · · *bags*
Þat mislykeӡ°me lade for luf at þis tyme · · · · · · *displeases*
Iche tolke mon°do as he is tan° tas
to° non ille · · · · · *each man must / placed / take it as*
1812 ne pine° · · · · · *nor grief*
Nay hende of hyӡe honours
Quoþ þat lufsum vnder lyne° · · · · · *lovely linen-clad lady*
Þaӡ I nade oӡt of youreӡ
1816 ӡet schulde ӡe haue of myne

XXVIII

Ho raӡt°hym a riche rynk° of red golde werkeӡ · · · · *offered / ring*
Wyth a starande° ston stondande alofte · · · · · · · · *shining*
Þat bere°blusschande bemeӡ as þe bryӡt sunne · · · · · *cast*

1808. on: MS, TG, D, W an; Go on an.
1810. for: Go for your.
1810. tyme. MS tyne.
1815. nade: MS, TG, D hade.

1801–02. Dorothy Everett (*Essays
on Middle English Literature*) notes
that here Gawain slips "from the for-
mal plural (ye, you) into the familiar
singular."
1802, 1810. *luf*: "for thy sake." See

1733*n*.
1808. *here on erande*: The simplest,
best reading is "here on business."
Morris, followed by Go, reads *here on
an erande*.

1820 Wyt ȝe wel hit watȝ worth wele° ful hoge°   *wealth / huge*

  Bot þe renk hit renayed° & redyly he sayde   *refused*

  I wil no gifteȝ for gode my gay at þis tyme   (f.115b)

  I haf none yow to norne° ne noȝt wyl I take   *offer*

1824 Ho bede° hit hym ful bysily° & he

   hir bode wernes°   *offered / eagerly / offer refuses*

  & swere swyfte by his sothe þat he hit sese nolde° *would not take*

  & ho sore° þat he forsoke° & sayde þerafter   *refused*

  If ȝe renay my rynk to ryche° for hit semeȝ   *costly*

1828 ȝe wolde not so hyȝly halden°be to me   *greatly beholden*

  I schal gif yow my girdel þat gaynes° yow lasse *profits*

  Ho laȝt a lace lyȝtly þat leke vmbe°

   hir sydeȝ   *was fastened around*

  Knit°vpon hir kyrtel° vnder þe clere mantyle *knotted / gown*

1832 Gered° hit watȝ with grene sylke & with golde schaped *made*

  Noȝt bot arounde brayden beten°

   with fyngreȝ *embroidered all around decorated*

  & þat ho bede° to þe burne & blyþely bisoȝt   *offered*

  Þaȝ hit vnworþi were þat he hit take wolde

1836 & he nay þat he nolde neghe in no wyse

   Nauþer golde ne garysoun° er God hym

   grace sende   *either gold or treasure*

1825. swyfte by: ᴍs swyftel.
1830. þat: ᴍs þat þat.
1832. golde: W gold.

1822. *for gode*: The context here indicates that this is certainly "for good, permanently." Go, following Wright, however, prints "for Gode."

1826. *ho sore*: "she was grieved" (Go).

1832. *schaped*: As D suggests, this is the participle of a verb derived from ᴏꜰ *chape*, "a metal mount or trimming."

1836. *nay*: TG and D take this to be a verb "said . . . not," the past tense of *nie (ᴏꜰ *nier*) formed by analogy with lay-lie. Since, however, as Go points out, *nie* does not appear in ᴍᴇ at all, it may be better to take *nay* as an adverb modifying a verb (some form of *say*) which has been omitted.

To acheue to þe chaunce° þat he hade
    chosen° þere   *adventure / undertaken*
& þerfore I pray yow displese yow noȝt
1840 & letteȝ be° your bisinesse° for I
      bayþe° hit yow neuer   *cease from / beseeching / will consent*
    to graunte
  I am derely°to yow biholde   *deeply*
  Bicause of your sembelaunt
1844   & euer in hot & colde
  To be your trwe seruaunt

XXIX

  Now forsake ȝe þis silke sayde þe burde þenne
  For hit is symple in hitself & so hit wel semeȝ
1848 Lo so hit is littel & lasse hit is worþy
  Bot whoso knew þe costes° þat knit ar þerinne   *qualities*
  He wolde hit prayse at more prys parauenture
  For quat gome so is gorde with þis grene lace
1852 While he hit hade hemely halched° aboute   *neatly looped*
  Þer is no haþel vnder heuen tohewe hym þat myȝt
  For he myȝt not be slayn for slyȝt° vpon erþe   *by any means*
  Þen kest þe knyȝt & hit come to his hert
1856 Hit were a juel for þe joparde þat hym iugged° were   *adjudged*

1848. &: Go þe.

1846–47. "Do you refuse this silk . . . as being unimportant in itself?"

1851ff. This reference and several others (2358ff., 161ff., 2038, 2431, 2485ff., 2515–18) to the green girdle and its magical qualities led Loomis (JEGP 42:149–84) to believe that the girdle was a familiar part of Celtic legend and that the poem as a whole was "much more deeply indebted to Irish tradition that Kittredge [and Hulbert] dreamed."

1853. *haþel vnder heuen*: An interesting echo of *Beowulf* 52, *haeleþ under heofenum.*

When he acheued to þe chapel his chek° for to
   fech°   *fortune / get*
Myʒt he haf slypped° to be vnslayn þe sleʒt
   were noble   *escaped*
Þenne he þulged with hir þrepe &
   þoled° hir to speke   *argument and suffered* (f.116a)
1860 & ho bere on hym þe belt & bede° hit hym
   swyþe°   *offered / earnestly*
& he granted & hym gafe with a goud wylle
& bisoʒt hym for hir sake disceuer° hit neuer   *reveal*
Bot to lelly layne°fro hir lorde þe leude hym
   acordeʒ   *loyally hide*
1864 Þat neuer wyʒe schulde hit wyt iwysse bot þay twayne
   for noʒte
He þonkked hir oft ful swyþe
Ful þro° with hert & þoʒt   *heartily*
1868   Bi þat on þrynne syþe°   *three times*
  Ho hatʒ kyst þe knyʒt so toʒt°   *strong*

XXX

Thenne lachcheʒ ho hir leue & leueʒ hym þere
For more myrþe of þat mon moʒt ho not gete
1872 When ho watʒ gon Sir Gawayn gereʒ° hym sone   *dresses*
  Rises & riches° hym in araye noble   *dresses*

                1858. Myʒt: ᴍꜱ Myʒ.
                1861. & (2nd): Go & ho.
                1863. fro: ᴍꜱ for.
                1872. ho: ᴍꜱ he.
                1872. Gawayn: ᴍꜱ G.

1859. *þulged*: Probably derived from ᴏᴇ *ðyldgian*, though Go thinks this derivation "phonologically impossible," and suggests a derivation from a metathesized form of ᴏɴ *þukla*, "to grope like a blind man," a reading which does not entirely suit the context.

1868. *Bi þat*: "By the time that."

Lays vp°þe luf-lace þe lady hym raȝt°   *puts away / gave*

Hid hit ful holdely þer he hit eft fonde

1876 Syþen cheuely°to þe chapel choses° he þe waye   *quickly / takes*

Preuely°aproched to a prest & prayed hym þere   *privately*

Þat he wolde lyfte his lyf & lern hym better

How his sawle schulde be saued when he schuld

    seye heþen°   *go hence*

1880 Þere he schrof hym schyrly & schewed his mysdedeȝ

Of þe more & þe mynne° & merci besecheȝ   *less*

& of absolucioun he on þe segge calles

& he asoyled hym surely & sette hym so clene

1884 As domeȝday schulde haf ben diȝt° on þe morn   *appointed*

& syþen he mace° hym as mery among þe fre ladyes   *makes*

With comlych caroles & alle kynnes ioye

As neuer he did bot þat daye to þe derk nȝyt

1878. lyfte: D, W lyste.

1875. *holdely*: TG, "faithfully, carefully"; Go, following Emerson, "loyally," "in accordance with [Gawain's] promise of 1864."

1876ff. This apparently invalid confession (because of Gawain's failure to tell the priest that he took and intended to keep the girdle) along with his later contrite "confession" to Bercilak (2379ff.) according to Burrow (MP 57:73–79) form a "contrast and so emphasize the theme of penance in the poem."

However, the poet insists that both the confession (1880) and absolution (1883–84) bestowed by the priest were complete and certainly Gawain's joy following his absolution is in marked contrast with his previous fearfulness. Bloomfield remarks that St. Thomas

Aquinas and others state that a man may lie to save his life and yet not be a sinner, though a willfully false confession may be another matter. Perhaps, as D remarks, the poet simply did not think Gawain's retention of the girdle to be sinful, even though he did in fact break his oath in failing to report the girdle to Bercilak. D, following a suggestion by T. A. Burrow (*A Reading of Sir Gawain and the Green Knight*, 105) emends *lyfte* in 1878 to *lyste*, the phrase *lyste his lyf* meaining "to hear his confession." However, the meaning of *lyfte his lyf*, "amend his life," is perfectly appropriate here.

1880. *schyrly*: "cleanly," of both mortal and venial sins (Bloomfield).

1888   with blys

Vche mon hade daynte° þare   *courtesy*

Of°hym & sayde iwysse   *from*

Þus myry he watȝ neuer are°   *before*

1892   Syn he com hider er þis

XXXI

Now hym lenge in þat lee° þer luf hym bityde   *shelter*

Ȝet is þe lorde on þe launde° ledande his gomnes   *field*

He hatȝ forfaren þis fox þat he folȝed longe

1896 As he sprent ouer a spenne° to spye þe schrewe°   *hedge / villain*

Þer as he herd þe howndes þat hasted hym swyþe   (f.116b)

Renaud com richchande° þurȝ a roȝe greue   *running*

& alle þe rabel in a res° ryȝt at his heleȝ   *rush*

1900 Þe wyȝe watȝ war of þe wylde° & warly abides   *creature*

& braydeȝ° out þe bryȝt bronde & at þe best casteȝ   *pulls*

& he schunt for° þe scharp & schulde°

      haf arered°   *swerved from / would / retreated*

A rach rapes° hym to ryȝt er he myȝt   *hound rushes*

1904 & ryȝt bifore þe hors fete þay fel on hym alle

& woried me þis wyly with a wroth noyse

Þe lorde lyȝteȝ bilyue & lacheȝ°

      hym sone   *alights quickly and seizes*

Rased hym ful radly out of þe rach mouþes

1908 Haldeȝ heȝe ouer his hede haloweȝ° faste   *halloes*

1906. lacheȝ hym: MS cacheȝ by.

1895. *forfaren*: Wright translated "intercepted" and Emerson "outstripped" from OE *forfaran*, "to get in front of." Go however, translates this verb "destroy" from analogies in *Patience* and *Purity* (see Go's note).

& þer bayen hym mony braþ° houndeȝ   *fierce*
Huntes hyȝed hem þeder with horneȝ ful mony
Ay rechatande aryȝt° til þay þe
  renk seȝen   *sounding the recall properly*
1912 Bi þat°watȝ comen his compeyny noble   *when*
Alle þat euer ber bugle blowed at ones
& alle þise oþer halowed þat hade no hornes
Hit watȝ þe myriest mute° þat euer men herde   *baying*
1916 Þe rich rurd þat þer watȝ raysed for Renaude saule
   with lote°   *cries*
  Hor houndeȝ þay þer rewarde
  Her hedeȝ þay fawne & frote°   *fondle and stroke*
1920   & syþen þay tan° Reynarde   *take*
  & tyruen° of his cote   *strip*

XXXII

& þenne þay helden to°home for hit watȝ nieȝ nyȝt   *went*
Strakande° ful stoutly in hor store° horneȝ   *sounding / mighty*
1924 Þe lorde is lyȝt° at þe laste at hys lef° home   *alighted / dear*
Fyndeȝ fire vpon flet° þe freke þer byside   *in the hall*
Sir Gawayn þe gode þat glad watȝ withalle
Among þe ladies for luf he ladde°much ioye   *had*
1928 He were a bleaunt°of blwe þat bradde°
  to þe erþe   *mantle / reached*

1909. braþ: ᴍs bray.
1915. men: W mon.
1919. Her: ᴍs Her her.

1909. *braþ*: Morris's emendation, followed by successive editors. Go suggests that "some such adverb as 'boldly' or 'bremely' is probably omitted" from this line.

1913. Savage suggests that only the aristocrats would carry bugles.
1917. See 639*n.*
1928ff. Savage (*The* Gawain-*Poet*, pp. 182ff.), following Cargill and

His surkot semed hym wel þat softe watʒ forred
& his hode of þat ilke henged on his schulder
Blande°al of blaunner° were boþe al
  aboute   *decorated | white fur*
1932 He meteʒ me þis god mon inmyddeʒ þe flore
  & al with gomen he hym gret & goudly he sayde
  I schal fylle vpon fyrst oure forwardeʒ nouþe
  Þat we spedly han spoken þer spared watʒ no drynk (f.117a)
1936 Þen acoles° he þe knyʒt & kysses hym þryes *embraces*
  As sauerly & sadly as he hem sette couþe
  Bi Kryst quoþ þat oþer knyʒt ʒe cach much sele
  In cheuisaunce of þis chaffer ʒif ʒe hade goud chepeʒ
1940 ʒe of þe chepe no charg quoþ chefly þat oþer
  As is pertly payed þe chepeʒ þat I aʒte
  Mary quoþ þat oþer mon myn is bihynde° *lesser*
  For I haf hunted al þis day & noʒt haf I geten
1944 Bot þis foule fox felle° þe fende haf þe godeʒ° *skin | goods*
  & þat is ful pore for to pay for suche prys þinges
  As ʒe haf þryʒt° me here þro suche þre cosses *thrust*

1936. þe: *Not in* MS.
1941. chepeʒ: Go pray; W porchas.

Schlauch (PMLA 43:119), relates Gawain's costume here to the garter robes. See note to *Honi Soit Qui Mal Pence.* 1938-41.

 "By Christ, you'd great happiness,"
  quoth then the host,
In getting these wares, if good
  were your bargains."
"Take no care for the cost,"
  the other said quickly,
Since plainly the debt that is
  due I have paid" (Banks)

1940. *chepe*: Wright suggests "goods," though "trade, price" seems better in context.

1941. *chepeʒ*: There is no need to emend this either to *porcheʒ* (TG's suggestion), or to *pray* (Go) in spite of its plural form. The *Middle English Dictionary* gives "price asked or offered" (Banks' "debt") as a perfectly standard meaning during the period. Bloomfield calls attention to the play on business terms in this passage.

so gode
1948 Inoȝ quoþ Sir Gawayn
I þonk yow bi þe rode°   *cross*
& how þe fox watȝ slayn
He tolde hym as þay stode

XXXIII

1952 With merþe & mynstralsye wyth meteȝ at hor wylle
Þay maden as mery as any men moȝten
With laȝyng of ladies with loteȝ of bordes
Gawayn & þe gode mon so glad were þay boþe
1956 Bot if þe douthe had doted oþer dronken ben oþer
Boþe þe mon & þe meyny maden mony iapeȝ°   *jests*
Til þe sesoun watȝ seȝen þat þay seuer moste°   *must part*
Burneȝ to hor bedde behoued° at þe laste   *must go*
1960 Þenne loȝly° his leue at þe lorde fyrst   *humbly*
Fochcheȝ° þis fre mon & fayre he hym þonkkeȝ   *takes*
Of such a selly soiorne as I haf hade here
Your honour at þis hyȝe fest þe hyȝe kyng yow
ȝelde°   *reward*
1964 I ȝef yow me for on of youreȝ if yowreself lykeȝ
For I mot nedes as ȝe wot meue tomorne

1962. selly: MS sellyly.

1948. *Inoȝ*: Go suggests, very shrewdly I think, that Gawain is anxious to cut short the discussion.

1952–53. See 118*n*.

1954. *bordes*: Kökeritz (MLN 58: 373–74) derives from OE **byrde*, "maiden" and translates the phrase "with the gay chatter of maidens."

1954. See 639*n*.

1954–56. "With the laughing of the ladies and the sounds of the feasts, Gawain and the lord could not have been merrier—unless they had become either childish or drunk." *Douthe* would seem here to refer simply to Gawain and Bercilak, though it could conceivably apply to the whole company.

1964. "I give you myself, if you'd like it, to serve you" (Banks).

&°ȝe me take° sum tolke to teche as ȝe
     hyȝt°   *if | give | promised*
Þe gate° to þe grene chapel as God wyl me suffer   *way*
1968 To dele on Nw ȝereȝ day þe dome of my wyrdes
In god fayþe quoþ þe god mon wyth a goud wylle
Al þat euer I yow hyȝt halde schal I rede°   *ready*
Þer asyngnes he a seruaunt to sett hym in þe waye
1972 & coundue°hym by þe downeȝ þat
     he no drechch° had   *conduct | trouble* (f.117b)
For to ferk° þurȝ þe fryth°& fare at
     þe gaynest°   *go | wood | most directly*
      bi greue
Þe lorde Gawayn con þonk
1976   Such worchip he wolde hym weue°   *offer*
Þen at þo ladyeȝ wlonk°   *lovely*
Þe knyȝt hatȝ tan his leue

XXXIV

With care & wyth kyssyng he carppeȝ hem tille
1980 & fele þryuande° þonkkeȝ he þrat° hom to haue   *hearty | urged*
& þay ȝelden°hym aȝayn ȝeply þat ilk   *return*
Þay bikende° hym to Kryst with ful
     colde sykyngeȝ°   *commended | grievous sighs*
Syþen fro þe meyny he menskly departes
1984 Vche mon þat he mette he made hem a þonke

1973. ferk: ᴍѕ frk.
1981. aȝayn: ᴍѕ aȝay.

1968. *dele*: "share (Wright).
1971ff. Wright thinks that the in-
troduction of the "seruaunt" supplies
another testing of the hero.
1975–76. "Gawain thanked the lord
that he had bestowed such an honor
on him," i.e., in furnishing him with
a guide. As Emerson points out, Ga-
wain has already thanked Bercilak for
his hospitality in 1962–63.

For his seruyse & his solace & his sere pyne
Þat þay wyth busynes had ben aboute hym to serue
& vche segge as sore to seuer with hym þere
1988 As þay hade wonde worþyly with þat wlonk euer
Þen with ledes° & lyȝt he watȝ ladde to his chambre   *servants*
& blyþely broȝt to his bedde to be at his rest
Ȝif he ne slepe soundyly say ne dar I
1992 For he hade muche on þe morn to mynne° ȝif
      he wolde   *think of*
         in þoȝt
      Let hym lyȝe þere stille
      He hatȝ nere þat°he soȝt   *nearby what*
1996   &° ȝe wyl a whyle be stylle   *if*
      I schal telle yow how þay wroȝt

PART FOUR

I

Now neȝeȝ° ȝe Nw ȝere & þe nyȝt passeȝ   *draws near*
Þe day dryueȝ° to þe derk as dryȝtyn biddeȝ   *follows*
2000 Bot wylde wedereȝ of þe worlde wakned þeroute
Clowdes kesten kenly° þe colde to þe erþe   *cast bitterly*
Wyth nyȝe innoghe of þe norþe þe naked to tene°   *punish*

1986. "Which they had been busy about in order to minister to him" (Wright).

1996–97. See 30–31n.

1998ff. An example of *descriptio opportuna* (see 2087–88n.).

1999. As TG point out, this line records the dawn, not the sunset, *dryueȝ* here meaning "makes onset against" (Go) or "makes its way (to)" (TG). Banks translates "the day, as the Lord bids, drives away darkness."

Savage (*The* Gawain-*Poet*, p. 78) notes that Gawain departs for the Green Chapel on the Feast of the Circumcision, on a day when Christ also shed blood.

2000. See 517n.

2002. *þe naked*: the "ill-clad" (TG); the "flesh" (Go).

Þe snawe snitered°ful snart° þat
  snayped° þe wylde   *shivered down | bitterly | nipped*
2004 Þe werbelande° wynde wapped° fro þe hyȝe *whistling | rushed*
 & drof vche dale ful of dryftes ful grete
 Þe leude lystened ful wel þat leȝ in his bedde
 Þaȝ he lowkeȝ° his liddeȝ ful lyttel he slepes   *closes*
2008 Bi vch kok þat crue he knwe wel þe steuen°   *appointed time*
 Deliuerly° he dressed vp er þe day sprenged *quickly* (f.118a)
 For þere watȝ lyȝt of a laumpe þat lemed° in his
  chambre   *shone*
 He called to his chamberlayn þat cofly° hym
  swared°   *promptly | answered*
2012 & bede hym bryng hym his bruny°& his blonk
  sadel   *mail shirt*
 Þat oþer ferkeȝ° hym vp & fecheȝ hym his wedeȝ   *gets*
 & grayþeȝ° me Sir Gawayn vpon°
  a grett wyse°   *clothes | in | magnificent manner*
 Fyrst he clad hym in his cloþeȝ þe colde for to
  were°   *ward off*
2016 & syþen his oþer harnays þat holdely° watȝ
  keped   *faithfully*
 Boþe his paunce°& his plateȝ piked°
  ful clene   *stomach armor | polished*
 Þe ryngeȝ rokked° of þe roust° of his riche
  bruny   *cleaned | rust*
 & al watȝ fresch as vpon fyrst & he watȝ fayn þenne
2020   to þonk°   *give thanks*
  He hade vpon° vche pece   *on him*

2011. hym: TG, W him.
2010. laumpe: ᴍs laupe.

2018. *þe ryngeȝ rokked*: Chain ar- filled with sand in order to burnish it.
mor was rolled (*rokked*) in a barrel

Wypped° ful wel & wlonk   *wiped*
Þe gayest into°Grece   *from here to*
2024 Þe burne bede bryng his blonk

II

Whyle þe wlonkest wedes he warp° on hymseluen   *put*
His cote wyth þe conysaunce°of þe
    clere werkeȝ°   *badge / fair embroidery*
Ennured°vpon veluet vertuus stoneȝ   *set*
2028 Aboute beten° & bounden enbrauded semeȝ   *set*
& fayre furred withinne wyth fayre pelures°   *furs*
ȝet laft he not þe lace þe ladieȝ gifte
Þat forgat not Gawayn for gode of hymseluen
2032 Bi° he hade belted þe bronde vpon his balȝe
    hauncheȝ°   *when / smooth hips*
Þenn dressed he his drurye° double hym aboute   *love token*
Swyþe sweþled vmbe° his swange°
    swetely þat knyȝt   *quickly wrapped around / waist*
Þe gordel of þe grene silke þat gay wel bisemed
2036 Vpon þat ryol° red cloþe þat ryche watȝ to
    schewe°   *royal / look at*
Bot wered not þis ilk wyȝe for wele þis gordel
For pryde of þe pendaunteȝ þaȝ polyst þay were

2027. Ennured: Go Enuirened.
2029. fayre (1st): Go ferly.

2026. *þe conysaunce of þe clere werkeȝ*: Savage notes that Blanche's *Cyclopedia of Costume* reveals that the word *conysaunce* was generally applied to the garment which displayed the wearer's armorial bearings. The phrase here refers to the pentangle device he wears *in schelde & cote* (637).

2035. *þat gay wel bisemed*: Go, rightly I think, read *bisemed* as "suited" and took *gay* as its object noun—"the girdle of green silk well suited that gallant." Emerson thought *biseme* to mean "seem" and Savage (MLN 49:232–34) took *gay* as an adverb modifying *wel*.

& þaʒ þe glyterande golde glent vpon endeʒ

2040 Bot for to sauen hymself when suffer hym byhoued

To byde bale withoute dabate° of bronde

      hym to were°   *defense / defend*

      oþer knyffe

    Bi þat° þe bolde mon boun°   *then / ready*

2044 Wynneʒ þeroute°bilyue   *goes outside*

    Alle þe meyny of renoun

    He þonkkeʒ ofte ful ryue°   *much*

III

    Thenne watʒ Gryngolet grayþe° þat gret

      watʒ & huge   *made ready* (f.118b)

2048 & hade ben soiourned sauerly° & in a siker wyse   *pleasantly*

    Hym lyst prik° for poynt° þat

      proude hors þenne   *it pleases to gallop / good condition*

    Þe wyʒe wynneʒ°hym to & wyteʒ° on his

      lyre°   *goes / looks / coat*

    & sayde soberly hymself & by his soth swereʒ

2052 Here is a meyny in þis mote° þat on menske°

      þenkkeʒ   *castle / courtesy*

    Þe mon hem maynteines ioy mot þay haue

    Þe leue lady on lyue luf hir bityde°   *befall*

    ʒif þay for charyte cherysen a gest

2056 & halden honour in her honde þe haþel° hem ʒelde°   *reward*

    Þat haldeʒ þe heuen vpon hyʒe & also yow alle

             2053. þay: Go, W he.
             2055. ʒif: Go Þus.
             2056. &: Go þat.

2041. *byde*: Neither Wright's "wait for" nor Go's "endure" gives the proper sense, which is "withstand, ward off."

2053. *þay*: Go needlessly emends to *he*. As Emerson points out, *þay* refers to all the retainers serving *þe mon*.

& ʒif I myʒt lyf vpon londe lede any quyle

I schuld rech yow sum rewarde redyly if I myʒt

2060 Þenn steppeʒ he into stirop & strydeʒ alofte

His schalk schewed° hym his schelde on
schulder he hit laʒt   *servant brought*

Gordeʒ° to Gryngolet with his gilt heleʒ   *spurs*

& he starteʒ° on þe ston stod he no lenger   *leaps forward*

2064   to praunce

   His haþel on hors watʒ þenne

   Þat bere his spere & launce

   Þis kastel to Kryst I kenne°   *commend*

2068 He gef hit ay god chaunce

IV

The brygge watʒ brayde° doun & þe brode
ʒateʒ°   *pulled / gates*

Vnbarred & born open vpon boþe halue

Þe burne blessed°hym bilyue & þe
bredeʒ° passed   *crossed himself / planks*

2072 Prayses þe porter bifore° þe prynce kneled   *who before*

Gef hym God & goud day þat Gawayn he saue

& went on his way with his wyʒe one

Þat schulde teche hym to tourne to þat tene° place   *dangerous*

2076 Þer þe ruful race he shulde resayue°   *receive*

Þay boʒen°bi bonkkeʒ þer boʒeʒ° ar bare   *went / boughs*

Þay clomben bi clyffeʒ þer clengeʒ þe colde

Þe heuen watʒ vphalt° bot vgly þervnder   *clouds were high*

2080 Mist muged° on þe mor malt° on þe mounteʒ   *drizzled / melted*

Vch hille hade a hatte a myst-hakel huge

2072–73. A slight interjection. Both
God and *goud day* are objects of *gef*,
"gave him a blessing and a farewell."

2076. *race*: TG, "onslaught"; Go,

"attack"; Savage, "blow, cut."

2081. *myst hakel*: "mist-cloak," a
unique and marvellously descriptive
phrase. Wright considered *hakel* to be

Brokeȝ byled & breke bi bonkkeȝ aboute

Schyre schaterande on schoreȝ þer þay doun
schowued°   *rushed*

2084 Welawylle°watȝ þe way þer þay bi
wod schulden° *very wild / must go* (f.119a)

Til hit watȝ sone sesoun þat þe sunne ryses
þat tyde°   *time*

Þay were on a hille ful hyȝe

2088 Þe quyte snaw lay bisyde

Þe burne þat rod hym by

Bede his mayster abide

V

For I haf wonnen yow hider wyȝe at þis tyme

2092 & now nar ȝe not fer fro þat note° place *noted*

Þat ȝe han spied & spuryed° so
specially after *have looked for and asked*

Bot I schal say yow forsoþe syþen I yow knowe

& ȝe ar a lede vpon lyue þat I wel louy° *love*

2096 Wolde ȝe worch°bi my wytte ȝe worþed° þe
better *do / would be*

2096. ȝe: Go yow.

---

related to dialect "hackle," the "straw covering of a bee hive," and so saw the hill as covered by a "cloud of mist rising ... in a huge cone-shaped mass."

2082. *byled*: Go derives this and *boyled* in 2174 from OF *boiller*, "to boil." Savage and Emerson's derivation from OE *bylgian*, "roar," however, better suits the context.

2083. See 506*n*.

2084. Sisam (*Fourteenth Century Verse and Prose*) notes the character-istic omission of a verb of motion after "shall," "will," etc.

2087ff. Though praised by Oakden (*Alliterative Poetry in Middle English*) and Go as examples of the poet's original, unconventional description, Pearsall (MLR 50:129–34) shows these lines to follow the pattern of *descriptio opportuna*, a "rhetorical am-plification of Gawain's state of mind," though the details are, of course, the poet's own.

Þe place þat ȝe prece° to ful perelous is halden *hurry*
Þer woneȝ a wyȝe in þat waste þe worst vpon erþe
For he is stiffe & sturne & to strike louies
2100 & more he is þen any mon vpon myddelerde
& his body bigger þen þe best fowre
Þat ar in Arþureȝ hous Hestor oþer oþer
He cheueȝ° þat chaunce at þe chapel grene *brings about*
2104 Þer passes non bi þat place so proude in his armes
Þat he ne dyngeȝ hym to deþe with dynt of his honde
For he is a mon methles & mercy non vses
For be hit chorle oþer chaplayn þat bi þe chapel rydes
2108 Monk oþer masse-prest oþer any mon elles
Hym þynk as queme° hym to quelle as *pleasant / alive to go*
      quyk go° hymseluen
Forþy I say þe as soþe as ȝe in sadel sitte
Com ȝe þere ȝe be kylled may þe knyȝt rede
2112 Trawe ȝe me þat trwely þaȝ ȝe had twenty lyues
      to spende

2105. dyngeȝ: ms dynneȝ.
2110. þe: Go yow.

2102. *Hestor*: Certainly Hector of Troy; the only Round Table knight this could refer to would be Hector de Mares, Lancelot's brother, but he surely would not be named above the other knights in prowess, though see Brett (MLR 22:457) and Onions.

2105. *dyngeȝ*: Napier's emendation.

2106. *methles*: TG, "violent"; Savage (MLN 58:46–7), "without principle."

2107. Savage deduces from the large number of such chapels in Lancashire and Yorkshire that the poet was a Lancashire or West Riding man, although the dialect would seem to point to North Staffordshire.

2111. Wright notes that "whereas the guide in his set speech uses the polite pronouns *ȝe* and *yow*, as soon as he finds Sir Gawain is quite determined to go his own way, he relapses altogether into the familiar *þou* and *þe* . . . ." Wright thus translates 2111 as "I may warn you, knight." More usual translations gloss *rede* as "choose" (Banks), "rule" (Go), "have his will" (TG and D).

He hatʒ wonyd here ful ʒore°   *long*
On bent° much baret bende°   *field | strife has led*
2116 Aʒayn his dynteʒ sore
ʒe may not yow defende

VI

Forþy goude Sir Gawayn let þe gome one°   *alone*
& gotʒ away sum oþer gate° vpon Goddeʒ halue   *way*
2120 Cayreʒ°bi sum oþer kyth° þer Kryst mot yow
spede   *ride | land*
& I schal hyʒ me hom aʒayn & hete° yow fyrre   *promise*
Þat I schal swere bi God & alle his gode
halʒeʒ°   *saints (f.119b)*
As help me God & þe halydam & oþeʒ innoghe
2124 Þat I schal lelly°yow layne &
lance° neuer tale   *faithfully | conceal and utter*
Þat euer ʒe fondet° to fle for freke þat I wyst   *hastened*
Grant merci quoþ Gawayn & gruchyng° he sayde   *reluctantly*
Wel worth°þe wyʒe þat woldeʒ° my gode   *be | wished*
2128 & þat lelly me layne I leue° wel þou woldeʒ°   *believe | would*
Bot helde þou hit neuer so holde &°I here passed   *faithfully if*
Founded°for ferde°for to fle in fourme°þat
þou telleʒ   *came | fear | manner*
I were a knyʒt kowarde I myʒt not be excused
2132 Bot I wyl to þe chapel for chaunce þat may falle
& talk wyth þat ilk tulk þe tale þat me lyste
Worþe° hit wele oþer wo as þe wyrde lykeʒ   *be*
hit hafe
2136 Þaʒe he be a sturn knape°   *man*
To stiʒtel° & stad with staue°   *control | club*

2124. lance: Go, W lauce.
2131. not: MS mot.
2137. &: MS & &.

Ful wel con dryȝtyn schape
His seruaunteȝ for to saue

VII

2140 Mary quoþ þat oþer mon now þou so much spelleȝ°   *say*
    Þat þou wylt þyn awen nye nyme°to þyseluen   *harm take*
    & þe lyst lese þy lyf þe lette I ne kepe°   *care*
    Haf here þi helme on þy hede þi spere in þi honde
2144 & ryde me doun þis ilk rake° bi ȝon rokke syde   *path*
    Til þou be broȝt to þe boþem of þe brem valay°   *wild valley*
    Þenne loke a littel on þe launde° on þi lyfte honde   *field*
    & þou schal se in þat slade° þe self chapel   *valley*
2148 & þe borelych°burne on bent°þat hit kepeȝ   *burly | field*
    Now fareȝ wel on Godeȝ half Gawayn þe noble
    For alle þe golde vpon grounde I nolde go wyth þe
    Ne bere þe felaȝschyp þurȝ þis fryth°on fote fyrre   *wood*
2152 Bi þat° þe wyȝe in þe wod wendeȝ° his brydel   *then | turns*
    Hit þe hors with þe heleȝ as harde as he myȝt
    Lepeȝ hym ouer þe launde & leueȝ þe knyȝt þere
        al one°   *alone*
2156   Bi Goddeȝ self quoþ Gawayn
    I wyl nauþer grete°no grone   *weep*
    To Goddeȝ wylle I am ful bayn°   *obedient*
    & to hym I haf me tone°   *committed*

VIII

2160 Thenne gyrdeȝ° he to Gryngolet
    & gedereȝ° þe rake   *puts spurs | follows* (f.120a)

2144. *ryde me*: Sisam (*Fourteenth Century Verse and Prose*) calls attention to this rare ethical dative, "which expresses some interest in the action of the verb on the part of one who is neither the doer of the action nor its object." D lists other occurrences in 1905, 1932, 2014, and 2459.

2154. *Lepeȝ hym*: "gallops." *Hym* refers to Gawain, not his horse.

Schowueȝ° in bi a schore at a schaȝe° syde   *pushes | wood*

Rideȝ þurȝ þe roȝe bonk ryȝt to þe dale

& þenne he wayted hym aboute & wylde hit hym þoȝt

2164 & seȝe no syngne of resette bisydeȝ° nowhere   *shelter around*

Bot hyȝe bonkkeȝ & brent° vpon boþe halue   *steep*

& ruȝe knokled knarreȝ° with knorned°

stoneȝ   *rugged crags | gnarled*

Þe skweȝ of þe scowtes skayned hym þoȝt

2168 Þenne he houed° & wythhylde his hors at þat

tyde°   *halted | time*

& ofte chaunged his cher° þe chapel

to seche   *looked in different directions*

He seȝ non suche in no syde° & selly hym þoȝt   *direction*

Saue a lyttel on a launde° a lawe° as hit were   *field | mound*

2172 A balȝ berȝ bi a bonke þe brymme° bysyde   *water's edge*

2171. were: MS we.
2171. Saue: TG Sone.

2163. *wayted hym aboute*: "looked around him."

2167. *skayned*: Morris reads *skay-ued*, "wild," from ON *skeifr* and translates the line: "The shadows of the hills appeared wild (desolate) to him." Wright connects the word with dialect *skeaf*, "a steep bank" or with *skave*, "askew," and translates *skweȝ* as a noun "uneven." Emerson, following Wright, glossed *skweȝ* as "precipitous bank." Both TG and Go derive *skweȝ* from ON *skȳ* (TG as "clouds," Go as "skies") and *skayned* from ON *skeina*, "grazed"; thus "the skies (or clouds) seemed to him grazed by the crags." Go's notes supply details of other possible derivations.

2171. *Saue*: This is clearly the MS reading, followed by Go and D, TG reading *sone*. "Except" here may be defended on purely rhetorical grounds as a transition from *he seȝ non such* [chapel] *in no syde* to Gawain's sudden perception of the *balȝ berȝ*.

2171ff. According to Schnyder (*Sir Gawain and the Green Knight*) the Green Chapel is the hell where Gawain, here a saint, must go to be tempted.

2172. *A balȝ berȝ*: "a smooth-faced mound," apparently a treeless burial mound by a stream. Go conjectures that it was "long rather than round, with a hole at the end and on each side. It was evidently an ancient barrow that had been broken into, and the contents carried off . . . . Further, it

Bi a forʒ of a flode þat ferked°þare   *ran*
Þe borne blubred° þerinne as hit boyled hade   *stream bubbled*
Þe knyʒt kacheʒ his caple° & com to þe lawe   *spurs his horse*
2176 Liʒteʒ doun luflyly & at a lynde tacheʒ°   *tree ties*
Þe rayne & his riche with a roʒe braunche

2177. &: W of.
2177. his riche: Go hit riched.

---

was a chambered barrow." Brewer, however, points out (NQ 193:194) that such "long barrow[s] in a narrow, steep-sided valley" are found neither in the analogues of the poem nor in northeast England and conjectures whether this barrow may not be a "remnant of Northern mystery and magic." Randall (SP 57:479–91) connects the *balʒ berʒ* with primitive ideas of the entrance into hell. Go's note also supplies a detailed commentary on *balʒ*.

Hulbert (MP 13:433–462, 689–730) noted that the description of the Green Chapel pointed to "a story involving Other-World beings, in the course of which the hero is tested by a 'shape-shifter' " (see 150*n*.).

Madden, acting on the assumption (shared by nearly everyone) that the poet is describing a scene familiar to himself and his audience, thought Volsty Castle in Cumberland and the neighboring Chapel of the Grene seen on old maps to be the scene of Gawain's meeting with the green knight. In fact, in the Percy Folio MS of *The Green Knight*, a condensation of *Sir Gawain and the Green Knight*, the castle is identified as Hutton Castle, which is probably Hutton-in-the-Forest

near Penrith, Cumberland. Oakden (*Alliterative Poetry*) believed the scene to be in the vicinity of John of Gaunt's castle at Clitheroe, Lancs. Mabel Day (in Go) identified the scene positively as a small cove at Wetton Mill, Staffs., but, according to L. H. Loomis (*Arthurian Literature in the Middle Ages*, 529) "confused it with Thor's cave (Thursehouse) a huge cavern in a cliff a mile away." The latest theorist, Ralph W. V. Elliott (The *Times*, May 21, 1958, 12), identifies the green chapel with Ludchurch, a fissure in the Castle Cliff rocks near Leek in northern Staffordshire.

2173. *a forʒ of a flode*: Loomis (JEGP 42:149–84) finds a parallel to the *forʒ of a flode* in the eleventh-century mabinogi of *Pwyll*. Randall (SP 57:479–91) notes that the crossing of a river to enter the spirit world is a "basic primitive belief."

Both TG and Go gloss *forʒ* as "waterfall," though Emerson, D, and Wright prefer "channel." Bloomfield very sensibly sees *forʒ* as *fors*, "rush."

2177. *his riche*: Probably, as TG said, "his noble [steed]," though these editors suggested that the line may have read *and hit riched*, "drew it to," a reading followed by Go. However,

Þenne he boȝeȝ to þe berȝe aboute hit he walkeȝ
Debatande with hymself quat hit be myȝt
2180 Hit hade a hole on þe ende & on ayþer syde
& ouergrowen with gresse in glodes aywhere
& al watȝ holȝ° inwith nobot° an olde caue   *hollow / nothing but*
Or a creuisse of an olde cragge he couþe hit noȝt deme
2184   with spelle°   *word*
        We° lorde quoþ þe gentyle knyȝt   *alas*
        Wheþer þis be þe grene chapelle
        Here myȝt aboute mydnyȝt
2188   Þe dele his matynnes telle

IX

        Now iwysse quoþ Wowayn wysty° is here   *desolate*
        Þis oritore is vgly with erbeȝ ouergrowen
        Wel bisemeȝ þe wyȝe wruxled° in grene   *wrapped*
2192 Dele° here his deuocioun on þe deueleȝ wyse   *perform*
        Now I fele hit is þe fende in my fyue wytteȝ
        Þat hatȝ stoken°me þis steuen° to strye°
        me here   *fixed / tryst / destroy*
        Þis is a chapel of meschaunce þat chekke hit bytyde
2196 Hit is þe corsedest kyrk° þat euer I com
        inne   *most accursed church*
        With heȝe helme on his hede his launce in his honde   (f.120b)
        He romeȝ° vp to þe roffe of þo roȝ woneȝ   *makes his way*

2187. Here: ᴍs he.
2198. roffe: TG rokke.

---

the line, awkward as it is, can read, as
Banks translates, "The knight . . .
tied to the limb/ Of a tree, right rug-
ged, the reins of his noble steed. . . ."
    2181. *glodes*: "Open spaces, patch-
es" (Go, D). Grattan, however, sug-
gests that it may be a variant of *clodes*.
    2186–88. "Whether (or not) this is

the Green Chapel, here the devil might
well say matins at midnight."
    2195. *chekke*: "harm," a term
which "originally referred to the check-
mate at chess" (TG); thus "may de-
struction befall it."
    2198. *roffe*: "roof." One can be
grateful to Go for restoring this ᴍs

Þene herde he of þat hyȝe hil in a harde roche
2200 Biȝonde þe broke in a bonk a wonder breme noyse
    Quat hit clatered in þe clyff as hit cleue° schulde   *break*
    As one vpon a gryndelston° hade grounden a syþe   *grindstone*
    What hit wharred & whette as water at a mulle°   *mill*
2204 What hit rusched & ronge rawþe° to here   *terrible*
    Þenne bi Godde quoþ Gawayn þat gere as I trowe
    Is ryched at þe reuerence me renk to mete
        bi rote
2208   Let God worche we loo
    Hit helppeȝ me not a mote
    My lif þaȝ I forgoo
    Drede dotȝ me no lote

<h2 style="text-align:center">X</h2>

2212 Thenne þe knyȝt con calle ful hyȝe
    Who stiȝtleȝ° in þis sted me steuen to holde   *rules*
    For now is gode Gawayn goande ryȝt here
    If any wyȝe oȝt° wyl wynne°hider fast   *wishes anything | come*
2216 Oþer now oþer neuer his nedeȝ to spede°   *help*
    Abyde quoþ on on þe bonke abouen ouer his hede

2203. mulle: MS mulile; TG, D, W mulne.
2205. as: MS at.

---

reading from the *rokke* of all previ-ous editions.

2199–204. This passage along with a sequence of others is used by Alain Renoir (Moderna Språk 54:245–53) to show how the poet has Gawain gradually decrease in stature in relation to his environment in *GGK* in order to give an "insight into the mounting anxiety of Gawain."

2208–9. TG translate the line "Let God work [his will]; [To say] Alas! helps me not a bit; though I lose my life, no noise shall make me afraid." Wright, however, takes the *Hit* of 2209 to refer to *þat gere* in 2205 and translates "It has no effect on me," which seems a strange comment for Gawain to make at this point.

2211. See 639*n*.

& þou schal haf al in hast þat I þe hyȝt ones°   *promised once*

ȝet he rusched on þat rurde rapely a þrowe

2220 & wyth° quettyng awharf° er he wolde lyȝt   *for | turned aside*

& syþen he keuereȝ° bi a cragge & comeȝ of a hole   *goes*

Whyrlande out of a wro°wyth a felle weppen   *nook*

A Deneȝ° ax nwe dyȝt° þe dynt with

to ȝelde°   *Danish | sharpened | repay*

2224 With a borelych bytte bende° by

þe halme°   *huge blade curved | handle*

Fyled°in a fylor° fowre fote large°   *sharpened | filing bench | wide*

Hit watȝ no lasse bi þat lace° þat lemed°

ful bryȝt   *thong | gleamed*

& þe gome in þe grene gered as fyrst°   *dressed as at first*

2228 Boþe þe lyre°& þe leggeȝ lokkeȝ & berde   *face*

Saue þat fayre° on his fote he foundeȝ° on þe erþe   *well | goes*

Sette þe stele° to þe stone° & stalked

bysyde   *handle | stony ground*

When he wan° to þe watter þer he wade nolde   *came*

2232 He hypped ouer on hys ax & orpedly strydeȝ

Bremly broþe° on a bent þat brode watȝ aboute   *fiercely savage*

on snawe

2223. to: MS O.

2223. *A Deneȝ ax*: The *NED* defines this as "a kind of battle-axe with very long blade, and usually without a spike on the back." This is certainly not the *giserne* (288 and 2265) that the Green Knight normally carries.

2226. *bi þat lace þat lemed*: A curious reference, since we have heard nothing of a lace turned about the handle of this ax, though the Green Knight's first ax (217–20) did boast such an ornament. Go suggests, and Malachey and Toelken discuss (JEGP 63:14–20), the possibility that the line may in some way refer to the green girdle which Gawain accepted from the lady.

2230. The Green Knight here uses the handle of his ax as a walking stick.

2232. *orpedly*: Go, "boldly"; TG, "actively"; Savage and Wright, "truculently."

Sir Gawayn þe knyȝt con mete°   *greeted* (f.121a)
2236 He ne lutte hym no þyng lowe°   *did not bow at all low*
Þat oþer sayde now sir swete
Of steuen mon may þe trowe

XI

Gawayn quoþ þat grene gome God þe mot
    loke°   *may look after*
2240 Iwysse þou art welcom wyȝe to my place
& þou hatȝ tymed þi trauayl as truee mon schulde
& þou knoweȝ þe couenaunteȝ kest° vs bytwene   *made*
At þis tyme twelmonyth þou toke þat° þe
    falled°   *took what | befell*
2244 & I schulde at þis Nwe ȝere ȝeply þe quyte
& we are in þis valay verayly oure one°   *alone*
Here ar no renkes vs to rydde° rele° as vs likeȝ   *part | reel*
Haf þy helme of þy hede & haf here þy pay
2248 Busk° no more debate þen I þe bede° þenne   *make | offered*
When þou wypped° of my hede at a wap° one   *slashed | blow*
Nay bi God quoþ Gawayn þat me gost lante°   *a spirit gave*
I schal gruch° þe no grwe° for grem°
    þat falleȝ   *begrudge | not a bit | harm*
2252 Bot styȝtel þe vpon° on strok & I schal stonde
    stylle   *limit yourself to*
& warp° þe no wernyng° to worch° as
    þe lykeȝ   *give | resistance | do*
    nowhare
He lened with þe nek & lutte°   *bowed*
2256 & schewed þat schyre° al bare   *white flesh*
& lette° as he noȝt dutte°   *acted | feared*
For drede° ne wolde not dare°   *fear | shrink*

2240. welcom: MS welcon.
2247. þy (1st): MS þy þy.

XII

Then þe gome in þe grene grayþed° hym swyþe   *readied*
2260 Gedereʒ vp hys grymme tole Gawayn to smyte
    With alle þe bur° in his body he ber hit on lofte   *strength*
    Munt° as maʒtyly° as marre° hym he
        wolde   *aimed / mightily / destroy*
    Hade hit° dryuen adoun as dreʒ as he
        atled°   *if it had / intended*
2264 Þer hade ben ded of his dynt þat° doʒty watʒ euer   *he who*
    Bot Gawayn on þat giserne glyfte° hym bysyde   *axe glanced*
    As hit com glydande adoun on glode° hym
        to schende°   *ground / destroy*
    & schranke a lytel with þe schulderes for þe scharp yrne
2268 Þat oþer schalk wyth a schunt° þe
        schene° wythhaldeʒ   *swerve / blade*
    & þenne repreued° he þe prynce with mony
        prowde wordeʒ   *reproved*
    Þou art not Gawayn quoþ þe gome þat is so goud halden
    Þat neuer arʒed° for no here by hylle ne be vale   *quailed*
2272 & now þou fles° for ferde° er þou fele
        harmeʒ   *flinch / fear* (f.121b)
    Such cowardise of þat knyʒt cowþe I neuer here
    Nawþer fyked° I ne flaʒe° freke quen
        þou myntest°   *flinched / fled / aimed*
    Ne kest° no kauelacion° in kyngeʒ hous
        Arthor   *made / cavilling*
2276 My hede flaʒ° to my fote & ʒet flaʒ I neuer   *flew*
    & þou er any harme hent arʒeʒ° in hert   *taken quail*
    Wherfore þe better burne me burde° be called   *I ought to*

2263. *dreʒ*: Go, "heavily"; Emerson, "continuously"; TG, "forcibly."

2271. *here*: Emerson conjectured that *here* might here mean "man." "Host," i.e., a company of warriors, however, seems a better reading.

þerfore

2280   Quoþ Gawayn I schunt oneʒ

      & so wyl I no more

      Bot þaʒ°my hede falle on þe stoneʒ   *if*

      I con not hit restore

XIII

2284 Bot busk° burne bi þi fayth & bryng me to þe poynt   *hurry*

      Dele to me my destine & do hit out of honde

      For I schal stonde þe a strok & start no more

      Til þyn ax haue me hitte haf here my trawþe

2288 Haf at þe þenne quoþ þat oþer & heueʒ hit alofte

      & wayteʒ as wroþely as he wode were

      He mynteʒ° at hym maʒtyly bot not þe mon ryneʒ   *aims*

      Withhelde heterly° his honde er hit hurt myʒt   *quickly*

2292 Gawayn grayþely° hit bydeʒ & glent°

      with no membre   *properly | flinched*

      Bot stode stylle as þe ston oþer a stubbe

      auþer°   *or else a stump*

      Þat raþeled° is in roche° grounde with roteʒ

      a hundreth   *entwined | rocky*

2280. Gawayn: MS G.
2290. ryneʒ: TG ryved.
2291. his: MS hs.
2296. bihoues: MS, TG, D, W bihous.

2289. *wayteʒ*: Go's derives from ON *veita* and glosses "behaves angrily," though the older editors had glossed "looks" from OF *waiter*. However, as Go says, the poet uses derivatives of *waiter* throughout his work to mean "search, watch," never "look" in this sense.

2290. *ryneʒ*: So Go and D, though older editions read *ryued*, "cleaved," Morris and TG, however, expressing some doubt. It seems better to insist that the Green Knight did not even "touch" Gawain with this second swing, much less "cleave" him.

Þen muryly efte con he mele° þe mon in
    þe grene   *again he spoke*
2296 So now þou hatȝ þi hert holle° hitte me
    bihoues   *courage whole*
Halde þe now þe hyȝe hode þat Arþur þe raȝt
& kepe° þy kanel° at þis kest° ȝif
    hit keuer° may   *save / neck / blow / survive*
Gawayn ful gryndelly° with greme þenne sayde   *fiercely*
2300 Wy þresch° on þou þro° mon þou þreteȝ to
    longe   *smite / fierce*
I hope þat þi hert arȝe wyth° þyn awen seluen   *quails at*
Forsoþe quoþ þat oþer freke so felly° þou spekeȝ   *fiercely*
I wyl no lenger on lyte lette° þin ernde   *in delay hinder*
2304   riȝt nowe
Þenne tas he hym stryþe° to stryke   *a stance*
& frounses° boþe lyppe & browe   *wrinkles*
No meruayle þaȝ hym myslyke°   *it displeases*
2308   Þat hoped of no rescowe

XIV

He lyftes lyȝtly his lome & let° hit doun
    fayre   *weapon and lets*

2299. Gawayn: MS G.
2303. lenger: W longer.
2305. he: MS he he.

2297. *hode*: Go's gloss, followed by D, "order, degree" as in knight*hood* is surely unnecessary. The Green Knight simply asks Gawain to hold his hood away from his neck. We are to presume, I think, either that the hood fell back over Gawain's neck when he flinched at the first blow or that the Green Knight is simply continuing his attempt to unnerve his victim.

2301. *hope*: "reckon, except" (King, RES 5:449–52) as in 140. King translates the line "I reckon that thy heart is afraid for thine own self."

2309. See 280*n*.

With þe barbe° of þe bitte° bi þe bare nek   *edge / blade* (f.122a)
Þaȝ he homered heterly° hurt hym no more   *struck fiercely*
2312 Bot snyrt° hym on þat on syde þat seuered þe hyde   *nicked*
Þe scharp schrank° to þe flesche þurȝ
       þe schyre grece   *sharp blank sank*
Þat þe schene blod ouer his schulderes schot to þe erþe
& quen þe burne seȝ þe blode blenk on þe snawe
2316 He sprit° forth spenne-fote more þen a spere lenþe   *sprang*
Hent heterly° his helme & on his hed cast   *seized quickly*
Schot° with his schulderez his fayre schelde vnder   *slung*
Braydeȝ° out a bryȝt sworde & bremely he spekeȝ   *pulls*
2320 Neuer syn þat he watȝ burne borne of his moder
Watȝ he neuer in þis worlde wyȝe half so blyþe
Blynne° burne of þy bur° bede° me no mo   *cease / violence / offer*
I haf a stroke in þis sted° withoute stryf hent   *place*
2324 & if þow recheȝ° me any mo I redyly schal quyte   *give*
& ȝelde ȝederly° aȝayn & þerto ȝe tryst°   *quickly / be sure*
       & foo°   *fiercely*
Bot on stroke here me falleȝ
2328 Þe couenaunt schop° ryȝt so   *appointed*

2320. burne: W barne.

2316. *spenne-fote*: A unique word, its probable derivation being ON *spenna*, "to clasp," the English term thus meaning "with feet close together" (*NED*). Indeed the most carefully worked-out interpretation of the phrase, that of J. H. Smth (MLN 49: 462–3), maintains that this is a translation of the French "joinz pez [a phrase used of Tristan in the *Folie Tristan*] or the like" and that Gawain as "a trained athlete would have jumped with his feet close together."

Go's note suggests other possible derivations.

2318. TG and D suggest that "Gawain had his shield slung on his back, and by a movement of his shoulders swung it in front of him so that he could use it for defence"; R. W. King (RES 5:449–452) glosses *vnder* as "under his left arm"; Go states that Gawain " 'got his body under his fair shield,' i.e., got his shield in front of him."

GAWAIN AT THE GREEN CHAPEL

Fettled° in Arþureʒ halleʒ   *arranged*
& þerfore hende now hoo°   *stop*

XV

The haþel heldet hym fro°& on his ax rested   *turned*
2332 Sette þe schaft vpon schore° & to þe scharp°
      lened   *ground | sharp blade*
& loked to þe leude þat on þe launde ʒede°   *field went*
How þat doʒty dredles deruely° þer
      stondeʒ   *fearless one boldly*
Armed ful aʒleʒ° in hert hit hym lykeʒ   *fearless*
2336 Þenn he meleʒ° muryly wyth a much steuen°   *speaks | big voice*
& wyth a rynkande rurde he to þe renk sayde
Bolde burne on þis bent be not so gryndel
No mon here vnmanerly þe mysboden habbeʒ
2340 Ne kyd° bot as couenaunde° at
      kyngeʒ kort schaped°   *acted | the covenant | directed*
I hyʒt° þe a strok & þou hit hatʒ halde° þe
      wel payed   *promised | consider*
I relece þe of þe remnaunt of ryʒtes° alle oþer   *duties*
Iif I deliuer° had bene a boffet paraunter   *nimble*
2344 I couþe wroþeloker° haf waret°to
      þe haf wroʒt anger°   *could more harshly | dealt | done harm*

2329. Fettled: ᴍꜱ *illegible*; TG, D fermed; W festned.
2337. rynkande: ᴍꜱ rykande.
2339. habbeʒ: ᴍꜱ habbe.
2343. Iif: Go ʒif.
2344. anger: ᴍꜱ *illegible*.

2329. The ᴍꜱ here is totally illegible: Go's *fettled* will "fill a pit as well as better" and certainly does as well as Menner and TG's *fermed*, Morris's *sikered*, and Knott's *schapen*.

2337. *rynkande*: "ringing," suggested by Napier. This is better than Emerson's "reign, rule" and Wright's "chatter, scold."

2339. *habbeʒ*: Napier's emendation.

2339. King (RES 5:449–52) translates "Nor [has any man] behaved but in accordance with the compact."

Fyrst I mansed þe muryly with a mynt one
& roue þe wyth no rof-sore with ryȝt I þe profered
For þe forwarde þat we fest in þe fyrst nyȝt   (f.122b)
2348 & þou trystyly° þe trawþe & trwly me
    haldeȝ°   *faithfully / keep*
  Al þe gayne þow me gef° as god mon schulde   *gave*
  Þat oþer munt° for þe morne mon I þe profered   *second feint*
  Þou kyssedes my clere wyf þe cosseȝ me
    raȝteȝ°   *you returned*
2352 For boþe two here I þe bede° bot two bare
    myntes°   *offered / feints*
     boute scaþe°   *without harm*
  Trwe mon trwe° restore   *a true man must truly*
  Þenne þar° mon drede no waþe°   *need / danger*
2356   At þe þrid° þou fayled þore°   *third exchange / there*
  & þerfore þat tappe ta° þe   *blow take*

XVI

  For hit is my wede þat þou wereȝ þat ilke wouen girdel
  Myn owen wyf hit þe weued° I wot wel forsoþe   *gave*
2360 Now know I wel þy cosses & þy costes° als   *manners*
  & þe wowyng° of my wyf I wroȝt hit myseluen   *wooing*
  I sende hir to asay þe & sothly me þynkkeȝ
  On þe fautlest freke þat euer on fote ȝede

2345–7. "First I threatened thee merrily with a feint only, and rent thee not with a grievous wound; justly did I aim at thee, in accordance with the compact."

2346. *rof-sore*: "cut." As Go suggests, this may "represent a lost Scandinavian *rof-sār*, a 'cut sod.'" Certainly this is a compound and *sore* cannot be taken to be, as Madden and Morris

thought, the object of *profered*.

2362. "I sent her to try you,
  and truly you seem
The most faultless of men
  that e'er fared on his feet."
          (Banks)
Such a reading is clearly superior to that of Go, who insists that *me þynkkeȝ* "cannot mean . . . 'thou seemest to me'," which it obviously does mean.

2364 As perle bi° þe quite pese° is of prys more   *compared to | pea*

So is Gawayn in god fayth bi oþer gay knyȝteȝ

Bot here yow lakked a lyttel sir & lewte° yow

wonted   *loyalty*

Bot þat watȝ for no wylyde werke ne wowyng nauþer

2368 Bot for°ȝe lufed your lyf þe lasse I yow blame   *because*

Þat oþer stif mon in study stod a gret whyle

So agreued for greme° he gryed° withinne   *grief | trembled*

Alle þe blode of his brest blende° in his face   *rushed*

2372 Þat° al he schrank for schome þat° þe schalk

talked   *so that | while*

Þe forme° worde vpon folde þat þe freke meled°   *first | spoke*

Corsed worth° cowarddyse & couetyse boþe   *cursed be*

In yow is vylany & vyse þat vertue disstryeȝ°   *destroy*

2376 Þenne he kaȝt to þe knot & þe kest lawseȝ°   *loosens*

Brayde broþely° þe belt to þe burne

seluen°   *flung fiercely | himself*

Lo þer þe falssyng° foule mot° hit

falle°   *betrayer | may evil | befell*

2364. One of the clearest links between this poem and *Pearl*. There are similar lines also in *Purity* (1068, 1116–32).

2366ff. Kitely (Anglia 79:131–37) states that a degree of cowardice may have been one of Gawain's traditional traits.

2366ff. Bloomfield notes that the shift to the second person plural pronoun may itself be a kind of rebuke.

2367. *wylyde werke*: Madden and Morris, "wild, amorous" deeds; TG, "intrigue" (ME *wīle*); Go, "a thing of choice workmanship" (ON *vildr*); D, an "excellent piece of workmanship"

(*wīle*). Go's derivation, though not his reading, is strained, and an allusion to the "rich girdle" would certainly fit the context.

2374–83. These lines are used by D. F. Hills (RES 14:124–31), along with 2505–10, to name *cupiditas*, "covetousness . . . a state of inordinate love for oneself," as Gawain's major transgression.

2376. *kest*: "fastening" (TG, D). King (*RES* 5:449–52) asks, however, if it cannot apply to the whole girdle and, if so, can it be translated "trick" here as in 2413.

For care° of þy knokke cowardyse me taȝt   *fear*
2380 To acorde° me with couetyse° my kynde
     to forsake   *associate / covetousness*
Þat is larges & lewte þat longeȝ° to knyȝteȝ   *belong*
Now am I fawty & falce & ferde° haf ben euer   *yet afraid*
Of trecherye & vntrawþe boþe bityde sorȝe
2384   & care
I biknowe° yow knyȝt here stylle   *confess to* (f.123a)
Al fawty is my fare°   *behavior*
Leteȝ me ouertake your wylle
2388   & efte° I schal be ware   *afterward*

XVII

Thenn loȝe° þat oþer leude & luflyly sayde   *laughed*
I halde hit hardily hole° þe harme
     þat I hade   *certainly healed*
Þou art confessed so clene beknowen° of
     þy mysses°   *absolved / faults*
2392 & hatȝ þe penaunce apert° of þe poynt of
     myn egge°   *evident / sword*
I halde þe polysed of þat plyȝt & pured as clene
As þou hadeȝ neuer forfeted syþen þou watȝ fyrst borne
& I gif þe sir þe gurdel þat is golde-hemmed
2396 For° hit is grene as my goune Sir Gawayn ȝe maye   *since*

2382. ferde: ᴍs fererde.
2390. hardily: ᴍs hardilyly.
2396. Gawayn: ᴍs G.

2387. "'Let me understand your will,' *i.e.* what do you want me to do now?" (Go). "Let your will take control of me" (Wright). Both readings assume that Gawain, having confessed, is here asking for penance, a request which Bercilak laughingly dismisses (2390ff.). However, TG's "Let me win your good will" seems to ignore the penitential nature of Gawain's request.

Þenk vpon þis ilke þrepe° þer þou forth
    þryngeȝ°   *contest | hasten*
Among prynces of prys & þis a pure token
Of þe chaunce of þe grene chapel at cheualrous knyȝteȝ
2400 & ȝe schal in þis Nwe ȝer aȝayn to my woneȝ
   & we schyn° reuel þe remnaunt of þis ryche fest   *shall*
    ful bene°   *pleasantly*
   Þer laþed° hym fast° þe lorde   *invited | earnestly*
2404 & sayde with my wyf I wene°   *suppose*
   We schal yow wel acorde
   Þat watȝ your enmy kene

XVIII

   Nay forsoþe quoþ þe segge & sesed hys helme
2408 & hatȝ° hit of hendely & þe haþel þonkkeȝ   *takes*
   I haf soiorned sadly sele° yow bytyde   *good luck*
   & he ȝelde°hit yow ȝare° þat ȝarkkeȝ°
    al menskes   *may he repay | fully | dispenses*
   & comaundeȝ me to þat cortays your comlych fere
2412 Boþe þat on & þat oþer myn honoured ladyeȝ
   Þat þus hor knyȝt wyth hor kest° han
    koyntly° bigyled   *trick | cunningly*
   Bot hit is no ferly þaȝ° a fole madde°   *marvel if | fool act madly*

2399. *at chevalrous knyȝteȝ*: " 'Mid chivalrous knights" (Banks). The phrase modifies either *þenk* or *þryngeȝ*, but is probably best understood as being in parallel construction with *among prynces of prys*. Bloomfield suggests that *at* here has the force of Fr. *cheȝ* or Ger. *bei* and compares *Troilus and Criseyde*, II, 984: "Till that thow be again at hire fro me." Sisam (*Fourteenth Century Verse and Prose*) would transpose *at* and *of* because "such a use of *at* is hardly conceivable."

2409. *sadly*: Go's and TG's "sufficiently, long enough, too well" seem much better to suit Gawain's frame of mind than Savage's and Emerson's "pleasantly, satisfactorily."

2410. See 2441–42n.

2414ff. R. W. King (MLR 29:435–36) notes that this anti-feminist passage is full of borrowings from the prose homilists of the period and has a "fairly close" parallel in the *Wars*

& þurȝ wyles of wymmen be wonen° to sorȝe   *brought*

2416 For so watȝ Adam in erde° with one bygyled   *actually*

& Salamon with fele sere° &

     Samson eftsoneȝ°   *many different ones | besides*

Dalyda dalt hym hys wyrde & Dauyth þerafter

Watȝ blended° with Barsabe þat much

     bale þoled°   *deluded | woe suffered*

2420 Now þese were wrathed wyth her wyles hit were

     a wynne huge

To luf hom wel & leue hem not a leude þat couþe

For þes were forne þe freest þat folȝed alle þe sele   *(f.123b)*

Exellently of alle þyse oþer vnder heuenryche

2424   þat mused

     & alle þay were biwyled°   *beguiled*

     With wymmen þat þay vsed

     Þaȝ I be now bigyled

2428   Me þink me burde° be excused   *I ought to*

XIX

Bot your gordel quoþ Gawayn God yow forȝelde°   *reward*

Þat wyl I welde° wyth guod wylle not for

     þe wynne° golde   *wear | pleasant*

Ne þe saynt° ne þe sylk ne þe syde

     pendaundes°   *girdle | long pendants*

2432 For wele ne for worchyp ne for þe wlonk werkkeȝ

2426. with: ᴍs with wyth.
2429. Gawayn: ᴍs G.

---

of Alexander, to which *GGK* may be related (see Go's Introduction, xiii–xviii).

   2420–24. " 't would be great gain To love them yet never believe them, if knights could.

For formerly these
   were most noble and fortunate,
More than all others
   who lived on the earth . . . ."
            (Banks)

Bot in syngne of my surfet° I schal se hit ofte   *fault*

When I ride in renoun remorde° to

    myseluen   *remorsefully recall*

Þe faut & þe fayntyse° of þe flesche

    crabbed°   *frailty / perverse*

2436 How tender° hit is to entyse teches°

    of fylþe   *liable / attract stains*

& þus quen pryde schal me pryk for prowes of armes

Þe loke to þis luf-lace schal leþe° my hert   *humble*

Bot on° I wolde yow pray displeses yow neuer   *one thing*

2440 Syn ȝe be lorde of þe ȝonder londe þer I haf lent°

    inne   *stayed*

Wyth yow wyth worschyp þe wyȝe hit yow ȝelde

Þat vphaldeȝ þe heuen & on hyȝ sitteȝ

How norne° ȝe yowre ryȝt nome & þenne no more   *call*

2444 Þat schal I telle þe trwly quoþ þat oþer þenne

Bercilak de Hautdesert I hat in þis londe

2445. Bercilak: MS, Go, D, W Bertilak.
2445. G *adds* [þat þus am aȝlych of hwe & al ouer brawden].

2433. *surfet*: Since virtue is a mean, superfluity becomes a sin (Bloomfield).

2438. *Þe loke to*: TG, "a glance at"; Banks, "the sight of."

2441–42. These lines, along with 1256, 1292, and 2410, are brought forward by Menner in his edition of *Purity* as examples of paraphrases for God very similar to those in *Patience* and *Purity*. Menner's conclusion that these parallels support his claim for common authorship is contested by Clark (MLN 65:232–36).

2445. *Bercilak de Hautdesert*: Printed as *Bernlak* by Madden and Morris, the correct form of the name was established by Hulbert (*Manly Anniversary Studies*: 12–19) who derived it from the Bertelak of the Vulgate Cycle, which Hulbert maintained the poet had read. Since *Bercilak* is the form used by most modern students, it seems a bit pedantic to print Bertilak, as do Go and D "on the evidence of the MS generally," though the letter itself is doubtful. *Hautdesert* here may mean "high hermitage," *desert* being an English form of Celtic *disert* from Lat. *desertum*, "a solitary place where an anchorite took up his abode" (TG), though, as D says," a specialized Celtic meaning is very unlikely to appear in

Þurʒ myʒt of Morgne la Faye þat in my hous lenges
& koyntyse of clergye° bi craftes wel lerned   *magic*

---

so characteristically French a compound as *Hautdesert*. "High wilderness" would be more appropriate to the seat of Bercilak's castle than to the Green Chapel.

Loomis suggests (*Celtic Myth and Arthurian Romance*) that Bercilak may be derived ultimately from a trisyllabic pronunciation of *bachlach*, "herdsman," a term applied to the disguised Curoi mac Daire, Cuchulainn's (Gawain's) shape-shifting host in *Bricriu's Feast*. Loomis (Romanic Review 15:266–84) also identifies the Burmalt figure in the Modena Sculpture (which attests to the spread of the Arthur story to Italy by the early 12th century) with the Curoi-Bercilak tradition.

Roland Smith, however (JEGP 45: 1–25), derives *Bercilak* from Ir. *bresalach*, "contentious," and relates the Green Knight to figures completely outside the Ulster cycle used by Loomis.

2445–46. Go, in an effort to clear up the somewhat twisted meaning of these lines, adds a line, *Þat þus am aʒlych of hwe & al ouer brawden*, following 2445 in order to give *þurʒ myʒt* something besides *hat* to modify. Emerson, on the other hand, suggests that the Green Knight's title "de Hautdesert" may indeed have been conferred on him "through the might of Morgan le Faye" in recognition of his *koyntyse of clergye* in which he is *wel lerned*.

My own feeling is that, as TG suggest by their punctuation, there should

be a full stop after *londe* and that 244–55 represents a rather long parenthesis, resembling that of 1512–19, identifying Morgan and explaining her powers to the bewildered Gawain.

2446. *Morgne la Faye*: Half-sister of Arthur and wife of King Uryens, she is the implacable enemy of Arthur and, especially, Guinevere, and her role of motivator of the action of the poem has fascinated recent students of the poem (see Introduction).

A thorough discussion of the early Morgan tradition can be found in Lucy Allen Paton's *Studies in the Fairy Mythology of Arthurian Romance*. In his efforts to explain her role in *GGK*, Loomis (JEGP 42:149–84) finds evidence in the *Didot Perceval* and elsewhere that Morgan was "a traditional *amie* of the wild Huntsman [in *GGK* the Green Knight] and was deeply involved in the annual combats at the ford. As a doublet of Bercilak's wife, she doubtless was taken into the plot of *GGK* at some earlier stage . . . ." Loomis also traces Morgan's ancestry to a number of ancient Gallic and Britannic goddesses as well as to figures of Irish legend.

Speirs (*Medieval English Poetry*), as might be expected, sees Morgan as representing in the poem the "old year," though Bercilak's statement that she is the prime mover of the action is dismissed by Speirs as "a bone for the rationalizing mind to play with" in the same way that Hulbert (MP 13: 433–62, 689–730) had dismissed it

2448 Þe maystres of Merlyn mony ho hatȝ taken°   *acquired*
    For ho hatȝ dalt drwry° ful dere sumtyme   *made love*
    With þat conable klerk þat knowes alle your knyȝteȝ
        at hame

2448. mony ho hatȝ: MS mony ho; D mony hatȝ.

---

years before and as Albert Friedman (Spec 35:260–74) does in claiming that Morgan's only function in the poem is that of a "foil to enhance the beauty of Gawain's temptress." Dale Randall, however (SP 57:479–91), takes Bercilak's statement quite seriously and claims sorceress Morgan to be an agent of Satan.

Laura Hibbard Loomis (*Arthurian Literature in the Middle Ages*), following a statement of Hulbert's in the *Manly Anniversary Studies*, traces Morgan's presence in the poem to the Vulgate *Lancelot* where Morgan having tried and failed to seduce Lancelot "sends her damsel, a younger self as it were, to effect the same end . . . . From this episode . . . , it is but a step to the two figures in *GGK*." Interestingly enough, Mother Angela Carson (MLQ 23:3–16), mainly on the basis of Morgan's reputation as a shape shifter, views Morgan and Bercilak's wife as the same person, the queen of an other-world domain whose husband lures Gawain to her in order to be tested.

Denver E. Baughan (ELH 17:241–51) takes Morgan to be what indeed Bercilak says she is, the sole motivator of the action, and her desire to humiliate Arthur as stemming from a desire to heal and purify the court (see also C. Moorman, Med Stu 18:158–72).

2448. *hatȝ*: Not in MS, originally added by Madden and supplied by subsequent editors.

2448. *maystres*: Almost certainly "masteries, magical powers" rather than "mistress" which was Madden's reading and would, I think, be anyone's first guess.

2448. *Merlyn*: First mentioned by Geoffrey of Monmouth in the *Vita Merlini*, where he is presented as a great Welsh prophet, though not as a magician. In his *Historia Regum Britanniae*, however, Geoffrey combines the Welsh *Merlin* with one Ambrosius mentioned by Nennius as a prophet and associates him with Uther Pendragon and with Arthur. Geoffrey also invents the famous story that Merlin was sired by the devil. Merlin in time, of course, comes in the legend to be responsible for Arthur's birth and training.

2449–50. Passages in the Vulgate *Lancelot* (Sommer's ed., IV, 124) and *Le Livre d'Artus* (Sommer's ed., VII, 134–5) describe this relationship. It might be noted that Morgan was regarded in the Arthurian tradition as *une des plus chaudes fames qui fust en toute la Grande Bretaigne*.

2450. *conable*: Madden and Morris, "famous, accomplished"; TG, "fitting"; Go, "affable, pliant"; Bloomfield, "knowledgeable." All derive

2452   Morgne þe goddes
        Þerfore hit is hir name
        Weldeȝ non° so hyȝe hawtesse°   *no one has | pride*
        Þat ho ne con make ful tame

XX

2456 Ho wayned° me vpon þis wyse to your
          wynne° halle   *sent | pleasant*
      For to assay þe surquidre° ȝif hit soth were   *test the pride*
      Þat rennes° of þe grete renoun of þe
          Rounde Table   *what is current*
      Ho wayned me þis wonder your wytteȝ to reue° *take away*
2460 For to haf greued Gaynour & gart°hir
          to dyȝe°   *caused | die* (f.124a)
     With glopnyng° of þat ilke gomen þat gostlych
          speked   *horror*

2459. wayned: Go wayued.
2461. glopnyng: ᴍꜱ gognyng.
2461. gomen: TG, D, W gome.

---

from ᴏꜰ *covenable*. Certainly Bloom-field's reading fits both the context and the received character of Merlin better than do the others'.

2450. *þat knowes alle your knyȝteȝ*: Savage is surely correct in rendering this clause as "all your knights know that," *i.e.* that "Morgan has had relations with Merlin."

2452. *Morgne þe goddes*: So called by Giraldus Cambrensis (*Speculum Ecclesiae*, dist. II, cap. 9) and by the writer of the Vulgate *Lancelot* (W. J. A. Jonckbloet, *Roman van Lancelot*, II, lxix). This title may also serve to link her with the Celtic goddess Morrigu or Morrigain (see Paton, *The Fairy Mythology of Arthurian Romance* and Loomis, *Celtic Myth and Arthurian Romance*, where she is presented as an enemy of Cuchulainn).

2459. *wayned*: Despite Go's defense of *wayued*, "cast upon," from ᴏɴ *veifa* "to wave," the more standard *wayned* seems to be sounder here.

2460. *Gaynour*: Morgan in the legend hates Guinevere because the queen had once caused her exile from court (see Introduction and D's note). Engelhardt, however, believes (MLO 16: 224) that this line is hyperbolic and that the Green Knight is attempting merely to reduce the queen's pride.

2461. *gomen*: Almost certainly "il-

With his hede in his honde bifore þe hyȝe table

Þat is ho þat is at home þe auncian° lady   *aged*

2464 Ho is euen þyn aunt Arþureȝ half-suster

Þe duches doȝter of Tyntagelle þat dere Vter after

Hade Arþur vpon þat aþel is nowþe

Þerfore I eþe° þe haþel to com to þyn aunt   *ask*

2468 Make myry in my hous my meny þe louies

& I wol° þe as wel wyȝe bi my faythe   *wish*

As any gome vnder God for þy grete trauþe

& he nikked° hym naye he nolde bi no wayes   *said*

2472 Þay acolen° & kyssen bikennen

    ayþer oþer°   *embrace / commend each other*

To þe prynce of paradise & parten ryȝt þere

    on coolde°   *cold ground*

Gawayn on blonk ful bene°   *fair*

2476   To þe kyngeȝ burȝ buskeȝ bolde

& þe knyȝt in þe enker° grene   *bright*

Whiderwarde-soeuer he wolde

XXI

Wylde wayeȝ in þe worlde Wowen now rydeȝ

2480 On Gryngolet þat þe grace° hade geten of his lyue   *gift*

Ofte he herbered in house & ofte al þeroute°   *outside*

2467. þyn aunt: ᴍs, TG, Go þy naunt.
2472. bikennen: *Not in* ᴍs; TG, D, W & kennen.

---

lusion, trick, enchantment" (Go), not "man" (TG).

2465. *Þe duches doȝter of Tynta-gelle*: *Þe duches* here is the wife of the Duke of Tintagel, Igerne, whom Uther with the aid of Merlin seduced. Apparently she had only one child by Uther, Arthur, though a number by her first husband.

2467. *þyn aunt*: There seems little reason to insist on the ᴍs division (See Savage, MLN 59:349).

2472. *bikennen*: Madden's addition.

2480. *þat*: Refers to *Wowen*, not *Gryngolet*.

& mony a venture in vale & venquyst ofte
Þat I ne tyȝt° at þis tyme in tale to remene°   *intend / recount*
2484 Þe hurt watȝ hole þat he hade hent° in his nek   *received*
& þe blykkande° belt he bere þeraboute   *shining*
Abelef° as a bauderyk° bounden bi his
    syde   *crosswise / baldric*
Loken vnder his lyfte arme þe lace with a knot
2488 In tokenyng he watȝ tane° in tech° of a faute   *taken / stain*
& þus he commes to þe court knyȝt al in sounde°   *safety*
Þer wakned° wele in þat wone when
    wyst þe grete°   *arose / great one*
Þat gode Gawayn watȝ commen gayn° hit hym
    þoȝt   *good*
2492 Þe kyng kysseȝ þe knyȝt & þe whene alce°   *also*
& syþen mony syker° knyȝt þat soȝt hym
    to haylce°   *trusty / greet*
Of his fare þat hym frayned° & ferlyly°
    he telles   *asked / marvelously*
Biknoweȝ° alle þe costes° of care þat
    he hade   *confesses / conditions*
2496 Þe chaunce of þe chapel þe chere of þe knyȝt
Þe luf of þe ladi þe lace at þe last   *(f.124b)*
Þe nirt° in þe nek he naked hem schewed   *nick*
Þat he laȝt° for his vnleute° at þe leudes
    hondes   *got / disloyalty*

2482. &: Go, W he.
2491. Gawayn: ᴍꜱ G.

2482. *vale & venquyst*: Go emends
to *vale he venquyst* and glossed *ven-*
quyst "turned aside from, escaped"
from ᴏꜰ *guenchir*. However, Savage
cites the phrase as an example of
condensed wording, "many a venture
in vale (he had) and overcame often,"
and there is no reason to avoid the
more obvious, and perfectly suitable,
meaning of *venquyst* as "vanquished."

2494ff. *he telles*: The usual prac-
tise of Arthur's knights is to report in
detail their adventures to the king.

GAWAIN AND ARTHUR'S COURT

2500   for blame

He tened° quen he schulde telle   *grieved*

He groned for gref & grame°   *shame*

Þe blod in his face con melle°   *rushed*

2504 When he hit schulde schewe for schame

XXII

Lo lorde quoþ þe leude & þe lace hondeled

Þis is þe bende of þis blame I bere in my nek

Þis is þe laþe° & þe losse þat I laȝt° haue   *injury | received*

2508 Of couardise & couetyse þat I haf caȝt þare

Þis is þe token of vntrawþe þat I am tan inne

& I mot nedeȝ hit were wyle I may last

For non may hyden his harme bot vnhap ne may hit

2512 For þer hit oneȝ is tachched° twynne° wil hit

       neuer   *attached | separate*

2506. in: *Not in* MS; Go on.
2511. non: D, W mon.

2505ff. *& þe lace hondeled*: This phrase, along with 2514ff., was taken by Savage to refer not to the Order of the Garter as proposed by Schofield (*English Literature from the Conquest to Chaucer*), Gollancz (*The Cambridge History of English Literature*), Cargill (PMLA 43:105–23), and Jackson (Anglia 37:393–423) and denied by Hulbert (MP 13:433–62, 689–730), Menner (*Purity*), and TG, but to the "Order of the Crown" (*Ordre de la Couronne*), an order "connected with" Enguerrand de Coucy whom Savage identifies with Gawain. See 620*n* and 2530*n*.

22505–10. See 2374–83*n*.

2506. *in*: Madden's addition, followed by Morris and TG. Emended to *on* by Go, who read the line "'this that I bear on my neck (*i.e.* the lace he is handling) is the *bende* (*i.e.* heraldic sign) of this blameworthiness' (of which he has just spoken)." Wright, however, offers the less tortured reading accepted by most readers: "This is the ribbon belonging to (or, cause of) this hurt I received in my neck."

2511. *bot vnhap ne may hit*: "without misfortune betiding" (Go). D emends *non* to *mon* in order to avoid the awkward double negative.

Þe kyng comfortez þe knyʒt & alle þe court als

Laʒen° loude þerat & luflyly acorden   *laugh*

Þat lordes & ladis þat longed to þe Table

2516 Vche burne of þe broþerhede a bauderyk schulde haue

A bende abelef° hym aboute of a bryʒt grene   *band crosswise*

& þat for sake of þat segge in swete° to were   *following suit*

For þat watʒ acorded þe renoun of þe Rounde Table

2520 & he honoured þat hit hade euermore after

As hit is breued°in þe best boke of romaunce   *written*

Þus in Arthurus day þis aunter bitidde°   *adventure befell*

Þe Brutus bokez þerof beres wyttenesse

2524 Syþen Brutus þe bolde burne boʒed° hider fyrst   *came*

After þe segge & þe asaute watʒ sesed at Troye

iwysse

Mony aunterez here biforne

2528   Haf fallen suche er þis

Now þat bere° þe croun of þorne   *he that bore*

He bryng vs to his blysse AMEN

HONY SOYT QUI MAL PENCE

2514. See 464*n* and 2505*n*.

2516. See 280*n*.

2523. *Þe Brutus brokeʒ*: This phrase might well stand for any of the chronicles of British history current in the poet's time. Cf. 33–6 and 389–90.

2524–25. See 1ff*n*.

2531. *HONY SOYT QUI MAL PENCE*: Possibly added by a scribe, this motto has been analyzed in great detail by I. Jackson (Anglia, 37:393–423), who claims that this line and a great number of passages in the poem demonstrate that "(1) The poem was written in 1362. (2) The topography points to a castle in Cheshire, Beeston in fact, as the Green Castle. (3) The poem closely describes a Garter feast and the dress of a K.G. (4) The Black Prince and Lady Joan link together Beeston Castle and Liddel Castle and harmonize the romance with history. (5) The lace, girdle, or garter, was a wedding favor. (6) The poem glorifies the Black Prince as Gawain; while the lace or garter was the wedding favour of his wife Joan, 'The Fair Maid of Kent'."

R. M. Garrett (JEGP 24:125–134), while denying that *GGK* is a "garter poem," feels that it is connected with a "refounded Round Table." See 2505ff*n*.

There is, however, no clear evidence connecting the poem with the Order of the Garter, the members of which have never worn green sashes.

· Glossary ·

(The following word list contains the most common meanings in their simplest forms of those words used eight or more times by the poet which are not immediately recognizable. No attempt is made to distinguish parts of speech.)

· A ·

abof: above.
abyme: abyss.
acorde: agreement.
aȝayn: back, in return.
aȝt: ought; eight.
alder: older.
anon: forthwith.
anvnder: under.
arayed: prepared; adorned.
armeȝ: arms; armour.
athel: noble.
auter: altar.
auther: either.
awen: own.
ay: ever; each.

· B ·

bale: torment, sorrow.
barne: child.
bede: command; offer.
ber: bear, endure; carry; support.
berde: beard.
bereȝ: bears.
besteȝ: beasts.

beten: beat.
bityde: happen.
blod: blood; mettle.
blonk: horse, steed.
blynde: blind; become dim.
blys: joy.
blysnande: gleaming.
blythe: gentle; merry.
boȝe: turn; go.
boȝt: buy.
boke: book.
bone: petition, prayer; good.
bonk: hill, ridge; shore.
bowe: bow; betake oneself.
bor: dwelling; boar.
borȝ: city; estate.
borne: stream.
bote: remedy; boat; shoe.
bothem: bottom.
boun: ready.
bounden: fastened; trimmed.
bour: bower.
bourde: maiden, damsel.
boute: without.
brayde: draw, pull.
brayn: brain.

· 445 ·

brede: bread; roast, meat; beget; grow.
breme: intense.
brest: breast.
breue: announce, declare.
brode: widely; broad
bronde: brand; piece of burnt wood.
bryddeȝ: birds.
bur: onslaught, blow; a strong wind.
burde: maiden.
burȝ: town.
burne: knight.
busk: get ready; array; hurry.
byde: remain, abide.
byȝonde: across, beyond.
bylyve: quickly.
bysyde: hard by, near.

· C ·

cach: catch.
carp: talk; conversation.
caȝt: caught.
cete: city.
clos: enclosure; fast.
com: come, arrive.
comly: fair.
con: did (auxiliary).
cors: course.
coruen: cut.
cote: coat.
couthe: evident.
cowthe: could.

· D ·

dalt: valley.
daunger: power; distress.
dece: dais.
ded: dead.
dede: deed; occupation.
deȝter: daughter.
dele: deal; mete out; perform.

deme: judge, consider.
derely: splendidly; courteously.
derf: bold, dreadful; grievous, severe.
derve: private, secret.
diȝt: dispose; set.
doel: lament; sorrow.
dom: judgment; doom.
dome: judge; decree.
douthe: company; army, nobility.
drawen: brought.
drof: came, entered.
dryȝe: heavy; endure.
dryȝtyn: lord.
dubbed: adorned.
durst: dared.
dyn: din, noise.
dynt: blow.

· E ·

eft: again; afterwards.
eke: also.
erde: land, region.
ere: ear.
ernde: message; errand.
ese: ease.
ethe: easy.

· F ·

falce: false.
fare: behavior; journey.
fast: firmly; earnestly; fast, quickly;
     binding.
fayn: glad, well pleased.
fayre: fair, beautiful; courteous.
fech: bring; strike (a blow).
fel: cruelly.
felde: field; fold.
fele: perceive; many.
felle: bold, fierce; skin; fell.
fende: fiend; devil.

fer: far.
ferde: fear.
fere: proud, bold; companion; fortune;
    rank.
ferly: wonderful; dreadfully; extraor-
    dinary.
fest: feast; fasten.
fete: feet.
fle: flee.
flesche: flesh, body.
flet: floor, ground.
flod: flood.
flot: grease, scum.
folde: earth, land; bend.
fole: horse; fool.
folȝed: followed.
folke: people.
fonde: try, test.
fonge: take, receive.
forsothe: truly, indeed.
forthi: therefore.
founden: found; started; dislodged.
fowle: fowl; shamefully; defile.
frayn: ask, inquire.
frayst: ask for; examine.
fre: noble, good; free.
freke: man; knight.
frely: readily, courteously.
fryth: woodland.
fyn: perfected; choice; fine.
fynde: find; pursue.
fyne: cease.

· G ·

gart: made, caused.
gayn: ready, prompt; avail; opposite.
gef: gave; wished.
gered: attired.
gif: give.
glam: noise of merrymaking; word.

glent: glance; deviated; shine.
glette: slime; filth; sin.
glydeȝ: glides; falls; advances.
gode: wealth; good thing.
gome: knight, man.
gomen: game, sport, pleasure.
goste: spirit.
goude: good, righteous.
graythed: arrayed; prepared.
graythely: aptly; promptly.
greme: wrath; resentment.
gret: greeted.
greueȝ: greaves.
greve: grove; afflict.
grymme: grim; horrible.

· H ·

habbe: have.
halche: embrace.
halde: hold; possess, maintain; take;
    preserve; measure; contain.
halden: restrained.
halue: half.
hande: hand.
happe: blessing; cover; wrap.
harme: injury, misfortune, evil.
haspe: clasp, fasten.
hathel: knight; man.
hatte: hat.
haylsed: greeted.
hed: head.
hede: observe.
hef: raise.
heȝe: high; hasten.
helde: turn; proceed, go; come.
hele: salvation; safety; heel.
hende: courteous: quiet, still.
hent: take; catch (up); seize.
hert: heart, mind; secret thoughts and
    feelings.

hete: promise; threaten.
heterly: bitterly; cruelty.
heued: head.
heuened: raised.
hiȝe: high, aloft.
hode: degree.
hoge: great.
hondes: hands.
hyde: conceal.
hyȝe: high; overbearing.
hyȝly: erect; highly.
hyȝt: hope; height.

· I ·

ilke: same; very.
ille: take amiss; wrongfully; evil.
ilyche: same.
inmyddeȝ: in the middle of.
innogh: enough.
iwysse: indeed.

· K ·

kaȝt: catch.
kene: wise; bold; bitter.
kepe: care; keep; regard.
kest: cast, throw.
kesten: scatter; set down.
keuer: recover; obtain.
knaw: know.
knawen: discovered.
kydde: acknowledge, show.
kyn: kind.
kynde: nature; courteous; proper.
kyst: chest, coffer.
kyth: native land.
kythe: show.

· L ·

lach: catch.
laghe: laugh.
laȝt: caught back; took.

lance: cut; utter.
lasse: less.
lauce: solve; do away with.
launde: glade, lawn; open space in
    woods.
lay: lay; stake; put aside.
layk: activity; sport, play.
layne: conceal.
lece: nonetheless.
lede: lead, led; man.
lef: dear; leaf.
lelly: loyally.
lemed: gleamed.
lemman: loved one, mistress.
lenge: stay; arrive; dwell.
lere: empty; teach; face.
let: let, allow.
lethe: soften.
lette: hinder.
leude: man; knight.
leue: permission; leave.
leueȝ: leaves.
leuen: believe.
lif: life(time).
lofte: aloft, on high, above.
loȝe: low; laugh.
loke: see, observe.
loken: part.
lome: tool; loom; vessel; lame.
lore: learning; teaching.
lote: sound; lot.
loude: loud.
loue: love; praise.
luf: love.
luflych: lovely; fair; courteous.
lureȝ: sorrows.
lyft: left.
lyfte: raise; set up; decree.
lyȝt: light; pure; treat with disrespect;
    descend.

lyke: please.
lyre: flesh.
lyst: pleasure.
lyste: hear; desire; be pleasing.
lyue: leave.

· M ·

madde: act madly.
maȝtyly: powerfully.
maked: created.
maner: manner; mode.
maskelleȝ: spotless.
mayn: great.
mayster: lord, knight.
mede: reward.
meke: gentle, submissive.
mele: mealtime; speak.
melle: mingle; stream; among.
mene: signify.
menske: honor.
merci: mercy.
mere: appointed place; noble; pool; boundary.
merked: situated.
meruayl: wonder.
mete: meet; equal; extending; food; proper.
meyny: household, company; multitude.
mo: more.
moȝt: could, might.
molde: earth.
mone: moon; complaint.
morne: grieve.
mot: may, must.
mote: moat; castle; walled city.
mukel: size; great.
myȝt: power.
mylde: gentle.
mynde: mind; memory.

mynne: think.
mysse: offence; lose.

· N ·

nade: have.
naȝt: night.
nas: was not.
nedeȝ: needs; of necessity.
neȝe: approach; nigh, nearly.
nem: took.
nerre: nearer.
nolde: would not.
nome: name.
note: work, occupation; practice; trouble; position.
nwe: new.
nyȝt: night.

· O ·

oȝt: anything.
ones: once; together.
oute: far and wide.

· P ·

passe: pass.
playn: plain, smooth; unobstructed.
plyt: plight; sin, guilt.
poynte: describe.
profered: offered.
pouer: poor.
preue: prove; valiant.
prys: capture; blast on horn when hunted animal is taken; excellence; exquisite.
pyȝt: place.
pyne: penance; torment; shut up.

· Q ·

quelle: quell; subdue; put to death.
quere: where.

quo: whoever; see.
quoso: whoso.
quoynt: skilful; happy.
quyl: while.
quyt: white.
quyte: requite; repay.

· R ·

radly: swiftly.
raȝt: offered.
reche: reck, care.
reken: righteous, pious; merry; ready;
    fresh.
rekenly: promptly.
reme: kingdom, realm; lament.
rengne: reign.
renk: knight; man.
riȝt: properly; justice; privilege.
roȝ: rough.
ronk: luxuriant: boldness.
ronoun: renown, glory.
ros: rise.
rote: custom; root.
runnen: flowed.
rurd: voice; cry.
ryȝtwys: righteous.

· S ·

saf: except; safe.
sale: hall, main room of a palace.
samen: gather; together.
Sauter: Psalter.
schalk: man.
schape: make; hasten; endeavor.
schelde: shield.
schene: bright, beautiful.
schewe: look at; expound.
schon: shine.
schore: shore, bank.
schot: sprang; rose.

schuld: should, would.
schulderes: shoulders.
schyr: bright.
segge: man.
seȝ: see.
sele: happiness.
selly: marvelous; strange; marvel.
semblaunt: demeanor; appearance.
seme: seemly; fair.
semly: fair; fitting.
sere: several; diverse; many; single.
serue: deserve; serve.
sete: seat; set; cause to be; esteemed,
    valued.
seten: sit.
sette: set; inflict; made merry.
siker: assure; sure.
sithen: afterwards, next.
soberly: gravely; decently.
soȝt: sought.
solace: pleasure; kindness.
sorȝe: sorrow.
soth: true; truth.
space: extent; short while; opportu-
    nity; region.
spare: waste; extent; spare.
stad: placed.
steuen: voice; appointment; command.
stif: stiff; fearlessly; undaunted.
stoute: strong.
stryf: resistance; contention.
sturne: grim; loud.
stylle: quiet; dumb; secretly.
stynt: cease.
sum: some; in general and particular.
sumtyme: once, formerly.
sute: suit; sort, kind.
sware: squarely built; answer.
swyn: boar, swine.
swythe: swiftly; strong.